ABERFAN
Government and Disasters

ABERFAN
Government and Disasters

Iain McLean
and
Martin Johnes

Welsh Academic Press

Published in Wales by Welsh Academic Press, an imprint of

Ashley Drake Publishing Ltd.
PO Box 733
Cardiff
CF14 2YX
www.welsh-academic-press.co.uk

First Impression – October 2000
ISBN 1 86057 033X

British Library Cataloguing-in-Publication Data.
A catalogue for this book is available from the British Library.

Typeset by WestKey Ltd, Falmouth, Cornwall.
Printed by Dinefwr Press, Llandybïe, Wales
Cover design by www.darkangel-design.com

CONTENTS

FOREWORD

We were very pleased to be asked by Iain McLean and Martin Johnes to contribute a few words to this important new work. *Aberfan: Government and Disasters.* Professor McLean has aided the cause of the bereaved of Aberfan and Merthyr Vale previously through several newspapers articles, which led to the reparation by the Government of £150,000 taken after the disaster from charity funds to clear the tip. This book is a meticulous examination of the documents and media reports relating to the disaster and, as such, is a landmark as the first serious lengthy academic treatment of Aberfan. Professor McLean and Dr Johnes have conducted their research with sensitivity and sympathy, and remained committed to uncovering the truth throughout. Their findings are as shocking as they are illuminating, and are a lesson to this and future governments as to how disasters should be handled. The bereaved of Aberfan and Merthyr Vale hope that such gross mismanagement and injustice is never again meted out to this in the most dire and unthinkable of circumstances.

H. Clifford Minett – Chairman of the Aberfan and Merthyr Vale Cemetery and Memorial Garden Committee.

PREFACE

The first thing I saw was the slag heap.

Big it had grown, and long, and black, without life or sign, lying along the bottom of the Valley on both sides of the river. The green grass, and the reeds and the flowers, all had gone, crushed beneath it. And every minute the burden grew, as cage after cage screeched along the cables from the pit, bumped to a stop at the tipping gear, and emptied dusty loads on to the ridged, black, dirty black.

On our side of the Valley the heap had reached to the front garden wall of the bottom row of houses, and children from them were playing up and down the black slopes, screaming and shouting, laughing in fun. On the other side of the river the chimney-pots of the first row of houses could only just be seen above the sharp curving back of the far heap, and all the time I was watching, the cable screeched and the cages tipped. From the Britannia pit came a call on the hooter as the cages came up, as though to remind the Valley to be ready for more filth as the work went on and on, year in and year out.

"Is the pit allowed to do this to us, Mr Gruffydd?" I asked him.
"Do what, my son?" Mr Gruffydd asked.
"Put slag here." I said.
"Nowhere else to put it, my son," he said.

Richard Llewellyn, How Green was my Valley, 1939.

If you are over 40, you probably remember exactly what you were doing on two days in the 1960s. One was 22 November 1963 when President Kennedy was assassinated. The other, also a Friday, was 21 October 1966, the day when a waste tip from Merthyr Vale Colliery slid down the mountain and engulfed Pantglas Junior School, Aberfan near Merthyr Tydfil in South Wales. The total death toll was 144, including 116 children. Aberfan horrified the nation as no other British disaster since 1945, except Dunblane, has done.

On the evening of 21 October 1966, like the rest of the nation, I (IM) stood transfixed in front of the TV to hear Cliff Michelmore, in tears, saying, 'Never in my life have I seen anything like this. I hope I shall never ever see anything like it again. For years of course the miners have been used to ... disaster. Today for the first time in history the roll call was called in the street. It was the miners' children'. Like everybody else, I wanted to do something. I did not have the courage to go and dig, so I started to raise money. The funds I raised went with thousands of others to the Disaster Fund announced by the Mayor of Merthyr on the evening of the disaster. As related below, some of that money ended up by paying for the removal of the National Coal Board's dangerous tips from above Aberfan.

The thirtieth anniversary of the disaster not only brought renewed media attention; it also meant the opening of governmental papers under the UK's 30-year rule. These papers have revealed new information, especially about the behaviour of the National Coal Board, the Ministry of Power, the Welsh Office and ministers in the Wilson government, in the aftermath of the disaster. Some of the injustices of the handling of Aberfan were widely known, or at least suspected, at the time. The new evidence confirmed and elaborated this knowledge.

This evidence led to an academic paper and a number of newspaper articles by IM.[1] In August 1997, when Ron Davies, then Secretary of State for Wales, repaid the £150,000 taken from the disaster fund to help pay for the removal of the tips at Aberfan, he cited IM as one of the people who had influenced his decision. From this research sprang a grant from the British Academy (APN 6714) to preserve and catalogue the archives held by Merthyr Central Library. The results of that work can be found on the internet at www.nuff.ox.ac.uk/politics/aberfan/home.htm. This book builds on the foundations of that earlier work. Funded by a grant from the Economic and Social Research Council (ESRC: grant no. R00022677), it revises some of the earlier conclusions, widens the scope of the study of the disaster and places it in the fuller and comparative context of developments since 1966.

The book begins with an account of the Aberfan disaster and its aftermath. This is based entirely on first-hand accounts with no editorial intervention. Chapter 2 is a revised version of the original academic article. It explains how and why the disaster happened. It documents the National Coal Board's (NCB) evasion of responsibility for the disaster in the face of the condemnation of it and its senior management in the Tribunal Report. It explains how nobody was sacked, demoted, sued, or prosecuted; and the roles of the Welsh Office, George Thomas, Harold Wilson, Lord Robens, and the Charity

Commission in securing the payment from the disaster fund for tip removal.

Chapter 3 explores the relationship between the NCB and Merthyr Tydfil County Borough Council. A small local authority whose citizens depended on the coal industry, was unable to challenge a large corporation. In the aftermath of the disaster, this unequal relationship continued to cause problems for the council whose resources were almost overwhelmed by the tasks that it had to confront. While other parts of South Wales were witnessing a rise in support for Plaid Cymru, in Merthyr, and particular Aberfan and Merthyr Vale, anti-government feeling was channelled into independent resident groups and the local MP, S. O. Davies, who had been expelled by the Labour Party. The chapter examines the lessons of Aberfan for disaster management.

Chapter 4 introduces the rest of the book. It explains why Aberfan is still remembered and still important before moving on to look at the field of disaster studies and how disasters are socially constructed. It outlines which disasters will be examined in the book and sets out the hypotheses that the subsequent chapters will challenge.

Nothing like Aberfan had happened since the Second World War, and nobody realised quite how large a task counselling the survivors would be. Chapter 5 documents what services were made available to help Aberfan in its recovery. It locates this within the contemporary understanding of traumatic stress and shows how there was some misunderstanding of the needs of the bereaved, survivors and community. The management of trauma after Aberfan is then compared with later disasters including Dunblane, Bradford and Hillsborough. Our understanding of the traumatic impact of disasters has increased significantly. Yet the kind of long-term problems suffered in Aberfan have continued to be witnessed after other disasters. Despite the advances in knowledge, there remains no clear consensus on how to help disaster victims while the misguided actions (and inaction) of different authorities continue to deepen the trauma that disaster creates.

The press labelled the Aberfan Disaster Fund 'the second Aberfan disaster'. The question of how to spend the huge sum of money donated caused arguments and further distress in the village. Chapter 6 investigates how the Charity Commission, duty-bound to uphold an outdated and inflexible law, intervened and obstructed payments by the charitable Disaster Fund to individual victims and for the cemetery memorial. It did not intervene to protect the Fund from a government raid on its money to pay for the removal of dangerous coal tips above Aberfan – a raid that seems dubiously

justifiable in charity law. The failures of regulation relating to the
fund are discussed; some of them have since been remedied, some
not. The chapter reviews why people donate to disaster funds and
how their administration has changed since Aberfan.

Chapter 7 examines the compensation paid after the negligent
death of a child. Damages for injuring an adult or killing a farm
animal are based on estimates of earning capacity forgone. Damages
for injuring or killing a child are not. Hence the Coal Board's contention in 1966 that £500 per child killed was 'a generous offer' to the
bereaved parents of Aberfan. Bereavement damages remain small
and available only to a narrow class of relatives. Parents of young
adults killed at Hillsborough received nothing. The chapter looks
critically at how this position has come about and the legal reasoning
for it.

Chapter 8 discusses how companies are to be held responsible for
corporate negligence that causes deaths. Attempts to bring charges
against those held responsible for subsequent disasters have met with
mixed fates. A prosecution for corporate manslaughter against the
operators of the *Herald of Free Enterprise* failed. Small or one-man
companies can be successfully prosecuted (as in the Lyme Regis
canoeing tragedy or the Wishaw *E coli O157* outbreak). In July 1999
a prosecution for corporate manslaughter of Great Western Trains,
the operator of the passenger train that crashed at Southall in
September 1997, failed, bringing further calls for a change in the law.
The chapter also discusses how the present law on health and safety
at work (written by a departmental committee chaired by Lord
Robens) has shaped the legal responses to disasters. It recommended
that the criminal law should be kept out of this area. British Rail's
acceptance of corporate liability for the Clapham disaster is
contrasted with other cases in the 1980s. This area of policy returned
to public attention after the Paddington (Ladbroke Grove) rail
disaster in October 1999.

The book's concluding chapter further discusses the issue of disasters, responsibility and regulation. It compares the contention made
in Chapter 2 (that the failure to hold anybody accountable for
Aberfan derives from the corporatist assumptions that pervaded
British politics at the time) with alternative possible explanations. It
includes an entirely fresh analysis of the *Titanic* disaster, showing
that for 80 years people have concentrated on side issues such as the
location of SS *Californian*, ignoring the glaring issue of the culpability of the Board of Trade, itself the body which commissioned the
disaster report. The whole process of how disasters can provoke
regulatory change is examined. Finally, the chapter draws together

the conclusions of the previous three, to show which of the events that followed Aberfan could happen again, and which would be unlikely to.

Academic rigour and ethical concerns demand that this book be as dispassionate and as objective as possible. Nonetheless, the history of disasters in Britain is littered with emotion, anger and injustice. It is unavoidable that we comment on such matters. Some believe that it is best to put the past behind us and 'leave the dead to rest in peace'.[2] However, for many survivors and bereaved families it is impossible to achieve this until they have seen justice for their losses. The failures of the legal system have meant that closure is impossible for many. Even when justice is done, the painful memories of disasters remain for the bereaved and survivors. After nearly 35 years, Aberfan is still sometimes a place of tears. The cardinal principle of our research has been not to intrude where we were not wanted or where we could cause harm. Except in the Dedication, we do not name individual victims of the disaster, even where such information is now in the public domain. It is hoped that this work will help highlight injustice rather than perpetuate grief.

Notes

1 'Heartless bully who added to agony of Aberfan', *Observer*, 5 January 1997. 'It's not too late to say sorry', *Times Education Supplement*, 17 January 1997. 'On moles and the habits of birds: the unpolitics of Aberfan', *Twentieth Century British History*, 8, 1997, 285–309.

2 See, for example, letter from Geoffrey Morgan, formerly secretary of the Aberfan Disaster Fund, discussing Aberfan and Hillsborough in *The Times*, 19 April 1999.

ACKNOWLEDGEMENTS

This book has been written with the help of a great many people. The Economic and Social Research Council funded the bulk of the research through a generous grant while the British Academy and the Glamorgan County History Society financed earlier stages of the work. Without these grants none of what follows what have been possible.

Carolyn Jacob, Geraint James and the staff of Merthyr Central and Dowlais Libraries kindly provided research facilities in the early stages of the work and continuing help throughout. Malcolm Todd assisted with access to the Charity Commission's records. The staff at Cardiff University libraries, Nuffield College library, the Bodleian Library, the National Library of Wales, the Glamorgan Record Office, the South Wales Coalfield Collection (University of Wales, Swansea), and the Public Record Office all provided valuable research assistance, as did Alistair McMillan at the outset of the work. Friends and family in London and Aberystwyth provided hospitality on what otherwise would have been lonely research trips.

Desmond Ackner, Kenneth Barnes, Alan Blackshaw, Bryn Carpenter, Barbara Castle, J. M. Cuthill, Alun Talfan Davies, Ron Dearing, Geoffrey Holland, Geoffrey Howe, Cledwyn Hughes, Gaynor Madgwick, Richard Marsh, Cliff Minett, Geoffrey Morgan, Cyril Moseley, Colin Murray Parkes, C. H. Sisson, John Taylor, Margaret Thatcher, Mr and Mrs W. Tudor, Harold Walker, Hugh Watkins and Tasker Watkins all kindly took time, in letters or discussions, or both, to share their memories of the disaster and its aftermath with us. Less formally, a host of people from across the world have kindly shared with us their memories of Aberfan and other disasters.

The following kindly provided details on the work of their respective organisations or other information: Air Accident Investigation Branch, Catherine Alderson, Jenny Bacon (Director-General, HSE),

Barrie Berkley (Disaster Action), A. Cooksey (HM Railway Inspectorate), Emergency Planning Division (Home Office), Hillsborough Families Support Group, Peter Hodgkinson (Centre for Crisis Psychology), Maureen Hughes (*Headway*), Peter Jones, John Lang (Chief Inspector of Marine Accidents), B. Langdon (HM Chief Inspector of Mines), Lynton Tourist Information Centre, National Mine Health and Safety Academy (US Department of Labor), David Pendleton, Deborah Perkin, Owen H. Prosser, Peter Spooner (Herald Charitable Trust) and Philip Stephens.

The following all kindly shared the benefit of their expertise in their respective fields; without such assistance the inter-disciplinary approach of this book would have been impossible: David Baldwin, Peter Bartrip, David Bergman, Fiona Bickley, Dave Billnitzer, Camilla Bustani, Richard Colbey, Alan Dalton, Simon Deakin, Dominic Elliott, Andrew Evans, Anne Eyre, Frances Gardner, John and Rhiannon Goldthorpe, Paul Johnson, Nicola Lacey, Stephen Lloyd, Laurence Lustgarten, Andrew McDonald, James Mallinson, Ross Manning, Richard Mayou, Derek Morgan, Ken Morgan, Michael Moss, Michael Napier, Morgan R. O'Connell, Clive Payne, Nick Roberts, Ted Rowlands MP, Patrick Schmidt, Phil Scraton, Celia Wells, Chris Williams, Stewart Wood, Charles Woolfson, William Yule, and a safety officer of a railway company. Those present at various papers given by us at Cardiff, Oxford and Southampton Universities also provided useful comments and observations.

Extracts from *I can't stay long* by Laurie Lee (Penguin Books, 1977, copyright © Laurie Lee, 1975), pp. 90, 94, and 96, are reproduced by permission of Penguin Books Ltd. Interviews first published in the *Daily Mail*, 5 October 1996 are reproduced by kind permission of the *Daily Mail* and Solo Syndication. Extracts from Gaynor Madgwick, *Aberfan: Struggling out of Darkness, A Survivor's Story* (Valley and Vale, 1996) are reproduced by kind permission of the author. Extracts from interviews first published in Melanie Doel and Martin Dunkerton, *Is it Still Raining in Aberfan? A Pit and its People* (Logaston Press, 1991) are reproduced by kind permission of the authors. Grateful acknowledgement is made to Philip Stephens (producer) and to Swansea Sound (part of the Wireless group) for kind permission to quote interviews recorded for the radio programme *Aberfan: an Unknown Spring*.

Earlier versions of some of the chapters in this book have appeared in *Twentieth Century British History*, *Legal Studies*, *Disasters* and *Welsh History Review*. We thank the editors and publishers of these journals for permission to reuse this material. Our publishers have shown great personal commitment and enthusiasm for this project. We are delighted to have such enthusiastic colleagues. On a more personal note – our families have been a source of love and support throughout.

Finally, the people of Aberfan, past and present, have shown us incredible forbearance in the course of this research. They have welcomed us into their homes, and taken the time and pain to share with us their memories and thoughts. Only those who have personally experienced a disaster can possibly hope to understand fully what they have been through. This book is dedicated to Aberfan and the memory of those it lost on the morning on 21 October 1966. The authors and publisher are giving a proportion of the royalties from this book to the Aberfan Memorial Charity, which exists for the maintenance and repair of the memorial garden and cemetery memorial at Aberfan, and for the relief in need of all those who have suffered as a result of the Aberfan disaster.

Iain McLean, Oxford
Martin Johnes, Cardiff
June 2000

ABBREVIATIONS

AAIB	Air Accident Inquiry Branch (DETR)
ADA	Aberfan Disaster Archive, Merthyr Tydfil public libraries
APRA	Aberfan Parents' and Residents' Association
CPS	Crown Prosecution Service
DETR	Department of the Environment, Transport and the Regions
DPP	Director of Public Prosecutions
EPD	Emergency Planning Department, Home Office
FA	The Football Association
FC	Football Club
GRO	Glamorgan Record Office
HM	Her/His Majesty's
HMI	Her/His Majesty's Inspector(ate)
HMRI	Her Majesty's Railway Inspectorate
H&S	Health and safety
HSC	Health and Safety Commission
HSE	Health and Safety Executive
HSWA	Health & Safety at Work (etc.) Act 1974
IMO	International Marine Organisation
MAIB	Marine Accident Inquiry Branch (DETR)
MEP	Member of the European Parliament
MP	Member of Parliament
MTCBC	Merthyr Tydfil County Borough Council
nd	No date
NCB	National Coal Board
PRO	Public Record Office
PTSD	Post Traumatic Stress Disorder
RoRo	Roll-on, Roll-off
SWCC	South Wales Coalfield Collection

Chapter One

THE LAST DAY BEFORE HALF-TERM

On the mountain

... I told him [Vivian Thomas] what I told him before, that the tip was sinking pretty bad and what were they going to do about it. ... He told me to go up to the tip, take a burner with me, and get the crane back as far as I could for we were to start another tipping site later on in the week. ...

[Q. When you got to the front of the tip, did you see how far it had sunk?] I should say about 18 to 20 ft. ... [The crane rails] had broken off and fell down into the hole. ... I told the boys that we would get the rails up from there and start and put the crane back. I said before we start we have a cup of tea, and we went back into the shack. We were not there five minutes ...

Tip gang chargehand[1]

I was standing on the edge of the depression, sir, I was looking down into it, and what I saw I couldn't believe my eyes. It was starting to come back up. It started to rise slowly at first, sir. I still did not believe it, I thought I was seeing things. Then it rose up after pretty fast, sir, at a tremendous speed. Then it sort of came up out of the depression and turned itself into a wave, that is the only way I can describe it, down towards the mountain ... towards Aberfan village, sir. ... And as it turned over, I shouted: "Good God, boys, come and look at this lot". ... I was looking down in the crevice, sir, down at the drop, and it seemed to me like as if the bottom shot out.

Tip worker[2]

We were not in there more than five minutes when I heard a shout. ... We all got out in a matter of seconds. ... We all stood there, sir, on the front of the tip. ... I saw the tip going in ... all I can tell you is it was going down at a hell of a speed in waves. I myself ran down the side of No. 3 tip, all the way down towards No. 2 and No.1 tip on the side. As I was running down I heard another roar behind me and trees cracking and a tram passing me. I stopped – I fell down in fact. All I could see was waves of muck, slush and water. I still kept running.... I kept going down shouting. I could not see, nobody could.... I was stumbling and I got stuck in a bit of the slurry. I could hear a rush behind me and all I could see was soaking wet slurry like waves coming down, more water than muck itself coming down.

Tip gang chargehand[3]

I never expected it would cross the embankment behind the village which I could not see because of the mist which covered the whole of the village. There was nothing I could do. We had no telephone to give an alarm or any warning device. I shouted, but it was no good.

Tip gang chargehand[4]

It never dawned on me or came to my thoughts, sir, that it had gone as far as the village.

Tip worker[5]

In Aberfan

I heard a noise, a big rumbling noise. ... I saw a tree and a telegraph pole coming towards me first, then I saw a big black mass of stuff. ... A black wave of muck.

Schoolboy, age 13.[6]

As I was walking up the hill where it turns left, I saw a big wave of muck coming over the railway embankment. It was coming straight towards me and I ran.... I saw trams, trees, trucks, bricks and boulders in it.

Schoolboy, age 14.[7]

[It sounded] Like a jet plane. ... and two or three seconds later I could hear stones and rubble, so I ran back down the hill. I thought it was the tip.... I said "I don't think it is a jet, it is the tip", and I shouted at them [two boys] to run, and they ran down behind me.... I remember in Moy Road I could see the front windows crashing in, and the front doors; it was like a pile of dominoes coming down.... I went into that lane for shelter; I didn't know what to do.... I had only got in about a yard and this top of the garage was down and a sheet of zinc came down and hit me on the head, hit me down.... I could not force it off me. There was a lot of bricks on it; it protected me.... [The noise] was suddenly cut off, just like the wireless being turned off.... It stopped as it hit the last house down No.1 Moy Road and there was a terrible silence.

Aberfan resident[8]

In that silence you couldn't hear a bird or a child.

Aberfan resident[9]

Pantglas Junior School

Mr Davis, our teacher, got the board out and wrote our maths class work and we were all working, and then it began. It was a tremendous rumbling sound and all the school went dead. You could hear a pin drop. Everyone was petrified, afraid to move. Everyone just froze in their seats. I just managed to get up and I reached the end of my desk when the sound got louder and nearer, 'til I could see the black out of the window. I can't remember any more but I woke up to find that a horrible nightmare had just begun in front of my eyes.

Pupil, Pantglas Junior School[10]

I was standing in front of the class and the thing I remember the most was what I thought was a couple of slates dropping off the roof; because they had been repairing the roof. And with that I looked up through the fog and I could see this enormous spinning boulder and there was a black line alongside it. And I had time to realise that that spinning boulder wasn't heading for me. I immediately looked at the class and with that it crashed into the room at the speed of a jet aeroplane and I was hurled from the centre of the room to the corner by the door. ... I could feel the room shaking and I could see the room filling up. I'm afraid my life didn't flash in front of me. What was happening I just didn't know. And then it stopped. And there was such an eerie silence I remember. From ... a tall old classroom ... with echoes and sounds, there was nothing, there was just this deadness. And I had a chance to reassess the situation. I was trapped up to my waist in desks and rubble and goodness knows what else. And I looked up to the roof and I could see a young lad in my class right up at the roof and climbing down what was then a tip inside my classroom. And I could hear children all, well they weren't screaming, they were trapped amongst their desks. And mercifully in my classroom no one was injured badly as far as I can remember, they were trapped but no one was injured badly. And I remember this boy climbing down and he climbed to the door, and I was trapped near the door, and he started kicking the top half of the door in. So I said to him 'What are you doing?' And he said 'I'm going home'. And the

reality still hadn't come home to me I don't think because I felt like
giving him a row for breaking the glass. So he kicked the top half of
the door and then he went out. And I thought well I better try and get
out of here.

Teacher, Pantglas Junior School[11]

I was about to start marking the register when there was a terrible
noise like a jet plane and I was afraid it was going to fall on the
school. So I said to my children 'Get under your desks quickly and
stay there'. And there was one little boy in front of me … and he kept
poking his head out, 'Why Miss? Why have I got to do that?' And I
said, 'Because I'm telling you to, get under your desk', and I had to
go and put his head under and stand by him. As it happened nothing
happened in our classroom, just this dreadful noise. It seemed like
ages but it must have been only a few minutes and there was silence.

Teacher, Pantglas Junior School[12]

My abiding memory of that day is blackness and dark. I was buried
by this horrible slurry and I am afraid of the dark to this day.

Pupil, Pantglas Junior School[13]

I went to the door of the classroom and tried the door of the class
room, the children were still under their desks, the door opened,
some rubble fell but when I looked out all I could see was black and
large lumps of concrete which were parts of the cloak room. But
when I looked I could see there was enough room for us to crawl
through sort of a tunnel. So I went back to the children and I said we
had a fire drill and I wanted them to walk out of class quietly. That
I'd go to the school door and open it and then I'd come back and they
were to go out one at a time. They weren't to talk, they were to go out
and stand in the yard and wait for fire drill. And every one of the children did as I asked them. They went out quietly and stood in the
yard. I came out then at the end and Mair had come down from the
room and we didn't know what had happened. We went round the
corner and when we looked around the corner well it just looked as if
the end of the school had just vanished, there was a just a black tip.

Teacher, Pantglas Junior School[14]

… when I got outside I looked at what was to become a famous picture of where the school, where three classrooms had been … the
school was smashed over with this rubble. And I remember standing
looking at that and thinking, well, the reality of it, I just couldn't believe it. And from where there were, at least to my calculations, a
hundred children there wasn't a sound.

Teacher, Pantglas Junior School[15]

I remember being thrown across the classroom when the stuff hit us, then I must have blacked out. I woke to the sound of rescuers breaking a window, then I saw [my friend]. I will never forget the sight. There was blood coming out of his nose and I knew he was dead. If I close my eyes I can still see his face as plain as that moment.

Pupil, Pantglas Junior School[16]

I was there for about an hour and a half until the fire brigade found me. I heard cries and screams, but I couldn't move. The desk was jammed into my stomach and my leg was under the radiator. The little girl next to me was dead and her head was on my shoulder.

Pupil, Pantglas Junior School[17]

The rescue

We are so used to having coal tipped near the school and this noise sounded just like coal being tipped only much more noise than usual; it was a heavy sound. ... I was going towards the school, and I suddenly realised the sound was coming nearer all the time, and the feeling it was the tip came to my mind straight away; so I ran back to the house; my little girl was in bed, so I got her and the wife outside and I went back to the school.

... The north side of the school was completely down, and the tip had come right down the road, Moy Road. I went straight into the boiler house of the junior school and raked out the fire. ... I came out of the boiler house and saw in the classroom next to the boiler house some children there and they were unable to get out, so I tried to smash the window to get the children out, but there was not enough space to get them out that way. The teacher managed to open the door somehow. ... I went in through the door and the children came out past me, out to the yard. Then I went round to the front of the school where Mrs. Williams' class was. I saw she was in there and she could not breathe – she shouted she could not breathe. So I went in through the window, the window was that height from the yard, you know. I climbed in through the window. There was some children trapped in the masonry; I got those children out, passed them out through the window. After that I went outside again and saw a little girl on top of the tank above Miss Jennings' classroom. She was right up and wanted to come down. How she got there I do not know. But I got up on the tank and got her down. Then I saw Mrs. Williams, a teacher, and went to the assembly hall and started digging them out.

After that I do not know, I cannot remember anything; all I know is my two boys were buried in the rubble.

School caretaker[18]

Then the next thing I remember was seeing a mass of men coming up from the colliery still with their lamp lights on. That was really moving because they were black, they'd just come off the shift and they'd been sent straight up. And they had their lights on. And after that they just took over from us.

Teacher, Pantglas Junior School[19]

I went down to work, changed, went down the pit and I hadn't been down the pit ten minutes when they sent for everybody to come up, that the tip had slid. Well we came up, I couldn't fathom it out; I'd never seen anything like it. The front of the school was there but there was no back. We went there and we dug and dug all day.

Miner and bereaved parent[20]

We had to break the front windows and then climb in. ... We had no tools – we used our bare hands and anything we could find. But there was nothing anyone could do, between the slurry and the water coming down. That was the worst, not being able to do anything. There's nothing as bad as that.

Bereaved parent[21]

The women were already there, like stone they were, clawing at the filth – it was like a black river – some had no skin left on their hands. Miners are a tough breed, we don't show our feelings, but some of the lads broke down.

Miner[22]

I have been asked to inform you that there has been a landslide at Pantglas. The tip has come down on the school.

Emergency call received by Merthyr Tydfil police,
9.25 a.m., 21 October 1966.[23]

We didn't know what to expect. I had no idea of the scale of the thing. It was a great shock. There was absolute chaos and somehow I had to organise that chaos.

Assistant Chief Constable[24]

I left by car for the scene of the incident. ... and I arrived at Moy Road ... at about 10 o'clock. That was near the infants' school. With the co-operation of the chief inspector I set up an incident post at a police car on the colliery side of the incident to maintain communications with police headquarters by radio telephone. ... I then made a reconnaissance of the whole area above the school, and I managed to get round to the streets to the other side, the north side of the incident at the Mackintosh hotel. This reconnaissance revealed that not only was the Pantglas junior school buried under approximately 20 to 30 ft. of debris, but a large number of houses in Moy Road and Pantglas had been demolished and submerged under a pile of debris and liquid mud.

... at 10.30 a large quantity of water was still pouring into the disaster area, and I was informed that it was coming from the mountain springs and two large water mains which had been fractured when the disused canal and disused railway embankment had broken.

Chief Constable of the County Borough of Merthyr Tydfil[25]

They [the vehicle and rescue workers] had to retire a little to avoid being swamped by the new rush of water and slurry. ... It certainly hindered the rescuers from the end that I was working and had that water not come quite a number of properties would have been saved.

Chief Inspector, Merthyr Tydfil County Borough Police[26]

As I was in the shop there was dirty black water coming down the hill, and as I was waiting my turn to be served I shouted out that we were going to be flooded. As I dashed back to the house with my little baby Alan, who was just one, in my arms, I fell over the milk bottles.

With that my friend Glenys from a few doors away arrived with her daughter Sian who was dirty. She said Sian had come home from class all covered in dirt, and she had thrust her into my arms before running back up to the school. I asked Sian what had happened and she said that the school had fallen down.

I didn't know what to do, so I went round to Glenys' house where the door was wide open and a stream of dirty water was just rushing through.

I ran up to the top then and when I saw the school had fallen down, my legs just turned to jelly. I couldn't walk. I just stood there dazed as all the time water flooded my home. Glenys came past and said she hadn't seen [my daughter].

Aberfan resident[27]

As I was being carried out I realised I had lost my jumper. It was a mustard-coloured one that my mother had knitted. There were five children in our family and you couldn't afford to lose a jumper, so I tried to go back and look for it because I thought I would get into trouble. I was taken straight to hospital and my parents did not come to see me until evening. They must have spent the whole day not knowing where I was, not knowing if I was alive or dead. But we never talked about it.

Pupil, Pantglas Junior School[28]

I could hear men's voices but I didn't know what they were doing or where they were. I heard someone crying and then this voice was asking me if I could see daylight and I could put my finger through it and then I was dug out.

I was passed through a chain of men, out through a window and into the yard and handed to the policeman, who carried me to the side of a wall where he placed me on the ground.... I looked back at the school and I just couldn't believe what had happened. It was completely flat.

Pupil, Pantglas Junior School[29]

At that time I'd bought felt pens and they were rather a new thing. They cost 2/6 at the time. And I had these three felt pens, a red one, a blue one and a mauve one. And I was more interested in getting these felt pens out. And the fire officer said to me, 'Forget those bloody felt pens and let's get you out'.

Pupil, Pantglas Junior School[30]

Men, women and children were tearing away the debris in an effort to reach the trapped children. As the men shovelled debris from spade to spade, children's books appeared. An odd cap was seen. A broken doll.

Mothers gathered around the school steps, some weeping, some silent, Some shaking their heads in disbelief....

The slurry had piled up 25 feet against the school, smashing its way through the building, filling the classrooms.

Teams of 50 men and boys worked in long rows from the school building, handing buckets of slurry up the mountainside from the classrooms.

On each side of the school mechanical shovels and bulldozers gouged the debris out. An endless line of lorries carried it away. ... At regular intervals everything would come to a halt – the roar of heavy machinery, the shouts, the scraping of shovels. Not a murmur would be heard among the thousand workers. Time stood still. And rescuers listened tensely for the slightest sound from the wreckage – for a cry, a moan, a movement – anything which would give hope to the mothers and fathers.

First journalist on the scene[31]

Nobody told me what had happened at the time. I asked somebody next to me, it must have been a couple of hours later, he said "What is this stuff?"; I did not know myself what it was, and I was under the impression it was an explosion of gas. I did not think the tip had slipped; I did not realise anything about the tip. It must have been a good two hours when somebody said "it's the tip that has slipped." I did not know; I was just knocked for six; I did not realise that it was that.

Bereaved parent[32]

It's like a blitz – as though a bomb had been dropped on the whole school.

We can only work in small groups, and gas is leaking. Progress is slow, as we have to prop up the beams and wall as we go in.

The chances of survival are negligible, but I'm hope I'm wrong.

Rescue worker[33]

You only have to mention what you want it and it comes. We've had no trouble at all to get anything.

Civil Defence worker[34]

The really incredible thing was that you couldn't walk five yards without a member of the WVRS or the Salvation Army or the Red Cross putting a cup of soup, a cup of coffee or a cup of chocolate into your hand.

Detective Constable[35]

We cut up cotton sheets for bandages, and gave blankets and pillows for the children as they were brought out on stretchers.. Rescuers came in for everything, and we gave all we could. All we thought of was that children's lives were at stake. Everything lost its value in comparison with those children.

Aberfan Resident[36]

No one was brought out alive after 11 o'clock.

Chief Constable of the County Borough of Merthyr Tydfil[37]

... the roads leading to the incident both from Merthyr Vale and from Troedyrhiw were blocked with vehicles with rescue workers and helpers, both official and voluntary, and similarly the A470 road between Pentrebach and the Travellers Rest was becoming congested, and in a number of places it had become completely blocked. ... The mortuary was set up in the early stages at Bethania Chapel, and I appointed an officer of the regional crime squad to take over the identification and handling of the bodies, and by 11.30 at night on the first day 67 bodies had been brought in and identification was then in progress.

Chief Constable of the County Borough of Merthyr Tydfil[38]

I reached the tragic village of Aberfan on Saturday morning. The initial panic and hysteria had died and now there was a well-ordered rescue operation under-way. But it was still a grim sight. There was a greyness everywhere. Faces from the tiredness and anguish, houses and roads from the oozing slurry of the tips. The grey-black mass seemed to have penetrated everywhere and all around were evacuated houses.

Merthyr Express[39]

There was an estimated 2,000 volunteers now [Saturday] at the scene. Many of them had been working for 24 hours.

First journalist on the scene[40]

Heavy rain started at 2.30 p.m. Saturday causing immense anxiety and fear that the huge tip would slide again and engulf the rescuers.... By this time about 2,500 workers were on the scene. Extra police were called in because in-experienced rescuers would not leave the scene.

Merthyr Express[41]

... no less than 144 men, women and children lost their lives. 116 of the victims were children, most of them between the ages of 7 and 10 ...

Report of the Tribunal appointed to inquire into the Disaster at Aberfan[42]

Bereavement

Up until then [Friday, 7 p.m.] I had hoped that the chapel was a hospital, but as I went into Bethania people were coming out who had been told their children had gone. Until I went in I still had hope that they were just lost. When I went all the pews were covered with little blankets and under them lay the little children. They picked up the blankets and showed me every girl until I came to [her] and said she was mine. There wasn't a mark on her except a little scratch over her mouth, even her clothes were clean.

What I missed most was the noise and fun around the house. [My daughter] was boisterous and full of fun. Our house was as quiet as a mouse after she'd gone.

Bereaved mother[43]

As soon as the word swept around Aberfan that the bodies were being taken to Bethania chapel, parents and relatives arrived at the front door. They waited in a long patient line to be permitted in, to try and identify the daughter, son, wife, husband, mother or father. Because of the cramped conditions in which we were operating we could only deal with two sets of relatives at a time.

When we established the age and sex of the person they were seeking they were shown all the bodies that matched. The task was not made easier by the fact that most of the boys wore grey short trousers and the girls a standard dress and cardigan.

Policeman working at the mortuary[44]

In the night we had to go to see if we could identify her in this chapel. I've never forgotten that. It comes back to me everyday. There's some part of the day that the picture comes back to me and I can never forget that. ... All these little bodies wrapped in blankets.

Bereaved father[45]

So they went back, my daughter, and my husband and her husband as he is now, to look and search for the child. Someone had said that the child was taken down to Church Village. So they went down to the hospitals there but no they couldn't see the child. I knew that when Emlyn came in the early hours of the morning that [she] was not going to be found. His face was grey and Angela was terrible, we knew then that the little one was gone.

Bereaved mother[46]

The streets were silent but for the sound of shuffling feet. Some mourners wept while others pent up their emotions until they reached the cemetery.

As the funeral singing began, hymn singing drifted down to the village below where everyone shared in the sorrow. All shops were closed; the doors of the public houses were bolted and normal life ceased.

At the graveside above, three thousand people gathered to pay their last respects.

The burial took place in the shadow of the now depleted tip.

Merthyr Express[47]

... all those little coffins in the grave. It was terrible, terrible. There was hundreds of people up there. Some screaming, some crying ...

Bereaved father[48]

Please use this small amount in any way you wish. I was saving it up for a new coat, O God I wish I had saved more. Yours sincerely, A Mother.

Letter to the Aberfan Disaster Fund[49]

Anger and determination

I was helping to dig the children out when I heard a photographer tell
a kiddie to cry for her dead friends, so that he could get a good picture – that taught me silence.

Rescue worker[50]

During that period the only thing I didn't like was the press. If you
told them something, when the paper came out your words were all
the wrong way round.

Bereaved father[51]

The brave front of the people of Aberfan cracked on Monday at an
inquest on 30 of the children.

There were shouts of "murderers" as the Coroner of Merthyr, Mr.
Ben Hamilton, began reading out the names of the dead children.

As one name was read out and the cause of death given as asphyxia
and multiple injuries, the father of the child said "No, sir, buried
alive by the National Coal Board".

One of the only two women among the 60 people at the inquest at
Sion Primitive English Methodist Chapel at Aberfan, shouted out
through her tears, "They have killed our children."

Then a number of people called out and got to their feet. The coroner tried to restore order and said: "I know your grief is such that you
may not be realising what you are saying."

The father repeated: "I want it recorded – 'Buried alive by the
National Coal Board.' That is what I want to see on the record. That
is the feeling of those present. Those are the words we want to go on
the certificate."

Merthyr Express[52]

It was impossible to know that there was a spring in the heart of this
tip which was turning the centre of the mountain into sludge.

Rt. Hon. Lord Robens of Woldingham,
Chairman of the National Coal Board, to a TV reporter[53]

A man who lost his niece at Aberfan broke through a police cordon
to talk to Lord Justice Edmund Davies – the man who is to head the
inquiry into the disaster – as he toured the stricken village on Tuesday.

The man, 61-year old Mr. Philip Brown, a disabled miner, told the
judge: 'Don't let strangers pull the wool over your eyes.'

The judge spoke to Mr. Brown for a couple of minutes and then
moved away to continue his tour.

Afterwards Mr. Brown said 'I asked him if I could speak to him for

five minutes. He told me, "Most certainly." He is a real gentleman.
   'I said, "Don't let strangers take up the mountain and pull the
wool over your eyes. If you must go up, go up with a local man who
knows the real facts."
   ... 'I told him the spring at the head of the mountain had always
been there.
   'It was not a hidden spring. The National Coal Board must have
known about it because everyone in the village did.'

Merthyr Express[54]

I was tormented by the fact that the people I was seeking justice from
were my people – a Labour Government, a Labour council, a Labour-nationalised Coal Board.

Bereaved husband and parent[55]

The Aberfan disaster was very much a disaster of the Valleys; it could
have happened in any part of them. It was the crowning disaster of a
dangerous industry, and its victims were the innocent.

Aberfan community worker[56]

Why there is bitterness

'During my childhood I played on that monstrous mountain of slag,
and in my youth I rummaged coal from it. Everyone knew that one
day – some day – this hideous scar on the landscape, this indiscrimi-
nate dumping of colliery refuse, would bring disaster. But little did
we think that when it did happen, it would leave such devastation
and heart-breaking sorrow in its wake.'
   These words are written by a native of Aberfan, an ex-pupil of
Pantglas school. They are contained in a letter to the editor expressing heartfelt sympathy to all those people who are suffering in this
hour of indescribable tragedy.
   There is today sadness in the hearts of everyone who lives in a mining valley. But there is bitterness too.
   The coal mining communities of South Wales have lived so long
with death as a companion that they reconcile themselves to accepting the peril that hangs over them.
   Everyone knows that coal tips move. Everyone fears that one day
the tip above their village will come rumbling down into the valley,
but it is a possibility that they accept.
   Without the tip above Aberfan the Merthyr Vale Colliery could
have closed down. Without the colliery the village would itself have
died.

This is the terrible fear that ate into the minds of the people of Aberfan.

Now the worst has happened. Tragedy of the most devastating kind has struck. A village has lost its children. Is not the bitterness, therefore, understandable?

Merthyr Express editorial[57]

My first impression of Aberfan was terrible. I couldn't imagine, I never imagined that it was like that. The village was dirty, my house was dirty, everything was dirty. The tip had left mud and slurry everywhere. I was fortunate in one way because I had no conception what this tip had done to us at Aberfan. It wasn't until a long time after that I came to terms with this. Then instead of being a passive person as I was before I became a fighter for Aberfan. I felt that we had a duty to the children who were left and those who were yet to be born. And it was a duty that we must build a better Aberfan for the children that were coming.

Bereaved parent on returning to Aberfan after the disaster[58]

The villagers had done admirably in rehabilitating themselves with very little help. A Government gesture was needed to restore confidence and only complete removal of the tips would do this. Many people in the village were on sedatives but they did not take them when it was raining because they were afraid to go to sleep. Children did not close their bedroom doors in case they should be trapped.

Official note of Aberfan social worker's comments at meeting with Welsh Office[59]

They took the money out of the disaster fund to pay for the removal of the tips, which was to me shocking. Absolutely unbelievable. And that's always been in me. I think they [the NCB] owe us. They owe the people of Aberfan a debt. Call it a debt of conscience if you like. I don't think we should beg for this And we need the money. There's the Memorial Garden to be maintained. And the cemetery. For many, many years to come. Where is it going to come from in later years when we're gone?

Bereaved parent, speaking in 1996[60]

Recovery

I tried to rescue people but I realised it could be dangerous just digging, not knowing what you were doing and I was getting in the way of people so I immediately switched over to pastoral work.... The end of chapter 8 of Romans is a great summary of faith – *What can separate us from the love of God?* – It's a passage I always use when there's a personal tragedy or disaster and that's a message we always try to emphasise – *I am certain that nothing can separate us from the love of God, neither death nor life, neither angels or other heavenly rulers nor powers, neither the present nor the future.*

Bereaved Baptist minister, speaking in 1996[61]

My work afterwards was more like that of a pastor. People had to face not only grief but bitterness, anger and even guilt. The first real thing that happened were the terrible nightmares people suffered, reliving the event time and time again. That went on for months. There was a terrible worry and pressure on people while the tip was still there, and every time there was a row over what was to be done about the tip my surgery would be full the next day. The stress and anxiety triggered off by what to do would affect people's health.

It was predicted at the time that a lot of people might suffer from heart attacks brought on by the stress and grief, but that didn't happen. Other experts predicted that there would be a number of suicides, but that didn't happen either. These people hadn't allowed for the resilience of the families involved. It was psychological problems that hit worst.

One thing that did happen within a short time afterwards was that the birth rate went up. Also many people were drinking a lot more and for some time after I had to deal with people who had serious drink problems, and for people who already had health problems, those problems increased.

From the time of the disaster for about the following six years I dealt with people who suffered break downs. There was no set pattern or any time when it could be expected to happen. It happened at different times for different people.

After the disaster I warned the community would have to come to accept its guilt. This guilt came out in many ways. There were the so-called guilty men who were blamed for what happened; they suffered themselves and were the victims of a hate campaign. But it wasn't only them. Women who had sent their children who hadn't wanted to go to school that day suffered terrible feelings of guilt. ... Grief and guilt came in many different ways. There was a strange bitterness between families who lost children and those who hadn't; people just could not help it.

Aberfan doctor[62]

I kept asking myself why I hadn't died and I blamed myself for allowing my brother and sister to die.

Pupil, Pantglas Junior School[63]

I've got to say this again, if the papers and the press and the television were to leave us alone in the very beginning I think we could have settled down a lot quicker than what we did.

Bereaved father[64]

... we were a community that were not used to being exposed on television or in papers. We are a community that wears our hearts on our sleeves. We're quite open and we were only doing in the time after the disaster, as far as I'm concerned, what we've always done for years, thrashing out and the press exploded it. The other thing I always felt was that many of the facts that they reported were, and if they kept the facts, were fairly accurate. But it did remind me of a scientist who has got a theory and then forces the facts to prove it. But what I wanted them to do was to take the facts and then decide what it told them. And the result was that they were coming in, and I remember more than one interviewing me wanting me to give certain answers.

Bereaved father[65]

We weren't prepared for it. We weren't geared up for what was happening. Like the people from the press. They came in. We hadn't seen any of this, ever, we didn't know, it's a different world to us. And they came from all over the place.... They were round with their notebooks and their pads and asking all these questions, 'How are you getting over it?' You can't ask me that now, never mind 30 years ago.

Bereaved parent, speaking in 1996.[66]

Fragments of the school itself still lie embedded in the rubbish – chunks of green-painted classroom wall.... Even more poignant relics lie in a corner of the buried playground piled haphazardly against a wall – some miniature desks and chairs, evocative as a dead child's clothes, infant-sized, still showing the shape of their bodies. Among the rubble there also lie crumpled song-books, sodden and smeared with slime, the words of some bed-time song still visible on the pages surrounded by drawings of sleeping elves.

Across the road from the school, and facing up the mountain, stands a row of abandoned houses. This must once have been a trim little working-class terrace, staidly Victorian but specially Welsh, with lace-curtained windows, potted plants in the hall, and a piano in every parlour – until the wave of slag broke against it, smashed the doors and windows, and squeezed through the rooms like tooth-paste.

Something has been done to clear them, but not very much. They stand like broken and blackened teeth. Doors sag, windows gape, revealing the devastation within – a crushed piano, some half-smothered furniture. You can step in from the street and walk round the forsaken rooms which still emit an aura of suffocation and panic – floors scattered with letters, coat-hangers on the stairs, a jar of pickles on the kitchen table. The sense of catastrophe and desertion, resembling the choked ruins of Pompeii, hangs in the air like volcanic dust.

....Prettily dressed and beribboned, riding expensive pedal-cars and bicycles, they [surviving children] are an elite, the aristocrats of survival, their lives nervously guarded and also coveted by those who mourn. By luck, chance, and by no choice of their own, they are part of the unhealed scar-tissue of Aberfan.

Laurie Lee, writer, on Aberfan one year on[67]

Of course, we could have lost the boy too. He was on his way up Moy Road when he saw the houses falling towards him. He ran off home; and I couldn't get a word out of him for months. He had to go to the psychiatrist.... Just wouldn't talk about it, and wouldn't mention his sister either. And the two of 'em worshipped each other. They was always together; slept in the same room, holding hands.... He used to hide when we went to the grave....

Then one night – about four months later it was – we was round at our brother's place. The boy went outside to the lavatory and I heard him call Dad! Ay, what is it, boy? I said. Come out here! he said. Sure, I said, what's the matter? It was a beautiful frosty night. He said, Look at that star up there – that's our Sandie, Dad. Sure, I said, that's our little Sandie.

The boy's all right now, and I'm going to see he's all right.... And I'll make damn sure he never goes down the pit. He's not going to grow up daft like me.

Bereaved father talking to Laurie Lee, 1967[68]

We were a generation that lost out. We lost out on our education and on our futures. I can't think of any of us who ever did really well and most of just stayed and grew up in the village. We haven't gone far at all.

Pupil, Pantglas Junior School[69]

In Mount Pleasant school, which was a similar school, I remember vividly the first day going in, I took the remains of the upper part of

the school, going into the classroom and sitting down there and outside was a railway line coming from the colliery and a diesel rumbled
past, very very slowly, and I can see the looks on the children's faces
and mine. But it turned out alright but the actual shock of getting
back to school was enormous and eventually everything went off alright and the children returned to normality.

Teacher, Pantglas Junior School[70]

There was none of the discipline we used to have ... We didn't go out
to play for a long time because those who'd lost their own children
couldn't bear to see us. We all knew what they were feeling and we
felt guilty about being alive.

Pupil, Pantglas Junior School[71]

As children we never got any sympathy. We were always told we
were lucky to be alive. I suppose everybody in the village was so
badly affected that nobody had the time to give us any sympathy. At
school, though, the teachers treated us differently. It was as if they
could not bring themselves to be strict with us. We lost a lot of
schooling after the disaster anyway, and most of us never really made
it up.

Pupil, Pantglas Junior School[72]

What happened in Aberfan that day was the dark little secret when
we were young and it still is. We knew we must not speak out. We
have been quiet for the sake of the other people, those who lost
children and those who did not want to hear about what happened, especially from the mouths of their own children.... What's
more, the survivors have never spoken to each other about it.
Most of us live in the same small village and have grown up together, yet we all kept everything locked away inside ourselves....
I think that, in some ways, it is harder for a man to deal with, especially around here. Here I am, a grown man, tough ex-miner and
all that, yet since that day I don't like the dark. Down the pit was
all right as long as I was in company. I made sure I was never alone
down there. Even being at home on my own at night makes me uneasy. I don't like being alone anywhere.... When we were young
there was almost nobody left. We wandered streets like lost souls.

Pupil, Pantglas Junior School[73]

In those days talking of your emotions was an embarrassment. As a
child you felt ashamed to tell someone what you were feeling, even if
you were crying. You didn't want them to know you were crying. I
only cried when I'd gone to bed in the evenings. If my mother heard
me she would come in to see me. But I couldn't talk to her about how

I felt – and in the morning I would feel embarrassed. In my family we never discussed what had happened. Nothing was said. Just tears and very quiet. It's the same round here today – people don't want you to see they're upset. I've never seen my dad to cry, never. When I went to bed I would speak to God. He was the only one I could speak to at the time. You don't get an answer back but you could feel there's somebody there. And that's a comfort. ... My Dad was very bitter for years. It was his only son, you see. My mother still won't talk about that time. She doesn't want to know. She's blanked it out. It was the only way she could cope. We always went to church and she turned atheist for a while, which was bad because it meant she had no comfort anywhere. But she started to believe again and I think it has given her back her strength.

Pupil, Pantglas Junior School[74]

We couldn't talk about the loss for some time. Our boy was only seven. It threw our family life completely off-balance. [My wife] was breaking down all the time. What can you say? You feel so helpless. You sit there and you can't do a thing.

Bereaved father[75]

It gives you a respect for living. You're thankful just to be here and all my friends seem to be very placid, I never argue with people. We seem to be different, for I never discuss the disaster with friends – I think you do tend to wipe it out.

Pupil, Pantglas Junior School[76]

Today, when a disaster happens, you bring in people who are trained counsellors to help the victims' families cope. But the counselling in Aberfan then was done by the community itself. That true Welshness, the sense of belonging and togetherness, came to the fore then.

Detective Constable[77]

By every statistic, patients seen, prescriptions written, deaths, I can prove that this is a village of excessive sickness. And the cause is obvious.... Psychiatrists came and wrote "Aberfan needs no help". Now they come to study what grief did to us. Nowhere else has grief been so concentrated. Lockerbie, Zeebrugge, King's Cross – everywhere they used the lessons this place taught them.

Aberfan doctor[78]

For many years after the disaster if I was sitting in an enclosed room and a jet aeroplane would approach I would absolutely quake and shiver until it had gone and actually feel the nerves running through

my body. I think it also affected my driving as well. I was very aware
of the environment and dangers in the environment. But gradually
over the years it sort of disappeared and now I'm all right. I can
rationalise a jet aeroplane.

Teacher, Pantglas Junior School[79]

As far as we're concerned now, we've still got two boys. We're only
separated for a time. One day we're going to meet. The parting and
the loneliness and being without him is terrible, but it's not for ever.

Bereaved Baptist minister, speaking in 1996[80]

Notes

1 Leslie Davies, *Transcript of Tribunal of Inquiry Proceedings*, day 5, pp. 265–268.
2 Gwynfor Elgar Brown, *Tribunal Transcript*, day 7, p. 364.
3 Leslie Davies, *Tribunal Transcript*, day 5, pp. 268–270.
4 Leslie Davies statement to Treasury Solicitor. Quoted in *Tribunal Transcript*, day 6, p. 316.
5 David John Evans, *Tribunal Transcript*, day 8, p. 413.
6 Gareth Groves, *Tribunal Transcript*, day 3, pp. 110–111.
7 Howard Rees, *Tribunal Transcript*, day 3, p. 107.
8 George Henry Williams, *Tribunal Transcript*, day 4, pp. 190–192.
9 George Henry Williams quoted in *Tribunal Transcript*, day 4, p. 192.
10 Gaynor Madgwick, *Aberfan: Struggling out of Darkness, A Survivor's Story* (Blaengarw: Valley & the Vale, 1996), p. 23.
11 SWCC Interview with Howell Williams, 1986, AUD/522.
12 SWCC Interview with Hetty Williams, 1986, AUD/523.
13 Susan Robertson quoted in *Daily Mail Weekend*, 5 October 1996, p. 13.
14 SWCC Interview with Hetty Williams, 1986, AUD/523.
15 SWCC Interview with Howell Williams, 1986, AUD/522.
16 Gerald Kirwan quoted in *Daily Mail Weekend*, 5 October 1996, p. 12. Name of deceased friend withheld.
17 Jeff Edwards quoted in *Daily Telegraph*, 18 October 1996.
18 Stephen David Andrew, *Tribunal Transcript*, day 4, pp. 193–194.
19 SWCC, Interview with Hetty Williams, 1986, AUD/523.
20 SWCC, Interview with Emlyn Richards, 1986, AUD/519.
21 Cliff Minett quoted in *Daily Mail Weekend*, 5 October 1996, p. 10.
22 Gwyn Davies quoted in *The Times*, 17 October 1986, p. 14.
23 Quoted in *Tribunal Transcript*, day 3, p. 100.
24 John Parkman, quoted in *Wales on Sunday*, 16 June 1991, p. 25.
25 T. K. Griffiths, Chief Constable of the County Borough of Merthyr Tydfil, *Tribunal Transcript*, day 3, pp. 101–103.
26 Chief Inspector R. Wilson, Chief Inspector in Merthyr Tydfil County Borough Police, *Tribunal Transcript*, day 3, pp. 113–114.
27 Jessie Meredith quoted in Melanie Doel & Martin Dunkerton, *Is it still raining in Aberfan? A Pit and its People* (Little Logaston: Logaston Press, 1991) p. 47. Name of daughter withheld.

28 Gerald Kirwan quoted in *Daily Mail Weekend*, 5 October 1996, p. 12.
29 Susan Robertson quoted in *South Wales Echo*, 21 October 1996, p. 2.
30 Jeff Edwards, *Timewatch: Remember Aberfan*, BBC2, broadcast on 15 October 1996.
31 Sam Knight, *Merthyr Express*, 28 October 1966, p. 6.
32 Robert Michael Minney, *Tribunal Transcript*, day 5, pp. 247–248.
33 Eric Hughes, quoted in *Merthyr Express*, 28 October 1966, p. 6.
34 Mrs Elizabeth Ingram quoted in *Merthyr Express*, 28 October 1966, p. 10.
35 Bob Evans quoted in *Western Mail*, 12 October 1996, Arena supplement, p. 3.
36 Mrs Francis Smith quoted in *Merthyr Express*, 4 November 1966, p. 3.
37 T. K. Griffiths, quoted in *Merthyr Express*, 28 October 1966, p. 6.
38 T. K. Griffiths, *Tribunal Transcript*, day 3, pp. 101–103.
39 *Merthyr Express*, 28 October 1966, p. 10.
40 Sam Knight, *Merthyr Express*, 28 October 1966, p. 7.
41 *Merthyr Express*, 28 October 1966, p. 11.
42 *Report of the Tribunal appointed to inquire into the Disaster at Aberfan on October 21st, 1966*, Chairman Lord Justice Edmund Davies, HMSO 1967, p. 26. (Hereafter *Aberfan Report*)
43 Jessie Meredith quoted in Doel & Dunkerton, *Is it still raining in Aberfan?*, p. 48. Name of daughter withheld.
44 Charles Nunn, 'The Disaster of Aberfan', *Police Review*, 16 October 1987, p. 2069.
45 SWCC, Interview with Emlyn Richards, 1986, AUD/519.
46 SWCC, Interview with Elaine Richards, 1986, AUD/520. Name of daughter withheld.
47 *Merthyr Express*, 4 November 1966, p. 5.
48 SWCC, Interview with Emlyn Richards, 1986, AUD/519.
49 Quoted in Benedict Nightingale, *Charities* (London: Allen Lane, 1973), p. 178.
50 Anonymous quote in *The Times*, 17 October 1986, p. 14.
51 SWCC, Interview with Emlyn Richards, 1986, AUD/519.
52 *Merthyr Express*, 28 October 1966, p. 18.
53 Quoted in Lord Robens, *Ten Year Stint* (London: Cassell, 1972), p. 251.
54 *Merthyr Express*, 28 October 1966, p. 24.
55 John Collins quoted in unaccredited press clipping in ADA, Merthyr Collection, D/17.
56 Erastus Jones, 'Working in Aberfan and the Valleys', *Social and Economic Administration*, vol. 9, no. 1, Spring 1975.
57 *Merthyr Express*, editorial, 28 October 1966.
58 SWCC, Interview with Elaine Richards, 1986, AUD/519.
59 Meeting with Aberfan Deputation at Welsh Office, London, 12 Noon, Wednesday 7th February 1968. PRO BD 11/3804.
60 Chris Sullivan, *Timewatch*, 15 October 1996.
61 Rev. Kenneth Hayes, in 1966 minister, Zion English Baptist Church, Aberfan, *Timewatch*, 15 October 1996.
62 *Dr Arthur Jones* quoted in Doel & Dunkerton, *Is it still raining in Aberfan?*, pp. 49–50.
63 Gaynor Madgwick, quoted in Doel & Dunkerton, *Is it still raining in Aberfan*, p. 43.

64 SWCC Bryn Carpenter, Interview with Bryn Carpenter, Rev. Kenneth
   Hayes & Doug Pearson, 1986, AUD/528.
65 SWCC Kenneth Hayes, Interview with Bryn Carpenter, Rev. Kenneth
   Hayes & Doug Pearson, 1986, AUD/528.
66 Chris Sullivan, *Timewatch*, 15 October 1996.
67 Laurie Lee, 'The village that lost its children' in *I can't stay long*
   (Harmondsworth: Penguin edn., 1977), pp. 90, 96.
68 Quoted in Lee, 'The village that lost its children', p. 94.
69 Gaynor Madgwick quoted in Doel & Dunkerton, *Is it still raining in
   Aberfan?*, p. 42.
70 SWCC, Howell Williams interview, AUD/522.
71 Gaynor Madgwick quoted in *Daily Mail*, Weekend, 5 October 1996,
   p. 11.
72 Janet Smart, quoted in *Daily Mail*, Weekend, 5 October 1996, p. 13.
73 Gerald Kirwan quoted in *Daily Mail*, Weekend, 5 October 1996, p. 12.
74 Gaynor Madgwick quoted in *Daily Mail*, Weekend, 5 October 1996,
   pp. 11–12.
75 Cliff Minett quoted in *Daily Mail*, Weekend, 5 October 1996, p. 12.
76 Gaynor Madgwick quoted in Doel & Dunkerton, *Is it still raining in
   Aberfan?*, p. 42.
77 Bob Evans quoted in *Western Mail*, 12 October 1996, Arena supplement, p. 3.
78 Dr Arthur Jones quoted in *Daily Mail*, 15 October 1991.
79 SWCC, Howell Williams interview, AUD/522.
80 Rev. Kenneth Hayes (1930–97), *Timewatch*, BBC2, 15 October 1996.

Chapter Two

ON MOLES AND THE HABITS OF BIRDS:
THE UNPOLITICS OF ABERFAN

We found that many witnesses, not excluding those who were intelligent
and anxious to assist us, had been oblivious of what lay before their eyes.
It did not enter their consciousness. They were like moles being asked
about the habits of birds.[1]

Tribunal of Inquiry Board

At 9.15 a.m. on Friday, 21 October 1966, a waste tip from Merthyr
Vale Colliery slid down a mountainside onto the mining village of
Aberfan, near Merthyr Tydfil in south Wales. It first destroyed a
farm cottage in its path, killing all the occupants. At Pantglas Junior
School, just below, the children had returned to their classes. It was
sunny on the mountain but foggy in the village, with visibility about
fifty yards. The tipping gang up the mountain had seen the slide start,
but could not raise the alarm because their telephone cable had been
repeatedly stolen. (The Tribunal of Inquiry later established that the
disaster happened so quickly that a telephone warning would not
have saved lives.) The slide engulfed the school and about twenty
houses in the village before coming to rest. One hundred and
forty-four people died at Aberfan; 116 of them were children.

So horrifying was the disaster that everybody wanted to do something. Hundreds of people stopped what they were doing, threw a
shovel into the car, and drove to Aberfan to try to help with the
rescue. It was futile; the untrained rescuers merely got in the way of
the trained miners. Nobody was rescued alive after 11 a.m. on the
day of the disaster, but it was nearly a week before all the bodies were
recovered. A disaster appeal quickly raised the unprecedented sum
of £1. 75 million (approximately £18.64 million in 1999 pounds).

A Tribunal of Inquiry was immediately set up under Lord Justice
Edmund Davies, a native of Mountain Ash, the next valley to the
west of Aberfan. The Tribunal reported in August 1967, finding that

> Blame for the disaster rests upon the National Coal Board ... The legal
> liability of the National Coal Board to pay compensation for the personal
> injuries (fatal or otherwise) and damage to property is incontestable and
> uncontested.[2]

These dry conclusions belie the passion of the preceding text. The
Tribunal was appalled by the behaviour of the National Coal Board
(NCB) and some of its employees, both before and after the disaster.[3]
It rejected accusations of 'callous indifference' on the part of the
NCB but instead concluded

> there are no villains in this harrowing story. In one way, it might possibly
> be less alarming if there were, for villains are few and far between. But the
> Aberfan disaster is a terrifying tale of bungling ineptitude by many men
> charged with tasks for which they were totally unfitted, or failure to heed
> clear warnings, and of total lack of direction from above.[4]

Colliery engineers at all levels concentrated only on conditions
underground. In one of its most memorable phrases, the Report
described them as 'like moles being asked about the habits of birds'.[5]
Desmond Ackner QC (now Lord Ackner), counsel for the Aberfan
Parents' and Residents' Association, said that Coal Board witnesses
had tried to give the impression that 'the Board had no more blameworthy connection with this disaster than, say, the Gas Board'.[6]
   The Tribunal concluded that the Board's defence, until a very late
stage in the inquiry, was that 'the disaster was due to a coincidence of
a set of geological factors, each of which in itself is not exceptional
but which collectively created a particularly critical geological environment'. It called aspects of the Board's post-disaster behaviour
'nothing short of audacious'.[7] Lord Robens, the Board's chairman,
had said soon after the disaster that 'it was impossible to know that
there was a spring in the heart of this tip'. The Tribunal had ignored
this on the grounds it was based upon hearsay and decided that
Robens could not help the Tribunal. However when Ackner
attacked Robens for this comment, the Tribunal offered Robens the
opportunity to reply. Under questioning by Ackner, Robens admitted that it was known that the disaster was foreseeable by the time the
inquiry began. Yet this was inconsistent with the geological argument put forward by the NCB at the inquiry. The NCB counsel
asked the Tribunal to ignore Robens' evidence. The Tribunal chose
to do so but maintained that if the Board had known that it was to
blame then it should have made this clear at the outset.[8]
   Despite the searing findings of the Tribunal, nobody was prosecuted, dismissed, or suffered a pay cut. Initially the Board postponed

a decision on the seven Coal Board employees who had been identified as in some degree blameworthy until the Director of Public
Prosecutions had announced whether he would be instituting
criminal proceedings or not. When it was announced that he was not,
the seven were interviewed by Lord Robens and W. V. Sheppard
CBE, his Director of Production, and six of them assigned to new
jobs.[9] The NCB's internal memorandum on the Tribunal Report
noted that, in dealing with the individuals criticised, it was not motivated by the desire to punish; they had already suffered severely. It
went on to note that the Board may have considered 'others in the
chain of command' at least 'equally blameworthy' and that those
who were singled out were 'but links in a chain of responsibility. ...
[There was n]o suggestion that in their work as a whole they showed
bungling ineptitude but they did not realise how dangerous an
unstable tip could be.'[10] The Board's desire not to further punish the
individuals concerned was also influenced by a feeling that the
Tribunal should not have named names, and if it had felt that it had
to, then it should have at least got the right names. Robens and
Sheppard interrogated Thomas Wright, the Area General Manager
for the area including Merthyr Vale. They treated Wright very differently to the seven blamed employees. To them, Robens had been
friendly and considerate (something he was not always behind their
backs). The hapless Wright bore the full brunt of his fury. Robens'
private office thought that Wright had escaped blame at the Tribunal
only because 'Edmund Davies took a shine to him'.[11] Robens and
Sheppard accused Wright of failing to deal with the personality clash
between civil engineer R. E. Exley and mechanical engineer D. L.
Roberts.[12] Wright lamely replied that the standard of area officers
was not up to that in his native Midlands:

> It was his experience in Wales that he could not make people do as they
> were told nor make them work.... As regards Mr Roberts, he was an
> unreliable character but a good engineer.... Generally, he [Wright] had
> thought long and hard about the events which had happened and could
> offer no explanation except that it was Wales and Welshmen.[13]

The Minister of Power accepted that the seven had suffered enough
and did not request the board take further action.[14]
    Robens and Sheppard were themselves among the people most
sharply criticised in the course of the inquiry.[15] Between the date of
the disaster and publication of the Report, but after Sheppard's
evidence had been described as 'astounding' by HM Chief Inspector
of Mines and Quarries for South Wales, Robens nominated

Sheppard for appointment to the main Coal Board. The Minister duly appointed him but refused Robens' 'strong representations' that Sheppard be made a deputy chairman of the board.[16] On publication of this report, 'Government sources' told the Press that the question of Robens' resignation had been considered; however, he did not offer to resign until four days later.[17] Richard Marsh, the responsible minister, asked him to stay for at least a month while the Coal Board responded to the inquiry's recommendations. At the end of the month, Marsh rejected Robens' resignation offer. Public opinion was heavily in favour of Robens staying. One dissenter was the Labour MP Leo Abse, who called the Robens-Marsh exchange a 'graceless pavane' and a 'disgraceful spectacle'.[18] However, all the other Labour MPs who spoke in the Aberfan debate in October 1967 supported Robens and the Coal Board. Opposition speakers (including the new Conservative front bench spokesman on power, Margaret Thatcher) complained about the failure of anybody to take responsibility, and about Coal Board headquarters' unsustainable argument that there had been no warning signs of impending disaster. She has written: 'Someone, I thought, should have resigned, though I held back from stating this conclusion with complete clarity'.[19] The briefing notes for Richard Marsh's speech in reply to the debate show that the Ministry of Power expected calls in the debate for the dismissal of Robens and/or Sheppard. In Sheppard's defence, the best the note could say was that 'he had more excuse than some for failing to realise the dangers', on the grounds that he did not come from South Wales.[20] Plaid Cymru was the only party to call for not only Robens' resignation but also Marsh's. Gwynfor Evans, the Plaid Cymru MP for Carmarthen, told the Commons that this was 'not a matter of having heads roll. This is a central matter for any social democracy. After all, to say that no one is responsible ultimately for the culpability of a State industry is an absurdity.'[21]

When Lord Robens neared the end of his contract as Chairman of the Coal Board, he was made chairman of a committee to review the law on health and safety at work. This committee reported that it was generally inappropriate to make negligence of health and safety at work a criminal offence, except in cases where the imposition of 'exemplary punishment would be generally expected and supported by the public'.[22]

Over thirty years have passed since Aberfan. The papers newly available at the Public Record Office[23] and elsewhere show that the Coal Board 'spin-doctored' its way out of trouble, controlling the public agenda from the day of the disaster until the tips were finally removed. The second section of this chapter documents that process.

The records show that Robens was able to control the agenda while ministers decided it was unnecessary to accept his resignation. The third section considers the 'unpolitics of Aberfan'. It is rare to be able to document why things one might have expected to happen did not;[24] however, the newly released records facilitate it in this case.

Apportioning blame: October 1966 – August 1968

The Coal Board was in session as news of the disaster arrived in London. Lord Robens decided not to go to the scene immediately, but to put the Divisional Director of Production in overall charge of rescue and stabilization operations. This was an entirely defensible decision and the normal policy in the aftermath of a disaster. However he proceeded with his planned installation as Chancellor of the University of Surrey on the Friday evening and Saturday, an event which produced news photographs of a smiling Robens in grand chancellarial robes. Meanwhile, somebody wrongly told the Secretary of State for Wales, Cledwyn Hughes, that 'Lord Robens ... has been personally directing this work.'[25] With Harold Wilson and the Duke of Edinburgh both having visited Aberfan on the Friday afternoon, Robens' failure to attend, and his subsequent presence in Guildford, exposed him to public criticism.

Robens had not attended university but was surrounded by members of his staff who all had degrees. Thus the ceremony at Guildford was personally important to him and he was keen for it to go ahead. For a man usually adept at public relations, this proved to be an uncharacteristic mistake. Nonetheless, the visits of Wilson and Prince Philip, complete with aides and security, temporarily blocked the roads to Aberfan. This did not cost lives but, in retrospect, it did perhaps vindicate Robens' decision not to visit Aberfan immediately.[26]

Robens left Guildford at lunchtime on the Saturday, pausing to condemn the 'ghoulish' media coverage,[27] and went to Aberfan, where he told two television and several newspaper interviewers about the 'natural unknown spring' in the tip. It was a statement based upon hearsay rather than considered opinion. Robens told a member of his private office that he had made the statement in an attempt to protect members of the tipping gang whom he understood to be the target of severe local criticism.[28] Whatever the motive, the statement was to haunt the NCB at the Tribunal of Inquiry.

Several Aberfan villagers immediately contradicted the unknown spring story. One of them was Leslie Davies, the tipping gang

chargehand, who was interviewed by Fyfe Robertson for BBC TV's
24 Hours. The most relevant section is:

> *LD:* Well, I don't know about an unknown spring, that spring has been
> there ever since I've known it.
> *FR:* Did you get instructions to tip on top of the spring?
> *LD:* No, all the instruction I got was tip, that's all. My instruction's to tip
> muck, isn't it?

At the end of the interview, Robertson turned to camera and said
that in previous pit disasters he had reported on, the final report had
nearly always been 'a frustrating exercise in official whitewashing'.[29]
It turned out that Davies' statement was entirely true (and that the
Tribunal report was not a frustrating exercise in official whitewashing). Nevertheless, the interview infuriated politicians. Sir Elwyn
Jones, the Attorney-General, issued a Commons statement that
unauthorised comment or speculation on the causes of the disaster
could constitute contempt of the Tribunal, which might be punishable as if it were contempt of court.[30] This statement was fiercely
criticised. Edward Heath, leader of the Opposition, said it was a
threat 'to the freedom of us all'.[31] Jones later conceded that it was
'badly drafted'.[32] Although there is no evidence that it was made with
the intention of shielding the NCB, it had that effect. Newspapers
reported the Tribunal proceedings very sparingly, and always in the
studiously neutral tone of court reports, ending with a phrase such as
'The tribunal continues today'.

Several of the Sunday newspapers (notably *The Sunday Times* and
The Sunday Mirror) had managed to get the cause of the disaster
approximately right in their issues of 23 October 1966, which went to
press only thirty-six hours after the disaster. After that, accurate
information went underground like an Aberfan spring, to emerge
only in August 1967. Disinformation continued to flow, despite the
Attorney-General's warning. Three days after the 'gag', Robens was
quoted in *The Sunday Times* as saying 'The Aberfan disaster has
produced a new hazard in mining about which we knew nothing
before'.[33] Given the history of tips sliding in South Wales, such a
comment was clearly in contempt of the Attorney General's
warning.

The Sunday Times of 26 February 1967 carried a remarkable
piece, which Ackner accused Robens of planting or inspiring:

> On most of the 48 days of the Aberfan inquiry so far the Coal Board has
> been under attack. The Board's main case for its defence will ... be ... that
> the disastrous slide of a waste-tip which buried alive 144 people was

'unforeseeable' because its root cause was 'a coincidence of geological factors', each of which in itself was not exceptional. No surface observation, the Board will claim, could have detected this particular danger. The attack by counsel on coalboard employees [is] now almost over.[34]

The story goes on to give a mostly accurate account of the weaknesses and failures which Coal Board witnesses had admitted. In fact, the Board had already started its 'unforeseeability' defence. On the second day, the NCB's counsel had said 'The prime cause of the disaster was therefore geological ... it would be unreal and unjust to credit any individual with foresight of this danger that only hindsight has revealed.'[35] Further references to a 'coincidence' of geological factors continued this line.[36] This defence was not finally abandoned until its counsel's closing speech on day 74 of the inquiry. But it already knew, and the inquiry forced Lord Robens to admit, that the 'unforeseeability' argument was untenable.[37] The springs over which waste was tipped are on an Ordnance Survey map of 1919 and a Geological Survey map of 1959; there had been a tip slide in 1939 of comparable magnitude just down the road; the Aberfan tips themselves had slid in 1944 and 1963; the unstable shape of the tips is obvious even to the untrained eye in photographs taken between 1963 and 1965 by parties other than the Coal Board.[38]

On 4 February 1909, at Pentre in the Rhondda, a colliery spoil heap collapsed. Witnesses claimed that the 'moving rubbish flung itself onward with the speed of an avalanche'. The noise was 'as if the whole mountain were moving'. Four houses were buried while a fifth was 'severed in twain' killing a young boy.[39] That incident was not discussed at the Aberfan Tribunal but the inquiry was a catalogue of warnings unheeded. Tip slides were neither unknown nor unforeseeable.

The last surviving member of Robens' private office staff at the time feels that the NCB had never tried to evade its blameworthiness, pointing to the fact that Robens had told reporters on 22 October 1966 that the Board accepted responsibility for the disaster. Instead, the NCB had fallen back upon a defensive position as a result of Desmond Ackner's confrontational approach to the Tribunal, which the Board felt was essentially turning the whole proceedings into a trial. He summarised the attitude of the NCB towards the Tribunal as 'not a conspiracy but a cock-up'.[40] But this does not clearly explain the lack of any clear initial acceptance of responsibility by the Board at the outset or the NCB's Counsel, Philip Wien, use of the unforeseeability argument on day 2. Robens' initial comments about an unknown spring may be excused on the grounds that they were

ill-informed but not only did the NCB not retract them, it added to
them with its arguments about geological conditions.

The NCB's memorandum on the Tribunal Report claims that its
experts had not made their final conclusions on the causes of the
disaster when Wien opened the defence on day 2. It goes on to state
that it was wrong for the Tribunal to take the evidence of individual
officials (who refused to accept they were to blame) as being submis-
sions by the Board itself. The memorandum also maintains that the
board had done its utmost to help the Tribunal throughout but that
it was not its role to 'make concessions and thus to anticipate the
conclusions on matters which ... cannot fail to have an impact on
other parties similarly represented.'[41] If this is all accepted, then the
Board appears to be condemning the behaviour of its chairman
(whom the memorandum did not defend) and its officials. The Coal
Division of the Ministry of Power commented on the memorandum
that the evidence, for whether the NCB knew that the disaster was
foreseeable before the Tribunal began, was conflicting:

> Lord Robens' own evidence on this point is confused and whilst it is clear
> that the Board's Chief Divisional Surveyor had concluded before the
> hearing began that a slip could clearly have been foreseen, it is far from
> clear that he had so advised the Board. Indeed from the minutes of a
> meeting in Hobart House two months after the hearing started it seems
> that Mr Sheppard still thought that the conditions at Aberfan were rare.[42]

Whoever was to blame, the attitude of the NCB and its officials
towards the Tribunal was confused, defensive and contradictory. The
essence of the disaster is perfectly clear. Tip 7 was built on top of
springs which were marked on the map and obvious on the ground.
Other tips in South Wales had slid before, including those at Aberfan.
There can hardly be a clearer case of a disaster waiting to happen.

A draft of the inquiry report reached ministers in July 1967.
Richard Crossman, then Leader of the House of Commons, is the
most candid witness:

Tuesday, July 15th [1967]
At Cabinet this morning we started with Aberfan. I'd had a row with the
PM about this on Saturday when he told me he intended to release a
statement before the publication of the report, which is immensely
damaging. ... When Cledwyn [Hughes, Secretary of State for Wales] came
to me yesterday to discuss publication I suggested that he shouldn't hurry
it but let the preparation run on, with maps and diagrams until, say, the
middle of August [i.e. after Parliament would have risen]. I would just
announce this in our adjournment debate. Cabinet agreed that I should

make the announcement this afternoon and meanwhile appointed Gordon Walker chairman of a Committee of Ministers to consider the implications of the Report.[43]

Harold Wilson wrote on his copy of this memorandum, 'I have now looked at the Report. It is devastating. Pl ask S/S Wales whether he should not make a statement to the House before publication.... While it is exceptional to make a statement *before* publication, the fact that the House is adjourning – combined with the deep public concern and the devastating nature of the Report makes this desirable.'[44] The Cabinet rejected the idea of delaying the Report. The Deputy Secretary at the Ministry of Power was sufficiently shocked by the Report to abandon the Ministry's customary protection of the Coal Board. He wrote to Marsh's private secretary that the Report

> calls in question his [Robens'] character and sense of proportion. In view of the tribunal's strictures, he may feel bound to resign. If so, his resignation should, in my view, be accepted but I do not think there is occasion to require his resignation. He is responsible for the organisation and efficiency of the industry. If there is a major failure anywhere in it, he must have some responsibility – wrong men in big jobs, inadequate overall direction from HQ.[45]

Gordon Walker's ministerial committee decided that since the Report did not blame Robens for the disaster, it was not sufficient to require his dismissal but the Government should not press him to stay if he offered his resignation.[46]

The Cabinet met again to decide on a course of action. Crossman noted:

Tuesday, August 1st
There was a big meeting about the presentation of the Aberfan Report.... [The Prime Minister] decided to take the chair ... and he called a lot of people to it. Patrick Gordon Walker had felt we should accept Alf Robens's resignation or even force it on him but without apparently realising that we should then have all the problem of the pit closures being sabotaged by Alf from outside. On the other hand it was equally dangerous to say, as Dick Marsh did, that we must on no account let him resign. I finally said to the PM, 'We ought to spend three weeks playing it out and request a report from the National Coal Board before we decide whether any resignations are accepted or not'.[47]

Ministers agreed to avoid detailed public discussion of the Report and to request the Board's observations before deciding whether to accept any resignations that might be offered.[48]

Marsh was therefore sent to confront Robens on 3 August with two statements authorised by the Prime Minister in his pocket: one to use if Robens offered his resignation, the other if not. The minutes of his meeting with Marsh however suggest that Robens' stance was not to lie down and be sacrificed.

> 5. Lord Robens said he hoped the Government would never again set up a Tribunal of this nature ... It has been an inquisition into the Board's affairs without the Board having the normal protection of the law ... The Tribunal had shown their bias in their criticism of his own evidence as not being consistent.
> 7. Lord Robens said that ... the Tribunal Report was conspiracy of silence as a result of which only the Board had been accused. The real cause of the failure of the Board ... was a breakdown of communication in that ... Mr Roberts ... and Mr Exley were not on speaking terms.[49]
> 9. The Minister said that any criticism of the Tribunal by the Board would be liable to misinterpretation and it would be best for the Board to confine itself to a factual statement.
> 10. After a good deal of further discussion, Lord Robens agreed that this was so and undertook to exclude any such comment from his Statement.
> 11. The Minister asked Lord Robens if he had come to any firm view on his own position.... Lord Robens said that ... he intended to give his resignation to the Government next Tuesday morning, 8 August. He could not possibly continue as Chairman of the NCB unless the Government expressed their confidence in him.
> 13. The Minister said that it was not inconceivable that at the end of the day the Government might have to announce the resignations of Mr Sheppard, Mr Kellett and Mr Morgan.[50] Lord Robens said ... that it would be hateful if people were to go round with long knives looking for victims.
> 15. Lord Robens reiterated that the Tribunal had been a conspiracy of silence for the benefit of the local people. They had even accepted that a man who had been tipping waste for over 20 years could not be expected to know anything about tip safety, whereas much of this was common-sense. The Tribunal had cleared everybody in Aberfan other than Board officials, and equally had cleared the Civil Engineers of Merthyr Tydfil.[51]

Robens' general demeanour is clear from these minutes. Whoever was to blame, senior Coal Board people were not. Perhaps Merthyr Borough Council was to blame for allowing a tip to slide on to its schools?[52] On 8 August 1967, an emotional Robens informed a full meeting of the Board of his decision to offer his resignation. No one tried to dissuade him.[53]

Robens had had a copy of the Report since 31 July 'on a very confidential "Privy Councillor" basis'.[54] On 4 August, Robens visited pits in Scotland, and pointedly criticised the Government decision to build a nuclear power station at Hunterston in Ayrshire. In making such a speech Robens was following his usual programme and agenda. Nonetheless, it helped cement his popularity within the industry: 'Lord Robens has had massive support from miners all over the country, who feel that he has done a fine job in standing up for their interests'.[55] Most areas of the National Union of Mineworkers (NUM) urged that he should stay, although its South Wales area executive was 'not unanimous'.[56] Robens' office drafted three form letters 'To Outsiders', 'To Unions', and 'To Management', to use in reply to incoming messages of support.[57] Details of the numbers of letters of support Robens had received were released to the press by the NCB, including one from former Prime Minister Harold Macmillan, who had appointed Robens to the Coal Board. Macmillan complained that he had not intended it for publication. The Press clearly perceived a 'Robens must stay' campaign orchestrated from Coal Board headquarters. *The Guardian*, which on the whole thought he should stay, nevertheless commented that 'Over the last few days the Coal Board's behaviour has ... been rather unseemly, in the circumstances'.[58] A Coal Board eyewitness maintains that while they and the NCB press office may have been trying to demonstrate public support for Robens, they were not doing so under his instructions.[59] In contrast, Richard Marsh believes that Robens had been personally manipulating the press 'the whole time ... He was a highly political animal and he was extremely good at it. It was quite natural because it was ... ongoing'.[60]

Robens' 'resignation' letter was issued on 8 August. A draft of the letter in his office papers, dated 3 August, was almost threatening: 'In going now I would be leaving it [viz. the reconstruction of the coal industry] incompleted [sic]. But without the confidence and support of the Government I cannot stay.'[61] The published letter omitted this, and referred only to the doctrine of ministerial responsibility. Robens had been a Labour politician before becoming Chairman of the Coal Board and those close to him at the time maintained that he valued this traditional doctrine.[62] Yet Robens must also have known that nobody had ever tried to claim that the chairman of a nationalised industry was liable, under the doctrine of ministerial responsibility, for the failings of his subordinates. The letter was published to the accompaniment of heavy hints from the usual sources that the resignation would be refused.[63]

Marsh complained about comment in the press relating to the resignation issue but did not actively try to prevent it.[64] He waited and watched, using the Coal Board's impending comments on the

Tribunal Report as an excuse not to take action on Robens' 'resignation'. What he saw was that public as well as industry opinion was in
favour of Robens staying. Gallup found that those it polled in
August 1967 believed that Robens should not resign by a margin of
74 per cent to 15 per cent.[65] The NCB submitted its comments on the
Tribunal Report to the Minister on 23 August. Robens' private
secretary described them as 'not too pugnacious and not too
contrite'.[66] On 30 August, Lord Robens left for New York on board
the *Queen Mary*. He left behind a tantalising hint that he might be
prepared to resign in March 1968. Sir David Pitblado, the Permanent
Secretary at Power, minuted,

> There are timing complications. The Minister would not be able to talk
> this over with Lord Robens until September 29th, since he will be in USA
> until September 14th, and at sea until September 20th. It will be impossible
> to postpone a public statement of the Government's attitude to his resig-
> nation until then. If this course of action commended itself to the
> Minister and the PM, it would be necessary to write to him (or to get him
> to fly back which might be dramatic).[67]

On 5 September, Marsh and Wilson decided, in the light of the public
and industry support for Robens, to reject his resignation. Marsh
telegraphed a draft letter saying so to Robens in New York, using the
British Ambassador to the UN, Lord Caradon, as a go-between.
Robens went to see Caradon, having already been informed by the
NCB Deputy Chairman that Marsh was probably going to reject his
resignation offer.[68] Caradon reported:

> I saw Lord Robens this afternoon and conveyed your message to him. He
> asked me to make the following reply. Begins. Provided the sentence 'It is
> the whole board, not the Chairman alone, which is appointed by the
> Minister and responsible to him for the operations of the industry' is
> deleted, my reply would be as follows. Thank you for your letter about
> my offer of resignation. In view of what you say I willingly agree to
> continue as chairman of the NCB. Ends.

Marsh's private secretary complained that the disputed sentence was
there for constitutional reasons – namely to explain that, if the
doctrine of ministerial responsibility implicated anybody, it implicated the entire Board. Nevertheless, Marsh issued the letter without
it, as instructed by Robens. It is indeed a powerful politician who can
dictate the letters he receives, as well as the letters he sends.[69]

The Commons debate on the report took place on 26 October. Reporting of it was dominated by allegations from S. O. Davies, the

constituency MP for Aberfan, that the remaining tips were not safe.
Marsh forcefully rebutted the allegations. *The Times* of 27 October
called it 'a bitter and unpleasant debate with a sense of pointlessness'.
The *Western Mail* referred to it as 'disappointing' and complained
that it dwelt upon the past rather than the future.[70] As well as Abse
and Thatcher, two opposition speakers (David Gibson-Watt, the
Conservative spokesman for Welsh affairs, and Colonel Claude Lancaster, a former coal owner) raised telling questions about Robens
and Sheppard. However, many of the criticisms anticipated in
Marsh's briefing note were not made. No further parliamentary action followed except the passage of the Mines and Quarries (Tips)
Act 1969.

But the remaining tips still towered above the village. The NCB
had argued throughout that removing them was not economically
feasible (unless somebody else paid), and that they posed no danger
to the village. They commissioned a report which priced six different
ways of removing the tips at between £1.014 million and £3.4
million.[71] The Tribunal Report accepted the NCB case that complete
removal was neither necessary nor economically feasible, giving an
estimated cost of £3 million (it is not known whether the Tribunal
saw the lower estimates).[72] From then until August 1968, Lord
Robens led a doughty fight to minimise the Coal Board's liability to
pay for tip removal. One exasperated Welsh Office civil servant
wrote to his Secretary of State that Robens' technique consisted of
'vaguely favouring a bigger scheme and allowing this view to be
known publicly. But ... adamant that the extra cost should be borne
by the Exchequer.'[73]

However, this approach faced three problems. The Chief Secretary
to the Treasury refused to pay;[74] evidence that the job could be done
more cheaply had to be suppressed or countered; some villagers
rejected anything short of complete removal, reportedly saying 'The
Coal Board put them there; the Coal Board can take them away.' A
local firm, Ryan Industrial Fuels, specialised in tip clearance and
salvage of reusable coal. Before the disaster, they had already
inspected the disaster tip with a view to tendering for coal removal
from it. After the disaster, they maintained that they could remove the
tips more cheaply than the Coal Board claimed it would cost. Finally,
in April 1968, they submitted an estimate to the Aberfan Tip Removal
Committee, which was forwarded to the Welsh Office. This was for
£660,000 if they were permitted to recover coal from the complex, and
about £1.25 million otherwise.[75] Something similar must already have
been on the table in October 1967, because the most eye-opening part
of the ministerial briefing is the advice given to the Minister on how he

should counter any claims in the Commons that the price of tip removal was being exaggerated. As no such claims were made, this part of the briefing note was never used.

> The chosen scheme [viz. an NCB landscaping scheme which did not involve removing the tips] could quickly transform the appearance of the area and total expenditure would amount to £3/4 million to £1 million. (This is deliberately ambiguous. NCB has spent £1/2 million so far and is continuing at £20,000 per week, say another £200,000, + £250,000 to the landscaping, making £1 million in all. Complete removal would cost £3 million.)

The note went on to say that the Minister should say that the question of tip removal was for the Welsh Office, not for him, and that the Tribunal Report had recommended against complete removal. On Ryan's offer, it continued that the minister should oppose coal recovery on the grounds that

> The sale of the coal is a problem:
> (i) it displaces deep mined coal when the mines cannot be closed fast enough and their stockpiles are swollen;
> (ii) if non-NCB tips are concerned the contractor can sell the coal cheaply to the detriment of the NCB.

The Minister was advised to say that Ryan had left other tips in 'a shambles', and that the NCB would confirm this.[76] When the Ryans tender arrived in April 1968, a Welsh Office official wrote to the Treasury that 'it is quite unrealistic to think in terms of Ryans doing the job when the NCB have their own contractors with men and equipment on the spot'.[77]

George Thomas, the new Secretary of State for Wales, told a deputation from Aberfan that cost was not the issue: 'One could not balance money against what had happened at Aberfan.' Landscaping was safer, quicker and caused less nuisance.[78] Yet, in private, money was always the issue. The NCB maintained it could not afford to pay in full, the Welsh Office was afraid money may be taken from its budget while there were wider Government concerns that it might commit itself to dealing with mine refuse elsewhere.[79] A Welsh Office under-secretary admitted that, despite the decision not to emphasise cost as an issue, 'it is the root of the matter and it seldom pays to cloud the main issue'.[80]

That under-secretary had been detailed by the Welsh Office to maintain liaison between the village and the Department. He reported frequently, almost in the manner of a colonial governor, expressing hopes that 'moderate' villagers, who were not calling for total removal of the tips, would prevail over 'militants', who were.[81] However, the 'moderates' were undercut by three things. First, by Lord Robens' public support for a bigger scheme (he did not say publicly that he would not pay for it). Second, by the 1965 NCB 'Powell Memorandum', quoted approvingly by the Tribunal, which showed that if it had been implemented, there would have been no disaster. This memorandum stated, 'Precautions to Prevent Sliding.... Where a slide would cause damage to property, no tip over 20 feet high should be placed on a hillside unless the ground is a compact gravel or of better quality than this'.[82] The remaining Aberfan tips were on a clay hillside, a ground of much poorer quality than compact gravel; one of them had already slipped in 1944; they were about 100 feet high. Finally and most decisively, by two storms in July 1968, which had brought slurry from the tips down into the disaster area.

Villagers used the Powell Memorandum as a lever to put pressure on the government, but to no avail.[83] A letter to George Thomas from Aberfan's Tip Removal Committee made clear the anger over the delays. It ended with the threat that unless a suitable reply was received, discussions would take place over 'what forms of militant action' to employ.[84] Further delays saw the threat become reality. After an unsuccessful meeting between Thomas and representatives of Aberfan, quantities of tip slurry were dumped inside the Welsh Office and the tyres on the Minister's car slashed. Thomas left the meeting in tears.[85] He wrote to Harold Wilson, describing it as 'one of the most harrowing and difficult meetings I have ever had'. Elsewhere he told Wilson that

> I believe they have worked themselves into an irrational state of mind on this issue but we have to contend with the intensity of their feelings, whether these are logical or not, and we also have to bear in mind the general reaction of the press and other commentators and also local opinion in the surrounding area.[86]

Thomas' memoirs record that he told Wilson on the telephone 'I am sorry, Prime Minister, but I can't do it. I just can't tell these people that the tip has to stay. They are afraid. Their protest has not been manufactured, it's a genuine fear from people who have been through a terrible experience.'[87] Wilson states that We met the next day; the tip had to go.' One might imagine that would have settled it. But Lord Robens still refused to budge: 'The Coal Board raised difficulties, and I asked the Minister to remind them of a few facts.'[88] The deal finally approved was for the Coal Board to pay £350,000, the disaster fund to pay £150,000, and the Treasury the rest up to a maximum of £1 million. Curiously, the Coal Board's estimate of the total cost had shrunk by two-thirds. The final tender price was £850,000; a price similar to that of Ryan Industrial Fuels for complete removal. Coal recovery was rejected on account on the heavy traffic it would involve and the danger of situating a washery high on the hillside.[89]

Forcing the Disaster Fund to pay part of the cost of removing the tip complex was controversial at the time, and it has not become any less controversial. The question first arose at a meeting between Robens and the two ministers concerned (Marsh and Hughes, the Secretary of State for Wales) in March 1967: 'Although in some respects there was something to be said for drawing on the Disaster Fund it was felt that, at this stage, such a suggestion would be far too explosive.'[90] However, by July 1968, with Robens still refusing to budge, ministers had to return to the Fund. George Thomas initially rejected the idea arguing that the general public would see the Government as 'shabby' and the 'village would be enraged'.[91] However an alternative plan was found: 'It was right that some of the money should be found locally, but the Government need not suggest that it should be taken from the Appeal Fund'.[92] This was disingenuous; everybody knew that there was no other public body in the valley with any money, and that no private body would see any reason to remove the Coal Board's waste from the Coal Board's property. An attempt was made to circulate donors to the Disaster Fund, asking them if they approved of its use in this way. About 100 replies were received, split evenly for and against. S. O. Davies MP resigned from the Fund's management committee in protest.[93] He wrote to the Prime Minister to complain about the situation calling it 'disgraceful and contemptible ... sheer blackmail.'[94] The terms of the trust deed of the Disaster Fund are:

> for the relief of all persons who have suffered ... and are thereby in need;
> for any charitable purpose for the benefit of inhabitants of Aberfan on 21 October 1966.[95]

The decision to contribute was not queried with the Charity Commissioners because of the poor state of relations between the Fund and the Commission. A form letter, drafted by the Welsh Office to send to members of the public who complained about this use of the funds, simply fails to answer the objection about charitable purposes at all; there is no record that the objection was raised in Cabinet.[96]

A reader today of the Tribunal Report might have difficulty in understanding how Robens, Sheppard, and Morgan could have kept their jobs. But outside Aberfan itself (and, in relation to those low down the NCB hierarchy, not even there), there was little demand for individuals to be punished. Cecil King noted that press comment on the Report itself was 'more hostile' than he expected.[97] Yet the disaster was still generally viewed as an accident. After more recent disasters, there have been persistent calls for heads to roll. After Aberfan, there were not. The nine named individuals were treated sympathetically by the press and there was even a local petition for the two still working at Merthyr Vale colliery to keep their jobs. The NCB's refusal to castigate them in public also strengthened their position.

The coal industry was united, whereas Aberfan was not. The private disquiet within sectors of the coal industry over the Tribunal's findings strengthened the position of Robens and his employees.[98] Given the publicity given to what was portrayed as bitter argument and division within Aberfan itself, there may also have been a quiet desire to avoid the further acrimony of sackings or even a trial. Robens was the only individual whose position was debated publicly. After publication of the report, the national press was divided on whether he should resign or not.[99] The government's refusal to accept Robens' offer of resignation immediately meant that the NCB had the opportunity to demonstrate the public support for Robens. His perceived value to the industry and popularity with the miners was stressed while running totals of the number of letters of support he received were published. The government was unlikely to let Robens go in the face of such support.

But it remains necessary to explore a number of things that did not happen at Aberfan, in order to establish why not. Even if the Coal Board and ministers had behaved quite differently, the outcome might not have been very different.

Why was there no legal action against the NCB or any of its employees?

At the parliamentary debate on the Aberfan tribunal report, Gwynfor Evans MP, said,

> If one drives a car dangerously and has the terrible misfortune to hurt somebody, or perhaps kill somebody proceedings can be instituted. It is possible for a driver to be convicted of manslaughter. But it is not

possible to take any sort of action against a public board. There seems to be one law for the private person and another for the public board. I am not suggesting that action should be taken against personal members of the Coal Board. I would not suggest that. But there should be some way of bringing a public board to justice.[100]

Theoretically there was no reason why the board could not be brought to justice. Corporations had been identified as separate legal persons since the late nineteenth century. Their liability to tort actions had been established through vicarious liability for the actions of their employees. However this principle was not applied wholesale to criminal law. Employers were only deemed responsible for their employee's criminal acts in cases of libel or public nuisance, or in other cases in accordance with the principles of secondary participation. The first case of corporate manslaughter brought in England and Wales involved the south Wales mining company Cory Brothers. During the 1926 miners' strike, the company had erected an electrified fence around its property. An unemployed miner was killed when he stumbled against it and the South Wales Miners' Federation brought private prosecutions for manslaughter against the company and three of its directors. However the trial judge decided that a company could not be indicted for offences against the person.[101]

In 1944, the law regarding corporate liability developed significantly through three cases that established the principle of identification.[102] This involved companies being deemed responsible in criminal cases normally requiring *mens rea* ('the criminal state of mind, accompanying an act which condemns the perpetrator of the act to criminal punishment; criminal intent' (*OED*)). Corporations of course do not have minds but it was established that a corporation could be guilty if a director or manager could be seen as acting, not for the corporation, but as it. Thus individuals could be identified as the corporation. In 1957, it was further clarified that where directors and managers are in effect the mind of a company, their actions could be said to be those of the company. Consequently, companies, through the actions of their senior officials, could be guilty of any criminal offence except those requiring a mandatory custodial sentence.[103]

In 1965, a welder-burner, Glanville Evans, was drowned when a railway bridge which his employers were demolishing collapsed into the river Wye. It was alleged that the workmen had been instructed by the managing director to burn the bridge into sections, starting in the middle, which the prosecuting counsel asserted was 'almost as ludicrous as telling a man sitting on a branch of a tree to saw that branch'. The jury at the inquest committed Evans' employers to court. Consequently, in *R v Northern Strip Mining Construction Ltd* (Glamorgan Assizes, 1965) the company was prosecuted for unlawful killing. The prosecuting counsel was Philip Wien QC; the defence counsel was W. L. Mars-Jones QC. The case against the firm rested upon the instructions having come from the Managing Director rather than the foreman, for whose actions the company was not necessarily liable. The prosecution failed because it was not shown that the instruction to begin demolition in the middle had come from the managing director. The validity of the indictment itself was not challenged.[104]

Eighteen months later and a few miles away, Philip Wien QC was counsel for the NCB at the Aberfan Tribunal, and W. L. Mars-Jones QC was counsel for the National Union of Teachers (representing the surviving Pantglas teachers and the relatives of those killed). Thus their roles were reversed; in effect Wien was counsel for the defence and Mars-Jones was one of the counsel for the prosecution. But there is no evidence that either of them regarded the *Northern Strip Mining* case as relevant to Aberfan. At Aberfan there were no allegations that the functional equivalent of 'managing director' of the Coal Board had instructed the tipping gang to build up the fatal tip. Lords Ackner and Howe, and Sir Ronald Waterhouse (three Aberfan counsel who are still alive) 'all share ... the recollection that criminal proceedings were never under consideration in this case'.[105] Nonetheless the criticisms in the Tribunal Report meant that the Attorney General did consider the bringing of charges against the individuals named blameworthy to varying degrees. On 4 August 1967, it was reported that he had announced that no proceedings would be taken. The decision met a mixed response in Aberfan.[106]

Aberfan residents had first raised the possibility of bringing manslaughter charges with their solicitors before the Tribunal had even begun sitting.[107] Their early belief in the NCB's culpability was demonstrated at the opening inquest at Aberfan, held on the Monday after the disaster when, amidst shouts of 'murderers', a bereaved parent called for the cause of death to be recorded as ' "Buried alive by the National Coal Board." That is what I want to see on the record. That is the feeling of those present. Those are the words we want to go on the certificate.'[108]

Following the publication of the Report the matter was again discussed. The press reported that some villagers were scouring the Report for evidence of negligence and if they found it they would demand legal action.[109] The issue was discussed at a meeting of the Aberfan Parents' and Residents' Association. Although some members of the village wanted to bring charges, Desmond Ackner told his clients that any prosecution against any of the nine individuals named in the Report as partly to blame would be unlikely to succeed. The decision was announced with a statement to the press:

> The Parents' and Residents' Association of Aberfan are unanimously and strongly averse to any prosecution of any Coal Board officials implicated in the Aberfan Disaster. No such prosecution will be brought by them or on their behalf.
> They fully accept the findings of the Tribunal. There is no question of their pursuing any vendetta or seeking retribution from those who have been found to be blameworthy.[110]

The consideration thus seems to have been of charges against the named NCB officials rather than the Board itself. The case against Northern Strip had involved alleged reckless conduct by the firm's managing director thus directly implicating the company itself. Prosecuting organisations for the combined fatal failures of its staff was simply not part of the legal culture of the 1960s. Indeed, health and safety offences in the workplace were not generally regarded as criminal matters (see chapter 8). Thus Aberfan was not viewed in the popular mind as a criminal act but a rather tragic accident. This drew upon and shaped the legal response.

It was thus not surprising that the 1970–2 Robens Committee on Health and Safety at Work argued that the use of criminal law was generally inappropriate, and even in fatal cases only prosecutions for breach of regulatory statutes were normally contemplated. (In any case there were no such breaches at Aberfan – see 'Why did the regulatory authorities fail' below.) It did not discuss corporate manslaughter.

After the sinking of the car ferry *Herald of Free Enterprise* in 1987, which killed 189 people, the inquest jury returned a verdict of unlawful killing against the coroner's advice. The ferry company and seven of its employees were prosecuted for reckless manslaughter. However, the trial judge halted the trial and directed acquittals before the prosecution case was completed, arguing that it was impossible to establish recklessness on the part of any one individual and thus the company. It is possible to compare the Aberfan Tribunal Report with the Sheen Report on the ferry tragedy point by point, whence it is fairly clear that the culpability of the Coal Board over Aberfan was comparable with that of Townsend Thoresen over the *Herald of Free Enterprise*.[111]

Yet even had any charges been brought against the NCB, they would have run into the same problems that faced the prosecutors of P & O (the owners of Townsend Thoresen). Despite the obvious failures of the company, the law simply did not allow the failures of individuals to be aggregated into criminal responsibility by their employer.

Between the criminal and the civil law yawned a great gulf. It has long been established in civil law that an occupier of land has strict liability for any damage caused by the escape of anything from that land. This doctrine was specifically applied to coal tips in a case which Ackner claimed 'any competent law student in his last year' would know (although Sheppard, the Director-General of Production for the Coal Board, did not).[112] Strict liability means that the plaintiff need not establish that the defendant was negligent. Thus the Coal Board was civilly liable for the deaths, injuries, and destruction of property caused at Aberfan, and would have been regardless of the culpability of individual employees. What, then, could the Tribunal achieve? Beyond investigating the possibility of criminal negligence, the Tribunal provided reassurance to both the bereaved and public that the disaster had not been taken lightly and that all would be done to identify those responsible and what was needed to avoid a repeat. There may have been no need to show negligence in civil law but there was a need to publicly establish the cause and fault, and perhaps for some people to say sorry. Yet only one witness – the most junior in the whole Coal Board hierarchy above the tipping gang, namely the colliery mechanical engineer – made any unforced admission of responsibility for any aspect of the disaster.[113]

Once the Tribunal Report was published a single inquest was resumed. It lasted just four minutes. The coroner announced that,

> It is not for me to decide any question of civil liability. As far as criminal liability is concerned, the whole matter has been investigated very thoroughly. The Tribunal assessment is tantamount to a finding of accidental death in each case.[114]

This interpretation is perhaps questionable given the force with which the Report had condemned the NCB. Accidental death was certainly not how many people in Aberfan felt about their losses and the press reported that some parents felt the verdict should have been manslaughter.[115] But that was not how the legal system worked. Nonetheless, at a meeting of the APRA, although some people felt that the coroner could have expressed himself more sympathetically, there was a general sympathy with the way he had handled proceedings. As the chairman of the meeting said, he had an 'unenviable task'.[116] Celia Wells, a Professor of Law, has described the political and legal responses to Aberfan as 'bizarre

and outdated'.[117] As she points out, it would be inconceivable that
the inquiry would be deemed as the end of the matter if such a
disaster occurred today.

Why did the government let itself be bullied by the NCB?

'The cost of all the consequences ... to an NCB in deficit, must fall in
the end on the Exchequer.'[118] So wrote the Welsh Office man in
Aberfan during the long unsuccessful campaign to persuade the
NCB to pay for removing the tips. All decision makers in govern-
ment agreed. No one felt that it was worth while to persuade the Coal
Board to pay more in the face of Lord Robens' obdurate resistance.
As Marsh points out, forcing the NCB to pay would only give
Robens an excuse to come and ask for bigger grants in the future.[119]

This is part of a much larger story. The coal industry had been
making heavy losses for a number of years. Even Merthyr Vale
colliery, although it made an operating profit in 1966 (and was one of
the last deep mines in South Wales to close, in 1990), was losing
money after finance charges.[120] If the Aberfan compensation claims
had been debited to Merthyr Vale, and still more if the cost of
removing the tips had been, it would have shown a heavy operating
loss. This could have had consequences for jobs that were so obvious
that they simmered below the surface of the inquiry, breaking out
acrimoniously once or twice.

Nobody, in 1966, proposed that the polluter should pay. The idea
that polluters should pay for externalities that they imposed on
society was commonplace in economics, but unheard of in practical
politics. Anti-pollution law such as the Rivers (Prevention of
Pollution) Act 1951 and the Clean Air Act 1956 relied on regulation
and the threat of prosecution, not on charges or permits. Therefore
politicians, of both parties, simply accepted that it was pointless to
saddle the NCB with costs that would merely increase its deficit. In
consequence, nobody faced the true cost of coal. As the *Financial
Times* put it soon after the Tribunal Report was published,

> [O]ne disadvantage of having industries run by the State that has been
> spotlighted by the Aberfan disaster is that, when Government stands in
> the role of owner of an industry, it will be apt to be less mindful of the
> need to care for the wider interests of the public in relation to that indus-
> try than it would be if it were dealing with private enterprise. It will be less
> inclined, for example, to ensure that due regard is paid to such consider-
> ations as the safety of the public and the avoidance of loss of amenities
> than would be the case if it were not so deeply concerned with the profit-
> ability of the industry.[121]

This failure extended to the Tribunal itself. Ackner said in his closing speech that, had the Coal Board been a private corporation facing claims for negligence, its counsel would have advised it that it had no defence.[122] However, as the cost of its seventy-six day defence was met by the taxpayer, it was not deterred.

Furthermore, the British coal industry was actively protected. Coal imports were effectively banned. Ministers were advised actively to discourage coal recovery – precisely on the grounds that it might be cheaper than deep mining. In general, the Coal Board under Robens' chairmanship was managing decline very competently. It was for this purpose that the Macmillan government had appointed Robens, a trade unionist and former front bench Labour politician. Robens succeeded in raising productivity per man-shift and in sharply cutting employment at the same time. This was no mean achievement. But it was one that Robens wished to manage on his own terms. These terms involved carrying mineworkers, and their powerful union, the NUM, with him whenever he could. As a former Labour politician, he knew exactly how and where to apply political pressure. He seems to have mesmerised ministers. Richard Marsh, who thought Robens must stay at all costs, nevertheless complained that in 1967 'Labour Members of Parliament were being openly briefed, on Alf Robens's direct instructions, at the Coal Board head-quarters'.[123] Barbara Castle, who complained that somebody 'already rivalling Robens in megalomania' might 'do a Robens on us by leaking to the press', was nevertheless the minister who appointed Robens to chair the health and safety committee.[124] In the summer of 1967, relations between Robens and ministers were at their lowest point. Ministers correctly saw that natural gas was about to become a cheap and clean fuel. They also believed, incorrectly, that nuclear power was about to do the same. These two beliefs necessarily implied that British coal production must decline more rapidly than previously unless it could find new product or export markets. Nobody seems to have attempted this, perhaps because it was common, but unspoken, ground that British coal was uncompetitive on world markets. Both Robens and Marsh perceive the main row of 1967 to have been not Aberfan but the government White Paper on Fuel Policy.[125] Although it promised to keep the coal import ban in being, and mentioned in passing that the pithead price of coal in the USA was less than half its price in the UK, Robens felt that its projections for future coal demand in the UK were too low, and fiercely lobbied against them. (In fact, demand for UK coal has fallen much faster than the 1967 projections.) Consequently he was an extremely popular figure with the NUM.

Why then were ministers so determined to keep Robens? Crossman feared: 'we should then have all the problem of pit closures being sabotaged by Alf from the outside'.[126] Richard Marsh is in no doubt that Robens would have pursued a campaign of attacking government fuel policy if he left the NCB. He also maintains that Robens' friendship with Cecil King, chairman of the Mirror Group, would have meant public backing for any attack from the *Daily Mirror*. The bitterness Robens felt towards the government, Harold Wilson and the Labour Party would have added to his zeal to criticise them publicly. To Marsh the whole issue of whether to keep Robens was nothing to do with Aberfan but everything to do with his intense dislike of the government's policy on fuel.[127]

Not only would there be the problem of an angry Robens outside the NCB tent but there was also the question of the lack of any suitable successor. It was then an axiom of British politics that no politician should ever be foolish enough to take on the NUM. It remained so until 1984. Robens alone, ministers felt, could shield them from the wrath of the NUM. Marsh noted

> If it were decided to accept the resignation it is relevant to bear in mind that Lord Robens' successor would appear to have been appointed in oppposition to the wishes of the industry ... His successor might therefore encounter some hostility. With the many serious difficulties that lie ahead of the coal industry, hostility between the chairman and unions would be a severe handicap.[128]

The monopoly power of the NUM, which made it so feared, was conferred by British governments themselves, notably in the bipartisan policy of banning coal imports. Ministers felt that Robens, however much he infuriated them, was indispensable.

Several Labour MPs for Welsh valley constituencies spoke in the Aberfan debate. With the sole exception of Leo Abse, they were intimately connected with the mining industry. Like other Labour Party members, they regarded the nationalisation of coal as a crowning achievement of the 1945–51 government. Therefore, they were uncomfortable with the notion that the NCB could do anything wrong. S. O. Davies, already under pressure from his local party, deepened his problems through his attacks on the Coal Board, all the more so as he was a former miner. He was deselected by the Labour Party but held his seat in the 1970 General Election as Independent Labour – the first deselected major party candidate to do so for a generation. Politically, the Labour government was in a difficult position in the South Wales valleys in 1967–8. There as elsewhere, it was massively unpopular with its own traditional supporters. In England, disillusioned Labour supporters had no obvious alternative party to turn to. In Wales and Scotland, they had the option of voting nationalist. Plaid Cymru (The Party of Wales) had won its first parliamentary seat at the Carmarthen by-election in July 1966, taking it from Labour. In two valley by-elections it came close. At Rhondda West in March 1967, it took 39.9 per cent of the vote, cutting Labour's lead from 67.4 per cent to 9.1 per cent. At Caerphilly in July 1968 it took 40.4 per cent, cutting the lead from 63.1 per cent to just 5.1 per cent.[129] Plaid Cymru also did reasonably well in local elections in South Wales in 1967 and 1968. In this context, accepting Robens' resignation might have been electorally dangerous.

Gwynfor Evans, the Plaid Cymru MP for Carmarthen, said, in the course of his speech in the Aberfan debate, that if the tips had slid on to 'Hampstead or Eton', the Government response to the disaster would have been stronger. He went on: 'The odds are that if Wales had had her own Coal Board, ... this disaster would never have occurred.'[130] The latter claim is scarcely borne out by the Tribunal Report. Evans' speech was less well-informed than three of the Conservative speeches, including Margaret Thatcher's. The most effective criticism of the Coal Board did not come from Plaid Cymru.

South Walians had at least two distinctive reasons for disillusionment with the Labour government in 1967–8. One was its failure to act over Aberfan; the other was the pit closure programme implied by the November 1967 White Paper on Coal. However, beyond calling for Robens' resignation, Plaid Cymru did not campaign specifically on Aberfan, nor have we found any evidence that government ministers had Plaid Cymru at the front of their minds in deciding how to react to the Tribunal and to Robens' subsequent behaviour. They may have felt that open criticism of the NCB or of Robens would play into Plaid Cymru's hands. But for all the talk of all seats being 'marginal now',[131] ministers would have been justified in believing that they could ride out the temporary popularity of Plaid Cymru in the valleys. At the Rhondda West by-election, Gallup asked a sample of voters, 'How would you vote if the contest were a general election and not a by-election?' Of those intending to vote for Plaid Cymru, 69 per cent said 'Labour' as against only 10 per cent who said they would still vote Plaid Cymru.[132] With this information in the public domain, ministers did not need make concessions to Plaid Cymru in the South Wales valleys.[133]

Why did the regulatory authorities fail?

The only body to escape lightly ·from the Aberfan Tribunal's
strictures was HM Inspectorate of Mines and Quarries. It is hard to
see why, when the Tribunal considered whether two entirely
innocent bodies – Merthyr Tydfil Borough Council and the NUM –
should bear some share of the blame. Its own evidence revealed
severe failure and regulatory capture.

Statutory regulation of coal mines in the UK goes back to 1842.
In 1954 it was consolidated into that year's Mines and Quarries Act.
That Act laid down very detailed powers of inspection underground.
These have evolved through the harrowing history of mine disasters,
some of which have involved higher death tolls than Aberfan. The
inspection procedures incorporated the workforce – union
representatives accompanied managers and inspectors. But moles
do not understand the habits of birds. Only accidents involving
injury or death to colliery employees were reportable under the 1954
Act. Because of the 'little short of miraculous' survival of the whole
tipping gang (they had gone for a cup of tea when the slide
started),[134] the Aberfan disaster was not even a reportable accident
under the 1954 Act.[135] On the day of the disaster, the Inspectorate
tried to dissuade Richard Marsh from visiting Aberfan. The Inspectors accompanying Marsh to the disaster pointed to the Mines and
Quarries Act to show that neither the Inspectorate nor the Minister
had any legal responsibility for tips or the disaster. Marsh
remembers the Inspectorate as 'working strictly to the book' with an
ethos not to get involved in things that they were not responsible
for.[136]

The Mines' Inspectorate annual report for 1966 begins with an
expression of sympathy that is careful to point out that the disaster
was not reportable under the 1954 Mines and Quarries Act for which
they were responsible. That year's annual report for the South
Western division of the Inspectorate, which incorporates Aberfan,
does not even mention the disaster.[137]

The records of inspections of Merthyr Vale colliery since 1961
were produced to the Tribunal. The Inspectorate visited the colliery
frequently between 1961 and 1966, but not once did they look at the
tips which towered over the valley. Yet the Chief Inspector for the
region covering Merthyr Vale freely accepted that he regarded tip
stability as part of the duties of the Inspectorate so as to protect the
men working there.[138] He was invited to describe what a tip inspection should cover. These are his words:

We would look at the tip itself, we would look for cracks, we would look for swellings, holes, and as long as the symmetry of the tip was satisfactory then we would regard that as being in order.[139]

The Aberfan tips had had almost all the faults he lists since 1944. The Inspector was cross-examined not by the fearsome Ackner but by his junior. The inquiry transcript shows that he was not hostile. In his response to further questions, the Chief Inspector revealed that he, too, was a mole. He was a former colliery engineer. Neither he nor any of his staff had professional expertise in soil mechanics; nor did they consult anyone with such expertise. Like the industry they were regulating, the Mines' Inspectorate was dominated by mining engineers. What happened to the mineral once it was extracted from the ground was simply not part of their conception of the industry.

This was self-evidently the capture of a regulatory body by, and in the interests of, those whom it regulates. This has commonly been observed with price and quantity regulation. But this example shows that it can occur with safety regulation also. The danger is greatest when regulatee and regulator are both public-sector bodies with a revolving door between them. The Tribunal commented on the 'greater alertness' of the former Powell Duffryn company to the 1939 slip than that of the Coal Board from 1963 onwards.[140] Regulation was devised by the miners for the miners, and although surface workers are miners too they are not the ones who make the running. Moles may make good rules for moles, but not for birds.

Ministerial briefing notes for the Aberfan debate show that the government was prepared for criticisms of the Mines' Inspectorate. In the event of any relevant question the Minister was to maintain that the Mines and Quarries Act made it clear that safety provision was the responsibility of the owners while the Inspectorate's role was to enforce that provision. Where provision had not been made through the failure to recognise danger then responsibility should lie with the mining profession. The briefing notes claim that it was unfair to argue that, with hindsight, the dangers should have been foreseen when no one had ever been killed by a tip.[141] The Minister was to concede that dangers could have been anticipated in South Wales where tips had slid before but, given that, it was strange that no one had ever asked the Inspectorate to assess tips. The brief also pointed out that when the Inspectorate was not carrying out its specific duties, it was looking at other areas of mining where experience had shown there were specific dangers.[142]

Such answers may have partially excused the failures of the Mines' Inspectorate but they hardly excuse the industry and its regulators' failure to look beyond the demands of extraction. This was the same narrow outlook that had left the industry behind the times in terms of marketing and sales. As a nationalised industry with a virtual domestic monopoly that had initially mattered little. However, natural gas, nuclear power and international competition had begun to challenge that complacency. Aberfan now shook it to its core.

The other regulator of the NCB was the Coal Division of the Ministry of Power. It was never realistic to suppose that a dozen administrative civil servants could effectively regulate an employer of hundreds of thousands of people (60,000 in South Wales alone, in 1966). But it did not have to be as egregiously captive as it was in 1967. The Coal Division most frequently told ministers that Robens was indispensable. The Coal Division argued that Ryans must not be allowed to produce coal more cheaply than the Coal Board, or to clear away the Aberfan tips. When the Tribunal recommended that the 1954 Act 'should be extended to include provision for safety of the general public', the Coal Division objected, calling this a 'revolutionary innovation'. (However, the revolutionary idea that the NCB had a duty to the public safety was incorporated obliquely into the 1969 Act and became a central feature in the 1974 Health and Safety at Work Act) We have found only three acts of symbolic rebellion over Aberfan: the Division refused to supply arguments in support of Robens' personal conduct, it argued unavailingly that Morgan should be dismissed, and it refused Robens' request to appoint Sheppard Deputy Chairman of the Board. Otherwise, it saw its role purely as protection of the public corporation it sponsored. The interests of the people of Aberfan and the wider national interest were not among its concerns.[143]

A consumer culture?

Britain in 1966, at the height of post-war corporatism, had a producer dominated political culture. That encouraging competition in coal might reduce prices was given as a reason against it. So ingrained was British corporatism that the Tribunal devoted a section of its report to discussing whether the NUM should be held partly to blame for the disaster. It answered no; but even raising the question implies that the union might be held formally responsible for running the industry.[144] Indeed, even Will Paynter, General Secretary of the NUM, felt that 'union leaders must accept some responsibility for the failure to anticipate and

take action to avert this terrible disaster.'[145] Corporatism provided
no remedy for corporations behaving badly. In aggregate, the most
shocking revelation from the new papers is that the arrogance and
obfuscation of the Coal Board continued unmodified after
21 October 1966.
Ostentatious moves to make government more consumer-friendly
were made from the late 1980s onwards. Commentators have not
taken the Citizens' Charter or the Cones Hotline very seriously. But
they symbolise a profound change in British political culture. For
better or worse, there was a sharp decline of deference after 1966.
The media would not now be frightened off by a warning such as
Elwyn Jones'. The *Sunday Times'* campaign against the company
that had marketed thalidomide led in 1973 to its conviction on contempt charges being upheld in the House of Lords, a conviction that
was only reversed by means of the European Court of Human Rights
some years later.

Various commentators at the time, including Richard Marsh,
made much of the fact that the only known laws anywhere in the
world on tip stability were in South Africa and North
Rhine-Westphalia. Therefore, Parliament was as guilty as anyone
else for failing to regulate the industry effectively. The trouble with
the plea that we are all guilty is that it lets off anybody in particular.
Lord Robens noted that at the Tribunal

> what was required of the National Coal Board was a simple plea of
> 'guilty'. This we were all ready to give, but we were misled by the terms of
> reference of the tribunal, which were framed to uncover facts rather than
> to apportion blame.[146]

Nobody else seems to have noticed the Coal Board's readiness to
plead guilty, nor does it emerge anywhere in the newly released
records.[147] Even saying sorry would have done no harm. But that was
not how things were done in those days.

Notes

1 *Aberfan Report*, p. 11.
2 *Aberfan Report*, p. 131.
3 One Coal Board engineer's 'unreliability as a witness proved as great as
  his manifest self-satisfaction' (*Aberfan Report*, p. 68). 'Does it really lie
  in the mouths of the members of the National Board to say that they ...
  are ... to be excused for having paid no attention to tip stability? They
  cannot be so excused.' (*Aberfan Report*, p. 84). On the Coal Board's
  refusal to make concessions 'this will not do. It will not do at all'
  (*Aberfan Report*, p. 88).

4 *Aberfan Report*, p. 25.
5 *Aberfan Report*, p. 11.
6 *Aberfan Report*, p. 86. The Cabinet decided that it was important for the Aberfan parents to be properly represented and thus provision was made for their legal costs to be recouped. They would not otherwise have been eligible for legal aid. PRO CAB 128/41 CC 52(66). All archival references in this chapter are from the PRO unless otherwise specified.
7 *Aberfan Report*, pp. 85, 87.
8 *Aberfan Report*, pp. 89–92.
9 Richard Marsh to Harold Wilson, 3 August 1967. POWE 52/212. Lord Robens, *Ten Year Stint* (London: Cassell, 1972), p. 259. The local lodge of the NUM petitioned the Board for Vivian Thomas to be retained in employment at Merthyr Vale colliery. Five of the seven were moved to 'jobs of smaller compass' without reduction of pay. The other two were left in comparable or more senior posts, despite the statements to the contrary in Robens' memoirs and in Parliament. COAL 73/5 W. R. King to Lord Robens, 10 September 1968. BD 521154, 'Brief for Aberfan Debate', unsigned [October 1967]; COAL 73/3, Staff Memo, 4 August 1967; COAL 73/4 Staff Administrative Branch Memo 5 January 1968; POWE 52/215, 'Harry' (Ministry of Power, Office for Wales) to R. Dearing, 18 August 1967.
10 POWE 52/212.
11 Interview, MJ and John Taylor, 28 May 1999.
12 D. L. Roberts (Area Mechanical Engineer) and R. E. Exley (Area Civil Engineer) were both instructed to inspect the disaster tip in 1965. Exley did not; Roberts claimed to have done, but the Tribunal was sceptical of his claim. Neither, therefore, reported on its obvious instability. *Aberfan Report*, pp. 98–100.
13 COAL 73/3 Meeting, Lord Robens, W. V. Sheppard, C. A. Roberts, T. Wright, 30 August 1967
14 POWE 52/212 Aberfan Disaster: Report of the Tribunal of Inquiry – Memorandum by the National Coal Board & The Report of the Tribunal appointed to inquire into the Disaster at Aberfan – A [draft] note by the Minister of Power. John Taylor interview.
15 Robens: *Aberfan Report*, pp. 89–92; Sheppard, *Aberfan Report*, pp. 84–5.
16 POWE 52/212 The Report of the Tribunal appointed to inquire into the Disaster at Aberfan – A [draft] note by the Minister of Power.
17 *The Times*, 4 August 1967, p. 1, subhead 'I Have Not Offered to Resign'; *The Times*, 8 August 1967, p. 1.
18 *Hansard*, Commons, 5th series, vol. 751, col. 1978. POWE 52/212 The Report of the Tribunal appointed to inquire into the Disaster at Aberfan – A [draft] note by the Minister of Power.
19 Margaret Thatcher, *The Path to Power* (London: HarperCollins, 1995), p. 143.
20 BD 52/154, 'Brief for Aberfan Debate'. Another copy is in POWE 52/68. Overall responsibility for the note rested with R. E. Dearing (now Lord Dearing), the head of the economic section of the Coal Division of the Ministry of Power (POWE 52/68, briefing note cover sheet, 9 September 1967, telephone interview with Sir Ron Dearing, 13 January 1997). On Robens, the briefer wrote, 'It is suggested that the Minister should not seek to defend Lord Robens' evidence.' He did not:

Hansard, Commons, 5th series, vol. 751, col. 2004: 'It is not for me to defend Lord Robens' conduct at the Tribunal.'
21 *Hansard*, 5th ser., vol. 751, col. 1959–60. POWE 52/212 The Report of the Tribunal appointed to inquire into the Disaster at Aberfan – A [draft] note by the Minister of Power.
22 *Safety and Health at Work, Report of the Committee,* Chairman Lord Robens, Cmnd 5034, 1972, para. 263.
23 Especially classes BD 11, BD 50, BD 52, CAB 164, COAL 29, COAL 73, POWE 52, and PREM 13. All Aberfan papers at the PRO were opened on 2 January 1997, although many of them would not normally have been opened until 1998 or later as they include documents from 1967 or later. Class BD 52 (records of the Tribunal of Inquiry) was opened in 1996.
24 The canonical example, whose title we borrow, is Matthew A. Crenson, *The Unpolitics of Air Pollution: a study of non-decisionmaking in the cities* (Baltimore: John Hopkins University Press, 1971).
25 *Hansard*, Commons, 5th ser. vol. 734, col. 643. In his closing speech to the Tribunal, counsel for the NUM, defending his clients against the charge that they should have realised that the tip was unsafe and alerted their managers, pointed out that if Coal Board officials could mislead the Secretary of State for Wales, they could also rnislead the Merthyr Vale lodge of the NUM. *Tribunal Transcripts*, day 71, p. 3973.
26 John Taylor interview. Similarly Richard Marsh recalls how a telephone line between a meeting of the heads of the rescue services and the disaster site was taken off the hook because it rang while Wilson was speaking. Richard Marsh, *Off the Rails* (London: Weidenfeld & Nicolson, 1978), pp. 114–115. Wilson did however tell to rescuers to carry on work after they were stopped in order for the Prime Minister to be introduced. The Queen did not visit the scene immediately for fear of disrupting the rescue. Tony Austin, *Aberfan: The Story of a Disaster* (London: Hutchinson, 1967), pp. 62, 69.
27 COAL 29/378, 'Radio and TV Transcripts: Aberfan'. Satirist John Bird said, 'Perhaps someone should have been there on that Friday to exercise some good taste but the Chairman of the NCB himself had a more pressing engagement to keep – he was at Guildford for the ceremony installing him as the University of Surrey's first Chancellor, so it wasn't until that night that he was able to get away to Aberfan and announce that he'd been sickened by the work of the TV reporters who'd been there for the previous day and a half'. (BBC TV, The Late Show, 5 November 1966).
28 John Taylor interview. Cf also letter from G. Morgan, D. Powell, C. Jones, D.L. Roberts, R.N. Lewis, R. V. Thomas and T. J. Wynne (i.e., the seven NCB employees blamed by the Tribunal) to Lord Robens 10.8.67: 'We were all very conscious that your comments to the press and on TV during the first days of the incident were designed to assist the local officials as much as possible. We are so sorry that this effort created so many difficulties for you at a later date'. COAL 73/3
29 Austin, *Aberfan*, pp. 150–3. A less coherent transcript is in PREM 13/1280.
30 *Hansard,* Commons, 5th series, Vol. 734, cols 1315–20.
31 Quoted in Austin, *Aberfan*, p. 148.

32 Lord Elwyn-Jones, *In My Time: An Autobiography* (London: Futura, 1988), p. 234. An interdepartmental committee later recommended that 'The law of contempt in its application to Tribunals of Inquiry should not prohibit or curtail any comment at any time about the subject-matter of the inquiry.' The government of the day (1973) stated that it accepted this recommendation. Cmnd 5313/1973, Appendix C. Lord Howe of Aberavon, who as Geoffrey Howe QC, was counsel for the British Association of Colliery Management and the National Association of Colliery Managers, was one of those who criticised Jones' warning: Geoffrey Howe, 'The Aberfan Disaster', *Medico-Legal Journal*, 38, 1968, 107–21.

33 Quoted in Austin, *Aberfan*, p. 159. Also see *The Sunday Times*, 30 October 1966, 'The Aberfan disaster has produced a new hazard in mining about which we knew nothing before.' Cf. also interview with Geoffrey Morgan, the engineer in charge of stabilization, in *The Times*, 26 October 1966: 'The tip had been properly inspected, he said ... "It is our opinion that the spring responsible for this incident [sic] was a recent eruption." '

34 *The Sunday Times,* 26 February 1967, p. 5; *Aberfan Tribunal Transcripts*, day 70, p. 3926. In the Tribunal's cutting of this story the passage above is sidelined and the word 'unforeseeable' underlined. PRO: BD 52/109. Lord Howe does not share Lord Ackner's belief that the article was NCB inspired.

35 Tribunal of inquiry, transcript of evidence, day 2, pp. 88, 90.

36 See *Aberfan Report*, pp. 85, 86.

37 *Aberfan Tribunal Transcripts*, day 70. Cross-examination of Lord Robens by Desmond Ackner, p. 3924: Q: 'Does it come to this, that by the time the inquiry started on 29 November you were then satisfied that the causes were reasonably foreseeable?' A: 'That is so'.

38 *Aberfan Report*, Fig. 1, Fig. 2, Plate 1, and Plate 3.

39 H. J. Siddle, M. D. Wright & J. N. Hutchinson, 'Rapid failures of colliery spoil heaps in the South Wales Coalfield', *Quarterly Journal of Engineering Geology*, 29, 1996, p. 105.

40 John Taylor interview. Howe felt that his role at the inquiry was 'acting as an insulator between those accused and the avenging fury of the public'. Geoffrey Howe, *Conflict of Loyalty* (London: Macmillan, 1994), p. 41. The only newspaper that reported Robens' acceptance of responsibility was the *Observer*. See Robens, *Ten Year Stint*, p. 249.

41 Aberfan Disaster: Report of the Tribunal of Inquiry, Memorandum by the National Coal Board. POWE 52/212.

42 Aberfan: Coal Division's comments on the NCB memorandum, 25 August 1967. POWE 52/212.

43 R. H. S. Crossman, *The Diaries of a Cabinet Minister. Vol. 2: Lord President of the Council and Leader of the House of Commons 1966–68* (London, 1976), pp. 440.

44 BD 11/3810, G. Daniel to B. Trend, 19 July 1967, PREM 15/1280, MS note on this memo in Wilson's hand.

45 R. B. Marshall to A. Blackshaw, 31 July 1967, POWE 52/94.

46 MISC 157(67) 1st meeting, 27 July 1967. CAB 130/328.

47 Crossman, *Diaries of a Cabinet Minister. Vol. 2*, pp. 440, 453.

48 MISC 157(67) 2nd meeting, 1 August 1967. CAB 130/328. Cledwyn Hughes later said that this was a mistake and that Parliament should have extended to allow a Commons debate. *Western Mail*, 1 January 1998.
49 See note 10.
50 A. H. Kellett was Chairman of the South Western Division of the Coal Board. G. S. Morgan was Production Director for South Wales. There was some feeling within the NCB that it was unfair that certain individuals had escaped censure when others had been named. MJ interview with John Taylor. Cf William Ashworth, *The History of the British Coal Industry, Vol. 5, 1946–1982: The Nationalized Industry* (Oxford: Clarendon Press, 1986), p. 287. Marsh expressed surprise at the above meeting that Kellett and Collins (the Board Member for Production) were not interviewed by the Tribunal. Marsh thought that Kellett would have been responsible for the liaison between division and HQ and that he might have reasonably been expected to know of the dangers of the Aberfan tips from the complaints in the local press. Paul Foot claimed that Kellett and Collins were told by Robens to stay at a conference in Japan 'which effectively prevented either man losing his head'. 'Footnotes', *Private Eye*, 28 April 1967.
51 POWE 52/94. The Aberfan Report and the NCB: note of a meeting held in the Minister's room, 3 August 1967.
52 A long series of letters from the Borough Engineer to the Coal Board in 1963–4, headed 'Danger from Coal Slurry being tipped at the rear of the Pantglas Schools', had encountered only evasions and falsehoods from the Coal Board (*Aberfan Report*, pp. 55–60, 107; copies of the letters are in Merthyr library's Aberfan Disaster collection).
53 John Taylor interview.
54 A. Blackshaw to R. Marshall, 31 July 1967. Earlier, Robens had complained to his Board about the 'difficulties encountered in obtaining advance copies ... it was essential that they should have access to the document well in advance of publication'. COAL 73/2, Secret Minute of the Board, 28 July 1967.
55 *The Times*, 7 August 1967, p. 1.
56 *The Times*, 9 August 1967, p. 2.
57 COAL 73/3, 8 August 1967.
58 Leader, 'Is it a Resigning Matter?' 7 August 1967.
59 John Taylor interview.
60 Lord Marsh interview with MJ.
61 COAL 73/2, draft resignation letter, 3 August 1967.
62 John Taylor interview.
63 For example, E. Silver, 'Lord Robens's Offer to Resign Not Accepted Yet', *The Times*, 8 August 1967: 'Although Mr Marsh is still keeping his own counsel, it is now thought unlikely in Whitehall that he will accept Lord Robens's offer.' Lord Marsh claims (*Off the Rails*, p. 116) that Robens had offered his resignation before the Tribunal reported, but that he then rejected it.
64 POWE 52/94. R. Marsh: 'Note for the Record Lord Robens', 9 August 1967.
65 Letter from The Gallup Organization to IM, 7 November 1996: POWE 52/93, letters from NOP and Government Social Survey to Press

Office, Ministry of Power, giving poll results, 6 September 1967 and 11 September 1967.

66 COAL 73/3, A. Alderson to Lord Robens, 17 August 1967. The comments (POWE 52/93, 'Aberfan Disaster: Report of the Tribunal: Memorandum by the NCB', 23 August 1967) pugnaciously rebut some statements in the Tribunal Report. There is little sign of contrition in them.

67 POWE 52/93. Memo from D. Pitblado to A. Blackshaw, R. Marshall, and C. Thorley, 31 August 1967.

68 John Taylor interview.

69 POWE 52/93. Draft of Minister's Reply: Telegram from Lord Caradon (both 5 September 1967); A. Blackshaw to R. Marsh, 6 September 1967.

70 Western Mail, 28 October 1967, editorial.

71 BD52/1/8. 'Proposed alternative methods of removing the whole of the tip complex', June 1967.

72 Aberfan Report, pp. 121–2.

73 G. Diamond to C. Hughes, 8 April 1968. BD 52/113.

74 BD 52/115 and 114, passim.

75 BD 52/113, letter from Aberfan Tip Removal Committee to J. Siberry, enclosing estimate from Ryan Industrial Fuels, 30 April 1968; BD52/114, memo by B. Houghton of meeting between Chief Secretary to Treasury and Secretary of State for Wales, n.d. July 1968.

76 BD 52/154, Brief for Aberfan Debate.

77 BD 11/3804. J. Siberry to G. Diamond, 2 April 1968.

78 BD 11/3804. Meeting with Aberfan Deputation at Welsh Office, London, 7 February 1968.

79 26 July 1968 Minute of Meeting 157(68). BD 11/3807.

80 J. Siberry to G. Diamond, 28 May 1968. BD 11/3804. (government concerns)

81 BD 52/113 and 114, reports by J. Siberry. On 10 February 1969, for instance, he reported, 'So the hurdle of the unpredictable emotions and reactions of Aberfan seems to be behind us.' BD 11/3807.

82 The 'Powell Memorandum', para 6.2, Aberfan Report, p. 142. This was the document which Roberts and Exley (see above) had failed to implement. The Powell memorandum is further discussed in Chapter 6.

83 BD52/113 Siberry to Daniel, 11 December 1967.

84 SWCC, Letter from T. S. Price to George Thomas, 18 June 1968, MNA/PP/16/37.

85 Interview with bereaved parent present at the meeting, Western Mail, 1 August 1997. MJ interview with Colin Murray Parkes, 28 April 1999.

86 G. Thomas to the Prime Minister, 23 July 1968. BD 52/114. Draft minute from G. Thomas to H. Wilson, 23 July 1968. COAL 73/5 & BD 11/3804.

87 George Thomas, Mr Speaker: The Memoirs of the Viscount Tonypandy (London: Century Publishing, 1985), p. 101.

88 Harold Wilson, The Labour Government 1964–70: A Personal Record (Harmondsworth: Penguin, 1974), pp. 694–5. George Thomas was also prepared to 'remind Robens of the outcome of the Inquiry and make it clear to him that he thinks the NCB have an obligation to the people of Aberfan'. He prepared to cancel a trip to Brunei, anticipating that even

this threat would not persuade Robens to pay. PREM 13/1281,
D. Andrews to H. Wilson, 26 July 1968.
89 BD 11/3804 Draft of statement to be made by Secretary of State re
Aberfan tips.
90 COAL 73/2, minutes of meeting on 6 March 1967. Less than a week
after the disaster, an editorial in the *South Wales Echo* had actually suggested using the fund for 'beautifying by afforestation' the tips above
the village. *South Wales Echo*, 26 October 1966.
91 BD 11/3804 Confidential note by Secretary of State., n.d. but July 1968.
92 BD 11/3807, minute of Misc. 157(68), first meeting, 26 July 1968.
93 *Second Report of the Management Committee of the Aberfan Disaster
Fund* (Merthyr Tydfil, 1970), p. 4; Joan Miller, *Aberfan: a Disaster and
its Aftermath* (London, 1974), pp. 60–2.
94 S. O. Davies to Harold Wilson, 30 July 1968. ADA, Dowlais collection
C/007/02.
95 *First Report of the Management Committee of the Aberfan Disaster
Fund*, 1968, p. 10.
96 Form letter: BD 11/3791, e.g. draft reply to letter from L. R. Beard to
the Prime Minister, 13 March 1970. Cabinet conclusion: CAB 128143.
CC (68) 37 (5). July 1968. In 1971 it emerged that the ongoing removal
was going to cost more than had originally been thought. The Welsh
Office rejected the idea of seeking a further contribution from the fund:
'Any such suggestion would stir up much trouble and unpleasantness.
To start a conflagration in Aberfan one has only to kick a stone accidentally'. J. Siberry to Mr Barker, 11 March 1971. BD 11/3807.
97 Cecil King, *The Cecil King Diary, 1965–70* (London: Jonathan Cape,
1972), p. 138.
98 Concern within the industry had been first raised after the appointment
of Edmund Davies. The *Colliery Guardian* argued that Davies' south
Wales background (which he emphasised after his appointment with
statements such as 'I want to be of the greatest service to the people to
whom I belong') made him partial and unsuitable for the 'cold dispassionate pursuit of facts' that was needed. *Colliery Guardian*, 28 October
1966. There was also private disquiet about the Tribunal Report outside
the coal industry. Geoffrey Howe felt that the Tribunal had inflicted an
'injustice' on some of those he represented. Howe, *Conflict of Loyalty*,
pp. 41–42.
99 See, for example, the summaries of press opinion given in the *South
Wales Echo*, 4 August 1967.
100 *Hansard*, 5ᵗʰ Series, vol. 751, col. 1956.
101 810 1 KB [Glamorgan Assizes] *R v Cory Brothers and Company Limited*.
1927 Feb. 2; Celia Wells, *Negotiating Tragedy: Law and Disasters*
(London: Sweet and Maxwell, 1995), pp. 170–171.
102 *DPP v Kent & Sussex Contractors Ltd* [1944] KB 146. *R v ICR Haulage
Ltd* [1944] 30 Cr App R 31. *Moore v Bresler* [1944] 2 All ER 515.
103 Law Commission, *Criminal Law: Involuntary Manslaughter*,
Consultation Paper no. 135 (London: HMSO, 1994), paras. 4.11–4.16.
104 *The Times*, 2, 4, 5 February 1965.
105 Letter from The Rt Hon The Lord Howe of Aberavon, CH, QC to IM,
2 December 1996; telephone interview with Lord Ackner, 27 November
1996.

106 *The Times*, 4–5 August 1967.
107 Note, 22 November 1966, file 1, Cyril Moseley Papers, NLW.
108 *Merthyr Express*, 28 October 1966, p. 18.
109 *The Times*, 4 August 1967.
110 Attendance re Aberfan, 10 August 1967, file 6, Cyril Moseley papers, NLW.
111 E.g., because of the false assurances given to Merthyr Borough Council: *Aberfan Report*, p. 56; BD 52/12, BD 52/199.
112 *Rylands v. Fletcher* [1868] LR 3. HL 330; *Attorney-General v. Cory Brothers & Co Ltd*, [1921] 1 AC 521 (*Cory* was the case of a tip slide, in the Rhondda Valley); *Aberfan Report*, p. 39; cross-examination of W. Sheppard by D. Ackner, *Aberfan Tribunal Transcripts*, day 51, p. 2824.
113 R. Vivian Thomas: 'I had no instructions at all about any tips ... but I was responsible. It is no good shirking it. I was responsible for the tip.' Such an admission must have taken great courage. *Aberfan Tribunal Transcripts*, day 17, p. 931; Howe, 'The Aberfan Disaster', p. 112. See also Howe's eloquent plea in mitigation of his clients, *ibid.*, pp. 112–4 and his defence of a Tribunal rather than other forms of redress for the victims, *ibid.*, p. 114.
114 *The Times*, 29 September 1967.
115 *The Times*, 29 September 1967.
116 Cyril Moseley papers, file 6, NLW, Attendance re Aberfan 28 September 1967
117 Celia Wells, 'Disasters: the role of institutional responses in shaping public perceptions of death', in Robert Lee & Derek Morgan (eds.), *Death Rites: Law and Ethics at the End of Life* (London: Routledge, 1996 edn.), p. 205.
118 J. Siberry to G. Daniel, 6 November 1967, BD 52/113.
119 Lord Marsh interview.
120 Unlabelled file of financial figures, collected from Engineer's Department, Merthyr Town Hall. In Merthyr Tydfil Central Library. Aberfan Disaster Collection.
121 *Financial Times*, 14 August 1967.
122 *Aberfan Tribunal, Transcript of Oral Evidence,* Day 70, p. 3940.
123 Marsh, *Off the Rails*, p. 111.
124 Barbara Castle, *The Castle Diaries 1964–70* (London: Weidenfeld & Nicolson, 1984), p. 370 (7 February 1968); cf. also p. 313 (25 October 1967). For comparably hostile comments on Robens see Wilson, *Labour Government*, p. 625; Crossman, *Diaries, II*, p. 751 (13 November 1967).
125 Cmnd 3438/1967. Robens, *Ten Year Stint*, pp. 178–222; Marsh, *Off the Rails*, pp. 109–11.
126 Crossman, *Diaries, II*, p. 453. Whether or not, Robens actually would have sabotaged the pit closures from outside is of course debatable. His obituary in *The Independent* (29 June 1999) notes that upon leaving the NCB in 1971 Robens deliberately kept a low profile on coal and energy matters. However, it also notes that by 1974 he was publicly attacking government energy policies. Nor does Robens' flirtation with Cecil King's plot for a coup d'etat suggest any particular inclination to ease the Government's path.
127 Lord Marsh interview.

128 Draft note by Minister of Power, 1 September 1967. POWE 52/94. Also see letter from James Callaghan to Harold Wilson, 31 July 1967.

129 Alan Butt Philip, *The Welsh Question: Nationalism in Welsh Politics 1945–1970* (Cardiff: University of Wales Press, 1975), p. 110.

130 *Hansard*, Commons, 5th series, vol. 751, col. 1958.

131 Miners' official to James Griffiths, December 1967. Quoted in K. O. Morgan, *Rebirth of a Nation: Wales, 1880–1980* (Oxford/Cardiff: OUP/UWP, 1981), p. 387.

132 *The Daily Telegraph*, 9 March 1967, quoted by Butt Philip, *Welsh Question*, p. 111.

133 A view backed up with regard to Aberfan by Cledwyn Hughes. Letter, Lord Cledwyn of Penrhos to MJ, 18 July 1999.

134 *Aberfan Report*, p. 30.

135 If they had died or been hurt in the slide, the disaster would have been reportable and there would have been a case to answer under the 1954 Act. But figures from the Robens Report show that the Mines and Quarries Inspectorate was remarkably unwilling to prosecute. Of the sixteen prosecutions under the 1954 Act in 1970, five had been initiated by the NCB itself, eleven by Procurators-Fiscal in Scotland and none at all by the Inspectorate. This total of sixteen prosecutions, in one of the two most dangerous industries in the UK, compares with 2,940 under the Factories Act 1961, 432 under the Offices, Shops, and Railway Premise Act 1963, and 311 under seven other regulatory statutes. Robens Report, Table 5.

136 Lord Marsh interview.

137 H. S. Stephenson, *Report of HM Chief Inspector for Mines and Quarries (under the Mines and Quarries Act 1954) for 1966* (London: HMSO, 1967). C. Leigh, *Reports of HM Inspectors of Mines and Quarries (under the Mines and Quarries Act 1954) for 1966, South Western Division* (London: HMSO, 1967).

138 *Aberfan Report*, p. 35.

139 *Aberfan Tribunal, Transcript of Oral Evidence*, Day 52. Evidence of Cyril Leigh, Chief Inspector of Mines and Quarries for Wales, p. 2868.

140 However, before nationalisation the Mines' Inspectorate was sometimes too close to the mining companies. Such a picture was clear after the Gresford disaster (Chapter 8).

141 Incorrect. A boy had been killed at Pentre in 1909 (see above).

142 POWE 52/212 Aberfan Debate – Draft Brief, 23 October 1967, role of HM Inspectorate of Mines & Quarries.

143 Aberfan Report, p. 132. Recommendation XVII Robens indispensable: POWE 52194, R. Dearing to C. Thorley, 1 September 1967; POWE 52/215, draft note for Minister to put to Cabinet, 25 August 1967. Ryan: see above. 'Revolutionary innovation': POWE 52/68. Coal Division memo on Tribunal findings, 26 July 1967. Refusal to endorse Robens' conduct: BD 11/3810, briefing note for Aberfan debate, Section 2, 'The Chairman's evidence to the Tribunal'. 'Require [Morgan's] resignation': POWE 52/94, R. Marshall to A. Blackshaw, 31 July 1967. Refusal to promote Sheppard: POWE 52/94. Dearing to Thorley, draft briefing note for Minister.

144 Just one corporatist move was frustrated. Wilson wanted to appoint a miner as a member of the Tribunal. Edmund Davies refused, pointing

out that if a miner was appointed, then a mine manager would also have to be, and that this would probably frustrate the Tribunal because the manager would be inclined to side with his negligent colleagues. PREM 13/1280, Prime Minister's office memo, 22 October 1966.

145 Will Paynter, *My Generation* (London: Allen & Unwin, 1972), p. 130.

146 Robens, *Ten Year Stint*, pp. 252–3.

147 Although Lord Robens has always insisted that he accepted liability on behalf of the Coal Board immediately after the disaster, this message did not reach the insurance department of the Coal Board. COAL 73/2, W. J. P. Webber memo, copied to Lord Robens, 25 April 1967: 'We considered earlier whether to admit liability. At that time there had been no general admission of liability and I decided ... that it would be unwise to do so. However, in view of what transpired when the Chairman visited the [Tribunal] hearing last week, my officials ... have decided that the time is now ripe to accept liability.'

Chapter Three

UNEASY RELATIONSHIPS:
ABERFAN, MERTHYR COUNCIL
AND LOCAL POLITICS

I was tormented by the fact that the people I was seeking justice from were my people – a Labour Government, a Labour council, a Labour-nationalised Coal Board.

Bereaved parent[1]

The causes of the Aberfan disaster were rooted in the shortcomings of individuals within the National Coal Board but also the attitudes, structure and economic power of the Board itself. This chapter will examine how this situation shaped the local political context, thus both contributing to the failure to prevent the disaster and governing aspects of its aftermath. It will go on to look at the impact of the disaster on the balance of power in local politics in the Aberfan area. Merthyr Tydfil County Borough Council not only had to reassess its relationship with the village, but itself suffered heavily in the disaster's aftermath.

'A state within a state'[2]: the NCB in South Wales

Before the Tribunal of Inquiry began its hearings, rumours and allegations had begun to circulate regarding the causes of the disaster. The National Coal Board was the obvious target of many of the accusations but people looked to the Borough Council too. After all, the local authority had been receiving complaints about the tip and the flooding it was causing for years; if the Council had forced the issue with the NCB then the disaster could have been avoided. At public meetings that quickly followed the disaster, the Borough

Council's Director of Education and his colleagues suffered what he described as 'bitter' criticisms and 'expressions of hatred' that were sometimes personalised.[3] In the atmosphere of disbelief and anger that follows disasters there is often a questioning of and antagonism towards officialdom.[4] Merthyr Tydfil County Borough Council (MTCBC) was the all-purpose local authority responsible for Aberfan and, in the immediate aftermath of the disaster, members of its education department were the nearest officials. The stressful circumstances were fully understood by those at whom the anger was directed but this cannot have made their experience any easier.

After the initial shock of the disaster, public anger in the village became more firmly focused on the NCB but the local authority was still in the dock as the Tribunal considered whether it should bear any responsibility for the tragedy. MTCBC had received complaints about flooding from the mountainside from 1949 and had expressed concern about the stability of the general tip complex from as early as 1944. Yet, despite pressurising the NCB on the matter, there was no resolution of the problems. The Tribunal noted that it could not understand why the Council could not reach 'an amicable settlement of what appears to be a simple drainage problem.'

While the flooding was less serious in its consequences, anxieties (not unconnected) over a tip slide were potentially far graver. The NCB told MTCBC that there was no danger but it would still investigate the matter. It did nothing and, in 1963–4, a series of letters headed 'Danger from coal slurry being tipped at the rear of the Pantglas Schools' were exchanged between the Borough Engineer's department and Mr. D. L. Roberts, the NCB's local Area Mechanical Engineer. The language in the MTCBC letters was strong enough that the Tribunal considered that the Coal Board should have investigated the matter. Roberts visited the tip complex but 'treated the matter so cavalierly as to render his visit useless.'[5] Further concerns were expressed by the Council during the discussion of the NCB's plan for an aerial walkway to allow further tipping on the mountain. Yet, the Tribunal noted, the Board's assurances that all was fine were accepted and Council officials never inspected the tips themselves (a visit by any of the Council's qualified engineers would have revealed the potential dangers), pressed their complaints higher than area level in the NCB or took legal action to deal with a situation that 'they thought dangerous to their burgesses.'[6]

The language used in the Council's complaints to the NCB suggests considerable worry over the stability of the tips. However, Mr. Bradley, the local authority's deputy engineer, told the Council's counsel that while he entertained fears of a substantial slip, he never imagined that it would lead to loss of life.[7] Yet even a small slip could have endangered lives and property but the Council still did not pursue the matter vigorously. However, the Tribunal felt that the Council should not be 'condemned on hindsight' and pointed to what it had done in alleviating it of any blame. It received 'no enlightening help' from the Welsh Office of the Ministry of Housing and Local Government, to whom it had written in 1957 arguing that the tipping area should not be extended. It had secured a promise that no more tailings (fine particles which are the final discard of modern coal filtration; the Council justifiably felt they were a cause of tip instability) would be tipped. It received assurances from 'high-ranking' NCB personnel that there was nothing wrong with the tip. The Council's engineers were felt by the Tribunal to have been perfectly reasonable in their assumption that the NCB had qualified experts inspecting the tips. Tragically this was not so.[8]

The Council's acceptance of the NCB's reassurances cannot be attributed to its trusting the Board's judgements and words alone. The local authority's counsel argued that,

> the local authority can make representations to whomsoever it pleases, but in making those representations it is governed by the fundamental character of its being, namely that it is an elected body. In doing so it mirrors the feelings and expressions of the people it represents. If there is no further demand for a certain course of action not prescribed as a legal duty, the local authority takes this course at its peril, and particularly when such a course may – or may not – jeopardise the daily bread of its people.[9]

Thus the Council's defence not only pointed towards what it did do but also argued that there was no popular demand for it to be more pressing in its concerns. Central to the absence of any such demand, despite the local concerns, was the impact any restriction of tipping might have on the future of the Merthyr Vale colliery on which Aberfan was economically dependant. After the euphoria that greeted nationalisation in 1947, the 1950s and 1960s were a more sombre period for the coal industry. A programme of pit closures was gathering pace which the NCB was felt to be executing unsympathetically.[10] Nor had the return of a Labour Government in 1964 halted the trend. That year there were 72,000 miners employed in the South Wales coalfield. By 1966 the figure was 58,000.[11] The impact on communities of the closure of collieries on which they were economically dependent reawoke the legacy of the dark days of the 1930s.[12] For those communities whose collieries were not deemed to be in immediate danger, the grim memories of the depression and the

more recent experience of their neighbours constituted a powerful warning. As MTCBC's counsel put it, the fear of unemployment must have been present in the minds of many in Aberfan.[13]
It was in this context that concerns over tip stability at Aberfan took place. The Tribunal spent almost two days considering whether fears over the future of the Merthyr Vale colliery had been a factor in the way local agencies handled the disaster. It concluded that the NCB was not considering closing the colliery, but did concede that such fears were not groundless in the event of tipping being restricted. MTCBC's counsel argued that this context did not overrule all other considerations (in other words safety) but it must be considered when assessing what actions the Council took.[14] S. O. Davies, the MP for Merthyr Tydfil, claimed to have been worried about tip stability and the danger to the village, but had not pushed the issue because of fears amongst the workers that such a dispute would lead to the closure of the pit. However, the Tribunal rejected his evidence arguing that he did not understand the grave implication of what he was saying and that he was affected by hindsight. Thus, while it would be wrong to assert that specific worries over the future of the Merthyr Vale colliery prevented action by the Council or other local bodies, the NCB's economic domination of the region did have repercussions on its general relationship with the local area. As the Tribunal argued, fears of over the future of the pit may have subconsciously affected coloured the attitudes and, in effect, the judgement of many. Taking the issue of tip safety too far could have had catastrophic consequences for Aberfan.[15]
Whether the fears over the tip and the future of the colliery were conscious or not, the result was a sense of guilt in Aberfan which hindered its recovery.[16] This issue thus coloured the debate on the removal of the tips. In 1967, an Aberfan resident told Richard Marsh,

> The real reason we want that particular tip removed is that we cannot stand the sight of it. Many of us are aware that the reason no complaint was made about the tip, which we knew had water in it, but which obviously we never thought would do the damage it did, was our belief that if action were taken to renovate it or make it safe for a time, the additional cost would have rendered a pit uneconomic, and would have resulted in its closure.

Marsh has suggested that it was this sense of guilt that made the urge to blame the disaster upon bodies outside the local community strong.[17]

Merthyr Tydfil had become a county borough in 1908, bringing new responsibilities to its Corporation that touched upon many aspects of local life.[18] In the year of the disaster, Merthyr was the smallest all-purpose local authority in Wales, and the fifth-smallest in Britain. Since becoming a borough, its population had fallen by nearly 20,000 to just 57,000.[19] Most of the other county boroughs of a similar size were prosperous county towns. The only ones smaller than Merthyr were Canterbury, Burton-on-Trent, Great Yarmouth, and Dewsbury. None of these had anything remotely like Merthyr's social problems, compounded by population decline and the lowest rateable value per capita of any county borough.[20] In 1967, it was claimed that Merthyr's rates were the highest of any county borough in England and Wales.[21] The 1967 white paper on local government in England and Wales suggested that Merthyr should cease to be a county borough. It noted that 'The Local Government Commission [for Wales, which reported in 1962] made a convincing case for regarding Merthyr Tydfil as too small and too lacking in resources to continue to carry out in modern conditions the full range of county borough functions and this case is strengthened by the further decline in its population since the Commission's report was published.'[22] The local authority's counsel at the Aberfan Tribunal argued that the Corporation was of 'modest dimensions but charged with functions as great as those of the cities of Cardiff, or Birmingham, or Liverpool' and that this should not be forgotten when considering the time and attention that it devoted to investigating the concern over the tips above Aberfan. Yet he still contended that it had done all that could be expected and acted with honour and dignity.[23]

Desmond Ackner QC, counsel for the parents' association, explained the Council's failures to push the matter by saying that,

... as the tips overshadowed, towered above, and indeed dwarfed the village, so did the National Coal Board the Council. Those whose function and duty it was to look after the welfare of the inhabitants of Aberfan discharged that function admirably in all other respects, but in regard to this matter, in relation to the National Coal Board, they were not big enough for the job.[24]

The Corporation's counsel retorted that the

National Coal Board from its very nature believed that no one outside its own confines could make an effective contribution, and if someone else other than the Merthyr Corporation, if the Welsh Office had made representations of the same character, they would have been treated likewise.[25]

Thus the problem extended beyond sub-conscious fears about the future of the colliery into the very nature of the NCB of itself. As MTCBC's counsel argued, the NCB was a powerful and arrogant organisation that felt it had a monopoly over all wisdom concerning the skills and precautions required in its industry. The question was not so much whether the Merthyr Corporation was too small but whether the NCB was so big that it was not easily approached or influenced and could thus treat those local authority officials that did approach it with disdain and contempt.[26]

Thus the causes of the disaster lay not just in the mistakes and fallibility of NCB employees but in the very nature and status of the Board itself. Its economic domination of the region meant that no one was keen to push complaints that might endanger the life of a colliery. Its nationalised monopoly meant it could brush aside the concerns of a small local authority whilst regulation of its practices were minimal in the corporatist atmosphere of the 1960s. Added to this was the Board's large and bureaucratic character that allowed the undetected breakdowns in communication between key members of staff that led to the tip not being properly inspected or maintained. For Aberfan, a village whose livelihood depended upon the NCB, the consequences of the Board's shortcomings proved to be fatal.

Aberfan and local politics

When a meeting was held in Aberfan after the publication of the Tribunal report to discuss the possibility of bringing criminal charges, it emerged that some people felt that the Tribunal should have blamed MTCBC as well as the NCB.[27] After suffering such tragic losses it was difficult to accept that the local authority had been warned about potential dangers and not taken every possible precaution. Individuals continued to feel let down by all those whose role it had been to protect their interests.

The general disillusionment with the Council ran far deeper than the circumstances surrounding the disaster. Villagers felt that the Corporation had a history of neglecting Aberfan. In the aftermath of the tragedy, a number of groups were formed in the village to consider how it could help itself cope and rebuild for the future. In the discussions that this entailed, the local authority were criticised for failing to provide safe play areas or adequate council housing, and for neglecting the environment and local infrastructure.[28] Such tensions were compounded by the Corporation's failure to solve the flooding problems in the village. The Council was naturally based in

Merthyr itself (five miles to the north of Aberfan) and, to people in the village, the borough seemed remote and high-handed with little understanding or sympathy for its smaller outlying communities.[29] In the months that followed the tragedy, the continuing Tribunal of Inquiry served to remind Aberfan of the local authority's failure to protect its interests. During the aftermath it also became clear how some people saw local politics as nepotistic and self-serving. One villager told the APRA solicitors that he did not complain about the tips because he felt that the councillors would not bite the hands that fed them. He regarded them as having 'cushy numbers' and easy jobs at the collieries.[30] While such an extreme view may have been a minority one, there was sometimes a general distrust of the three councillors who represented the ward of Aberfan.[31] Thus the disaster exposed some of the latent anger over the way the village, like other mining communities in South Wales, had been treated by local government.[32] It was seen as a tragic manifestation of years of neglect by the local authority.

This neglect was rooted in, and symptomatic of, the Labour Party's domination of the politics of South Wales at both local and parliamentary level. Labour's integral links with the mining unions and its work during the depression, when other parties offered little more than despair and inactivity, established it as the political voice and soul of the South Wales coalfield. However, after the triumph of its national successes in 1945–51 and lacking any realistic opposition, Labour in South Wales became complacent and somewhat removed from the communities it was meant to serve. While there were individuals who were popular, the political climate of the region had become stagnant. The party's national policies were also beginning to lose their way. Advance factories were slow to make up for the pit closures (which in themselves were hardly the expected outcome of nationalisation) and unemployment was rising in a stagnant economy. Yet, in the March 1966 general election, Labour had reached a zenith by winning thirty-two of the thirty-six Welsh seats. Passive disillusionment with the party may have been growing but Labour were still entrenched, not only in the politics of the region, but also in its culture. Until a credible, radical alternative emerged, it was unlikely that this position would change.

Plaid Cymru's unexpected victory (helped by the disillusionment of local miners[33]) in the 1966 Carmarthen by-election provided that alternative. Suddenly the party was thrust into the limelight and seemed to become a serious alternative to the Labour hegemony. In July 1967, residents of Aberfan visited Westminster demanding an inquiry into the administration of the disaster fund. With their local representative, S. O. Davies, being a trustee of the fund, they instead asked for the 'MP for Wales', Gwynfor Evans, the new member for Carmarthen. Evans was not there but later refused to take up the cause for fear of being seen as making political capital out of the disaster.[34] The refusal of Plaid Cymru to become involved in the affairs of the disaster fund caused some minor consternation in Aberfan and a small group staged a demonstration in Cardiff claiming that the party had let them down.[35] Evans responded by saying that 'It would be unforgivable if Plaid Cymru did or said anything that would influence in any way the unhealed wound left by the tragedy. If we have disappointed some who wanted us to fight more publicly for a certain policy, the sole reason is our anxiety to do that which is best for all who are involved.'[36] The well-publicised disputes over the disaster fund made any external intervention potentially controversial and emotionally provocative.

Yet, given the public support for Aberfan's desire for a more generous distribution of the fund, this may have been a missed opportunity. Nonetheless, Plaid Cymru continued to make electoral advances in South Wales during the late 1960s. The party was threatening to become the radical new voice, not just of Welsh-speaking Wales, but also of ignored and marginalised industrial South Wales. The growth in Plaid Cymru's support across the South Wales valleys was rooted in the same general disillusionment that Aberfan felt with its Labour local authority. The link was not overt but the disaster did seem to symbolise all that was malignant about the political culture of South Wales.[37] For a brief period, out of the stagnation of Labour politics in South Wales and the tragedy of Aberfan, a new political force seemed to be emerging.

In 1968, S. O. Davies resigned from the management committee of the disaster fund in response to its agreement to pay £150,000 towards the removal of the remaining tips that overlooked Aberfan. Because of government pressure, the committee had little choice but to pay the money and the situation angered Davies enormously, causing him to write a stinging letter to the Prime Minister. He asked Harold Wilson, 'Don't you think that the Aberfan Tips have already taken, far, far too much out of this village ... ?'[38] The situation and later outbursts against Wilson further alienated Davies from his constituency party. His position was already in serious jeopardy because of his advanced age and sympathy for Welsh nationalism. In 1970, Davies was deselected but, in the general election later that year, he was re-elected to Parliament as an independent Labour candidate; the first such case in Britain since 1945. His success was achieved despite some Labour 'dirty tricks' related to S. O.'s 87 years.[39]

Table 3.1 Labour and Plaid Cymru share of the vote (percentage) in the eastern half of the South Wales coalfield (Merthyr and neighbouring constituencies), 1966 and 1970 General Elections[40]

	Aberdare	Bedwellty	Caerphilly	Pontypridd	Rhondda East	Rhondda West	Merthyr
1966	Lab 73.3 PC 8.6	Lab 86.2 PC 0	Lab 74.2 PC 11.1	Lab 74.9 PC 0	Lab 77.4 PC 7.5	Lab 76.1 PC 7.5	Lab 74.5 PC 11.5
1970	Lab 60.0 PC 30.0	Lab 74.6 PC 10.0	Lab 61.8 PC 28.5	Lab 58.5 PC 10.4	Lab 68.6 PC 24.3	Lab 74.8 PC 14.0	Ind. Lab 51.9 Lab 28.7 PC 9.6
% Mining *	21.2	23.5	23.9	10.7	17.1	18.7	12.4

* Percentage of employed engaged in mining or quarrying
NB No Plaid Cymru candidates stood in Bedwellty and Pontypridd in 1966

Across Wales, Plaid Cymru's share of the vote had risen from 4.3 per cent in the 1966 general election to 11.5 per cent in 1970. In some valley constituencies, Plaid's vote had risen to over twice this figure. The constituencies in which the Plaid Cymru vote went up by 10 per cent or more between 1966 and 1970 were, with only one exception, all either mining seats or Welsh speaking seats.[41] The Party of Wales was emerging as an alternative voice for those unhappy with Labour. However, in Merthyr, with Davies taking the left-wing anti-Labour vote, Plaid Cymru's share actually fell.[42]

Before the 1970 election, Davies had written to Harold Wilson to ask for the fund money to be repaid, arguing that the Labour Party's chances in Merthyr might be destroyed if this was not done.[43] His stance over Aberfan was only one contributory factor to Davies' re-election but it reinforced his reputation as an honest and principled politician at a time when the image of many of his profession, in both Parliament and Merthyr Town Hall, was somewhat different. Thus, at least temporarily, in the late 1960s there was a degree of political backlash against the Labour Party in the South Wales coalfield. Whereas in the past, the political stagnation had met with muted disquiet or indifference, voices of objection were now being raised. The link with Aberfan was not direct but it was a factor in exposing Labour's failings and, in the Merthyr constituency, it contributed to an independent rather than Plaid Cymru candidate taking much of the anti-government vote.

The disillusionment with the local political situation was compounded by some naive and ill-thought out actions by MTCBC following the disaster. A duplicated standard letter of sympathy sent to the bereaved from the Mayor hardly conveyed an image of sincere personal empathy, but more serious errors of judgement were to follow.[44] A significant mistake was arranging for the pupils that had attended Pantglas school to be educated at nearby Merthyr Vale. This school stood under a disused tip and gave a clear view of the Aberfan cemetery where friends and relatives were buried. Attending the school would also have involved crossing a busy road. These factors naturally upset the parents and they lobbied for alternative arrangements. While the Council's plans would have been reasonable in other situations, they failed to take account of the special circumstances and consequently were seen as unnecessarily bureaucratic. The Council eventually gave way and erected a temporary classroom in Aberfan but the affair had already further damaged relations with the village.[45]

The Corporation's control over the disaster fund also increased tension between the local authority and the village. Disaster fund meetings took place in Merthyr not Aberfan which, as a care worker in the village later pointed out, 'might have been a thousand miles away'.[46] It took a representation from the NUM before the fund released any money to help immediate problems. The fund's hesitation centred upon the legal problems of giving out donations before a trust deed with clear objectives had been drawn up. However, such technicalities were hardly of concern to those in Aberfan in need of the money that had been donated for their benefit. Even as funds were slowly released, the village's representation on the provisional committee was limited to just one local councillor from its ward; although the lobbying of the Parents and Residents Association's solicitor ensured that the villagers' wishes were at least listened to.[47] Again however, there was reason for this since under charity law recipients could not be trustees. Concern also arose over the fact that the money was temporarily invested in the Corporation's mortgage stock. While this was logistically sensible, with the village's minimal representation on the fund's provisional committee, it further aggravated a worsening relationship.[48]

Thus many of the tensions were a problem of communication and misunderstanding. The initial minimal-representation of the village on the disaster fund lay not in a wish to deny Aberfan a voice but the Council's misconception that there was no leadership in the village.[49] Given the lack of significant community involvement in local authorities across Britain, the misconception was perhaps understandable but foresight of the community activity that disasters provoke could have prevented some of the problems. The relationship between Aberfan and the Council was further harmed by the failure of the local authority to communicate adequately the details of its activities to the village. The Council did gradually come to recognise its duty to fully inform villagers of its plans and consequently the atmosphere of distrust receded. Simple actions such as pinning minutes of Council meetings to notice boards in Aberfan went some way to repairing the relationship. The village did not just passively accept its grievances. It formed residents' groups to put forward its opinions more clearly and effectively, which in turn contributed to the self-respect and confidence of the village. The Aberfan Parents' and Residents' Association, aided by the efforts of its solicitor, campaigned hard and became the village's public voice in a way that MTCBC, and even the ward's councillors, were not. The formation of such groups led to further tension in the village's relationship with the Council. A brief written for the Prime Minister noted that,

> This vigour of a kind of ad hoc democracy caused friction for a time with the Corporation (and in particular the Merthyr Vale Ward Members who cover Aberfan) who saw these organisations as usurping the functions of the elected Council members.[50]

Where lobbying failed, elements of the village were prepared to take more radical action to ensure that their grievances were not ignored. Nineteen residents briefly refused to pay their rates because of a dispute over the uneven treatment given to different sections of the village and anger over the delay in cleaning up the disaster site and removing the school's ruins. The APRA accused Merthyr Council of 'sickening indifference' to the village. Again, the dispute owed much to the Council's failure to communicate its plans properly while the full clearing of the disaster site was awaiting the Tribunal's decision on who was liable. While this dispute continued, the debris from the disaster remained in the disturbing state described by Laurie Lee (chapter 1 above). The dispute was quickly resolved but nonetheless, it did illustrate the new determination in Aberfan to stand up against the traditional agencies of power.[51] As chapter two showed, it was the frustration over the government's delay in deciding whether to remove the remaining tips from above the village that most clearly revealed the greater resolve the disaster had brought about. The threats and limited use of militant action was a last resort but one that had been forced by the inaction of the NCB and government. It also signified the new determination in Aberfan to ensure its interests were not marginalised.

The reaction of Aberfan in forming groups to represent its needs and issues was characteristic of community reactions to disasters. In the wake of a significant disaster within a community there is normally a mass mobilisation of people and resources in order to meet immediate priorities such as rescue work. Subsequently a period of consensus follows with high levels of community participation. This often leads to the questioning of decisions made by traditional authorities and demands for greater consultation.[52] Events in Aberfan followed this model through residents, including those not directly bereaved, trying to assume a degree of control in local affairs for themselves. When the relationship with the local authority appeared to be in disarray there were plans to secure a greater say through standing against established councillors for election to the Borough Council in 1967. The seats were to be contested on a personal rather than party basis for the first time. Thus Aberfan began to follow a trend already established elsewhere in the valleys of residents' associations putting up candidates against Labour because of the failure of 'political monopoly by one party'.[53] In a high turnout (68 per cent), the residents association won 'considerable' support in Aberfan. However, overall in the Merthyr Vale ward, Labour managed to retain the two contested seats but it could no longer be assured of its position.[54] Later that year, Eddy Thomas, a famous former boxer from Merthyr, planned to stand as a Plaid Cymru candidate against the Mayor, while attacking him personally over the disaster fund.[55] The fact that he was from outside Aberfan was an indication just how deeply the disaster had coloured people's perceptions of local politics.

It is a further characteristic of the aftermath of disasters that the recovery period is marked by disillusionment and conflict.[56] The stresses of the situation and the already broken social norms can lead to behaviour that would otherwise be untypical. The cases of conflict within Aberfan are infamous yet very greatly exaggerated. Much can be put down to the work of unscrupulous journalists taking comments out of context and misusing them.[57] Nonetheless, a perception of a divided community at Aberfan has survived to an extent and has been instrumental in more recent disasters taking careful steps to prevent any sort of similar public conflict, real or imagined.[58] Such divisions and disillusionment often leads to a gradual reduction in community participation in local politics and again Aberfan followed this pattern. No candidates from the Aberfan Ratepayers' Association stood at the next set of local elections. In the by-election following the death of S. O. Davies in 1972, the official Labour Party candidate was elected; normal party politics had clearly resumed.[59] The election of a Conservative government in 1970 had revitalised Labour's blanket support across South Wales demonstrating that the rise of Plaid Cymru had been largely a transient reaction to the disillusionment with Wilson's administration rather than the beginning of a genuine political realignment.

Yet in Aberfan, despite the renewal of the Labour hegemony, community groups remained active in the village to a far greater extent than they ever had been before the disaster. To this day, Aberfan boasts groups from a local nursery to a village magazine whose origins lie in the community activity that developed in response to the disaster. There is also a determination in Aberfan not to let bureaucracy and authority allow dangers to go unseen or implement schemes that would be harmful to the community.[60] Consequently the village is much stronger for it.

Disaster management and Merthyr Tydfil County Borough Council

For all the justifiable complaints thrown at it, the disaster left MTCBC in a difficult position to which it adapted to its credit. It found itself having to cope with many and varied practical tasks in the days, months and even years that followed the tragedy. Its initial involvement was in the rescue operation where Council employees naturally played an important role. Yet even then they were subject to criticism. A Civil Defence Officer, who was decorated for his efforts in the operation, accused Council officials of not having made themselves prominent or even known.[61] The accusations were naturally strongly denied, and although there was some confusion in the rescue operation, the Council appears to have conducted itself admirably.

The disaster dominated the attention of the Council in the following months. Individual senior Council officials, particularly the Town Clerk and the Director of Education, found themselves having to cope with excessively large workloads. Tasks such as compiling evidence for the Tribunal from its archives and finding alternative housing and educational facilities were time-consuming, emotional and controversial duties that had to be carried out in difficult circumstances. The Director of Education wrote, 'in those early days of shock and intense grief it was far from easy to think coolly, perceptively and with future horizons in mind'.[62] In his department the limited number and experience of the staff made the problem worse. Consequently, the responsibility, 'strain and pressure ... weighed heavy' on them.[63] Even non-urgent work such as dealing with the sackfuls of letters that arrived at its offices every day was beyond the Council's means. It was forced to take on volunteers who worked late into the night acknowledging the donations that arrived.[64] The impact of the small size of the Borough upon its Council's resources was being exposed by the disaster. Inevitably, some normal services were forgotten in the early chaos.[65] Normal Council meetings were temporarily suspended and other tasks were put aside. One Aberfan pensioner for instance complained that her meals-on-wheels had not been delivered.[66] Yet the fact that the whole process of local government in Merthyr did not temporarily collapse was a tribute to the resourcefulness and energy of the Council staff.

As well as having to cope with the extra administrative tasks, some Council members and officers also had to live with the guilt that they could have personally done something to prevent the disaster. Even after the Tribunal Report exonerated the Council, individual officials must have wished that they had pressed their concerns harder.[67] Adding to the pressure was the constant attention of the world's media. In particular, Stanley Davies, the Mayor, found himself in the spotlight and subject to levels of pressure that he could never have imagined his period of office would entail. The confusion and cases of misinformation that followed the disaster did not help his position either. Incidents such as publicly accepting an offer that had never been made of a new school from the Canadian government were embarrassing for the Mayor and added to his difficulties.[68] Davies' health deteriorated under the pressure and he died suddenly in 1969. As one villager put it, 'The burden of his cares for us in Aberfan really brought about his death'.[69]

In the course of the rescue operation, the various organisations, companies and individuals involved, had ignored or bypassed usual procedures in an effort to help the victims and their families. The inevitable result was confusion and a bureaucratic nightmare. Voluntary and public departments wanted equipment back while companies and traders wanted compensation for goods and services supplied. With no obvious alternative body to take responsibility, claims were sent to the Council. Thus it was left with the unenviable task of assessing who was liable for what and for how much. In the confusion and haste of the rescue operation, equipment such as picks and shovels had been lost and goods eaten or used before they could be accounted for. In many cases there was simply no way of verifying that the value being claimed was justifiable or indeed that the goods had even been supplied at all. Government departments might be understanding over the loss of their shovels but others were not always so.[70] The prolonged arguments over who should foot the bill for 100,000 paper cups illustrated the extremes that arose.[71] One firm appears to have tried to take advantage of the confusion by asking for payment for 100,000 sandbags which were allegedly never supplied or ordered. The invoice was passed between different organisations amidst denials of being responsible for ordering the bags. It took an investigation by the Welsh Office to reveal the possibly fraudulent nature of the claim by the suppliers.[72] Such confusion simply placed more pressure on the already beleaguered Council.

The growing number of claims had its own momentum thus adding to the workload. A fish and chip proprietor from Aberfan noted that he had supplied goods, with no intention of claiming costs, as part of what he took as a common effort. It was only since all other shopkeepers were submitting claims that he felt he should do the same.[73] A trust deed for the disaster fund was not drawn up until January 1967 and a secretary/treasurer not appointed until May that year. Before then, sorting out much of this bureaucratic nightmare fell on the shoulders of the Council's town clerk and treasurer who respectively acted as honorary secretary and treasurer of the provisional committee of the disaster fund. They were tasks that brought great anxieties and little credit.

Dealing with the housing problems that many villagers faced was perhaps the most difficult task the Council faced. Houses had been destroyed, others damaged and many people evacuated as a safety precaution. Organising alternative accommodation and repairing damaged houses was no easy task. It required patience, tact and hard work on the part of the Council. With some evacuated residents wishing to return to their houses immediately, irrespective of any danger, and others expressing completely understandable but almost irrational fears, finding a compromise was not easy.[74] In the end, the Council had no option but to let individuals decide for themselves. The Secretary of State for Wales was asked to appoint independent consultants to assess the damage to houses.[75] This was a task that would have normally been undertaken by the Council's own housing department but in the circumstances they felt it was best done by outside experts. With the world's eyes upon Aberfan, should the Council make a mistake or do anything that could be deemed thoughtless or inappropriate then a swift backlash would be inevitable. The people of Aberfan had already suffered enough at the hands of authority and there was likely to be little sympathy for anyone else who was deemed to be hindering the village further. The residents of Aberfan too were more likely to accept the word of outside experts rather than that of the local establishment who had already let them down.

Many of the logistical and legal problems that the Council faced were entirely new to it. It had neither the experience nor ability to foresee many of the potential problems. In overcoming such hurdles, the Council was helped greatly by the Welsh Office which fulfilled its role as an important link between local and central government. For example, it tried to persuade the Council and NCB to communicate over the disaster fund to ensure the money was handled sensibly.[76] Civil servants also anticipated problems over donors to the fund wanting large sums given to the bereaved families regardless of need. Thus the Welsh Office advised some sort of consultation with the large donors to avoid any such problems.[77] It also stressed the need to make clear publicly that the village was being consulted over the use of the fund and suggested that the Council should encourage the formation of a residents' group with whom visible liaison could take place.[78] Of course, as a Government department, the Welsh Office was anxious to avoid any controversy that might cast further bad light on the establishment. However, its advice and active help aided significantly the local authority in dealing with the disaster's problematic aftermath. Much of the good work it did was forgotten in the controversy that surrounded its obstinate role in the funding of the removal of the remaining Aberfan tips. However, although a great deal of the Welsh Office's work was not visible to the public, Merthyr Tydfil Borough Council fully appreciated it.[79] The fledgling department was proving its worth.[80]

Yet at the same time, the Welsh Office under-secretary designated to liaise with Aberfan saw the village as 'emotionally wrought', wrote of moderates and extreme factions in the village and sought local allies to help him deal with the 'Aberfan folk'.[81] When it came to the tip removal, he thought the village would expect a degree of consultation on technical matters 'beyond what would be reasonable, and they may have to be spoken to firmly.'[82] He believed he had a friendly relationship with the village,[83] but he later said that he would not read all of the second report of the disaster fund and recommended that the Secretary of State for Wales not read it at all.[84] The Welsh Office undoubtedly helped the local council but its more direct dealings with the village disclosed a civil service that seemed more concerned with finance and minimising the public outcry than seeing to the needs of the village.

The disaster also left the Council with a financial burden as it tried to meet the numerable administrative costs and much of the price of the rescue operation. While the NCB did compensate the Corporation for the loss of the two Aberfan schools, it was slow in paying up. Even in March 1970, the NCB had only paid £50,000 of the Council's

£200,000 claim. It did not settle in full until August that year. This must have had serious effects on the cash flow of the smallest County Borough in Wales.[85] Similarly, while it had been agreed in principle that the State should meet the expenses incurred by the Corporation at the Tribunal, securing payment was a lengthy problematic process that encountered repeated delays and queries. The series of letters between MTCBC and various government departments are a clear indicator of the excessive bureaucracy that plagued the public sector before the days of citizen charters.[86] Financial remuneration was ultimately forthcoming but the continual delays were yet another headache for Council officials to cope with.

The Council officials were as touched by the disaster as everyone else in the region and they did try and alleviate the suffering in the village in the months, and years, that followed. Hence the Council almost immediately supported the complete removal of the remaining tips overlooking the village and argued that there were strong psychological grounds to demolish rather than rebuild the Pantglas schools.[87] Yet its previous neglect of Aberfan, implication in the disaster's cause and a series of clumsy errors in the aftermath meant that much of the Council's good work and own problems were obscured. Achievements such as securing money for a nursery despite a government moratorium on such spending or the sympathetic and flexible handling of bereaved children returning to school were significant.[88] Such work did much to make up for the Council's earlier mistakes and deserves credit.

Merthyr Tydfil County Borough Council undoubtedly learnt from its mistakes. After the furore over the initial minimal representation of villagers on the committee of the disaster fund, it helped devise a very carefully considered plan to elect representatives from Aberfan. The exact election process caused further controversy but this time the Council officials involved made every effort to ensure that it was done fairly and took into consideration the views of all concerned.[89] Similarly, there was a new determination in the Council that the NCB fulfil all its safety obligations in the future. After the tragedy, there was concern in the neighbouring village of Merthyr Vale over the safety of a tip there. The Merthyr Council wasted no time in ensuring that it was fully inspected and declared safe. No further risks were to be taken, no matter how small.[90] The Council was also no longer willing to tolerate misdemeanours of any kind by the coal board. Hence the dropping of refuse on the road by lorries travelling from the Merthyr Vale colliery now brought harsh warnings where in the past it would have been ignored.[91]

A number of lessons for disaster management can be derived from
Merthyr Council's handling of the Aberfan disaster. Disasters
present considerable administrative and logistical problems that
must be handled sensitively if the suffering of the victims is not to be
exacerbated. Such difficulties can only be surmounted through a
flexible approach that is willing to depart from bureaucratic norms.
Central to that approach must be a consideration of the interests of
the bereaved and survivors. Merthyr Council gradually learnt this
lesson but not until it after it had angered people in Aberfan and
damaged its relationship with the community. Today, the need for a
versatile approach that prioritises victims and the bereaved is set out
in the disaster management guidelines laid down by the Emergency
Planning Department of the Home Office and similar bodies.[92]

Such guidelines are invaluable. Merthyr Council made mistakes
because of its inexperience in dealing with any situation remotely
comparable with the disaster. Most local authorities today would find
itself in a similar position should they have to cope with disaster. Thus
the attempts to disseminate the lessons and experiences of earlier
disasters are vital if future mistakes are to be avoided. There is also
perhaps an argument for the creation of a specialist and experienced,
government-funded, disaster response team. Such a unit would advise
and help those services and authorities dealing with the aftermath of a
disaster. The idea of a lead 'disaster squad' was rejected by the government in 1989 in order to keep 'prime responsibility' for handling
disasters at the local level.[93] In the absence of any such body, policy
guidance and the dissemination of lessons and information takes on
added importance and there has indeed been much work to learn from
the experiences of the disasters of 1980s. How effectively those lessons
have been learnt and disseminated remains to be seen.

'My people'

The anger that followed the Aberfan disaster was contributed to by
the political context in which the tragedy and its aftermath took
place. As one bereaved father remembered 'I was tormented by the
fact that the people I was seeking justice from were my people – a
Labour Government, a Labour council, a Labour-nationalised Coal
Board.'[94] The disaster presented the local political establishment
with a colossal challenge. It was to be a challenge that both revealed
the strengths and shortcomings of Merthyr Tydfil County Borough
Council. The disaster had its origins in the inability of the Council to
overcome the arrogance of the NCB arising from the latter's

dominant position in the local economy and the former's limited resources. The intense public concern and pressure that followed the disaster changed that relationship but the Council was still left with an immense administrative task in the tragedy's aftermath. It was a tribute to the energy and resourcefulness of its staff that the extreme workload that the disaster created was coped with, despite intensive media attention and the extremely difficult and emotional circumstances. Initially mistakes were made but these were gradually overcome and a new relationship established with the inhabitants of Aberfan.

The disaster left an indelible mark on the village and the lives of those who lived there. Yet an examination of local politics in the area illustrates how some good has come out of the tragedy. Before the disaster, the interests of Aberfan and other similar communities were marginalised by both local and national government due to the entrenchment of the Labour Party in Welsh politics. This did not represent a deliberate policy on the part of the local Labour establishment but instead was based in a lack of competition inducing a state of complacency. The interests of those communities who had helped create the Labour hegemony were consequently marginalised since there was no need on the part of the local party to seek votes or new ideas.

Although not a realistic parliamentary threat, the rise of Plaid Cymru drew upon the resultant dissatisfaction and forced the Labour Party to reassess both its position and policies in Wales. In Aberfan, this dissatisfaction and the anger that emerged out of the disaster was partly aimed at the Merthyr Corporation; a local authority that, under a burden of excessive work and in the stagnant political atmosphere, had also lost touch with its outlying communities. The disaster revealed the fatal danger of the complacency that prevailed in the Council and especially the cumbersome NCB. Consequently, it reawoke the political will of the village and ensured that they were no longer willing to tolerate apathy and mismanagement from above. The more extreme challenges to the local establishment that arose may have been relatively short-lived but their legacy was a number of active community groups and projects in Aberfan that continue to serve the village today. Once the local establishment began to recover from the heavy burdens that the disaster placed upon it, it too took a more active interest in the welfare, and in particular the safety, of those who it served. The new voices from below were now finding ears above that listened. Such empowerment has not been able to overcome wider economic trends. In 1989 the Merthyr Vale colliery shut and

Aberfan today suffers from the same hardships that the rest of the South Wales valleys are experiencing. Nor can anything ever make up for the tragedy of 21 October 1966 but the revitalisation of the local political context is a welcome development and its legacy should ensure that Aberfan and other similar communities are never so catastrophically ignored again.

Notes

1 Bereaved parent quoted in unaccredited press clipping. ADA, Merthyr collection, D/17.
2 IM interview with Alan Blackshaw.
3 SWCC, Interview with John Beale (Director of Education, Merthyr Tydfil County Borough Council), 1986, AUD 521.
4 David Cohen, *Aftershock: The Psychological and Political Consequences of Disaster* (London: Paladin, 1991), p. 65.
5 *Aberfan Report*, p. 99.
6 The Tribunal's findings on the Council can be found in *Aberfan Report*, pp. 107–110. Quote from Attorney's Questions to the Tribunal. *Aberfan Report*, para 246. Given that the problem was one of safety not planning, the Tribunal's implications that the Council could have used its planning powers (or indeed a summons for nuisance) to restrict tipping at Aberfan are unfair.
7 *Tribunal Transcript*, day 53, p. 2983.
8 Quotes from *Aberfan Report*, para. 109.
9 *Tribunal Transcript*, day 71, p. 4002.
10 Hywel Francis & David Smith, *The Fed: A History of the South Wales Miners in the Twentieth Century* (London, 1980), p. 457.
11 Francis & Smith, *The Fed*, appendix IV.
12 See Francis & Smith, *The Fed*, pp. 452–458.
13 *Tribunal Transcript*, day 71, p. 4003.
14 *Tribunal Transcript*, day 71, p. 4003.
15 *Aberfan Report*, p. 111.
16 MJ interview with Colin Murray Parkes.
17 Quoted in Marsh, *Off the Rails*, p. 117. Lord Marsh interview.
18 R. S. Evans, 'The Development of Local Government', in *Merthyr Tydfil: A Valley Community* (Merthyr, 1981), pp. 252–253. County boroughs (abolished in 1972 but re-created in Wales in 1996 under the title of unitary authorities) are all-purpose local authorities responsible for all local services.
19 'Merthyr Tydfil Local Government Reorganisation', PRO BD 11/3791.
20 *Registrar General's Statistical Review of England and Wales for the Year 1966* (London: HMSO 1967), Part I, Table 13. Bruce Wood, *The Process of Local Government Reform, 1966–74* (London: George Allen & Unwin, 1976), p. 117.
21 James Belt, a Residents' Association candidate in the Cyfarthfa Ward in Merthyr, also said that the average county borough rates in England and Wales were 12/9 in the £ while in Merthyr they were 17/6. *Merthyr Express*, 5 May 1967.

22 *Local Government in Wales*, Cmnd. 3340 (Cardiff: HMSO, 1967). The Welsh Office noted that the council was 'violently angry about the proposal that the town should cease to be a county borough, arguing that their services are excellent. They have made particular reference to the way in which their education department coped with the aftermath of the Aberfan disaster.' Merthyr Tydfil Local Government Reorganisation, PRO BD 11/3791.

23 *Tribunal Transcripts*, day 71, p. 4006; day 73, 4069.

24 *Tribunal Transcript*, day 69, p. 3902.

25 *Tribunal Transcript*, day 71, p. 4005.

26 *Tribunal Transcript*, day 71, p. 4005.

27 NLW, Moseley papers, Attendance re Aberfan, 10 August 1967, file 6.

28 Ken Roberts, *The Reconstruction of 'Community': Aberfan* (Coventry: Warwick Working Papers in Sociology, 1985), p. 11.

29 Miller, *Aberfan*, p. 20.

30 NLW, Moseley papers, Note dated 16 November 1966, file 1.

31 Austin, *Aberfan*, pp. 172, 180–181.

32 Elsewhere in the valleys this disillusionment had already led to Residents' Associations putting forward candidates at local elections. See, for example, *Merthyr Express*, 5 May 1967.

33 Francis & Smith, *The Fed*, p. 453.

34 Robert Griffiths, *S. O. Davies: A Socialist Faith* (Llandysul: Gomer, 1983), p. 280.

35 *South Wales Argus*, 11 August 1967; *South Wales Echo*, 12 August 1967.

36 *Western Mail*, 14 August 1967.

37 Man-made disasters are often seen as points of reference that symbolise the political and social conditions of a particular moment.

38 ADA, Dowlais collection, C/007/02.

39 See Griffiths, *S. O. Davies*, pp. 279–290 & Alun Morgan, 'The 1970 Parliamentary Election at Merthyr Tydfil', *Morgannwg*, XXII, 1978.

40 The exception is Cardiff West: no PC candidate in 1966, 10.06 per cent PC vote in 1970.

41 Calculated from information in Arnold J. James & John E. Thomas, *Wales at Westminster: A History of the Parliamentary Representation of Wales, 1800–1979* (Llandysul: Gomer, 1981).

42 Derived from James & Thomas, *Wales at Westminster*; 1966 sample census; *The Times Guide to the House of Commons* (London: Times Newspapers Ltd, 1970).

43 SWCC, S. O. Davies to Harold Wilson, 7 May 1970, MNA/PP/16/37.

44 Austin, *Aberfan*, p. 178.

45 Miller, *Aberfan*, pp. 116–117; Austin, *Aberfan*, p. 179; SWCC, Interview with Mair Jones (headmistress), 1986, AUD 526; John Beale, 'Aberfan: Recovery', unpublished paper in ADA, Merthyr collection, I/02, p. 1.

46 SWCC, Interview with Audry Davey (Aberfan social worker), 1986, AUD 524.

47 *The First Report of the Management Committee of the Aberfan Disaster Fund*, 1968, p. 10. For an example of close communication between the Fund and the solicitors representing the Aberfan residents see ADA, Dowlais, C/006/26 & C/006/29. As one villager acknowledged, having prominent members of the Welsh establishment on the committee did

open doors that Aberfan could not have opened on its own. SWCC, Interview with Cyril Vaughan (former member of Disaster Fund management committee & Parents' & Residents' Association), 1986, AUD 527.

48 Benedict Nightingale, *Charities* (London: Allen Lowe, 1973), p. 180.
49 Miller, *Aberfan*, p. 111.
50 Prime Minister's Visit to Aberfan, Notes of people and affairs in the village, PRO BD11/3814.
51 Quoted in Nightingale, *Charities*, p. 182; Miller, *Aberfan*, p. 101; *Merthyr Express*, 17, 24 February 1967.
52 Kathleen J. Tierney, 'The Social and Community Contexts of Disaster', in Richard Gist & Bernard Lubin (eds.), *Psychosocial Aspects of Disaster* (New York: Wiley, 1989), pp. 23–24, 32.
53 Councillor from Dowlais Ratepayers' Association quoted in *Merthyr Express*, 3 March 1967.
54 *Merthyr Express*, 19 May 1967.
55 The personal nature of the attacks attracted much criticism and led to the local Plaid Cymru branch threatening to withdraw its support. Thomas eventually decided not to stand. *Merthyr Express*, 18 June 1967.
56 Tierney, 'Social and Community Contexts of Disaster', p. 31.
57 SWCC, Interview with Rev. Kenneth Hayes, Bryn Carpenter & Doug Pearson. AUD 528.
58 For example see Roger W. Suddards, *Administration of Appeal Funds* (London: Sweet & Maxwell, 1991), ch. 2.
59 Ted Rowlands secured the seat in 1972 with a majority of 3,710 over Plaid Cymru whose vote had increased by 385 per cent. In the 1970 general election, S. O. Davies had won a majority of 7,467 over the official Labour Party candidate. Normal politics had resumed but the rising tide of Plaid Cymru was still evident. Indeed, in 1976 Plaid Cymru won a majority on the Merthyr Council. Figures calculated from James & Thomas, *Wales at Westminster*, p. 176.
60 SWCC, Hayes, Carpenter & Pearson interview, AUD 528. This determination reached its peak in the village's successful campaign to overturn plans to run the new A470 through Aberfan. The planned route would have cut the village off from the cemetery. The route finally chosen runs above the cemetery and through the disaster slide site.
61 The Civil Defence Officer was responding to allegations from the Chief Constable that he had been decorated for something he didn't do. ADA, Dowlais, B/007/08.
62 Beale, 'Aberfan: Recovery', p. 1.
63 SWCC, Beale interview, AUD 521.
64 Miller, *Aberfan*, p. 30; Austin, *Aberfan*, p. 180.
65 Such an administrative overload was characteristic of the problems experienced by other local government in post-disaster situations. See Allen H. Barton, *Communities in Disaster: A Sociological Analysis of Collective Stress Situations* (Ward Lock Educational, 1969), pp. 284–294.
66 ADA, Dowlais, B/002/17.
67 *Aberfan Report*, pp. 107–110.
68 See Austin, *Aberfan*, pp. 170–171.
69 SWCC, Vaughan interview, AUD 527.

70 See the correspondence between the Council and the Ministry of Health. ADA, Dowlais, B/002/09.
71 ADA, Dowlais, B/001/47.
72 See ADA, Dowlais, C/009/03.
73 ADA, Dowlais, C/009/03.
74 For example see ADA, Dowlais, B/004.
75 ADA, Dowlais, B/001/26.
76 ADA, Dowlais, B/002/06.
77 Similarly, the Council were legally advised to avoid having too many representatives on the management committee of the Fund for fear of giving the impression that it was using the Fund to escape its own responsibilities. ADA, Dowlais, C/005/25–26.
78 ADA, Dowlais. C/005/42.
79 For example see the thanks to the Education department in Beale, 'Aberfan: Recovery', p. 7.
80 The historian K. O. Morgan has suggested that, by bringing government closer to the people, the Welsh Assembly will prevent the type of injustices that Aberfan suffered at the hands of government. K. O. Morgan, 'Welsh devolution: the past and the future' in Bridget Taylor & Katarina Thomson, (eds.), *Scotland and Wales: Nations Again?* (Cardiff: University of Wales Press, 1999), pp. 199–219.
81 PRO, Siberry to PSO, Welsh Office, 8 June 1967, BD 11/3802. Also see, for example, Siberry to Treasury, 27 February 1968, BD 11/3804.
82 PRO, Siberry to Daniel, 11 December 1968, BD 11/3806.
83 PRO, Siberry to Erastus Jones, 17 October 1968, BD 11/3814.
84 PRO, Siberry to King, 5 October 1970, BD11/3814.
85 McLean, 'On Moles and the Habits of Birds', pp. 289–290; *Merthyr Express*, 20 August 1970.
86 Even the price of curtains for the Tribunal was queried by the Ministry of Works. See ADA, Dowlais, D/001/68–69.
87 ADA, Dowlais, C/005/32 & C/005/51.
88 SWCC, Beale interview, AUD 521.
89 *First Report of the Management Committee of the Aberfan Disaster Fund*, pp. 11, 20. Also see ADA, Dowlais, C/006/13, C/006/16.
90 For example see ADA, Dowlais, B/001/45.
91 ADA, Dowlais, B/001/36.
92 See, for example, Emergency Planning Society, *Responding to Disaster: The Human Aspects*, Guidance Document, 1998.
93 See *Hansard*, 6th ser., vol. 154, col. 512, written answer by Douglas Hurd.
94 Bereaved parent quoted in unaccredited press clipping. Merthyr Tydfil Public Libraries, ADA, Merthyr collection, D/17.

Chapter Four

ABERFAN AND OTHER DISASTERS

Of recent years the houses in the valleys and on the lower slopes are still
further overshadowed by the huge coal-tips which are being piled on the
breasts and upper slopes and which, besides making the landscape
hideous, will in time endanger the very lives of those dwelling in the
valleys below.

The 1917 Commission of Enquiry into Industrial Unrest;
No 7 Division, Wales and Monmouthshire, Cd 8668.

Aberfan in Welsh history

In 1984, a judge presiding over a libel case ruled that the word
Aberfan 'had passed into the currency of ordinary language and that
it requires no explanation'.[1] What happened at Aberfan on
21 October 1966 left an indelible mark on the valleys of South Wales.
Even today, the name Aberfan evokes sadness and contemplation.
The shock was felt beyond South Wales too. Most British people
born before 1960 remember what they were doing when they heard
the tragic news. The television coverage allowed a collective witnessing of the disaster and turned it into a national tragedy. Parents,
children, mining communities, Welsh exiles, people who had been
evacuated to the area during the Second World War – so many
people across Britain and worldwide felt a deep personal empathy
and sympathy with those who suffered in the disaster. The surviving
50,000 letters of condolence sent to the village are a testament to that
sympathy.[2] David Kerr MP, (Labour, Wandsworth Central) said in
Parliament that 'this tragedy has reminded people a long way from
Wales that we are still one nation.'[3]
Aberfan was a defining moment in Welsh history and it has
become part of the nation's collective memory. Certain historical
events assume such positions because of the signals they give out

about our lives and place within society. Disasters in particular are laden with such cultural resonances.[4] The tragedy of Aberfan was exacerbated by the fact that the NCB was supposed to serve and be part of the community. Coal nationalisation was widely seen as a just recompense for years of hardship and exploitation and the crowning achievement of the 1945–51 Labour government. Thus the creation of the NCB was greeted with goodwill and enthusiasm in South Wales despite some concern at managerial personnel retaining their jobs. This goodwill was evaporating in the 1960s as collieries were closed and miners lost their jobs.

For many people in South Wales and beyond, Aberfan was confirmation or realisation of this disenchantment. It brought back memories of the pit disasters of Senghennydd (1913 – 439 killed) and Gresford (1934–265 killed) and the numerous less-known accidents that killed and maimed individual miners. Such fatalities continued to occur in the wake of 1947 but miners accepted the dangers inherent in their occupation. Aberfan however was different. This time it was their children who were killed, and by implication, a part of the future was lost. To many, Aberfan was evidence of the failures of the nationalisation dream. The NCB's responsibilities to the people whose labour underpinned it were not being fulfilled.

The continuing social and economic problems of the South Wales valleys have ensured that the Aberfan disaster has remained part of the collective memory of the region and indeed Wales. The tragedy does not belong to a poverty-stricken bygone age but a period of exploitation and deprivation that still exists for many. Many of the tips in Wales have since being removed or landscaped[5] but the physical, economic and emotional scars left by the coal industry and its decline remain prominent in the valleys. While nearby Cardiff has developed into a prosperous and cosmopolitan city, the valleys remain markedly separate to the surrounding areas.[6] Although housing in the valleys is much cheaper than in Cardiff, there has been little movement up-valley of commuters. The lack of any real economic replacement for the closed collieries means that the valleys are a region unable to escape their past. The dominant narrative of that past is one of united and vibrant communities struggling against a tide of exploitation and deprivation. Along with strikes, dole queues and soup kitchens, the Aberfan disaster is part of a history that still casts its long shadow over the South Wales coalfield.

But Aberfan has significance far beyond Wales. In the remaining chapters of this book, we trace various threads from Aberfan through a series of other disasters up to 1999. Each chapter – on the management of trauma, on the management of disaster funds, on the compensation payable on the death of a child, and on changes in safety regulation – begins with Aberfan. But all of these things have both affected, and been affected by, later disasters as well. First, we have to define what is meant by 'a disaster'.

Defining Disaster

The *Concise Oxford Dictionary* defines a disaster as 'a great or sudden misfortune' thus paving the way for the variety of personal and social interpretations. From dropping a favourite teacup to the death of thousands in an earthquake, the word is a classic example of the impreciseness of language.[7] Even the academic field of disaster studies is not agreed on what constitutes a disaster.[8] While practitioners have concentrated upon the physical manifestations and dimensions, academics have emphasised the fluidity of interpretations of events as disasters.[9] What may be a disaster on a personal scale, can be unnoticed on the wider social platform. As Horlick-Jones points out, disasters 'take place, and are perceived in, specific socio-economic, historical, cultural and chronological contexts.'[10] Such contexts go far towards determining what is regarded as a disaster. Thus the whole question of which events are seen as disasters provides important insights into the priorities and concerns of the media and society.

Some scholars have tried to define 'disaster' more objectively. For example, Drabek uses the following definition:

An event in which a community undergoes severe danger and incurs, or is threatened to incur, such losses to persons and/or property that the resources available within the community are exceeded.[11]

Similarly, Fritz's definition is

an event, concentrated in time and space, in which a society, or a relatively self-sufficient subdivision of a society, undergoes severe danger and incurs such losses to its members and physical appurtenances that the social structure is disrupted and the fulfilment of all or some of the essential functions of the society is prevented.[12]

But both of these definitions, with their references to 'a community' and 'a society', show that 'disaster' is largely a social construct.

The unexpectedness of the event is of particular importance in determining its interpretation as a disaster. Multiple deaths on the road are almost commonplace and thus rarely viewed as disasters.

Similarly, thousands can be killed in wartime without ever being viewed as a disaster because of the wider context. Even more 'conventional' disasters in wartime are quickly forgotten. A classic example is the death of 173 people in a crush as crowds rushed into Bethnal Green tube station to escape an air raid on 3 March 1943. Similarly, Britain's worst rail crash was on 22 May 1915 at Quintinshill near Gretna Green; 227 people, mainly soldiers, were killed but the disaster was submerged in the wider context of the carnage of the Great War. It had relatively little contemporary impact and is rarely remembered except by railway specialists and local people.

Similarly deaths in the workplace are relatively common and are thus normalised rather than seen as disasters. Of the series of the disasters in the mid-late 1980s, Piper Alpha was the second deadliest (see Table 4.1). Yet its popular impact was small compared to Bradford, Hillsborough and King's Cross (or, indeed, the death of Diana Princess of Wales), which each killed significantly fewer people. The deaths occurred offshore in a dangerous industry. It was not something most people related to and was thus treated with a degree of fatalism. This fatalism reflected the attitude of many workers within dangerous industries to smaller fatal accidents and injuries. Although management and trade unions maintain that safety is a priority, workers in dangerous industries such as coal do become accustomed to fatal accidents.[13]

Meanwhile, other events which only kill relatively small numbers, but in unique circumstances, can be perceived quite differently. For example, the loss of the space shuttle *Challenger* was unique and powerfully symbolic because of the importance of space exploration to US prestige and because it unfolded live on TV. Consequently, across the United States, the loss of the craft was viewed as a serious disaster. Similarly, deaths, which take place in a context that raises serious questions about public safety or public institutions, are often regarded as disasters because of their wider implications. Horlick-Jones, for example, argues that the Cannon Street train crash of 1991, in which two people were killed, was a disaster because of the wider context of the debate over the funding and performance of British Rail.[14] The crash signified the problems of an important public institution with possible repercussions for the safety of the general public.

Social constructions of events as disasters are also determined by the tragedy's causes. Fatal road traffic accidents are so common that they rarely achieve much attention. In 1966, 879 children aged 14 and under were killed in road traffic accidents in the UK.[15] Yet, in contrast to the 116 children killed at Aberfan, they are forgotten

Table 4.1 Disasters in the UK with a death toll greater than 30, 1966–99

Name	Date	Death toll	Cause
Aberfan	21 October 1966	144	Tip slide
Hither Green crash	05 November 1967	49	Broken rail
Ibrox Park	02 January 1971	66	Crowd crush at football match
Summerland fire	02 August 1973	50	Fire in leisure complex
Moorgate	28 February 1975	42	Train fails to stop at dead end of terminal tunnel.
Bradford City Fire	11 May 1985	56	Fire in wooden stand at football match
Manchester aircraft fire	25 August 1985	55	Aircraft catches fire during take off
Herald of Free Enterprise	06 March 1987	193	Car ferry capsizes
King's Cross fire	18 November 1987	31	Fire in London underground station
Piper Alpha	06 July 1988	167	Explosion on North Sea oil rig
Clapham train crash	12 December 1988	35	Train collision
Kegworth air crash	08 January 1989	47	Aircraft crash-lands on motorway
Hillsborough	15 April 1989	96	Crowd crush at football match
Marchioness	20 August 1989	57	Dredger collides with pleasure cruiser on the Thames
Ladbroke Grove	05 October 1999	31	Train crash

outside their own families. Individual murders are also common-place enough to be rarely perceived as disasters. Yet mass-murders such as the bombing of Pan Am Flight 103 or the Dunblane shootings lead to widespread shock and horror and have significant impact on the communities in which they take place. They are thus popularly described as disasters. In contrast, most terrorist bombings in Northern Ireland before the peace settlement of 1998 rarely had a profound impact in mainland Britain where the public had become almost normalised to the regular killings. The view of Lockerbie and Dunblane as disasters meant that there were strong parallels in both the public and political reaction to the events with more 'conventional' disasters.

Disasters are not necessarily single, dramatic events. The outbreak of *E. Coli* in Central Scotland in 1996 killed 18 people over a course of several weeks but would not normally be regarded as a disaster because of the lack of a single impacting event. Yet the outbreak could be traced back to negligence by a butcher's company and should be viewed in this light.

In this study, we will try to be as objective as possible by defining a disaster as 'an event causing multiple deaths, primarily attributable to negligence'. It would be macabre and insensitive to define too precisely how many deaths are required for a disaster to be defined as such, but here we will primarily concentrate on disasters since 1966 with a death toll of thirty or above (see table 4.1). The scale of these disasters is actually small when compared to contemporary natural disasters, mostly in the developing world, or nineteenth century disasters in the UK. When a pleasure cruiser, the *Princess Alice*, sank on the Thames in 1878, seven hundred lives were lost.[16] The 1999 earthquake in Turkey killed about 15,000 people. Outside Britain, there has been much research on natural and environmental disasters, particularly those in the developing world. In the UK, we are fortunate that such disasters are rare. The last fatal earthquake in Great Britain, for example, was in 1884 when one person in Rowhedge (Essex) was killed. Natural disasters also induce significantly different reactions since there is no obvious human agency to blame. This study will therefore concentrate on disasters where there is a clear human agency.

Yet because a variety of events are constructed as disasters, the analysis here can not only concentrate on those tragedies in table 4.1. Thus the events in table 4.2 will also be considered where relevant. Some are disasters outside the UK or our time period. Some (for example, Gillingham) are not disasters under our definition but had important legal consequences. Others (for example, Dunblane, Lockerbie) are not disasters under our definition because they were caused deliberately.

Disaster response and preparation

The attitude of government towards disasters, and the need to prepare for them, is naturally shaped by this social construction. When an event is normalised then the response can be minimal but where the public outrage is strong, it can be quite different.

During the twentieth century, disasters have produced specific legal responses. From the lifeboat laws after the sinking of the *Titanic*, to the tip safety legislation after Aberfan and the banning of handguns after Dunblane, government responses have been aimed at preventing a specific repeat of the disaster. But it was not until the late 1980s that there were government attempts to respond on a wider scale to the questions and issues that disasters raised.

Emergency planning in Britain developed out of the civil defence programme. The Civil Defence Act 1948 imposed a duty on local

Table 4.2 Other disasters/events discussed in the text

Name	Date	Death toll	Cause
Tay Bridge	28 December 1879	75	Railway bridge collapses
Titanic	14–15 April 1912	1490	Liner collides with iceberg and sinks
1923 FA Cup Final (Wembley)	28 April 1923	30	Overcrowding at football match
Gresford	22 September 1934	265	Gas explosion in colliery
Bolton Wanderers	9 March 1946	30	Crush in football crowd
Lynmouth floods	12 August 1952	34	Flooding
Gillingham bus crash	4 December 1951	24	Bus ran into group of Royal Marine Cadets
Buffalo Creek (USA)	26 February 1972	125	Dam of mining waste, mud and water burst and flooded valley
Flixborough	01 June 1974	28	Explosion at chemical works
Hungerford	19 August 1987	16	Shootings
Glanrhyd	19 October 1987	4	Train swept into swollen river
Penlee life boat	19 December 1981	8	Life boat lost at sea in rescue operation
Grangemouth	2 accidents in March 1987	3	Explosion and fire at refinery
Lockerbie	21 December 1988	270	Aeroplane destroyed in mid-air by terrorist bomb
Purley train crash	4 March 1989	5	Train collision
Bilsthorpe	18 August 1993	3	Roof collapses in mine
Ramsgate	14 September 1994	6	Walkway collapses
Dunblane	13 March 1996	16	Shootings at a primary school
E.coli O157 outbreak, central Scotland	November 1996– January 1997	18	Outbreak of infection from foodborne illness
Death of Diana, Princess of Wales	6 September 1997	3	Road accident
Southall	20 September 1997	7	Train crash

authorities to draw up plans to protect the local population in the event of an attack by hostile external forces. By the early 1980s the overall scheme was in disarray with left-wing local authorities refusing to draw up plans because of their opposition to nuclear weapons and/or a belief that civil defence would be futile in the event of nuclear attack. This led to regulations imposing a duty on authorities to draw up and maintain civil defence plans. However, since the resources allocated for this were small, the motives seem to have been political rather than to protect the public.

The 1972 Local Government Act allowed a local authority to incur expenditure in averting, alleviating or eradicating the actual or potential effect of any disaster or emergency in its area. Nonetheless, there remained no duty on local authorities to plan for disasters and the level of preparedness varied significantly across Britain.[17] Thus it was in this context that public and government concern grew in relation to the disasters of the 1980s. In 1986, local authorities were granted a statutory power to divert civil defence budgets into emergency planning. In 1989, following a government review of emergency responses, the government appointed a civil emergencies advisor. To support him, he was assigned a Home Office secretariat while the civil defence college at Easingwold was given a new remit and renamed the Emergency Planning College. Media and local authority calls for a 'national disaster squad' and a statutory requirement to plan for disasters were refused. The appointment of the advisor represented the beginning of a further review of disaster arrangements culminating in 1992 with the publication of the report *Dealing with Disasters*.[18] Despite the impetus that the disasters of the 1980s and the end of the Cold War have given emergency planning in the UK, the British system remains fragmented: the responsibility of local authorities and lacking in strong central direction.

Disaster Inquiries

When disaster does strike everybody wants to ensure that it never happens again. Each tragedy we discuss has been followed by an inquiry that endeavours to understand why the disaster occurred. Steps are then taken to ensure it will not happen again. However, at times inquiry recommendations (particularly when technical) can become submerged in consultation and consideration periods. When the recommendations involved are expensive to implement there is a danger of a 'war of attrition' over the exact terms between the regulator and the regulated. This led a post-*Marchioness* inquiry to recommend that the Government conduct and publish an annual review of the progress in implementing the recommendations which follow national disasters.'[19]

Shutting the stable door after the horse has bolted may prevent the next horse escaping but in all likelihood the next 'disaster' would be altogether different. Disasters are rarely exact repeats of past events and if they are to be learnt from, and thus forecast and averted, then wider lessons need to be drawn that are applicable to other industries. Addressing the specific problem that caused past tragedies is not enough; cultural re-adjustments are required. Rules will not be internalised until those subject to them see the risk as real.

A clear commitment to safety is needed. This has been repeatedly acknowledged at disaster inquiries. Lord Cullen noted after Piper Alpha: 'It is essential to create a corporate atmosphere or culture in which safety is understood to be, and is accepted as, the number one priority.'[20] This culture must run through all levels of an organisation and requires leadership and guidance from not only the top of the company but also the regulators. As an inquiry into river safety after the *Marchioness* noted: 'a safety culture does not come naturally to those who work the river for reward. They need to be led into this culture by their owners and by the regulators.'[21] Safety should thus not be seen as a side issue in a company's operations but an integral part of its responsibilities.[22] For that to occur then there has to be a reappraisal of wider political and economic demands while the tendency to only scrutinise safety measures after something goes wrong has to be overcome.

The process of accepting and apportioning blame is hindered by the different official response to disasters. Official inquiries, inquests and criminal trials into the same event can all produce different conclusions. Interpretations of the causes of, and responsibility for, disaster varies according to the different remits and priorities of the investigators. When painful evidence is repeated in different inquiries, particularly when contradictory conclusions are then reached, the result can be tension and distress for the bereaved.

The chairmen of inquests and inquiries have considerable leeway in how they interpret their role. This is at the heart of some of the problems that subsequently arise. The conclusions do not always meet the expectations of the bereaved. For example, the ongoing dissatisfaction with the Hillsborough inquests results from the coroner's discretionary decision not to hear evidence from after 3.15 pm on the day of the disaster. The discretion of chairmen also means that disaster inquiries do not necessarily seek culprits. The Popplewell inquiry into the Bradford fire felt it was not its role to apportion blame, but simply to investigate the facts. Even statutory inquiries can follow similar lines. The Marine Accident Investigation Branch (MAIB) of the Department of Transport does not see its role as being to ascribe liability or apportion blame beyond what is necessary to determine the cause of an accident.[23] The NCB always maintained that was how it interpreted the Aberfan inquiry and that if it had realised it was required to plead guilty it would have done so. This diversity of interpretation of the responsibility of inquiries does not help the clear apportioning of responsibility or the recovery of survivors and the bereaved.

Technical, statutory inquiries are generally regarded more satis-factorily.[24] There was some disillusionment with the MAIB's initial handling of the sinking of the *Marchioness* but the disaster was the department's first experience of a major incident and it concedes that if it were to happen today many aspects would be handled differently.[25] Both the Railway Inspectorate and MAIB feel that their investigatory processes work well and there is little evidence to contradict such conclusions. The inpectorates are staffed by individuals with first-hand experience of the industry they are regulating. Rather than leading to regulatory capture (see Chapter 8), this is necessary in order to ensure a thorough understanding of the field.

Where transport inquiries have deviated from their statutory norms then the results have been less satisfactory. For example, within the rail industry there has been a tendency for inquiries of large accidents to be chaired by judicial figures rather than individuals from the rail inspectorate. This has resulted in parties seeking legal representation and being unwilling to openly concede mistakes and the like for fear of incriminating themselves.

Yet there are also supporters of legal representation in inquiries. Lord Howe, counsel for the colliery managers at Aberfan and later a long-serving cabinet minister under Mrs Thatcher, severely criticised the Scott Inquiry into arms trading with Iraq for denying witnesses legal representation. He maintained that without it witnesses are left vulnerable to public criticism without the opportunity to defend themselves properly. Howe points to his representation of NCB officials at the Aberfan inquiry as an example where those subject to censure, inside and outside the Tribunal, were in clear need of the legal representation they received.[26]

To overcome some of these problems, a 1997 Home Office working party recommended changes to the formal relationship between inquests and public inquiries into disasters. It recommended that an inquest should initially be held to establish the medical causes of death and allow the death to be registered. The inquest should then be adjourned while a public inquiry established the full causes of death. Under the recommendations, it would be the coroner's discretion whether the inquests were resumed. It is envisaged that a resumption would not normally happen unless there were circumstances such as new evidence or unease with the inquiry's findings. In the case of a resumed inquest, the working party recommended that the legislation regarding the need for a jury and the use of written evidence should be relaxed to avoid repeating distressing evidence.[27] Given that the bereaved and survivors have tended to be happier with the

findings of inquiries than those of inquests, the recommendations offer a welcome development. At the time of writing, they
are being implemented through the Access to Justice Act 1999
and appropriate secondary legislation.[28] The operation of technical, statutory inquiries is also under consideration. At the time of
writing, the Department of Environment, Transport and the Regions (DETR) was considering the possibility of setting up a single transport inspectorate. One of the benefits envisaged is that it
would avoid 'too cosy' a relationship existing between the regulator and the regulated. Another is that it should avoid any inquiry
feeling constrained about criticising its own regulation after an
accident.[29]

Disaster Studies

Disaster studies is a growing and inter-disciplinary field that draws
together the sciences, social sciences, law and humanities, as well as
non-academic practitioners. The field originated in the early 1950s in
the USA in the context of the Cold War. Sponsored by Federal
Government, the focus of research was on human behaviour in collective stress situations. It was hoped that the findings could be extrapo-
lated to determine the likely public response to a nuclear attack.[30]

Since then disaster studies has diversified and can be divided into
three broad but central concerns: disaster management, disaster
prevention and legal responses to disasters.

(a) Disaster management
The study of disaster management examines the handling of disasters
by the relevant responsible agencies. The rescue operation, the social
and psychological care given to survivors and victims and the overall
administrative response to the event are all subjected to close
scrutiny. Overall, the emphasis is on preparedness, response and
recovery. Practitioners writing of their experiences have been prominent here. The objective of analysing disaster management is to
improve the response to future disasters.

Much of the early work on disaster victims concentrated upon the
psychological impact of disasters. This complemented the work on
war veterans that was to eventually lead to the classification of
Post-Traumatic Stress Disorder (PTSD) as a distinct psychological
condition (see chapter 5). Disasters have since become an important
research ground for the development of knowledge about PTSD and
the psychological impact of traumatic events.

(b) Disaster Prevention

Disaster prevention attempts to learn lessons from the causes of previous disasters. It also incorporates the wider fields of risk and hazard management. Much of the work uses theoretical approaches. Rather than viewing disasters as acts of gods or the specific failings of individuals and technology, they are seen as 'phenomena that arise from the behaviour of complex social-technical systems and the interaction of these systems with their environments'.[31] Barry Turner, in particular, has emphasised how this enables common system failures to be identified in disasters, the lessons from which can be applied to other spheres.[32]

The account provided by the Tribunal Report of the failures within the NCB that led to the Aberfan disaster, has provided a powerful case study for those working in the field of disaster management and prevention. As Turner has shown, Aberfan illustrated the limitations and introspective nature of many management systems and the dangers of communication failures within organisations.[33] Like so many disasters, Aberfan is also powerful evidence of the danger of unheeded warnings. Thus its place as an example in much of the disaster prevention literature is unsurprising.[34]

Driven by commercial interests and needs, the scientific study of risk management has developed into a field of its own. In disaster studies, much of the emphasis on risk has been on the difference between scientific measures of risk and the subjective interpretations of those at risk.[35] Communities and individuals will often live knowingly in potentially dangerous conditions and an understanding of why is important in assessing and managing other risks. The work of Mary Douglas in particular has contributed a different, sociological and anthropological, approach to the study of risk. Her work locates perceptions and responses to risk within social and cultural structres.[36]

(c) Legal responses to disasters

The third, smaller but developing, area of disaster studies looks at legal responses. The legal processes such as inquiries, inquests and criminal trials are all central to a full understanding of the place of disasters in society. Victims of disasters often feel the legal responses perpetuate their grief and exacerbate the injustices they suffer. Consequently, the victims' pressure group Disaster Action has commissioned research into the legal responses to disasters.

Anne Eyre has argued that there is a strong need for a bridge to be established between the two cultures of disaster practitioners and academics. The building of this bridge has begun through the professionalisation of emergency management and growth in training and education programmes in the subject. Yet the space between the practitioner and the academic remains as wide as it does in so many other fields. Even within academia, research and dissemination is often too confined to the discipline of the researcher.[37] If disaster studies is to achieve its objective of helping the prevention and management of future disasters then there is a need for practitioners and academics to work together. Drabek argues that more is known about disasters than has actually been implemented.[38] Much of the academic work is often decidedly theoretical and perhaps somewhat inaccessible,[39] while the more accessible work aimed at practitioners[40] is sometimes overlooked by academics. The distinctive roles and perspectives need to be respected and understood but the gap has to be bridged if our understanding and management of disasters is to be improved.[41]

The significance of disasters

In 1989, a *Guardian* journalist wrote 'How we respond to ... disasters as a community – and how the Government responds on our behalf – is a measure of our own society.'[42] The unfolding of events in the aftermath of the Aberfan disaster raised important questions about corporate and media responsibility, the accountability and power of nationalised industries, definitions of charity law, the condition of social and psychological support services and the abilities and priorities of local and central government. Aberfan offers an insight into the very nature of the State and society in 1960s Britain.

In the 1960s, tragedies like Aberfan seemed thankfully rare but by the 1980s, even Margaret Thatcher noted the 'appalling disasters that seemed to plague us'.[43] In 1988, *The Guardian* labelled Britain a 'Disaster Zone', summing up what seemed to be the opinion of many.[44] Consequently, the wider public began to ask 'why' more forcefully than had previously been the case. Disaster inquiries repeatedly highlighted mismanagement, ignored warnings and apathy towards safety. In the face of such evidence, it was becoming difficult to see the catalogue of disasters as accidental or coincidental. As the Director General of the British Safety Council put it, 'It is no use putting these accidents down to acts of God. Why does God always pick on badly managed places with sloppy practices?'[45]

The horror at the British disasters of the mid-late 1980s was reinforced by the concentrated media coverage. Despite the criticisms, the reporting of Aberfan had been largely responsible and respectful. In contrast, the tone of the coverage in the 1980s was quite different:

> A public discourse of shock, sympathy, blame and accountability tends to be orchestrated through the media and a well-rehearsed narrative is imported which polarises the 'heroes' and the 'villains', regardless of the appropriateness of these constructions.[46]

The tone of this narrative, most notably at Hillsborough, was sometimes intrusive and graphic. The tabloid press in particular presented its accounts in such a fashion as to emphasise the tragedy. The youth, beauty, families and futures of victims were all often highlighted to underline the sense of loss, while the story was dramatised by the immediate search for culprits.[47]

In a period of free enterprise, the catalogue of disasters was suggesting to some that profits were being prioritised at the expense of safety.[48] In 1989, Opposition MPs attacked the Government following a series of fatal train crashes. There were accusations that a lack of investment had caused a rise in the accident rate and that the Government was 'seeking to get safety on the cheap'. The attacks were underpinned by similar statements from a former head of safety and signalling at BR.[49] The link between safety and cost was identified explicitly in the inquiry into the King's Cross fire where it was shown that certain fire precautions had not been implemented because management felt that such investment would be ruled out in the 'financial climate'.[50]

Disasters were this increasingly becoming contested spaces where wider debates were acted out. The injustices suffered by Aberfan quietly slipped from the wider public attention. In contrast, the continuing campaigning of victims of disasters in the 1980s, not only questioned the traditional view of victims as helpless, but also ensured that the controversies were not forgotten.[51] Survivor and victim pressure groups fought to ensure their cases remained in the public eye and were not brushed over by government. For some of the survivors and bereaved, the need for justice became all encompassing: 'The truth must be known – only then can we feel that we can 'move on'.'[52] Their personal experience ensured media attention and a moral authority on the subject. Disaster Action, an umbrella organisation acting as both a mutual support and pressure group, actually commissioned research into the handling and prevention of disasters, motivated by the feeling that '[w]e don't want anyone else to go through what we've been through.'[53] Alongside these developments were wider concerns about the environment in the late 1980s and the priorities and responsibilities of the corporations allegedly threatening it.[54] Progress was often slow – it was not, for example, until ten years after the *Marchioness* disaster that a public inquiry was granted – but the campaigning of victim groups ensured the handling of disasters remained in the public and political arena. Thus the legal and moral issues that disasters raised were not only becoming better known, they were also beginning to be challenged. The disasters of the 1980s forced questions and changes in British law and culture in a way that Aberfan did not; the Southall (1997) and Ladbroke Grove (1999) rail disasters seem certain to lead to more changes still.

Disasters have tended to be confined to tragic footnotes in academic British history. Yet their impact on wider society can be profound. Disasters raise questions about humanity's control over technology and safety. They demonstrate our vulnerability at the hands of nature and what we have created. Where they happen in everyday situations such as on public transport or at a leisure event they create strong signals that any of us could have been a victim. The large sums raised by some disaster funds are often an acknowledgement of this as well as a demonstration of sympathy and empathy. Yet such funds can also cause division and argument amongst the beneficiaries. Visits to disaster sites and survivors by politicians, royalty and other dignitaries offer further recognition of this wider sympathy rather than practical comfort. Indeed, while the appearance of dignitaries can cause security concerns for the local authorities, for a victim it can even be unpleasant.[55] Thus a key theme in this book is how the popular and governmental responses to disasters do not always accord with what survivors and the bereaved actually want or need.

Government departments and the law react mechanistically to events. However procedures normally acceptable can cause distress in the aftermath of a disaster. The popular and political responses to disasters can be very different to the actual needs of those directly affected by the tragedy. For a disaster response to be efficient, just and caring, it has to be flexible and have the interests of the victims at its core. It is hoped that this book is a demonstration of that need. It is often predicted that in the future there will be more disasters because of the increasing population density in many areas, the increased settlement in high-risk areas that are hurricane or earthquake prone, and the increased technological risks.[56] If this is the case then the need to learn the lessons of the past is even more important. Yet prevention is better than cure and the great lesson of disasters past is that most were predictable.

Notes

1 *Kerria Developments Ltd and Another v The Reporter Ltd*, 31 July 1984, HC Lexis.
2 The letters are in the care of Merthyr Central Library. Further details on the collection can be found at www.nuff.ox.ac.uk/ politics/ aberfan/condol.htm
3 *Hansard*, 5th ser., vol. 734, col. 649.
4 Peter Hinton, 'Introduction: Some Observations on Disasters', in Peter Hinton (ed.), *Disasters: Image and Context* (Sydney: Sydney Association for Studies in Society and Culture, 1992), p. 1.
5 The disaster was a spur for the creation of the Welsh Office Derelict Land Unit which slowly reclaimed land, including tip sites, across Wales for economic purposes. See Gwyn Griffiths, 'Regaining the Wastelands', in David Cole (ed.), *The New Wales* (Cardiff: University of Wales Press, 1990).
6 Even before the Second World War, when the prosperity of Cardiff was based upon exporting coal from the valleys, there remained clear social divisions between the two areas. See Dai Smith, 'The Valleys: Landscape and Mindscape', in Prys Morgan (ed.), *Glamorgan County History vol. VI: Glamorgan Society 1780–1980* (Cardiff: Glamorgan County History Trust, 1988).
7 The sixteenth century meaning of the word 'disaster' was 'unfavourable aspect of a star' (*Oxford Dictionary of English Etymology*). This is a reflection of contemporary views about the divine power over the fate of man. The development of the word's meaning is further indication of the social construction of what actually constitutes a disaster.
8 See, for example, E. L. Quarantelli (ed.), *What is a Disaster? A Dozen Perspectives on the Question* (London: Routledge, 1998).
9 Anne Eyre, 'Calling for a Disasters Study Group: A Proposal', Paper given at British Sociological Association Conference, 1999.
10 Tom Horlick-Jones, 'Modern Disasters as Outrage and Betrayal', *International Journal of Mass Emergencies and Disasters*, vol. 13, no. 3, p. 306.
11 Thomas E. Drabek, *Social Dimensions of Disaster: Instructor Guide* (Emmitsburg: Federal Emergency Management Agency, 1996), pp. 2–4.
12 Charles E. Fritz, 'Disaster', in Robert K. Merton & Robert A. Nisbet (eds.), *Contemporary Social Problems* (New York: Harcourt, 1961), p. 655.
13 E.g., Alan Blackshaw (in 1966, Private Secretary to the Minister of Power); interview, IM, August 1999
14 Horlick-Jones, 'Modern Disasters as Outrage and Betrayal', p. 306.
15 Letter from A. W. Evans to IM, 4 June 1999.
16 Mick Hamer, 'Lessons from a disastrous past: Victorian disasters in public places have much in common with more recent tragedies, except that many more lives were lost', *New Scientist*, 22 December 1990, vol. 128, no. 1748.
17 The history of local government's role in emergency planning is reviewed in Ian Henderson, 'Local Government's Role in Emergency Planning', *Local Government Studies*, vol. 12, no. 4, July/August 1986.
18 This section is derived from Celia Wells, *Negotiating Tragedy: Law and Disasters* (London: Sweet & Maxwell, 1995), pp. 60–62 & *Hansard*, 6th

ser., vol. 154, cols. 512–513. The advisor's review was published as Home Office, *Dealing with Disaster*, HMSO, 1992. There have been two subsequent revised versions. There was also an earlier and separate Home Office report into the social services response into disasters. See Disasters Working Party, *Disasters: Planning for a Caring Response, Part One: The Main Report* (London: HMSO, 1989).

19 John W. Hayes, *Report of the Enquiry into River Safety*, Cm 1991 (London: HMSO, 1991), paras. 9.28, 11.10. This inquiry also noted that as the consultation process continues the memory of the tragedy recedes the department responsible may settle for the 'lowest common denominator' in safety regulations. Para. 9.28.

20 Lord Cullen (chairman), *The Public Inquiry into the Piper Alpha Disaster*, Cm. 1310 (London: HMSO, 1990).

21 Hayes, *Report of the Enquiry into River Safety*, para. 11.2.

22 For a discussion of the need for safety cultures within companies see Peter Spooner, 'Developing the Corporate Mindsets which will Help to Reduce Man-made Disasters', *Disaster Prevention & Management*, vol. 1, no. 2, 1992, 28–36.

23 DETR, Transport Safety, A1.15.

24 Home Office, *Report of the Disasters and Inquests Working Group*, 1997.

25 Letter from J. S. Lang (Chief Inspector of Marine Accidents) to MJ, 29 July 1999.

26 Howe, 'Management of Public Inquiries', p. 302.

27 Home Office, *Report of the Disasters and Inquests Working Group*, 1997.

28 Changes do not apply to Scotland where the use of fatal accident inquiries means that the whole investigatory process is different.

29 DETR, Transport Safety Consultation Paper, 1998, paras 2.10, 2.22.

30 Tierney, 'Social and Community Contexts of Disasters', p. 13.

31 Horlick-Jones, 'Modern Disasters', p. 306.

32 Barry A. Turner, with Nick F. Pidgeon, *Man-Made Disasters* (Oxford, Butterworth-Heinemann, 2nd edn, 1997).

33 Ibid.

34 Also see, for example, Peter Young, *Disasters: Focussing on Management Responsibility* (London: HFA, 1993).

35 Horlick-Jones, 'Modern Disasters', p. 308.

36 E.g., Mary Douglas, *Risk and Blame: Essays in Cultural Theory* (London: Routledge, 1992).

37 Anne Eyre, 'Calling for a Disasters Study Group' & 'Bridging the Gap: Research-based Emergency Management', *Emergency Management*, Spring 1999, p. 9.

38 Thomas E. Drabek, 'Following Some Dreams: Recognizing Opportunities, Posing Interesting Questions, and Implementing Alternative Methods', *International Journal of Mass Emergencies and Disasters*, March 1997, vol. 15, no. 1, p. 33.

39 For example, Brain Toft and Simon Reynolds, *Learning from Disasters: A Management Approach* (Oxford: Butterworth-Heinemann, 1994).

40 For example, Chris Llewelyn, *Learning Lessons from Disasters* (Cardiff: Welsh Consumer Council, 1998).

41 Anne Eyre, 'Calling for a Disasters Study Group'. Drabek, 'Following Some Dreams', pp. 35–36.

42 *Guardian*, 15 June 1989, p. 21.

43 Margaret Thatcher, *The Downing Street Years* (London: HarperCollins, 1993), p. 756.
44 *Guardian*, 15 June 1988, p. 21.
45 Quoted in *Guardian*, 22 August 1989, p. 1.
46 Anne Eyre, 'More than PTSD: Proactive Responses Among Disaster Victims', *The Australasian Journal of Disaster and Trauma Studies*, 1998–2.
47 John Taylor, 'Death's Grim Bazaar', *New Statesman & Society*, 15 December 1989, 30–32.
48 Arthur Marwick, *British Society Since 1945* (Harmondsworth: Penguin, 1990 edn.), pp. 320–323. In April 1989, the Socialist Workers' Party produced a poster which depicted a lone and distraught Liverpool fan sitting in front of the mangled fences at Hillsborough. Its caption read 'Thatcherism: Ten Years of Disasters'. Ian Taylor, 'English football in the 1990s: taking Hillsborough seriously?', in John Williams & Stephen Wagg, Stephen (eds.), *British Football and Social Change: Getting into Europe* (Leicester: Leicester University Press, 1991), p. 10.
49 In particular see John Prescott in *Hansard*, 6th ser., vol. 148, cols. 609–611. Quote – Michael Martin (Glasgow, Sprinburn), *Hansard*, vol. 148, col. 758.
50 Desmond Fennell (chairman), *Investigation into the Kings' Cross Underground Fire*, Cm 499 (London: HMSO, 1988), p. 149.
51 Much of the academic literature on disaster victims has also emphasised the negative aspect of their experiences, such as PTSD, rather than the more positive and proactive action undertaken by survivors and the bereaved. See Eyre, 'More than PTSD'.
52 Pamela Dix, bereaved relative of Lockerbie/Flight 103 victim. *The Guardian*, 25 July 1998.
53 Quoted in Eyre, 'More than PTSD'. Disaster Action's objectives are to encourage companies to take Health and Safety more seriously and to change the law on corporate manslaughter and responsibility. Telephone interview between Barrie Berkley (Disaster Action spokesperson) and Martin Johnes, 14 February 1999.
54 The clearest manifestation of the rising environmental awareness was the 15 per cent for the Green Party at the 1989 European election.
55 A critically ill survivor of Hillsborough later recalled 'The last thing I needed was to wake up in a hospital bed to be patronised by Margaret Thatcher'. Phil Scraton, *Hillsborough: The Truth* (Edinburgh: Mainstream, 1999), p. 116.
56 For example see E. L. Quarantelli, 'The Environmental Disasters of the Future will be More and Worse but the Prospect is not Hopeless', *Disaster Prevention and Management*, vol. 2, no. 1, 1993.

Chapter Five

THE MANAGEMENT OF TRAUMA

[One bereaved father would at times go] into a room on his own and sit
down and just grieve and he was then in agony trying to visualise what his
wife and his children went through before they died. ... [T]his is what is
happening in dozens of homes in the village.[1]

Note by APRA solicitor

Post Traumatic Stress Disorder

The survivors, bereaved and wider community have to face many
traumatic problems in the aftermath of a sudden and unexpected
man-made disaster. Acute grief, denial and detachment, anger and
hypervigilance are all common responses that have to be managed
before lives can be rebuilt. For some victims these reactions can be
severe and long lasting. Since 1980, this has been classified as Post
Traumatic Stress Disorder (PTSD); a condition that acknowledges
that extremely traumatic events can produce chronic responses in
normal individuals.[2] The traumatic experience need not be catastrophic but any event that is exceptional and threatens the physical
well being or integrity of self or others.

Before the diagnosis of PTSD was professionally accepted,
extreme response to trauma was usually ascribed to some pre-
existing psychiatric problem. Because such abnormal grief is not
necessarily the result of pre-existing problems, mental health professionals argue that different forms of counselling and psychiatric care
can help individuals and communities come to terms with the impact
of disasters.

The concept of PTSD grew out of work on Vietnam veterans and
victims of other man-made disasters such as the Holocaust, the atom
bomb and hostage taking.[3] The observation of chronic responses to
trauma has a longer history dating back to studies of what was then

called 'shell shock' in troops who served in the First World War. However, before the diagnosis of PTSD, prolonged disorders following trauma were often conceptualised as anxiety or depressive neuroses. In such cases, disasters or other causes of extreme stress were considered 'nonspecific triggers that might serve to release, exacerbate, or prolong a predictable diathesis to psychiatric symptoms.'[4] With PTSD, the emphasis is placed upon external stressors rather than pre-existing psychological conditions.

However, the prevalence and exact nature of PTSD are still controversial.[5] Many of its symptoms overlap considerably with general anxiety and stress disorders thus questioning the validity of its classification as a separate condition. It is also questionable whether the emphasis should be on the actual event itself or the cultural and social significance that is placed upon it. Different people and cultures can regard similar events in different fashions. Many people who experience traumatic events do not develop PTSD. Thus the cause can not always be the event itself.[6] Pre-existing psychological conditions and other individual variables should not therefore be discounted as contributing factors.

Nonetheless, the recognition of PTSD and the emphasis on the role of the external stressor has, theoretically, led to more proactive and supportive help for the victims of disaster. Experience of disasters has shown some doctors that an individual's character or environment is not always the prime cause of psychological illness. Such experiences have helped confirm in their eyes the validity of diagnoses such as PTSD.[7] The recognition of PTSD has also provided a route to financial compensation from any party whose negligence contributed to the trauma. (However, the financial benefits of this are not always straightforward; at least one victim of an UK disaster has been denied life insurance following a diagnosis of PTSD.[8]) Its importance in our understanding of the aftermath of disasters is thus central.

In the past, most families experienced personal tragedy. War, child mortality, working conditions all claimed victims regularly, while widespread religious beliefs, and/or sheer fatalism, helped lessen the grief. However, in post-war Western Europe, such tragedies have become infrequent, so that people are less experienced in coping with sudden bereavement. Modern technologies and medical progress have created a world in which the experience of trauma is not inevitable.[9] This, together with an increasingly secular society and a more scientific approach to psychology and psychiatry, has contributed to the growth of all manner of professional (and quasi-professional) counselling.

By the late 1950s, there was a growing awareness in the USA of the potential long-term psychological effects of disasters. However, much of the evidence for what was termed 'disaster syndrome' was anecdotal.[10] Its influence in Britain was marginal. There were varied views and opinions about how to deal with the problems but very little conclusive evidence about what techniques actually worked. American social workers felt their professional skills could have a critical role in helping victims come to terms with their experience. Yet the UK centre of academic evidence-based psychiatry in 1966, Maudsley Hospital, did not accept that social workers had a primary role.[11] Survivors of disasters thus had to rely on local support networks and whatever facilities local authorities made available. However, there was very little outpatient psychiatry in Britain for non-psychotic illness and few people working in related disciplines.[12] Victims were therefore generally reliant on traditional forms of counselling and help such as visits from friends, family and ministers of religion and messages of condolence. Yet such immediate sources of comfort could not be expected to last until time gradually eased the pain.

Trauma and Aberfan

Aberfan was a disaster with no real precedent in contemporary British history.[13] The loss of so many children in a small community was bound to have severe psychological consequences. Bereavement by disaster is more intense than by expected death and thus more difficult to come to terms with. The grief also tends to be more acute in cases where children are lost and where the disaster is man made rather than natural.[14] It was obvious that the traditional networks of support would struggle to cope adequately, particularly since so many people in the village were affected. There were also forecasts that the disaster would lead to psychological problems on a scale that would be too large for local professional services to cope with.[15] Consequently the local services were inundated with offers of help.[16] Yet even the resources available elsewhere, in terms of trained people, were minimal while there were no agreed or proven methods.[17] Offers of help may have been forthcoming but, in these circumstances, they may not have been effective.

The depth of the trauma that the disaster had inflicted quickly became apparent. A solicitor representing the Aberfan residents wrote in his papers a month after the disaster that one bereaved father would at times go 'into a room on his own and sit down and just grieve and he was then in agony trying to visualise what his wife and his children went through before they died. ... [T]his is what is happening in dozens of homes in the village.'[18] Trauma affects different people in different ways. In the first few weeks after the disaster a psychiatrist noted the following groups of symptoms: disorders of sleep, changes of mood, anxiety symptoms, changes in behaviour, phobic reactions, physical or psychosomatic symptoms.[19] Of the 86 children he assessed, 55 were found to have fairly or moderately severe symptoms, although none were classified as very severe. Of the 83 adults examined, 90 per cent were classified as having moderate to severe symptoms.[20] It is likely that some individuals came to manage their grief and suffering while others were distressed for varying but prolonged periods. Today they would probably be diagnosed as suffering from PTSD.

Local doctors and social workers acknowledged that Aberfan would need professional psychological and social work support. But there was no guarantee that Aberfan would accept it. The stigma of seeking psychological help was stronger in the 1960s than it is today. Outpatient psychiatric and neurosis treatment was still very much in its infancy and consequently psychiatric services were associated with asylums and severe mental illness. Psychiatric medicine is still popularly associated with vulnerability, failure and a sign of weakness.[21] In a mining community such as Aberfan, that had lived through the desperation of the inter-war depression, the constant dangers of working underground and the pressures of the Second World War, the stigma of being given help for emotional and psychological problems was probably stronger. Indeed, even the surviving children felt it. One child wrote in 1970,

> There was talk amongst the survivors that their parents had letters for each child that survived to see a psychiatrist. I was totally horrified to hear this from my friends. God, what would people think seeing in my eyes a SHRINK? I confronted my parents and told them bluntly there was no way that I was going for these head tests and talks. A few weeks went by and Susan Maybanks had her letter to go, and my boyfriend, David. As far I knew I did not get one. I questioned them when they came back from their appointment, and I thought it was a very disturbing thing they put them through. Hadn't they been through enough? But I was very adamant that I was not going. My parents tried their best to reason with me, and told me of the importance, but each time I got very upset of even the thought.[22]

This reluctance to see the psychiatrist was despite the fact that he was only assessing the children in order to help them claim damages. The general distrust of authority and outsiders that had developed after the disaster complicated the situation further and added to the reluctance to accept the help of mental health professionals.[23] Press reports that psychiatrists were about to descend on the village did not help matters either.[24] After one mother had to be admitted to hospital, there were rumours that anyone visited by the local mental welfare officer would be taken to a mental hospital. This was, after all, what the officer's work normally entailed. The rumours led to the welfare officer being taken off work with bereaved families.[25] It is thus not surprising that the local consultant psychiatrist reported that he found it difficult getting people to realise they needed help.[26]

Psycho-social care at Aberfan

This was the context in which Merthyr Tydfil County Borough Council took the decision to handle the disaster using its own welfare services. The offers of outside help were 'tactfully declined' and 'fended off'.[27] Local services had set to work very quickly, although their work was deliberately not publicised for fear of making the situation worse.[28] Dr English, the consultant psychiatrist responsible for Aberfan, wrote to the *British Medical Journal* saying that the existing service was adequate. He continued,

> What we wish to avoid is the risk of predisposition to mental illness as a consequence of people outside the area anticipating such among the bereaved families, and allowing their fears to be made known to the residents of Aberfan. … If, however, there is a marked increase in cases of breakdown directly due to the disaster, the doctors treating the patients must understand the community as it is in normal circumstances, to be aware of the fears and thoughts they share in day-to-day living, and this can best be done by the doctors whom they know well and whose advice they trust.[29]

Thus the decision not to accept external assistance was rooted in a desire to help Aberfan. The continuation of this policy was influenced by outside bodies' proposals to carry out research in association with the assistance they were offering. The people of Aberfan were already suffering from the glare of publicity and had no wish to become guinea pigs. Thus research plans were declined and the existing services struggled on alone.[30]

In line with the then current thinking, some of the relevant officials thought that residents of Aberfan who were seriously disturbed by the disaster had prior family problems or, in the case of children, pre-existing difficulties such as enuresis or temper tantrums.[31] 'Broadly speaking' wrote the local child psychologist,

> the children who were most affected were those with other anxiety creating situations in their backgrounds. Of the first few cases that were referred, several were from families in which there had been a striking number of grief situations in the past, and this seemed to have made them and their parents more vulnerable.[32]

The tendency to view the situation through such a lens must have clouded the view of the need for a more comprehensive scheme of counselling and psychological support.

Helping Aberfan thus fell largely on the shoulders of the local available services and, in particular, two psychiatrists and the local general practitioners. The three GPs in the area were under tremendous pressure; indeed one had lost a child himself in the disaster. Two left within a year of the tragedy. Finding replacements proved problematic and those doctors who were brought in were not Welsh and, in a community distrustful of outsiders, had problems winning the confidence of their patients.[33] There was outside support and advice available to the psychiatrist, general practitioners and social workers, especially from the Tavistock Institute in London. Its advice was found useful but its plans for an outside team to help and research in Aberfan meant that it never seems to have fully won the trust of the local services.[34] The work of the psychiatrists was complicated by their different terms of reference.[35] Dr Cuthill had clients referred to him primarily by the Parents' and Residents' Association's solicitors. He was to assess them for the purpose of compensation claims but not to treat them. Adult clinical work fell on the shoulders of Dr English (the consultant psychiatrist who was based in Bridgend, a town outside the local area) while the local authority's child psychiatrist was designated to work with the children.

Of the 218 bereaved adults who continued to live in the area, 83 were examined or treated by a psychiatrist.[36] There was a consensus of feeling amongst the psychiatrists involved that there were many more adults probably in need of help.[37] Some did not want it; others were not referred by their GPs. There was speculation that the GPs concerned were unaware that Cuthill was initially assessing for compensation rather than treating clients. Certain GPs were also said to have an antipathy towards psychiatry.[38] Even the out-patient facilities in the local psychiatric hospital were not fully utilised. Cuthill's fears that the adults he had seen were probably just the tip of the iceberg thus seem well founded.[39]

Children were initially referred to the child psychologist (who worked for the education department) through their schools. Therefore, the child psychologist did not see children who showed no sign of disturbance at school but did so at home. Subsequent research has shown how both schools and parents report fewer signs of psychopathy in children than children themselves. Particularly in cases where the parents are also affected by the trauma, children learn not to unburden their problems on others and thus their suffering can go unnoticed or misunderstood. Given that children as young as eight are thought of as being vulnerable to PTSD, the consequences can be significant.[40]

A long-standing administrative division between the education and health departments of the local authority hindered communication between those treating adults and children. It took prompting by an external advisor to get the two groups to meet to discuss the services they were offering. They found, not surprisingly, that they were working with clients from the same families. The well being of children and their parents influenced each other but organisational divisions had initially obscured this and any possible solution.[41]

Even within the borough council there was a feeling that the service available to the children was inadequate. Such shortcomings mirrored a wider shortage in child psychiatry across Britain and the underdeveloped field of children's psychology. The education department's fears of being held liable for the disaster do not seem to have helped the co-ordination of services either. The psychiatrist assessing the children for legal purposes did review their condition periodically for eight years and was able to thus offer some treatment or alert others to those in need of help.[42] Nonetheless, a number of children awarded compensation for psychological damage never received medical help for it.[43]

Subsequent research has suggested that early proactive support can help prevent chronic stress and trauma.[44] Much of the support social workers give today is actually practical rather than counselling: helping with funeral arrangements, compensation claims and the like. This eases the logistical concerns of the bereaved and establishes a relationship with social workers which helps counselling at a later date. Aberfan did get such support early on. An advice centre was quickly set up and staffed by members of the Wales and Monmouthshire Council of Social Service. It did much-needed work in helping people fill in claim forms and deal with the offers of compensation.[45]

The initial daily support on offer from the local authority was hampered by the council's limited resources. It had two mental health officers and five trained social welfare officers, three of whom were classified as home teachers to the blind while the other two covered a wide range of general tasks from helping the elderly and disabled to dealing with 'problem families'. Initially, the non-psychiatric help given to Aberfan was their responsibility. They did their best but were not trained for such a situation.[46]

Consequently, with the help of the Tavistock Institute, Audrey Davey, a family caseworker, was appointed in November 1966. Initially there were some misgivings, and even opposition, to her appointment within the local authority. Such doubts were based on a feeling that it would only keep the disaster fresh in people's minds.[47] Davey's initial task involved just visiting and listening to bereaved families, enabling people to come to terms with their loss. Such work was invaluable; the ability to face up to what has happened is integral to recovery. Some people, but fewer than she expected, turned her away because she was a social worker. Given the distrust of officials and experts in the village, trust had to be won rather than assumed.[48] All bereaved families were visited at least twice and those with special needs received more intensive help.[49] Davey gradually won the trust and respect of the community to such an extent that she was invited to be part of a village delegation that lobbied the government for the removal of the tips.

Although she was acting with external professional advice and support, much of her work appears to have been based upon common sense, kindness and empathy. She encouraged people to talk and form support groups that were inclusive rather than exclusive to certain groups such as the bereaved. This undoubtedly had beneficial effects, not only for the individuals concerned, but also the whole community. As one report on her work concluded, 'Audrey is still the piercing point. She is the link between the personal and the social, and between the people and the helpers.'[50]

However, Davey was overworked and in need of additional help. Lack of time meant she had to focus on the bereaved parents, the most vulnerable group, meaning that others in need of support may have not have initially received it.[51] There were thus moves to bring in further outside support. The Tavistock Institute, the Welsh Board of Health and local psychiatrists acknowledged the need for additional caseworkers to help Davey.[52] All felt though that any additional support should be introduced gradually so as not to overwhelm the village. However, some GPs and others in the local authority were against the idea for extra help and it came to nothing. After two years in Aberfan, Davey still felt that her job was unfinished. The local consultant psychiatrist wrote to the Welsh Board of Health emphasising the need for Davey to continue in her post. However the local authority refused to pay for her to stay or to employ another social worker, while the disaster fund would not finance work which it felt other authorities had an obligation to support. At least one observer, a local solicitor, felt that by allocating money to 'bricks and mortar' rather attending to the social needs of the village, the fund had not got its priorities right.[53] There was certainly an awareness of the likelihood of long term psychological problems amongst the children at least, but a lack of money meant no further daily help for Aberfan was forthcoming.[54]

Community help in Aberfan

Alongside the professional help available, a form of community self-help had been developing. It provided a network of support for the bereaved that was to prove effective in overcoming many problems. There is naturally a degree of romanticism in the idea of self-supporting, tight-knit, Welsh mining communities. Such notions gloss over the fractures that exist within small communities and that can detract from the value of community networks of support. At Aberfan, the strength of this community support was also hindered to an extent by the fact that few people were not directly affected the disaster. According to the child psychologist, this reduced the support families, friends and neighbours could give each other.[55] Similar circumstances and effect have been noted at Buffalo Creek where there was also a high proportion of victims to non-victims.[56] Nonetheless, the strength of community is cited by many in Aberfan as having being integral in the road to recovery.[57]

Local ministers of religion provided not only spiritual care but a wider emotional support too. Consequently ministers, especially the Rev. Kenneth Hayes, the minister of Zion English Baptist Church, came to the fore as community leaders and earned the respect of a wide audience. Many of the survivors and bereaved talk about how their faith helped them cope to terms with their losses. The faith of some was strengthened by the whole experience while a few non-religious residents became members of chapels and the church.[58] Others had their faith tested or even destroyed by the tragedy.[59]

One minister who played an important role in helping Aberfan was another 'outsider', Erastus Jones. He was invited to Aberfan by the local council of churches to serve the community in whichever ways he thought appropriate. Initially, Jones and his wife, working from a caravan they named Tŷ Toronto (Welsh for Toronto House –

Jones' work was funded by a gift from the Welsh community of Toronto) slowly built up local contacts and helped the tip removal campaign with practical administrative work. Through such efforts they
became accepted in the village.

The work of Tŷ Toronto led to the formation of an umbrella community association and the holding of conferences to embrace and
encourage dialogue between the different groups in not only Aberfan
but also the adjoining village of Merthyr Vale. Community rehabilitation needed the community to overcome its divisions. The first
conference, entitled 'The Way Ahead', was successful in helping to
bring down barriers between different churches, the bereaved and
the non-bereaved, those who had lost houses and those who had not.
It also embraced outside authorities, such as the Disaster Fund and
Merthyr Council, who were involved with affairs in Aberfan. An important part of the first conference was a paper on how people react
after disasters. This showed the people of Aberfan that their own reactions were not abnormal but instead to be expected in the traumatic circumstances. Through enabling dialogue and discussion, the
hope was that the anger that existed in Aberfan would be channelled
into the more creative purpose of community development.[60]

The focus of Tŷ Toronto was communal rather than individual
because

> we thought that a healthy community could best help its individual
> sufferers through to recovery, since the very numbers of those personally
> in need were beyond our resources. We thought also that perhaps friends
> and relatives could do a better job than strangers and professionals, given
> the encouragement of a purposeful community.[61]

This also helped overcome one of the initial problems that the official
help was concentrating on the bereaved, rather than being freely
available to all. Tŷ Toronto grew ambitiously and culminated by de-
claring 1974 the 'Year of the Valleys'. It developed a programme that
embraced grassroots groups and academics from across South Wales
in an attempt to 'deepen their [the valleys'] self awareness and to
open new doors to a region whose economic, cultural and social
cohesion was undergoing such rapid change'.[62] The programme's
long-term goals of aiding the valleys' socio-economic regeneration
failed but within Aberfan Tŷ Toronto helped the community rebuild
itself.

Also important in helping Aberfan's recovery were the donations
and messages of condolence the village received. The disaster fund
received nearly 88,000 donations, most of them accompanied by a

letter or card.[63] In the words of one bereaved mother, 'People all over the world felt for us. We knew that with their letters and the contributions that they sent ... They helped us to build a better Aberfan.'[64] For all the problems the fund later caused, it and the simple gesture of writing a note of condolence meant a great deal to the people of Aberfan. Contemporary disaster theory makes it clear that social workers can often initially do little more than listen to victims. In doing this they help the victim acknowledge that the trauma is indeed awful and can not be prevented. In witnessing it the social worker is telling the victim that they are not alone.[65] The sympathy and donations sent to Aberfan had much the same effect. It verified the pain and thus was a small step towards recovery.

Obstacles to recovery in Aberfan

The recovery of Aberfan was hindered by a number of factors which made the village infamous. In 1968 a psychiatrist noted a greater degree of suffering in the village than he would have anticipated from the disaster alone. He attributed the prolonged problems to post-disaster affairs in the village.[66] In the wake of the disaster, people in Aberfan understandably felt uneasy living in the shadow of the remaining tips. During the campaign for the removal of the tips, Kenneth Hayes wrote to the Prime Minister:

> Every time it rains people are afraid to go to bed, ... and all of us subconsciously are awaiting the alarm to sound.... The mental wellbeing of the community today, and the safety of the unborn generations depends on the removal of tips.[67]

The arguments, delays and haggling over the cost caused considerable anger in Aberfan for the two years before the government agreed to remove the tips. Such an atmosphere was hardly conducive to recovery.

Stimuli that resemble or symbolise the original traumatic event are thought to exacerbate the symptoms of PTSD.[68] Indeed, avoidance of stimuli associated with the trauma is one of the symptoms of PTSD. At Lockerbie, the local community had to live with the visible impact of the disaster for many weeks as wreckage and bodies were slowly recovered. This continued exposure to the disaster contributed to a high rate of PTSD.[69] The continued presence of the tips at Aberfan seems to have had a similar effect, exacerbated, perhaps, by feelings of guilt that they were created by the village's own economic raison d'être. It is also a common feature of disasters that the victims fear a repeat of the tragedy; thus the people of Aberfan were reacting rationally in demanding the removal of the tips, despite the official assurances that they were safe.[70] The child psychologist responsible for the village felt that recovery only really began to take place when the aggression towards forms of authority began to subside. Specifically, she saw the continued presence of the tips as aggravating the fears people had of situations such as sleep, the dark and extreme weather.[71] A local GP also noted that worry and controversy over the tips was affecting people's health.[72]

The family caseworker made a strong appeal to the Welsh Office for complete removal. The meeting's minutes recorded her arguments:

> The villagers had done admirably in rehabilitating themselves with very little help. A Government gesture was needed to restore confidence and only complete removal of the tips would do this. Many people in the village were on sedatives but they did not take them when it was raining because they were afraid to go to sleep. Children did not close their bedroom doors in case they should be trapped.[73]

The injustice of the delays and resultant anger and hurt was all the worse since it was unnecessary and political.

Those helping Aberfan felt strongly that the insensitive, and sometimes unscrupulous, attention of the press hindered the village's recovery.[74] The facts reported were usually correct but the interpretations could be less reliable. Unused to dealing with the media, villagers found their comments being taken out of context and twisted. Debate in the village on what to do was portrayed as argument and the words or actions of a minority depicted as the norm.[75] At least one freelance reporter went further by supplying newspapers with untrue stories and encouraging villagers to spread false rumours.[76] Controversies over the use of the disaster fund and arguments between individual residents made sensational stories for a hungry press but did not give a complete picture of village affairs. There was a feeling that the press was uninterested in happy stories about the village and only published those that told of conflict.[77] Concerns were raised in the information division of the Welsh Office that the stories would reflect badly upon Wales unless action was taken.[78] Yet there was little a government department could do without being criticised for attacking the freedom of the press, something that had already happened at Aberfan. Thus the Welsh Office told Merthyr Tydfil County Borough Council that it could not intervene in shielding Aberfan from media attention on the first anniversary of the disaster.[79]

Guilt and anger are normal sequels to a disaster. Disasters create situations where emotions run high and many of the previous social barriers are broken down. Anger is also a symptom of PTSD and a reasonable response when people are being treated inappropriately by authority. Thus disasters create situations where pre-existing and new tensions often boil over. The press's failure to recognise these circumstances meant that Aberfan was often portrayed as 'some kind of delinquent community'.[80] The village was thus caught in a vicious circle. The normal angry response of victims to a disaster was added to by problems with the local authority, disaster fund and NCB. This resulted in the community being misunderstood and misrepresented which in turn ensured that its demands and needs were not heard.

People's attitudes and beliefs are important in determining how they recover from traumatic experiences.[81] In Aberfan traditional working class notions of masculinity appear to have hampered the recovery process. Miners in particular are associated with notions of strength and emotional resilience. Davey was worried about the fact that fathers could not talk about their feelings while at least one survivor felt that it was harder for him to come to terms with the events because he was a man.[82] In 1968, a psychiatrist wrote that while some bereaved mothers were getting back to normal, there was some evidence that the health of the fathers was tending to deteriorate. An external advisor had earlier noted that the men, and in particular the bereaved men, were not in a frame of mind to accept the designated help. He suggested providing help that was not associated with psychiatry, religion or any of the other 'helping professions.[83] A bereaved fathers' group had only lasted two meetings in contrast to the successful mothers' group. Instead much male grief was denied rather than shared and faced.[84]

Aberfan and recovery

In 1967 the Medical Officer for Merthyr said he was satisfied that everything was being done that was possible for Aberfan. Colin Murray Parkes, the consultant from the Tavistock Institute in London who was voluntarily supporting the work, said in 1971 that he agreed and accepted that his plan for a team of outside help had been inappropriate.[85] Despite the initial problems, the care on offer did gradually improve and those involved in helping the village felt that in the second year after the disaster there were significant improvements in the village's morale and well being.[86] Yet, at the time, there was perhaps not a full awareness of the long-term consequences of personal tragedies. In some contemporary literature, disasters were even seen as having therapeutic effects including 'frequent cases of remission of pre-existing neurotic and psychosomatic symptoms'.[87] Research into the long-term impact of disasters in the USA and Australia during the 1970s and 80s showed that the long-term psychological consequences can be severe.[88] Survivors of Second World War concentration camps have been known to suffer forty to fifty years of continuous PTSD symptoms.[89] No two disasters are alike, so drawing valid comparisons is difficult. Nonetheless, subsequent research does suggest that long-term effects would be likely at Aberfan.

Fourteen years after the 1972 disaster at Buffalo Creek, 193 survivors were examined. Sixty per cent of the sample suffered from PTSD initially while 28 per cent had the condition fourteen years later, including a number who had not been originally diagnosed.[90] One of the explanations given for this continuing high rate of PTSD was that it took 2–3 years before the disruption to life in the community settled down. There were continuing lawsuits, much of the housing had been destroyed, the community had been broken up and people rehoused in temporary trailer parks that did not reflect pre-existing social groupings. Thus people were separated from the support of their friends and neighbours. Another cause of the long-lasting trauma was that the disaster became a central reference point in the lives of the community's inhabitants.[91]

Aberfan experienced a similar prolonged rupture and constant reminders which was thought to be holding back its recovery.[92] But unlike Buffalo Creek, the structure of the community at Aberfan was preserved and actually strengthened through community activities. Parkes, an external advisor, felt that the community support and development programmes prevented Aberfan from suffering the scale of psychological damage experienced at Buffalo Creek.[93] Today group therapy is regarded as a useful therapeutic exercise for mild to moderately affected victims while professional help is acknowledged as being secondary to the support of friends, family and community.[94] It allows traumas and fears to be listened to and confronted in an understanding and supportive environment. There is a lack of actual controlled evidence on the benefits of various grief and PTSD treatments, but there is a consensus that different forms of social support are important.[95] Communal expressions of grief, such as the annual Aberfan memorial services, can also help cement that social support. At Aberfan, the community groups allowed people to talk through their experiences and emotions and channel their anger into something creative, while the caring work of individuals like Davey and the clergy helped the bereaved come to terms with their losses.[96] Studies of the Three Mile Island accident concluded that while social support networks reinforced the ability of individuals to cope, and minimised the unpleasantness of post-disaster stresses, they did not grant the ability to terminate such problems.[97] This appears true of Aberfan where psychological problems remained in both the short and long term. In 1968, Davey, estimated that there were still thirty-plus families that needed constant care and attention.[98] Later that year, a bereaved mother died of an overdose of barbiturates. In recording an open verdict the coroner noted,

> I have no hesitation or doubt in saying that the Aberfan disaster contrib-
> uted very materially to this woman's death. You can see the picture of her
> lying in bed ill, and the only solace and comfort to her in her illness was
> the photograph of the child she was clutching.[99]

This was an example of the tragic extremes that the disaster's after-math brought. A village GP noted that after the disaster, Aberfan suffered from excessive drinking, stress, disturbed sleep and psycho-logical problems. For people already with health problems their conditions got worse while there was a series of breakdowns in the village for about the next six years.[100] In 1971, a follow up prognosis of those who had claimed compensation classified the recovery of 80 per cent of the adults as 'pretty poor', although 66 per cent of the children were rated good or excellent.[101] The local consultant psychi-atrist noted that year that he was worried that morbidity regarding the disaster was higher in the village than had hitherto been revealed.[102] A local GP believed that at least twenty mothers and fathers died prematurely after the disaster while many other suffered health problems linked to the mental anguish. He felt he was still seeing the effects of the disaster in 1991 and claimed that Aberfan had more prescriptions issued and a higher incidence of illness than other parts of Mid Glamorgan.[103]

Much of this evidence is qualitative rather than quantitative but nonetheless suggests that the long-term psychological impact of the disaster was significant. Much of the suffering may not be strictly de-finable as PTSD since it can not be clearly attributable to the disaster itself. But to the victims such arguments are academic. Of course, not everyone in Aberfan suffered in this way. Individuals varied accord-ing to their personal circumstances but recovery was a slow and gradual process. Yet Davey felt that the villagers grew out of adversity and benefited from the unity that the disaster brought about.[104]

Those taking part in the rescue and welfare operations that follow disasters can also suffer psychological injuries. Today it is generally recommended that workers be debriefed and offered counselling themselves after being involved with a disaster, its survivors and the bereaved.[105] Fourteen police officers, who dealt with the dead and injured inside the terrace pens at Hillsborough, received compensation from South Yorkshire Police, Sheffield Wednesday FC and the club's engineers totalling £1.2 million in an out of court settlement for psychological injuries.[106] In December 1998, the House of Lords overturned similar awards to other officers on the grounds that the claimants had not been in physical danger and that such an award would be unfair when bereaved families had lost their case for compensation for psychological injuries.[107] Nonetheless, it is undeniable that all workers involved can experience severe trauma because of disasters. The Hillsborough police officers who lost their cases for compensation had all been diagnosed as suffering from PTSD.

At Aberfan, approximately 2,500 people were involved in the rescue operation. Many witnessed and took part in the horrific recovery of bodies. Many were digging for the children of friends, family, even their own. Others were less intimately involved, having driven from across the country to help, but sometimes equally vulnerable. The burden on the education authority meant that some teachers had to endure the traumatic experience of entering the junior school on the Monday to try and recover teaching materials.[108] A police officer, who worked at the Mortuary, wrote that he and his colleagues suffered no after effects beyond a few stomach upsets and a general tiredness brought on by the long hours.[109] Nonetheless, the experience for many had a lasting traumatic effect for which, under today's laws, compensation could have been recoverable from the coal board. The press told of grown men crying as they dug. Relatives have told us of rescuers suffering from flashbacks on their deathbeds thirty years later and depression culminating in suicide.

Today, it is standard practice for victims of disasters suffering from PTSD to claim compensation. Claims for psychological damage were not unknown before the classification of PTSD and were referred to as nervous shock. By 1901 courts were willing to award damages for nervous shock where the plaintiff had been in fear of his or her safety.[110] However, medically proving trauma or nervous shock in the majority of cases was extremely difficult before the classification of PTSD. Some children and adults did receive compensation from the coal board for psychological damage in an uncontested out of court settlement. However, given the paucity of knowledge about the long-term effects and the distrust of psychiatrists, the numbers who claimed were small. Had PTSD been classified in 1966, then there is no doubt that more parents and children at Aberfan could have been awarded substantial sums by the coal board.

In 1990, a woman, who had been an eleven-year-old pupil in the adjoining senior school at the time of the disaster, issued a writ against the NCB for psychiatric injury. In around 1978, after having seen a television programme about the disaster, she began to suffer psychiatrically. The plaintiff maintained that, in her treatment, no connection was made between her condition and her experiences as a child. However, the judge rejected this assertion and decided that the plaintiff was in a position then to bring an action. Because she did not issue the writ until 1990 – partly because her symptoms had not been continuous – the court ruled that she could not proceed with her claim. Its reasoning was that the delay would cause significant problems for both sides in adducing and testing the evidence.[111] Thus because it is difficult in court to prove past difficulties, the residents of Aberfan appear to have lost out financially because psychiatric medicine was not as developed in 1966 as it is today.

Colin Murray Parkes wrote in October 1967 that it would be 'utterly wrong' to imply that the local authority had 'failed to provide adequate care'. He went on, 'I think on the contrary that they have done a tremendous lot for the community, and it is only as time passes that it has become possible for us to see where additional help is needed.'[112] As a senior civil servant noted in 1971, mistakes were made but no one had any expertise in the area and it was pointless and perhaps unkind to criticise them.[113] Aberfan was a new experience for the local social and medical services. More advice and support could have been sought elsewhere but other experts too lacked the experience to know how to handle the situation. Parkes admitted that his idea to send in a trained research team to help had been unsuitable. The people of Aberfan had suffered enough without being descended upon by teams of outside experts. Yet without the research component that Parkes' plan would have entailed, lessons were not learnt for the handling of future disasters.

After Aberfan: developments in psycho-social care

Aberfan initiated little change in the way that the psychological effects of disasters were handled. Its lessons were never widely publicised and thus its mistakes remained to be repeated. Before 1988, formal training for disaster support workers was non-existent, nor was the subject covered in the training for UK mental health qualifications.[114] According to two of the leading British practitioners in disaster counselling, the 'longer term psychosocial needs of victims ... has been conspicuously absent from disaster planning in the UK.' Thus at the time of the Bradford fire 'there was no conception of what to do'. However, Bradford proved to be a turning point in establishing the importance of proactive care. Its lessons were passed on from disaster to disaster but it did not lead to the establishment of a clear blueprint for psychological care and support. Nor did the classification of PTSD have any immediate effect on disaster planning. The organiser of the Herald Assistance Unit had never heard of PTSD when he set up the unit.[115] Few of the general practitioners involved at Lockerbie had heard of PTSD either and none had any working knowledge of the condition. Yet once they given material on it by psychologists, it made treating their patients much easier. They were now able to make sense of the symptoms they were seeing. It formalised the way they treated patients and enabled to know what to look for in people they thought might be suffering.[116]

The lack of foresight in planning for the long term care of disaster victims that existed in the mid–1980s was clearly illustrated after the Zeebrugge disaster. Under Dover District Council's emergency plan, the local housing department was responsible for dealing with the aftermath of disasters. The rationale for this was 'Disaster = Homelessness'. Yet it was the counselling and care that could be provided by social services that was in need – and social services were the responsibility of Kent County Council, not Dover District Council. Kent social workers did not travel to Belgium to see survivors for four days and it was another eight days before social services, local health authority, voluntary agencies and Dover council met to discuss the longer term care of survivors and the bereaved. Distrust between social services and the police meant that no database of names and addresses of the deceased, survivors and bereaved was generated for two months. Consequently, it was two and a half months before people were informed of the services available and proactive visiting began. Given the importance of immediate help the whole process was 'painfully slow'.[117]

The spate of disasters that hit Britain in the mid-late 1980s brought practical experience of the needs of disaster victims and developed the awareness of the long term psychological impact of such trauma. Consequently professional support was available in a way that it had not been before Bradford, in theory, dedicated teams of social workers and counsellors, telephone helplines, information leaflets, assistance with the formation of self-help community groups are now standard in the aftermath of disasters. Indeed it is now expected that social workers will be involved in a disaster's aftermath.[118] Many of these techniques were also used at Aberfan but on a smaller scale and only after an initial delay. Today response is quicker and more systematic but still far from perfect. The growing knowledge and understanding of post-disaster psycho-social care has yet to be fully utilised meaning that local authority plans and preparedness vary significantly.

As at Aberfan, lack of funding hampered the efforts of services set up to help disaster victims during the 1980s. For example, the decision to disband the two teams of social workers set up to help the victims of the Zeebrugge disaster was taken on financial rather than clinical grounds.[119] Similarly, the Hillsborough teams covering the Wirral closed prematurely as a result of spending cuts by the local authority.[120] Today disaster planning takes place in an environment of 'a stripped back mental health service'.[121] The funding is not available for dedicated long-term support. The effects of disasters are long-lasting but in practical terms dedicated support cannot continue indefinitely. Thus the phasing out of services must be done gradually, whilst making provision within the pre-existing social services for those who need it.[122] Some form of provision is also important for key points in the long term, such as anniversaries when media coverage can be intense and painful memories triggered. Financial shortcomings need not mean help is unavailable.

A 1998 report on the lessons of disasters stressed the need for co-operation and co-ordination between all the organisations involved.[123] In the past that process has been disrupted by rivalry between the agencies involved. Disasters offer the opportunity for an organisation to demonstrate its abilities in a high-profile forum. Thus situations can arise where different groups even sometimes within a single agency, separately offer their services. The result is that victims are converged on with offers of help. One survivor of the Clapham train crash was subjected to six approaches by different counselling services in a single day. She refused them all.[124] The problem of co-operation at disasters in the 1980s was often made difficult by the geographical dispersion of the victims, particularly in transport disasters. This meant that the social services of several local authorities could be involved with no co-ordination. While some victims were converged on, others in areas outside the disaster scene were sometimes ignored by their local services who were unaware of their needs and the wider situation.[125]

Even when better organised, proactive and early help from social services may not be appropriate or wanted. When social workers visited survivors of Hillsborough in the first week after the disaster they were sometimes seen as intrusive or insensitive.[126] Similarly, and echoing the experience of Aberfan, at Lockerbie there was some local feeling that there was a problem of outside counsellors going around looking for people to counsel rather than just making it known that help was available.[127] This is partly a reflection of the lack of co-ordination between official and voluntary services and the involvement of concerned groups and individuals who lack specific experience in disaster responses. However, the old problems of an antipathy towards the psychiatric and social work professions do remain meaning people are both reluctant to accept help and realise that it would benefit them. At Lockerbie, it was only the need for a medical report in order to claim compensation for psychological injuries that forced some people to see their GP and prevented them from suffering in silence.[128]

The 1980s led to a gradual acceptance of the role of social welfare services in the aftermath of disasters. This was recognised by Government and, in 1989, the Department of Health set up a disasters working party after pressure from voluntary and local authority organisations.[129] No two disasters are alike, making the drawing up of a blueprint for responses difficult. Nonetheless the working party produced two reports, one of which looked at the response of the caring professions and made recommendations on courses of action based upon the lessons of the 1980s. In 1997, the Home Office published a revised edition of its handbook on dealing with disasters. It acknowledged that there will be a need for immediate support for those suffering from the effects of a disaster and that 'social and psychological support services should be set up in the immediate aftermath and will undoubtedly be needed in the longer term'. This represented a significant improvement on the earlier 1992 report which only acknowledged that such services might be 'possibly' needed in the longer term.[130] Research on PTSD appears to be eventually making an impact.

There continues to be a lack of a clear and easily accessible forum through which the lessons of psycho-social care after previous disasters can be adequately learnt.[131] Many are not well documented and the process of communicating often relies too heavily on key individuals and their ability to convey information. The danger of this is that individuals change positions or retire, and that their knowledge is lost.[132] The psychological care outlined in disaster plans continues to vary from local authority to local authority. There is now a statutory requirement for local authorities to plan for civil emergencies but the place of psychological care within them is still only a recommendation. The recommendations of the disasters working party on the response of the caring professions have not been widely implemented.[133] With the absence of any major disaster[134] in Britain from 1990 to 1998, the subject has receded from the public eye. Consequently, local authorities, who are under growing financial pressures, have concentrated on what is statutorily required of them.[135] Changing that may not avoid the long term problems found at Aberfan but it may minimise their possible effects.

Not all disasters have led to widespread long lasting psychic distress nor do all victims suffer to the same degree.[136] However, there is not yet any concrete evidence that the help given actually benefits survivors in the long term.[137] Even in the short term, high levels of trauma are found after disasters where there has been a significant level of counselling at an early stage.[138] As Gist and Lubin have pointed out, 'Psychologists cannot take the pain away or keep it from happening; they can only make it easier to experience and to grow beyond'.[139] Nor has the classification of PTSD necessarily helped prepare social workers and others for the tasks they face in the aftermath of disaster.[140] Thus while the reaction of the caring professions to disasters since Aberfan has improved significantly, the lack of any clear and structured framework for co-operation and the dissemination of knowledge and experience has meant that responses to disasters remain far from perfect while the actual benefits are far from clear.

Some believe that certain counselling techniques can actually hinder the recovery of disaster victims. Clegg claims that it is widely stated that counselling helps people with normal grief but that those with 'abnormal' grief (in other words PTSD) should be treated by professional psychiatrists and psychologists.[141] For one survivor of Clapham, at least, the debriefing he received after the disaster has enabled him to live with the pain but not move on and put it behind him.[142] Similarly, it has been argued that bereavement counselling creates a dependency on 'experts' and undermines traditional community help and responses.[143] The Dunblane shootings exposed some of the fears of both specialists and lay observers. Princess Anne commented that there was a need for 'less counselling' and 'more common sense'. Likewise, Peter Hodgkinson of the Centre for Crisis Psychology commented that the surviving children needed the support and care of those who they knew rather than outside counsellors.[144]

For survivors and the bereaved, disasters are not single happenings but a series of inter-related events that continue to cause trauma. From the immediate aftermath, to the funerals, to the inquiries, the suffering is an on going process. Many of the psychological reactions that can be found in the aftermath of disaster, are not necessarily a reaction to the disaster itself, but also the resultant bereavement, physical dislocation, financial and social problems. At Hillsborough for example, the ongoing legal battles for justice have prevented many families putting the disaster behind them and extended the pain.[145] Some members of Disaster Action have ended up feeling as angry at the systems of inquiry and inquest as they are at the actual deaths. For them 'death is only the beginning of the disaster'.[146] The legal system is thus denying them not only justice but also the ability to achieve some form of closure that would help in their psychological recovery.[147]

The increasing awareness of the need to respond to the trauma that disasters can cause in the medium and long term has perhaps obscured the actual importance of the immediate response to a disaster itself. Davis and Scraton have illustrated how delays and confusion in the processing and identifying of bodies at Hillsborough, Lockerbie, Dunblane and *Marchioness* caused severe distress to bereaved relatives which was a factor in their later trauma. They attribute many of the immediate problems that arise to the conflict of interest brought about by the priority given to the needs of the legal investigation of the circumstances and control of the disaster scene. For example, the bereaved's wish to see the site of the death of their loved one and know all the relevant information can conflict with the police's wish to treat the disaster site as a scene of crime and only release minimal information to avoid hindering their investigations. From the questioning parents at Hillsborough about the drinking habits of the son whose body they had just identified to the removal of the hands of some victims of the *Marchioness* for fingerprinting, the legal concerns of the police and inquests have clearly sometimes been at odds with the needs of the bereaved. The legal investigations and the increased awareness of helping the bereaved in their trauma are undeniably important but, by improving the methods used in dealing with the bodies of their relatives, then some of the causes of the trauma may actually be reduced.[148]

Thus different stressors inter-react with each other causing severe trauma. Because PTSD places the emphasis on the initial event itself, rather than the sequence of events that it triggers, then it fails to fully acknowledge the complexity of determinants in traumatic disorders. But whatever the definitional problems that arise with the concept of PTSD, its classification has at least developed the awareness of the problems that disaster victims suffer and the need to take a proactive stance in helping them. Clear evidence of which methods and techniques work is yet to be found but lessons and experiences are now being communicated between practitioners after different disasters. If this goes even a small way towards easing the pain victims feel than that is an achievement.

Conclusion

From their research on Buffalo Creek, Gleser, Green and Winget list six factors which contribute to the psychopathological impact of disasters.[149] All six are highly applicable to the Aberfan disaster and its aftermath. Using this theoretical framework, the effects of the disaster on the people of Aberfan are likely to have been severe.

1) The extent to which the disaster poses a serious and unexpected life threat to individuals, their friends and family, resulting in existential fears, feelings of powerlessness and vulnerability, and threat of sudden loss.

The Aberfan disaster was sudden, unexpected and a very real life threat to those in the vicinity of the tips.

2) The degree of bereavement suffered by the victims as a result of the disaster.

Again, the sheer scale of the loss of life and the age of so many of the victims made the degree of bereavement severe.

3) Prolongation of physical suffering, life threat, and the lack of normal necessities over an extended period of time, coupled with the impossibility of changing or ameliorating the situation.

The remaining tips were perceived as a threat and the fear of another collapse was very real in Aberfan. The prolonged refusal of the Government and the NCB to agree to complete removal of the tip complex not only extended this period of threat, it also engendered a feeling of helplessness regarding the situation. Even the wreckage of Pantglas School and the destroyed houses had not been cleared away by October 1967.

4) The extent to which the disaster victims must face displacement or changes in their former environment and new modes of living after the disaster.

For some inhabitants there was significant displacement as they were evacuated from the disaster area. However for everyone in the village the disaster brought significant changes to their lives and environment. Not least was the constant media attention and sightseers which left the villagers unable to rebuild their lives in peace.

5) The proportion of a community or group affected by the disaster. Thus, victims who are part of a community that is relatively untouched by the disaster will recover better than victims in isolated groups or communities where almost all the individuals are affected by the disaster.

Aberfan and Merthyr Vale comprise a small, distinct community, which, by British standards, is quite isolated. Pantglas School was the community school, to which every village family sent their children. The loss of 144 lives in a community of 4000 meant that everyone was bereaved, either through family or friends. The impact of this was bound to be profound but at the same time it did at least ensure that the grief was put in the open and not hidden and denied.[150]

6) The cause of the disaster, that is, whether it was natural or manmade. Disasters that are man-made are likely to result in a widespread feeling of having been betrayed by those who were trusted. Such loss of trust can lead to conflicts, recriminations and alienation that lessen the sense of community.

Not only was Aberfan a man-made disaster but it was perpetrated by the dominant local employer, the NCB, an organisation that people had struggled hard to bring into existence. The failures of the long desired nationalised coal board and the local authority meant a widespread feeling of betrayal and anger. The fact that bereaved fathers worked for the NCB in the colliery that created the tip waste must have exacerbated such feelings.

Even without quantitative evidence, the scale and duration of the trauma in Aberfan can be said to have been significant. Only a small proportion of people affected by disaster ever develop full PTSD but a wider acute trauma and grief is often common. The resources to help manage this were swamped as they are at every disaster.[151] Thirty years on, the memories, pain and anger are still there. Incidents, small and large, can trigger off a memory. In Aberfan, memories of the disaster were brought back by news of the Dunblane killings. The parallel of the loss of the children inside their school was

poignant and painful.[152] Aberfan understood the pain of those who
had lost their children that day in a way that few others could. Such
bonds of understanding have been instrumental in the formation of
groups such as Disaster Action and the host of organisations that
help the victims of violent crime. People who have not experienced
such tragedies can not hope to fully understand the pain and trauma
that disasters cause.

Looking back, one psychiatrist involved in 1966 felt that if the
Aberfan disaster were to happen today, the services offered would be
very different but not necessarily any better.[153] Aberfan suffered from
conflict between the agencies helping it and an apparent disregard
from the media and government. Such problems are all too familiar to
victims of the UK disasters of the 1980s.[154] Yet even if this were overcome, and despite the advances in the knowledge about PTSD and
counselling, there is still little conclusive evidence about which techniques actually work or who should administer them. Nonetheless,
the awareness of the need for rapid intervention represents a significant advance. After the 1999 Ladbroke Grove train disaster, counselling services were set up immediately in all the commuter towns where
there were a number of victims: a clear testament to the developing
awareness of the psychological problems that disasters can bring.

There are clear lessons for future disasters from Aberfan. The
value of existing support networks within the community should not
be underestimated or neglected. Professional services can be
swamped by a lack of financial resources and expertise. Yet external
help should be only be brought in carefully and sensitively with full
regard for the wishes and needs of those it is supposed to help. Above
all, government and the media must be aware how their actions after
a disaster impact on the recovery of those they are supposed to serve.

Notes

1 NLW Cyril Moseley Papers, File 2, 'Note', 22 November 1966.
2 For the full definition of PTSD see Appendix.
3 Peter E. Hodgkinson & Michael Stewart, *Coping with Catastrophe: A
  Handbook of Disaster Management* (London: Routledge, 1991), p. 11.
  For a synthesis of the development of the knowledge of trauma in war
  veterans see Judith Lewis Herman, *Trauma and Recovery: From Domestic Abuse to Political Terror* (London: Pandora, 1994), pp. 20-28.
4 Rachel Yehuda & Alexander McFarlane, 'Conflict between Current
  Knowledge about Posttraumatic Stress Disorder and its Original Conceptual Basis', *American Journal of Psychiatry*, 152 (12), 1995.
5 L. N. Robins, 'Steps towards evaluating post-traumatic stress reaction
  as a psychiatric disorder', *Journal of Applied Social Psychology*, 20,

1990, 1674-1677. It can be argued that diagnostic tools for PTSD are subject to a Western bias and thus not always appropriate in different cultural contexts.

6 Gerald C. Davison & John M. Neale, *Abnormal Psychology* (New York: John Wiley, 7th edn, 1997), p. 147.

7 Margaret Mitchell, 'The Role of the General Practitioner in the Aftermath of the Lockerbie Disaster' in Tim Newburn (ed.), *Working with Disaster: Social Welfare Interventions during and after Tragedy* (London: Longman, 1993), p. 92.

8 Personal knowledge.

9 David L. Rosenhan & Martin E. P. Seligman, *Abnormal Psychology* (New York: W. W. Norton, 3rd edn. 1995), p. 237.

10 For a summary of thinking on the syndrome see Martha Wolfenstein, *Disaster: A Psychological Essay* (Glencoe: The Free Press, 1957).

11 Richard I. Shader & Alice J. Schwartz, 'Management of Reactions to Disaster', *Social Work*, vol. 11, no. 2, April, 1966, pp. 102-104. Letter from Prof. Richard Mayou to IM, 1 March 1999.

12 Letter from Richard Mayou to IM.

13 The only comparable British disaster was in 1883 when 190 children were killed in a crush in a Sunderland theatre. See Michael Wynn Jones, *Deadline Disaster: A Newspaper History* (Newton Abbot: David & Charles, 1976), pp. 20-21

14 Jane Littlewood, *Aspects of Grief: Bereavement in Adulthood* (London: Routledge, 1992), p. 143. The Disasters Working Party, *Disasters: Planning for a Caring Response, Part One: The Main Report* (London: HMSO, 1991), p. 5. Also see Charles B. Wilkinson & Enrique Vera, 'Clinical Responses to Disaster: Assessment, Management and Treatment' in Gist & Lubin (eds.) *Psychosocial Aspects of Disaster*, pp. 240-241. Yehuda & McFarlane, 'Conflict between Current Knowledge about Posttraumatic Stress Disorder and its Original Conceptual Basis'. Shader & Schwartz, 'Management of Reactions to Disaster', p. 102.

15 See letter from David T. Maclay, *British Medical Journal*, 29 October 1966, p. 1075.

16 R. Bevan to Chairman, Welsh Board of Health, 9 November 1966. PRO: MH 96/2179.

17 Letter from Richard Mayou to IM.

18 NLW Cyril Moseley Papers, File 2, 'Note', 22 November 1966.

19 James M. Cuthill, *The Aberfan Disaster – A Study of the Survivors*, Unpublished paper, p. 5.

20 Ibid, pp. 5, 10.

21 See Hodgkinson & Stewart, *Coping with Catastrophe*, p. 104.

22 Madgwick, *Aberfan*, p. 45. Madgwick wrote this book as a 12-year-old child in 1970.

23 *The Times*, 12 October 1971. Although for those who did receive help, the fact that it was from someone beyond the local community appeared to alleviate some concerns. Interview between MJ and Dr J. M. Cuthill, 20 April 1999.

24 Cuthill interview.

25 Miller, *Aberfan*, p. 63.

26 A. Gray to A. Owen, 6 November 1967. PRO: MH 96/2179.

27 R. Bevan to Chairman, Welsh Board of Health, 9 November 1966. PRO: MH 96/2179. *The Times*, 12 October 1971.
28 F. Williams to Lady Traherne, 10 November 1966. R. Bevan to Chairman, Welsh Board of Health, 9 November 1966. PRO: MH 96/2179.
29 Letter from Dr H. L. English, Morgannwg Hospital, Bridgend, *British Medical Journal*, 19 November 1966, p. 1266.
30 Gaynor N. Lacey, 'Observations on Aberfan', *Journal of Psychosomatic Research*, vol. 16, 1972, p. 258; *The Times*, 12 October 1971; A. Gray to A. Owen, 6 November 1967. PRO: MH 96/2179. Also see Austin, *Aberfan*, p. 181.
31 *The Times*, 12 October 1971.
32 Lacey, 'Observations on Aberfan', p. 259.
33 A. Owen to J. W. M. Siberry, 15 November 1967. G. Prys Davies to James Griffiths, 22 November 1971. PRO: MH 96/2179.
34 Parkes interview. See the discussion of the Institute's plans in the Welsh Board of Health records. PRO: MH 96/2719.
35 R. Bevan to A. Owen, 7 December 1971. PRO: MH 96/2179.
36 Cuthill, *The Aberfan Disaster*, p. 11.
37 Cuthill interview. Detailed notes of discussion with Dr Cuthill, 6 December 1968.
38 Cuthill, *The Aberfan Disaster*, p. 11. G. Prys Davies to J. Griffiths, 22 November 1971; A. Jones to A. Owen, 25 November 1966. PRO: MH 96/2179. Parkes interview.
39 Detailed notes of discussion with Dr Cuthill at the meeting held on 6th December 1968. Aberfan Disaster Fund Management Committee minutes. GRO: D/D X295/12/1/3.
40 William Yule, 'The Effect of Disasters on Children', *Bereavement Care*, vol. 9, no. 2, Spring 1990, pp. 2-3, 4. Knowledge about PTSD in children is still underdeveloped. One child survivor at Aberfan noted her inability to speak to her parents about the disaster, Gaynor Madgwick quoted in *Daily Mail Weekend*, 5 October 1996. A study of 13 surviving children from the *Herald of Free Enterprise* disaster concluded than more than half had suffered from PTSD. *The Times*, 1 September 1988.
41 Parkes interview.
42 Cuthill interview. G. Prys Davies to J. Griffiths, 22 November 1971. PRO: MH 96/2719.
43 *The Times*, 12 October 1971.
44 The Disasters Working Party, *Disasters: Planning for a Caring Response, Part One: The Main Report* (London: HMSO, 1991), p. 5.
45 The Council of Social Service for Wales and Monmouthshire, Citizen's Advice Bureaux, Department Participation in Aberfan Information Centre, Report January 1967. PRO: MH96/2179.
46 E. Lewis to A. Owen, 9 November 1967. PRO: MH 96/2719.
47 Miller, *Aberfan*, p. 88. Welsh Board of Health Memo, E. Lewis, 6 January 1967. PRO: MH 96/2179.
48 Miller, *Aberfan*, pp. 92-93. Audrey Davey interview, SWCC: AUD/524. Davey also had to cope with opposition to her appointment from members of the children's department in the Merthyr Council. E. Lewis to A. Owen, 9 November 1967. PRO: MH 96/2719. That Davey was Welsh, a consideration in her appointment, seems to have helped her in winning the confidence of Aberfan. Parkes interview.

Aberfan, Wales – 21 October 1966 – 144 killed

© The Western Mail

1.

2.

3.

4.

5.

6. Prime Minister Harold Wilson (centre), Secretary of State for Wales George Thomas (right) and Cledwyn Hughes MP (left) visit Aberfan. © The Western Mail

Ibrox, Glasgow - 2 January 1971 – 66 killed

Zeebrugge, Belgium - 6 March 1987 - 193 killed

Piper Alpha, Scotland – 6 July 1988 – 160 killed

Hillsborough, Sheffield – 15 April 1989 – 96 killed

49 *The Times*, 12 October 1971.
50 Confidential note 're Miss Audrey Davey' sent by Bishop to Llandaff to Sir Cennydd Traherne, 13 March 1968. In Diocese of Llandaff papers, box 6, NLW.
51 Parkes interview. Some of the non-bereaved in Aberfan did feel that they had not been offered enough support or advice on how to cope with their trauma. After Aberfan and other disasters, some survivors did feel isolated and as if their trauma was not seen as important or valid as that of the bereaved. Mention is sometimes made of a 'hierarchy of grief'. For such problems after Hillsborough see Simon Hattenstone & Tom O'Sullivan, 'Those who were left behind', *The Guardian Weekend*, 8 May 1999, 23-30.
52 A. Gray to A. Owen, 6 November 1967 PRO: MH 96/2719.
53 G. Prys Davies to J. Griffiths, 22 November 1971. PRO: MH 96/2719.
54 *The Times*, 12 October 1971. English to Bevan, 22 March 1968. PRO: MH 96/2719. Lacey, 'Observations on Aberfan', p. 260.
55 Lacey, 'Observations on Aberfan', p. 259.
56 Kai T. Erikson, *In the Wake of the Flood* (London: George Allen & Unwin, 1979).
57 *The Times*, 12 October 1971.
58 SWCC interviews.
59 See for example interviews in *Daily Mail Weekend*, 5 October 1996.
60 Outlining that extreme feelings are normal responses to traumatic situations continues to be a cornerstone of post-disaster counselling today. Such information is now usually conveyed quickly through the distribution of appropriate leaflets to those people affected.
61 This account of the work of Tŷ Toronto and the Way Ahead conference is derived from Erastus Jones, 'Working in Aberfan and the Valleys', *Social and Economic Administration*, 9 (1), 1975. Quote at p. 34. Cf Parkes interview.
62 Paul H. Ballard & Erastus Jones (eds.), *The Valleys Call: A Self-Examination by People of the South Wales Valleys during the 'Year of the Valleys,' 1974* (Ferndale: Ron Jones Publications, 1974), p. 15.
63 *First Report of the Aberfan Disaster Fund Management Committee*, p. 4.
64 Elaine Richards interview, SWCC: AUD 519.
65 Hodgkinson & Stewart, *Coping with Catastrophe*, pp. 116-117.
66 Detailed notes of discussion with Dr Cuthill at the meeting held on 6th December 1968. Aberfan Disaster Fund Management Committee minutes. GRO: D/D X295/12/1/3.
67 Rev. K. Hayes to H. Wilson, 29 January 1968, PRO BD 11/3791 PM's papers after Aberfan Disaster.
68 R. E. Kendell & A. K. Zealley (eds.), *Companion to Psychiatric Studies* (Edinburgh: Churchill Livingstone, 1993, 5th edn.), p. 518.
69 Kendell & Zealley (eds.), *Companion to Psychiatric Studies*, p. 519.
70 Miller, *Aberfan*, p. 89.
71 Lacey, 'Observations on Aberfan', p. 258.
72 Arthur Jones quoted in Doel & Dunkerton, *Is it still raining in Aberfan?*, p. 49.
73 PRO BD 11/3804. Meeting with Aberfan Deputation at Welsh Office, London, 7 February 1968.

74 Davey interview, SWCC: AUD/524. Lacey, 'Observations on Aberfan', pp. 257-258. The insensitive, and sometimes inaccurate, attention of the media has been a problem for many victims of violent crimes and disasters, most notably after the Hillsborough disaster. For a survey of the impact of the media upon survivors of violent crime and disaster see Ann Shearer, *Survivors and the Media* (London: Broadcasting Standards Council, 1991).

75 Kenneth Hayes interview, SWCC: AUD/528.

76 P. L Marshall to B. H. Evans, 1 September 1967. PRO: BD 11/3809. The false stories were not published.

77 Audrey Davey interview, SWCC: AUD/524.

78 P. L. Marshall to B. H. Evans, 1 September 1967. PRO: BD 11/3809.

79 Siberry to Town Clerk, 9 October 1967. PRO: BD 11/3809.

80 Miller, *Aberfan*, p. 93.

81 Hodgkinson & Stewart, *Coping with Catastrophe*, p. 21.

82 Audrey Davey interview. SWCC: AUD/524. Gerald Kirwan quoted in *Daily Mail*, Weekend, 5 October 1996, p. 12. There was a similar reluctance amongst male survivors of Hillsborough and older males in Lockerbie to seek help. Tim Newburn, *Making a Difference? Social Work after Hillsborough* (London: National Institute for Social Work, 1993), p. 50. Margaret Mitchell, 'The Role of the General Practitioner in the Aftermath of the Lockerbie Disaster' in Newburn (ed.), *Working with Disaster*, p. 90.

83 H. L. English to A. Bevan, 22 March 1968; C. M. Parkes to L. Abse, 24 October 1967. PRO: MH 96/2719.

84 Miller, *Aberfan*, pp. 90, 94. Parkes interview.

85 *The Times*, 12 October 1971.

86 Parkes interview.

87 Fritz, 'Disasters', p. 206.

88 Disasters Working Party, *Disasters: Planning for a Caring Response, Part One: The Main Report* (London: HMSO, 1989), p. 5. Also see Beverley Raphael, *When Disaster Srikes: A Handbook for the Caring Professions* (London: Unwin Hymen, 1990 edn.), ch. 8.

89 Kendell & Zealley (eds.), *Companion to Psychiatric Studies*, p. 519.

90 Rosenhan & Seligman, *Abnormal Psychology*, p. 241. Bonnie L. Green, Jacob D. Lindy, Mary C. Grace, Goldine C. Gleser, Anthony C. Leonard, Mindy Korol & Carolyn Winget, 'Buffalo Creek Survivors in the Second Decade: Stability of Stress Symptoms', *American Journal of Orthopsychiatry*, vol. 60, no. 1, January 1990, 43-54.

91 Bonnie L. Green, Mary C. Grace, Jacob D. Lindy, Goldine C. Gleser, Anthony C. Leonard & Teresa L. Kramer, 'Buffalo Creek Survivors in the Second Decade: Comparison with Unexposed and Nonlitigant Groups', *Journal of Social Applied Psychology*, vol. 20, no. 13, August 1990, p. 1046. Also see Erikson, *In the Wake of the Flood*.

92 Detailed notes of discussion with Dr Cuthill at the meeting held on 6th December 1968. Aberfan Disaster Fund Management Committee minutes. GRO: D/D X295/12/1/3.

93 C. M. Parkes, 'Planning for the Aftermath', *Journal of the Royal Society of Medicine*, vol. 84, January 1991, p. 22 & preface & conclusion in Erikson, *In the Wake of the Flood*.

94 Disasters Working Party, *Disasters: Planning for a Caring Response*, p. 3.

95 Davison & Neale, *Abnormal Psychology*, pp. 151-152.
96 The channelling of anger was something identified by Parkes in his plans for community development aided by a team of outside experts. C. M. Parkes to Leo Abse, 24 October 1967. PRO: MH 96/2719. Cf Parkes interview.
97 Hodgkinson & Stewart, *Coping with Catastrophe*, p. 58.
98 Bishop of Llandaff to Sir Cennydd Traherne, 'Re Miss Audrey Davey - Confidential note', 13 March 1968. In Diocese of Llandaff papers, box 6, NLW.
99 *Merthyr Express*, 10 October 1968.
100 Arthur Jones, Aberfan GP in Doel & Dunkerton, *Is it still raining in Aberfan?*, pp.49-50.
101 *The Times*, 12 October 1971.
102 G. Prys Davies to J. Griffiths, 22 November 1971. PRO: MH 96/2179.
103 Arthur Jones in *Campaign Merthyr/Cynon Valley*, 8 November 1991 p. 1.
104 Davey interview SWCC.
105 Hodgkinson & Stewart, *Coping with Catastrophe*, ch. 7.
106 Simon Allen, 'Rescuers and Employees – Primary Victims of Nervous Shock', *New Law Journal*, 7 February 1997, 158-159.
107 *The Times*, 4 December 1998. *The Guardian*, 4 December 1998.
108 Interview between MJ and Hugh Watkins, 8 April 1999.
109 Charles Nunn, 'The Disaster of Aberfan', *Police Review*, 16 October 1987, p. 2071.
110 Shyamala Rajan-Vince, 'Nervous Shock!', LAWTEL, document no. 0981210. www.lawtel.co.uk.
111 Crocker v British Coal Corporation, *The Times*, 5 July 1995. [1996] JPIL Issue 1/96. LAWTEL, Document no. C0002592. www.lawtel.co.uk
112 C. M. Parkes to Leo Abse, 24 October 1967. PRO: MH 96/2179.
113 R. Bevan to A. Owen, 7 December 1971. PRO: MH 96/2179.
114 Hodgkinson & Stewart, *Coping with Catastrophe*, p. 205.
115 Hodgkinson & Stewart, *Coping with Catastrophe*, p. 77. Personal communication, Peter Hodgkinson to MJ, 20 November 1998.
116 Margaret Mitchell, 'The Role of the General Practitioner in the Aftermath of the Lockerbie Disaster' in Newburn (ed.), *Working with Disaster*, pp. 86, 90.
117 Hodgkinson & Stewart, *Coping with Catastrophe*, pp. 82-83.
118 Tim Newburn, 'Conclusion: Caring after Tragedy', in Christine Mead (ed.), *Journeys of Discovery: Creative Learning from Disasters* (London: National Institute for Social Work, 1996), p. 90.
119 Hodgkinson & Stewart, *Coping with Catastrophe*, p. 85.
120 Newburn, *Making a Difference?* p. 8.
121 Peter Hodgkinson, personal communication.
122 See Parkes, 'Planning for the Aftermath', p. 24.
123 Chris Llewelyn, *Learning Lessons from Disasters* (Cardiff: Welsh Consumer Council, 1998), p. 27.
124 This section is derived from Hodgkinson & Stewart, *Coping with Catastrophe*, pp. 85-86.
125 Janet Johnston with Liz Beeson, 'Social work in the aftermath of the Zeebrugge Ferry Disaster', in Newburn (ed.), *Working with Tragedy*.

126 Newburn, *Making a Difference?*, p. 8.
127 *The Scotsman*, 15 March 1996. Hints of such approach at Aberfan can be seen in Edward England, *The Mountain that Moved* (London: Hodder & Stroughton, 1967).
128 Mitchell, 'Role of the General Practitioner', p. 86.
129 Disasters Working Party, *Disasters: Planning for a Caring Response.*
130 Home Office, *Dealing with Disaster* (London: HMSO, 1992 & 1997 edns), paras. 3.25 & 4.25 respectively.
131 This is being addressed by the Emergency Planning Society, who plan to tour local authorities in 1999-2000 offering guidance on disaster plans. There are also attempts in academia to facilitate such knowledge-sharing through study groups and training programmes for practitioners and others.
132 Chris Llewelyn, *Learning Lessons from Disasters* (Cardiff: Welsh Consumer Council, 1998), pp. 27-28. For an example of the process of individuals voluntarily conveying their experience to those handling other disasters see David Whitham & Tim Newburn, *Coping with Tragedy: Managing the Responses to Two Disasters* (Nottingham: Nottinghamshire County Council, 1992), pp. 23-24.
133 Parkes interview.
134 In the sense in which we define 'disaster' in Chapter 4
135 Peter Hodgkinson, personal communication.
136 Goldine C. Gleser, Bonnie L. Green & Carolyn N. Winget, *Prolonged Psychosocial Effects of Disaster: A Study of Buffalo Creek* (New York: Academic Press, 1981), p. 139.
137 Kendell & Zealley (eds.), *Companion to Psychiatric Studies*, p. 519. Also see Disasters Working Party, *Disasters: Planning for a Caring Response.*
138 Although the help on offer is not aided by the fact that some counsellors feel ill-equipped to deal with disasters. See Howard Davis & Phil Scraton, *Beyond Disaster: Identifying and resolving Inter-agency Conflict in the Immediate Aftermath of Disasters*, A Research Report for the Home Office Emergency Planning Division, 1997, p. 44.
139 Richard Gist & Bernard Lubin, 'Implications for Research and Practice', in Gist & Lubin (eds.) *Psychosocial Aspects of Disaster*, p. 342.
140 Newburn (ed.) *Working with Disaster*, p. 4.
141 Francis Clegg, 'Disasters: Can Psychologists help the Survivors?', *Psychologist*, April 1988, p. 134.
142 Personal knowledge.
143 For a summary of such arguments see Davies & Scraton, *Beyond Disaster*, p. 34.
144 *The Independent*, 18 March 1996. Rita Carter, ' "The last thing young children need is to be confronted by strangers': why the professional counsellors must approach with caution", *The Times*, 14 March 1996.
145 *Hillsborough: The Legacy*, BCC1, 11 April 1999. Hilary Arnott, 'Justice: Hillsborough's final victim', *Legal Action*, April 1992, p. 8.
146 Eyre, 'More than PTSD'.
147 It is important to note however that the clinical link between injustice and continuing trauma is not always conclusive. See Michael J. Soloman & James Thompson, 'Anger and Blame in Three Technological Disasters', *Stress Medicine*, vol. 11, 1995, 199-206.

148 Howard Davis & Phil Scraton, 'Failing the Bereaved: Inter-Agency Relationships in the Immediate Aftermath of Disaster' in *Picking Up the Pieces: Report of a Multi-Agency Workshop to develop Post-Major Incident Psycho-Social Support Plans* (Bedford: Bedfordshire County Council, 1996) & *Beyond Disaster*. Such conflicts between the needs of the bereaved and the medico-legal system are acknowledged in the Home Office document *Dealing with Disaster*.

149 Gleser, Green & Winget, *Prolonged Psychosocial Effects of Disaster*, pp. 148-149.

150 Parkes interview. In this sense Aberfan was very different to most other disasters.

151 Parkes interview.

152 For example, see the comments of people from Aberfan in *The Times*, 14 March 1996.

153 Cuthill interview.

154 Davis & Scraton, *Beyond Disaster* & 'Failing the Bereaved: Inter-Agency Relationships in the Immediate Aftermath of Disaster'.

Chapter Six

REGULATING GIFTS OF GENEROSITY:
DISASTER FUNDS

[B]efore any payment was made each case should be reviewed to ascertain whether the parents had been close to their children and were thus likely to be suffering mentally.[1]

Since the nineteenth century, relief funds have been a common response to disasters. Yet they are fraught with potential problems that can further distress those whom they are designed to help. The administration of funds is restricted by the legal and social norms of the day. This is not always conducive to a harmonious and smooth distribution.

The problems that courted relief funds in the nineteenth and early twentieth centuries can be illustrated by reference to the Senghennydd disaster of 1913 in which 439 miners were killed – the highest death toll for a mining accident in British history. A public appeal was quickly launched which raised over £126,000 (just over £8 million in £1999). It received donations from royalty, the colliery owners and the general public. Yet despite this generosity, payments from the fund were carefully limited and distributed in small but regular sums in order to assure recipients were not lifted beyond their previous station in life. This practice was also determined by fears that working class widows would not be able to manage large lump sums. Widows thus received weekly payments of between 3 and 10 shillings each with a further five shillings for each dependent child.[2] Charity law limited payments to relieving need but contemporary interpretations of need nonetheless remained narrow even in such tragic circumstances. The result of distributing funds in such small instalments was that the funds had long active lives. The Senghennydd fund was not wound up until 1952, 39 years after the disaster. Funds set up to help those bereaved in the *Titanic* disaster were still operating in the 1990s.

Paying out sums in small instalments also allowed a measure of scrutiny of over the beneficiaries. Two weeks after the Senghennydd disaster, a meeting of Caerphilly District Council heard:

> Mr Mark Harding said he had seen the grocery bill of a person who had received a grant of 10s., and this bill included a quarter of a pound of tobacco, two pounds of bacon at 1s. 3d., butter at 10d. a pot. He did not think these were necessary things.[3]

Like many state and local welfare payments of the day,[4] payments were also subject to a character test. Some beneficiaries of the fund later had their payments stopped for such 'immoral' behaviour as giving birth to an illegitimate child.[5] Disaster funds may have represented the public sympathy for the bereaved but there was both social and legal reluctance to see people enriched by their tragic losses, particularly if they were thought to be behaving beyond the realms of respectability.

Overseeing the running of charitable disaster funds was the Charity Commission. The Charity Commission has regulated charities in England and Wales since 1853. Its role before the Second World War was very much a distant one with little practical intervention in the operation of charities. In 1960, the Charity Commission had its duties revised and laid down in the Charities Act of that year. 'By the act the powers of the commission were strengthened with the general purpose of promoting the effective use of charitable monies'.[6] In 1974, the first year for which the *Civil Service Yearbook* prints the mission statements of Government departments and agencies, that for the Charity Commission states, 'The general functions of the Charity Commissioners include maintaining a register of charities in England and Wales, protecting the endowment of charities by controlling disposals of permanent endowment, advising trustees, and providing the services of an Official Custodian of Charities.'[7] By 1999, this has evolved to: 'The Charity Commission is here to give the public confidence in the integrity of charities'.[8]

None of these statements, except perhaps the last, clarifies in whose interest the Charity Commission operates. Three identifiable groups require protection: donors, beneficiaries, and the general public. The first and second need to be assured that money raised charitably is spent as donors want it to be on the appropriate beneficiaries. There is a public interest in preventing fraud and in ensuring that charitable tax advantages go only to organisations that deserve it. It is thus the role of the Charity Commission to protect the interests of these groups within the constraints of the law.

This chapter examines the regulation of the Aberfan Disaster Fund by the Charity Commission in the years 1966–69.[9] We show that the Commission protected neither donors nor beneficiaries. It was caught between upholding an outdated and inflexible law that had its origins in the Statute of Charitable Uses 1601, and fulfilling the varied expectations of donors, beneficiaries and the fund's management committee. The process and outcome were unsatisfactory, and even upsetting, to all concerned.[10]

The origins of the Aberfan Disaster Fund

The Mayor of Merthyr, Stanley Davies, issued an appeal on the evening of the disaster for money to help relieve and rehabilitate the village. He was later to recollect that immediately after the disaster he had no specific ideas as to how the money was to be used, beyond that it was 'to help the people of Aberfan generally including the children and anybody else who needed help'.[11] The Mayor's fund quickly raised a total of £1.75 million (worth about £18.64 million at 1999 prices).

As soon as money from the public started to flood into the Aberfan fund, all the lawyers involved realised that it was important to avoid the problems that had arisen after some other disasters, including the 1951 Gillingham bus crash and the 1952 Lynmouth floods. If the disaster fund were constituted as a charity, then it would be difficult or impossible for the village to be represented on the management committee of the fund. Every inhabitant of Aberfan was a potential beneficiary, and therefore *prima facie* ineligible to be a trustee. Also, charity law would restrict the objects that the fund could be spent on, specifically excluding straightforward cash handouts except as required to relieve 'need'. This raised the possibility of a substantial surplus. For the fund to remain charitable in law, the trust deed would have to specify that any surplus would be used for the public benefit. The Gillingham trustees had been forced to try to trace donors and give them back their money, because, after having spent all that was possible on the primary objects of the fund, the secondary terms of the appeal were not deemed exclusively charitable.[12]

Since the initial Aberfan appeal had been made without clear objectives, there was no single and specific intention amongst donors while the sheer number of Aberfan gifts made a later consultation impossible. (About 50,000 letters accompanying donations survive, and there were approximately 88,000 donations altogether). Yet it was obvious that many of the donors saw their gifts as charitable. The Charity Commission had warned in its 1965 Annual Report that disaster funds were not automatically charitable. But if the Aberfan Disaster Fund were not to be a charity, it would be subject to taxation. As Chesterman has pointed out, Aberfan illustrated that 'charitable status does not automatically follow even where the element of altruism is entirely "pure" and spontaneous... [T]he law had to distort the intentions of many of the donors to make them fit the mould of legal charity'.[13]

It took some time for the Trust Deed to be drafted, and all the while the money was pouring in. In November 1966, the Charity Commissioners discussed Aberfan for the first time. They were concerned that no objects had been stated when the Mayor of Merthyr made his appeal, and that it was essential to find out the trusts on which the fund was now held.[14] That month, an assistant commissioner met with the Mayor of Merthyr and the fund's provisional committee to advise on the terms of a draft deed which had been drawn up by an eminent QC.[15]

The Deed as finally drafted gives the purpose of the charity:

The Fund as to both capital and income shall be applicable at the discretion of the Management Committee:

(1) For the relief of all persons who have suffered as a result of the said disaster and are thereby in need; and

(2) Subject as aforesaid for any charitable purpose for the benefit of persons who were inhabitants of Aberfan and its immediate neighbourhood (hereinafter called 'the area of benefit') on 21 October 1966 or who now are or hereafter become inhabitants of the area of benefit and in particular (but without prejudice to the generality of the last foregoing trust) for any charitable purpose for the benefit of children who were on 21 October 1966 or who now are or hereafter may become resident in the area of benefit.

Following a (probably planted) parliamentary question,[16] the Commission corresponded with the Treasury on how to ensure that disaster funds were properly set up and run. The Treasury had drafted a brief circular to be sent to other government departments drawing attention to the powers and experience of the Charity Commission.[17] For the next 18 months, the Commission took a close and sometimes threatening interest in whether gifts to individuals or work at the Aberfan cemetery were consistent with the charitable purpose of the Trust. However, their surviving records reveal no discussion of whether a donation to remove the tips was consistent with its charitable purposes.[18]

The Fund and the Charity Commission

On 7 July 1967, the Commission heard that the Fund was proposing to spend around £40,000 on providing a memorial at Aberfan cemetery to take the form of a series of arches and pillars surrounding the area in the cemetery where the children who died in the disaster are buried. They were alarmed that it had apparently not occurred to the trustees that the provision of a memorial of this sort might not be charitable or within the trusts. This fund, they said, was very much in the public eye and the proposal to erect a monument might be a target for criticism. It was therefore important to make sure that, in accordance with the trust deed and the law, the money was used for charitable purposes which were also for the benefit of inhabitants of Aberfan.

The Commissioners discussed the problem at length. They reasoned that it was doubtful whether the provision of a memorial was in itself a charitable purpose. However maintaining or beautifying a burial ground would be a charitable purpose even when the cemetery was owned by the local authority, as the Aberfan cemetery is. If therefore the proposed colonnade improved or beautified the cemetery, its provision would be charitable, the fact that it also served as a memorial would be incidental. The cemetery was close to and could be seen from Aberfan so that improving or beautifying the cemetery would be for the benefit of the inhabitants.[19]

By this (it might be thought) tortuous reasoning, the Commission brought itself to approve the memorial, which was duly built and still stands. The question of payments to survivors was more intractable. The first report of the disaster fund's management committee noted that 'bereaved parents were desirous of receiving major cash benefits without delay and simply as a class irrespective of other conditions.' The bereaved parents felt that the money had been donated to relieve their situation and thus should be distributed accordingly.[20] However any payments to the bereaved as a class, regardless of need, would have gone against the terms of the trust deed and charity law. Suggestions by the management committee that, in making payments, it distinguish between families on the grounds of need met with 'resistance en bloc'. The families were united in their grief and became more so upon any proposition that individuals be treated differently. Meanwhile, the deliberations were causing considerable anxiety in Aberfan about the management committee's intentions. Thus the committee concluded that it could well be 'disastrous' to follow the obvious interpretation of charity law and distribute funds according to need.[21]

The words 'in need' had added resonance in the South Wales coalfield. The 1930s had witnessed whole communities – men, women, and children – taking to the streets in protest against the means test which strictly governed unemployment benefit according to families' financial resources.[22] A deep-rooted tradition in South Wales and other working-class areas regarded means-tested payments as humiliating and degrading. This helps to explain why the rhetoric of the post-war welfare state was built on the principle of universality not need. Any suggestion of having to go cap-in-hand asking for money would find scant support anywhere in the south Wales valleys. As one bereaved mother remembered, going to the fund to ask for money was almost like begging. The first secretary/treasurer of the fund was a former officer from a social security office. This was not how the bereaved families envisaged the fund. The Aberfan Parents' and Residents' Association had expressed concern about the words 'in need' being in the trust deed when it was being drawn up. However, their solicitors told them that this was necessary if the fund was to be charitable.[23] Although the presence of this wording in the trust deed annoyed local people and caused problems in the fund's distribution, it was a requirement of charity law and thus the Charity Commission had little option but to enforce it.

In July 1967 the management committee met the Charity Commission to discuss the situation. At first the commissioners expressed the view that any major cash grant to the bereaved, irrespective of need, would be contrary to the terms of the trust deed. Upon discussion, they recognised what they called the 'unprecedented emotional state' of Aberfan and advised that the fund could pay £500 to each set of bereaved parents because of the 'devastating effect of the disaster upon all the people concerned and the intense and mounting state of emotion which had resulted from it'.[24]

A lawyer member of the management committee sought the advice of the Attorney General on the upper limit for payments from the fund. Elwyn Jones, the Attorney-General, reportedly said 'the law was the law'. However the parents and the management committee were not prepared to accept this and both wanted a higher payment.[25] The parents understandably sought a significant payment in recognition of their bereavement. This was not to be compensation for the loss of their children – no financial sum could

provide that – but rather an acknowledgement that money had been
donated to the fund in sympathy for the deaths of their children.[26]
Alun Talfan Davies QC, vice-chairman of the management
committee, drafted a memorandum outlining the reasons for making
a payment of £5,000 rather than £500. The committee argued that the
sum was to relieve mental stress and strain rather than compensate
the parents for their losses. £5,000 would allow parents wishing to
move away from Aberfan to do so while giving a new start to those
who wished to stay.[27] In September 1967, W. E. A. Lewis OBE, one
of the Commissioners, and an Assistant Commissioner attended a
meeting of the disaster fund management committee where the memorandum was discussed. There was a 'great deal of argument' and the
commissioners were told that grants of £5000 would be made
whether they liked it or not.[28] The Commission conceded that the
payments were permissible but gave apparently conflicting advice on
the methods that should be followed. They said that all the bereaved
should be treated alike (which was what the management committee
wanted to do) in that all should receive the same sum, but also that

> before any payment was made each case should be reviewed to ascertain
> whether the parents had been close to their children and were thus likely
> to be suffering mentally.[29]

This would imply that parents who were found, on examination, not
to have been close to their children would not be allowed to benefit.
Perhaps fortunately, this advice was not taken. At this meeting, the
Aberfan representatives resigned from the committee in order to
avoid being both trustees and beneficiaries with the intention that
they or other local people should be re-elected after the fund had paid
out individual grants. The remaining trustees then agreed the
bereaved parents who had lost children 'and are thereby in distress'
should receive £5000 per family. The policy of making flat-rate
grants to each family avoided any finding that some bereaved
parents were not thereby in distress.

In November 1967 the management committee met a deputation
of parents whose children had not been physically injured. They
reported that their children were afraid of the dark and loud noises,
and that many of them would not sleep alone. Even if they seemed
normal at school, their parents had noticed many differences from
their previous behaviour at home. The committee discussed whether
these children and their parents were eligible for payments from the
fund. One trustee said that he felt that all children who were mentally
injured should make compensation claims from the coal board.[30]

The committee nevertheless considered making payments to all the physically uninjured children and the Charity Commission were again consulted. The secretary/treasurer presented the case for payments to the uninjured children and their parents as a class but Commissioner Lewis stated that such payments would be 'quite illegal' and if made the Commission would have to intervene. This was reported at the next meeting of the management committee to the dismay of the chairman, Stanley Davies, who had founded the fund. He stated that it had been his intention for the money to help the people of Aberfan generally and that he did not like the obstacles being put in the way. He did not want a repeat of the Senghennydd and Lynmouth funds and in many ways he now wished that the fund had not been made into a charity and felt that the people of Aberfan would not accept the Commission's decision.[31] Another trustee remembered dealings with the Commission as a battle, recalling the Commissioners as 'interested in legal matters, not justice... acting like lords'.[32]

A meeting of the other Commissioners agreed that the grants proposed would not be charitable. 'The grants made to the parents who had been bereaved were very close to the borderline'. If the management committee ignored this ruling, the Commission considered whether it would refer the matter to the Attorney General with a view to making the members of the management committee refund the amount misapplied, to remove the present committee members from office or to order the charity's bankers not to pay the cheques. They were reasonably certain that if the management committee decided to make such grants that someone on the committee would inform the commissioners immediately.[33]

Confrontation was averted, however. At the next meeting of the Commissioners, Lewis reported that the management committee had not pressed very hard for authority to make grants to the parents of uninjured children, that the deputation had listened 'very reasonably' to what he had to say and had asked him to confirm it in writing.[34]

The committee did receive legal advice that payments to the physically uninjured children were probably lawful because they would ease psychological suffering.[35] However, given the stance of the Charity Commission, the fund's first report noted,

It is, of course, apparent that the thread of justification for the issue of grants in the case of these surviving children who had not been physically injured, is much finer but the Management Committee is anxious and intends to consider ways and means of affording them such benefit as would be proper in the circumstances.[36]

While considering such means, £100,000 was to be set aside by the management committee to meet the present and future needs of children who were physically and psychologically injured. Solicitors for residents in Aberfan had enlisted a local psychiatrist to examine those child survivors who seemed to be distressed. The psychiatrist reported in alarming terms to the management committee in December 1968. Of the 81 children he had seen, two-thirds were found to be moderately to severely affected.[37] The intended payments from this reserve fund were shaped by the parameters of charity law. Rather than making general payment to all the physically uninjured children, those assessed were to receive financial assistance based upon the extent of their psychological injuries.[38] However, after 'considerable thought', rather than making people apply to this reserve fund, one-off grants were made to physically and known psychologically injured children, based upon medical reports on their injuries.[39]

Significantly, the consultant psychiatrist had not seen all the surviving children and it is likely that others too suffered from the symptoms he described. As shown in Chapter 5, in the late 1960s, little was known about the set of conditions now labelled 'post-traumatic stress disorder'. Because of this lack of awareness of the possible full extent of the trauma, not all the children saw a psychiatrist, either for treatment or assessment for compensation. Were Aberfan to happen now, a comprehensive examination of all the physically uninjured children would be likely for medical and compensatory reasons. Many perhaps would be able to make substantial claims for PTSD or related conditions.

The donation for removing the tips

The Commission's activism on grants to the memorial or to survivors contrasts starkly with its silence on the proposed donation from the disaster fund towards the cost of removing the remaining tips that overlooked Aberfan. People in the village wanted them removed because of the constant reminder they provided of the disaster. If their very presence was not enough, slurry from them was washed down into the village streets by a storm in August 1968. The coal board and government both refused to remove them, leading to a strong and vocal campaign by the villagers. In the end a compromise was reached where the disaster fund contributed £150,000 with the coal board and government meeting the remaining cost.

The fund's management committee does not appear to have sought the Charity Commission's consent to make this payment.[40] The matter was not recorded in the minutes of any meeting of the Charity Commissioners up to the end of 1969. It is odd that a donation which was bitterly controversial in Aberfan was not discussed, whereas two donations that were not controversial in Aberfan took up a lot of the Commissioners' energy. A Welsh Office memorandum however notes that the Charity Commission had confirmed that such a contribution would be in accordance with the trust deed.[41]

Villagers in Aberfan campaigned vigorously for the complete removal of the tips. This culminated in 70 villagers bursting into the Welsh Office demanding to see George Thomas, who replaced Hughes as Secretary of State in April 1968, and then dumping a handful of coal slurry on the table in front of him. They were aided by the lobbying of a dozen Welsh Labour MPs and rumours that Thomas would resign if the decision was not taken. The Government eventually agreed to the complete removal of the tips but only if local interests were to contribute £250,000. In March 1967 Ministers had thought seeking a contribution from the fund 'far too explosive'.[42] But in the face of NCB and Treasury refusal to pay, that explosion was now risked. George Thomas said that the Government was willing 'to play its part, but extra money for Government expense of this sort has to be found at the cost of some other project, such as hospitals and roads. It is, therefore, only reasonable to expect that local interests should contribute as well.'[43] What local interests were was not specified, but with the local authority quick to point out that it had no money for such a project, it could only mean the disaster fund.

The Government's decision was announced at a meeting between Thomas and a deputation from the village and the disaster fund in July 1968. The initial news that the tips were to go was received joyously. Talfan Davies said that the management committee would be sympathetic if their help was necessary. He claimed that it would fulfil one of the fund's main purposes, the rehabilitation of Aberfan.[44] Yet once the euphoria was over the implication of the phrase 'local interests' began to sink home. Stanley Davies, the Fund founder and chairman, stated that he was against it making any contribution while there was said to be anger in Aberfan itself. S. O. Davies, the local MP and member of the fund's management committee, called the decision 'disgraceful' and 'the meanest thing I have seen in 34 years in Parliament'. An editorial in the only national newspaper in Wales declared 'It is enough that the villagers have suffered so much and lived for so long in fear without making them pay for the removal of the tips as well.'[45]

The opinion of donors was sought after an appeal by the secretary of the Parents' and Residents' Association. Only about 100 replies were received. They were divided evenly for and against the donation, as were letters received by George Thomas himself.[46] A Welsh Office briefing note warned officials that, in the original letters accompanying donations, only £33/10/- had been earmarked for tip removal and that 'local people would make much' of this fact.[47] The final decision, to contribute a maximum of £150,000 out of the £250,000 being demanded, was taken by the fund's management committee on 8 August 1968 in the Welsh Office after a meeting with George Thomas. The swaying factors appear to have been a promise that the fund's contribution would not have to be made for another two years, allowing further interest to accrue, and the realisation that there appeared to be no alternative if the tips were to be removed. George Thomas had told the committee

> If, however, the local interests do not feel strongly enough to wish to make a contribution themselves then the case for spending a big sum of tax payers' money over and above what is needed for purposes of amenity and safety is greatly weakened ...[48]

S. O. Davies was the only member of the committee who voted against the fund contributing. He promptly resigned.[49] The Committee was then faced with the task of explaining its decision to the Aberfan Parents' and Residents' Association. This was done at a meeting on 13 August 1968. Fifty members of the association attended to hear the committee's explanation and only one person voted against supporting the decision.[50] This is not to say that it was widely supported, merely that there appeared to be no alternative.

Stanley Davies, the fund chairman, maintained strongly that the management committee had not been blackmailed into contributing. He said that George Thomas had told them what the Government and NCB could afford to contribute and that they had to face that 'bald fact'.[51] Blackmail may not be the right noun but it is difficult to see what alternative the fund had. It had taken nearly two years to get the Government to agree to the full removal that people wanted so desperately. With the Government's insistence that there was no more public money available, no one in the fund or Aberfan wanted to risk the tips staying because of a failure to raise the remaining capital needed.

In the broadest interpretation of the fund's objects, removing the tips could be seen as for the benefit of Aberfan. At the meeting with George Thomas, Tasker Watkins QC, who was a trustee of the fund, noted the need for careful wording for the committee's decision. He suggested the following statement:

> The Committee having very carefully considered not only the statement of the Secretary of State for Wales but many other aspects of the problem and having had in mind very much the relief which will come to the people of Aberfan by the removal of the tips, have decided to make a contribution but the size of this contribution cannot be determined until the Committee has had time to consider its various commitments.[52]

There is no bar on a charity providing a service that would otherwise be supplied at the expense of the state and taxpayer.[53] However, given the NCB's liability for the disaster and its previous failure to observe its own recommendations on tip safety, it is surprising that the coal board did not remove the tips on its own initiative. This was especially so since, even with assurances that the remaining tips were safe, material had continued to wash down into the village from the spoil heaps after the disaster.

The 'Powell Memorandum' had played a large part in the tribunal of inquiry. This was circulated in April 1965 to all NCB area mechanical and civil engineers in South Wales. It adapted and expanded a 1939 memorandum from the Powell Duffryn coal company. The tribunal found that if the 1939 (or indeed the 1965) document 'had ... been properly circulated, studied and applied ... the probability is that there would have been no disaster'.[54]

The Powell Memorandum is headed 'The Sliding of Colliery Rubbish Tips'. Among its recommendations are:

> 6.1 Where a slide would cause damage to property, no tip over 20 feet high should be placed on a hillside unless the ground is a compact gravel or of better quality than this.
> 6.2 The advancing tip should be so aligned, along a sloping surface, that water draining off the ground above it can be collected, if necessary, by a system of drains cut in the ground, and led past and clear of the tip....
> 6.3 On the dip side of the tip, deep drains (not less than 18 inches) should be cut leading downhill to prevent water accumulating and to keep the ground dry....
> 6.4 Tipping should never be extended over springs of water, whether continuous or intermittent, or over bogged and water-logged ground.[55]

These requirements are in the 1939 document, and repeated verbatim in the 1965 reissue. The disaster tip had broken them all. Tips 4 and 5, which remained after the disaster, broke requirements 6.2, 6.3, and 6.4 by a generous margin. They were around 100 feet high. They were on boulder clay and fissured Pennant sandstone, a (much) poorer quality of ground for its purpose than compacted gravel. Tip 4 had previously slid in 1944, so that not only were they not drained as required by the Powell Memorandum, but the 1944 slip had offered a naturally lubricated surface for the disaster slide[56] and would do the same for any future slide. Tip 4 had been drained when it started to bulge, but tip 5 had promptly been started right on top of the drain by the man (Geoffrey Morgan) who had authorised the drain. Both tips bulged out of conical shape.[57]

It is true that the technical experts retained by both sides at the disaster inquiry concurred that tips 4 and 5 were safe, and that removing them would be an impracticably vast job.[58] Richard Marsh repeated in Parliament that they were safe in reply to S. O. Davies' attacks during the Aberfan debate.[59] However, as noted above, the coal board had led the Tribunal to believe that removal would cost more than three times its internal estimate.[60] Aberfan residents did not believe anything the coal board said. The opening of papers under the 30-year rule has shown how wise they were. If NCB assurances about price were worthless, what reason is there to trust NCB assurances about safety?

The fact that tips 4 and 5 seriously breached the coal board's own standards may not in itself be sufficient to show that the coerced contribution from the disaster fund was unlawful under charity law. The coal board had a strict (civil) liability to compensate anybody injured, or any property damaged, by a sliding tip.[61] It did not (yet) have a legal duty to make them safe.[62] Nevertheless, these facts are powerful evidence against the propriety of forcing the disaster fund to contribute to the removal of tips 4 and 5.

The controversial contribution was not forgotten. S. O. Davies continued to lobby on the issue (see chapter three). His successor to the seat, Ted Rowlands, lobbied successive Labour leaders on the issue. Aberfan residents asked Conservative governments three times for the money to be repaid. Despite the fund's careful investments, hit by inflation, it had problems in managing the disaster's memorials. In 1987, it was forced to hand over control of the Aberfan community centre to the local authority because of financial difficulties.[63] Such problems made the case for a refund all the stronger. In July 1997, Ron Davies, the new Secretary of State for Wales, announced that the Government would repay the money contributed to the removal of the tips by the disaster fund, adding that the fund should never have been asked to contribute in the first place.

While the decision was welcomed for helping to guarantee the future maintenance of the cemetery and remembrance garden, there was also a degree of resentment. £150,000 was to be refunded, the exact figure agreed to in 1968, rather than the £1,534,410 that the contribution would be worth in £1997.[64]

It seems unlikely that the real value, including interest forgone, of the original contribution will ever be repaid. Unless the contribution were deemed not in accordance with the fund's trust deed, then there appears to be no legal avenue open for recovering it. If the contribution were deemed illegal then it would place the trustees of 1968 in a difficult position. They would have broken their duty to ensure that the money was spent in accordance with the deed although it is unlikely that they would be held personally financially liable for the decision. Given the pressure from the NCB, the Wilson Government and the residents of Aberfan on the trustees, their decision seems entirely understandable. Had the Commission intervened, then the whole protracted question of the tip removal might have lasted even longer.

In its annual report for 1967, the Commission drew attention to its general function under the Charities Act 1960 of

> Promoting the effective use of charitable resources by encouraging the development of better methods of administration, by giving charity trustees information or advice in any matter affecting the charity and by investigating and checking abuses.

In the same document, the Commission draws attention to some services that seem relevant to the circumstances of the Aberfan Disaster Fund: for example: 'charity trustees who ... feel uneasy about the way in which it has been the practice to administer their charity should not hesitate to come to the Charity Commissioners for advice'.[65] But when the law was ill-equipped to deal with the kind of problems that the Aberfan fund faced, and the government was creating impossible situations, then the advice of the Commission could not provide a distribution of money that was to the satisfaction of all concerned. Consequently the regulation of the Charity Commission failed and it was left unclear in whose interest it was operating.

The fashion for mission statements had not yet arisen. They might, for once, have been some use in this case. The Commission did not make it clear how it balanced its duties to the general public, to charity donors, to charity beneficiaries, and to charity trustees. The result was that at Aberfan, the interests of the local people, and of those donors who objected to their gifts going towards the removal of the tips, were not protected. In 1968, 1969, and 1970 a number of members of the public wrote to MPs or Ministers to object to this use of the fund. The form letter drafted by the Welsh Office to reply to these complaints does not address the complaint about alleged abuse of charitable purpose at all.[66]

Why people give

To some local and national observers, the problems at Aberfan had their origin in the size of the fund. Yet disaster funds have remained the most common way for people to respond to disasters in the UK. Given the notorious problems that funds encounter or sometime cause, why do people continue to donate? Charity fund raising events such as Band Aid or Children in Need rely on a common sense of an unique occasion to raise large sums of money. The success of disaster funds is also determined by a common feeling of grief at an extraordinary tragedy. Parkes and Black have argued that disaster funds enable the general public to express symbolically their sympathy with those who have suffered.[67] At Aberfan there was a sense of a national and shared tragedy. Because of the media and an increasingly global culture, the communities affected by a disaster extend beyond the immediate site of impact. Shared values and culture ensure a wider sense of loss and tragedy beyond the bereaved and survivors.[68] Disaster funds can be seen as one manifestation of this.

The role of disaster funds as a gesture of a shared sense of grief developed further in the 1980s with the advent of donations from the UK government. The Herald of Free Enterprise and Piper Alpha funds received £1m each, the Clapham and Bradford funds £250,000, and the Lockerbie fund £150,000. These payments can be seen as an expression of the nation's horror at a disaster.

That sense of something extraordinary, which helps raise money for disaster funds, is further illustrated by the relatively low sums raised by more 'everyday' disasters such as rail crashes. The victims of car crashes, even where there are multiple deaths, do not have funds set up for them at all. To win the sympathy of the public, a disaster must be something apart from the everyday reality; motor accidents are simply too common to bring about widespread public sympathy.

Yet this cultural response to tragedy is by no means a global phenomenon. For example, whereas the death of children at Aberfan and Dunblane led to large funds in the UK, there was no equivalent fund raising after the various US high school mass murders of the 1990s. Disaster funds are part of a much wider cultural tradition in Britain of supporting deserving causes – be it injured soldiers, the nation in war-time, disaster victims or the aged poor.[69] The precise final use of that money was not central in the decision to give. Instead donations were gestures of sympathy or even responsibility in the absence of any obvious alternative. A letter to the Aberfan Disaster Fund noted 'I know that no amount of money can buy these children's lives, but what else can one do?'[70] Some observers have regarded this giving without any clear need as 'of course, irrational ... There was goodwill in abundance; but not always good sense'.[71] But it is not for the commentator to say that one or another use of someone else's money is rational or irrational. People have their preferences, and that is all one can say. The lady who gave the money she had been saving for her winter coat to the disaster fund (Chapter 1) was expressing a preference and a wish – 'Please use this small amount in any way you wish'. It was a wish the Charity Commission failed to protect. The trustees did not wish donors' money to be put to removing tips 4 and 5. Only at most 77 out of 90,000 donors gave their express approval.

The amount of money raised by disaster funds varies significantly (see table 6.1). That donations are statements about ourselves has been stressed by some commentators. The journalist John Humphrys, who reported from Aberfan, has written 'as with giving money to Aberfan and Dunblane, decisions are taken primarily to satisfy our fickle moral vanity rather than to do the right thing.'[72] In other words, donations, rather than being given to relieve any specific need, are statements that the donors care. As such they are influenced by the media and our own circumstances rather than the disaster or tragedy itself. This is no way reduces the duty of trustees and regulators to donors.

In 1987, a *Sunday Times* journalist wrote of the public's reaction to disasters: 'There should not be a league table of horror, with Aberfan at one end of it and everyday fatal accidents at the other. But there is'.[73] The size of the Aberfan fund signifies the impact it had on people across Britain and beyond. Its size is even more remarkable when the increasing ease with which it has become possible to donate to more recent funds (telephone hotlines, credit card donations, the involvement of local banks etc.) is considered. It is possible to discern a number of contributing factors to the extent of the public's generosity. The size of the Dunblane and Aberfan funds indicates that the death of children leads to widespread sympathy. Tragedies that occur close to the traditional family period of

Christmas (notably Penlee – see below) can also generate large funds. Where the deceased are part of a wider but clearly identifiable group, there is a strong degree empathy that attracts sympathy beyond that of the common culture of the nation. Many of the letters to the Aberfan fund were from parents imagining how awful it would be lose their own children. The Ibrox, Bradford and Hillsborough funds all raised very large sums partly thanks to the empathy of other football fans who had experienced similar conditions of overcrowding or dilapidated grounds. It did not require much imagination to see how their own experiences could easily have become disasters.

The media plays a significant role in constructing an event as a tragic disaster. The media's power in shaping such popular perceptions can be seen by contrasting the *Marchioness* disaster with the death of Diana, Princess of Wales. The relatively small sum raised by the *Marchioness* fund is often attributed to the media portrayal of the deceased as party-going 'yuppies'.[74] Whatever the reality of this depiction, it was unlikely to stimulate widespread sympathy. In contrast the UK media portrayed the death of Diana, in an ordinary car crash caused by speeding and drunk driving, as a global tragedy. She of course already enjoyed an icon-like status and the genuine affection of many people, especially those whose charities she had helped. Nonetheless, the period after her death witnessed her canonisation by the UK (maybe World) media. Consequently her death took on a new significance and her memorial fund became a way of not only demonstrating grief at her death but an acceptance of her values. Table 6.1 below estimates the amount raised by disaster funds in constant pounds, and in constant pounds per fatality, for the set of disasters defined in Chapter 4. Table 6.2 repeats the exercise for some events outside our definition of disasters where funds were raised.

Fig 6.1 charts the amount raised per fatality in constant prices, after the disasters in Tables 6.1 and 6.2. It excludes the Diana Memorial Fund. Although that appears in Table 6.2 because it dramatically illustrates the effect of an event that provoked a huge emotional response, it was not a disaster fund on the same basis as the others. It did not seek to relieve the needs of the bereaved.

We have not (yet) analysed these data statistically. But some features of Fig. 6.1 jump out a mile. A group of four disasters at the top end (Bradford, Aberfan, Hillsborough, and Dunblane) involved children and young people, all killed in tragic circumstances. But so did Summerland, which is low on the table. Surprisingly, the most reliable predictor for a massive disaster fund is not children but community. The two football stadiums (three including Ibrox, the next

Table 6.1 Disaster Funds since 1966

Disaster	Year	Death toll	Disaster Fund, £ (some figures approximate)	Equivalent in £1999*	Equivalent in £1999, per fatality**
Aberfan	1966	144	1,750,000	19,620,593	136,254
Ibrox Park	1971	66	315,000	2,570,423	38,946
Summerland	1973	50	84,782	554,953	11,099
Moorgate	1975	42	8,500	41,140	980
Bradford City	1985	56	4,250,000	7,725,750	129,845
Manchester Aircraft Fire	1985	55	None known	0	0
Herald of Free Enterprise	1987	193	4,000,000	6,802,409	26,434
King's Cross	1987	31	628,000***	1,067,978	34,451
Piper Alpha	1988	167	4,590,000	7,365,487	34,496
Clapham	1988	35	483,796	776,338	10,719
Kegworth	1989	47	None known	0	0
Hillsborough	1989	96	12,200,000	18,198,326	189,566
Marchioness	1989	57	86,000	128,283	2,251

Round numbers indicate approximate figure. Sources for fund totals: respective trustees' reports and contemporary Press estimates
* All funds expressed in £1999 (third quarter). Source: RPI (latest), from Office of National Statistics, Economic Trends, various issues.
** Col 6 = Col 5 divided by Col 3, after deducting government and company gifts to funds.
*** Sum raised in first month only.
*** First 4 weeks only

Table 6.2 Funds following other tragedies

Disaster	Year	Death toll	Disaster Fund, £ (some figures approximate)	Equivalent in £1999*	Equivalent in £1999, per fatality**
Flixborough	1974	28	50,000	291,679	10,417
Penlee	1981	8	4,000,000	9,208,824	1,151,103
Lockerbie	1988	270	2,000,000	3,209,363	11,887
Dunblane	1996	16	7,000,000	7,615,784	475,987
Death of Diana	1997	3	100,000,000	105,481,198	35,160,399

See note to Table 6.1 for sources and methods

on the list), the Penlee lifeboat (see below), and the two schools were all institutions at the heart of communities. Donors react much more generously when disaster hits a community than when it hits a collection of people gathered together at work, or by chance in a boat or train or plane.

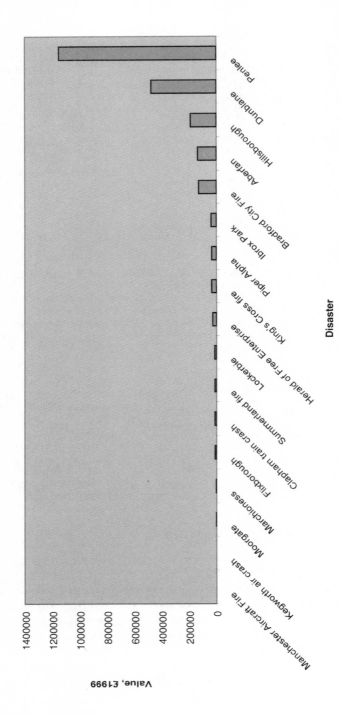

Figure 6.1 Value/victim (1999 prices, excluding govt and company contributions)

Developments since Aberfan

Aberfan spelt out the problems of charity law and large appeal funds without very specific objectives. The controversies led the Liberal MP Jeremy Thorpe to introduce a private member's bill into Parliament for the creation of a national disaster fund, from which disaster victims would benefit when and wherever necessary. The single fund was to avoid the problem of surplus money being left over once the needs of survivors, the bereaved and the community had been dealt with. Despite its good intentions, the bill failed to attract government support or reach the statute book. Harold Wilson argued that a national fund would be difficult to administer and, by not being related to a specific disaster, it might not attract the level of donations required.[75] Thus Aberfan did not bring about any immediate changes in the operation and administration of disaster funds.

In 1981, around £4 million was raised in an appeal for the families of eight lifeboat crew from Penlee, Cornwall, who drowned while attempting to rescue a tanker. The tragedy took place six days before Christmas bringing widespread sympathy. The sum raised surprised the fund's organisers who tried to divert some of it to help the Royal National Lifeboat Institute. This, however, went against the terms of the original appeal, which was to help the bereaved families. The response of donors to this change was mixed but it caused controversy in the local community. After intervention from the Attorney General and Charity Commission, the fund was declared noncharitable allowing it to be distributed in its entirety between the bereaved families rather than according to need.[76]

After Penlee, the Attorney-General published guidelines for disaster appeals. They encourage consideration from the outset of whether the appeal should be charitable or not. The trustees of the fund that was set up to help the survivors and 56 victims of the 1985 Bradford City fire followed this lead by not registering as a charity.[77] This made the fund liable to taxation but ensured that the trustees were free to dispose of it as they saw fit. Before drawing up the terms of the Bradford fund, the administrators consulted those involved with other disaster funds, including Aberfan. They were determined to avoid the type of problems stemming from charitable status that are chronicled here. The Bradford City fund's determination and success has set a bench mark that other funds have followed yet the payment of tax on sums donated by the public to help the victims of disasters seems unjust. It also means that there are potential problems of the unaccountability of the trust while the public may not always be happy to contribute to a fund that is not a registered charity. This led to a second smaller but charitable fund being set up by the Bradford trustees.[78] The Hillsborough fund followed the Bradford lead but ran into its own problems over mistrust of the confidential assessment criteria and the impact of payments on beneficiaries' entitlement to DSS benefits.[79] Non-charitable trusts bring their own problems.

The Bradford solution side-steps the problematic law rather than offering a long-term solution to the need for reform. The 1996 Deakin Report of the National Council for Voluntary Organisations (NCVO) proposed a change in the definition of charity to the flexible and wide-ranging 'benefit to the community'. The Charity Commission's current Review of the Register also contemplates a similar move away from the 1601 definition.[80]

Even a fund which avoids the legal pitfalls can still face a difficult, perhaps almost impossible, task in satisfying all its beneficiaries and donors. There remains some public disquiet about the whole concept of using money to compensate for grief and the trauma of loss on the grounds that such emotions are uncompensatable.[81] Such reservations about disaster funds have been increased by the well-publicised disputes amongst beneficiaries. Like Aberfan, Dunblane and Lockerbie both witnessed local arguments, possibly exaggerated by the media, over how the money should be used. Non-discretionary trusts may allow the money to be distributed in accordance with the Trustees' wishes but the question still remains how much is the right sum to give someone who has lost a loved one? The example of the Bradford fund, where the sums paid out to individuals were confidential does offer a solution but one which the inevitable rumours and gossip can still undermine. Furthermore, complete agreement on the most suitable memorial or which local community activities should benefit can rarely be achieved while the use of surpluses also raises questions.

Regulating the purportedly irrational

The Charity Commission was not the only regulatory agency to fail the public over Aberfan; so did HM Inspectorate of Mines and Quarries (see chapter 2). Part of the fault lies with a regulatory culture that did not make it clear in whose interest the regulator was regulating. Nor was there any mechanism to prevent regulatory capture. There is a large literature on how regulators can be captured by the interests they regulate. This was clearly the case with the mines inspectorate, which was staffed by colliery engineers and reduplicated both the strengths and, tragically, the blind spots of those it regulated.

The case of the Charity Commission is more complex. The Commission was faced with the difficult task of upholding a narrow law that failed to meet the expectations of the different parties involved. The Commissioners did make attempts to find ways around the law as their actions over the memorial and payments to the bereaved demonstrated. However, the reasoning was tortuous and perhaps even insulting to the people of Aberfan. Thus the Commission compounded the injustices of the law. Had their advice always been strictly followed then the situation would have been worse. The Commissioners may have only being doing their job, but the whole affair raises question about in whose interests they should have been working. Regulation of the Aberfan Disaster Fund did not clearly work in the interest of Aberfan.

Many things have changed since Aberfan; some have not. The Charity Commission is currently reviewing its Register of Charities

> to consider, within the law, whether those organisations which currently benefit from charitable status should continue to do so, and whether there is scope to develop further the boundaries of charitable status. Both will be done by the flexible use of our powers to apply and interpret the law.... whilst public opinion cannot determine what is or is not charitable, it is an important factor to be taken into account in the shaping of the legal understanding of charity.[82]

Both social and legal cultures in relation to disasters differ widely across countries. In some countries there is a tradition of charitable giving for disaster victims; in other countries there is not. It is clear that the law in England and Wales was highly unsatisfactory in 1966 and the first few years thereafter. The approach and flexibility of the Charity Commission may have improved but a reform of the out-dated law that was at the heart of the Aberfan Disaster Fund's problems is yet to happen. However, even if such a reform was enacted, it is important to remember that no fund can ever compensate for the loss people suffer in disasters.

Donors, too, need protection. The opinion that donors to disaster funds are 'irrational' is surprisingly widely held in some legal and administrative circles. The amounts shown in Tables 6.1 and 6.2 vary so wildly that it is easy to see how some people have reached this conclusion. Yet it has been deeply damaging. We repeat: it is not for others to question donors' motives in giving to a charity. Rationality is a property of means, not of ends. If people respond to an appeal, their wishes should be respected. At Aberfan, they were not. The diversion of the disaster fund's money to removing tips 4 and 5 depended on the mindset according to which the donors were irrational and the recipients were quarrelsome.

Notes

1 W E A Lewis, Charity Commissioner, *Minutes of Aberfan Disaster Fund Management Committee* (hereafter *ADF mins*), 8 September 1967. GRO D/D X 295/12/1/1.
2 John Benson, 'Charity's Pitfalls: The Senghenydd Disaster', *History Today*, vol. 43, November 1993. Catherine Welsby, 'Warning her as to her future behaviour': The Lives of the Widows of the Senghenydd Mining Disaster of 1913', *Llafur*, vol. 6, no. 4, 1995.
3 Quoted in Benson, 'Charity's Pitfalls', p. 7.
4 For example eligibility for aid under the Poor Law was dependent upon the approach of the local Board of Guardians, the more extreme of whom would exclude those of 'immoral' character. This attitude was also reflected the 1908 Old Age Pensions Act which excluded known drunks and others of disreputable behaviour.
5 See Welsby, 'Warning her', pp. 104–105.
6 Charity Commission statement 1974. Quoted from the *History of the Organisation of Central Government Departments 1964–92* database at http://www.nuff.ox.ac.uk/politics/whitehall/
7 Charity Commission statement, 1973–4.
8 Quoted from the mission statement on the front page of the Charity Commission's website, February 1999: http://www.charity-commission.gov.uk/
9 The study stops in 1969 because no more recent files are yet open to the public under the thirty year rule.
10 Michael Chesterman, *Charities, Trusts and Social Welfare* (London: Weidenfeld and Nicolson, 1979), pp. 339–346, discusses the situation as it then appeared, although he did not have access to the records or to local interviews.
11 *ADF mins*, 2 February 1968, GRO D/D X 295/12/1/2.
12 *Re Gillingham Bus Disaster Fund* [1957] 3 WLR 1069. A bus had crashed into a line of marching cadets, killing 24 of them. The bus company's insurer met most of the claims, leaving a large charitable fund with a small number of direct beneficiaries. The last of the money was not disposed of until 1993, 42 years after the cadets were killed.
13 Chesterman, *Charities*, p. 344.
14 Charity Commission meeting of 8 November 1966. PRO CHAR 9/2.
15 *Report of the Charity Commissioners for England and Wales for the Year 1966* (London: HMSO, 1967), paras 10–11, p. 6.
16 PQ by Alexander Lyon (Lab, York) and replies by the Prime Minister, 25 October 1966. *Hansard*, Commons, 5th ser, vol 734, 825–6.
17 Charity Commission meeting of 27 January 1967. PRO CHAR 9/2.
18 Surprisingly in view of the salience of Aberfan, the Charity Commission case file on Aberfan has not survived.

19 Charity Commission meeting of 7 July 1967. PRO CHAR 9/2.
20 *First Report of the Management Committee of the Aberfan Disaster Fund*, p. 27.
21 *First Report of the Management Committee of the Aberfan Disaster Fund*, p. 28.
22 Francis & Smith, *The Fed*, ch. 8.
23 Interview, MJ and Mr & Mrs T. (bereaved parents, names withheld), 1 February 1999.
24 *First Report of the Management Committee of the Aberfan Disaster Fund*, p. 29. £500 was the same figure as the NCB was prepared to award per child killed.
25 Telephone interview, MJ and fund trustee (name withheld), 7 December 1998, recalling an interview between the trustee and Elwyn Jones, 1967; *First Report of the Management Committee of the Aberfan Disaster Fund*, pp. 26–30
26 Interview, MJ and Mr & Mrs T.
27 *ADF mins*, 8 September 1967, appendix B, GRO D/D X 295/12/1/1. *First Report of the Management Committee of the Aberfan Disaster Fund*, p. 29.
28 Noted in minutes of Charity Commission meeting of 7 February 1968. PRO CHAR 9/2. Interview, MJ and fund trustee.
29 W E A Lewis, Charity Commissioner, *ADF mins*, 8 September 1967. GRO D/D X 295/12/1/1.
30 *ADF mins*, 9 November 1967. GRO D/D X 295/12/1/1. Initially, all families with at least one surviving child who had been a pupil of either of the Aberfan schools at the time of the disaster received £200 if they had not also been bereaved. *First Report of the Management Committee of the Aberfan Disaster Fund*, pp. 35–36.
31 *ADF mins*, 2 February 1968. GRO D/D X 295/12/1/2.
32 Interview, MJ and fund trustee.
33 Charity Commission meeting of 7 February 1968. PRO CHAR 9/2.
34 Charity Commission meeting of 6 March 1968. PRO CHAR 9/2; cf *ADF mins*, 1 March 1968. GRO D/D X 295/12/1/2.
35 *ADF mins*, 29 May 1968.
36 *First Report of the Management Committee of the Aberfan Disaster Fund*, p. 36.
37 Detailed notes of discussion with Dr Cuthill at the meeting held on 6th December 1968. *ADF mins*. GRO D/D X295/12/1/3. The psychiatric impact of the disaster is discussed at length in chapter five.
38 *First Report of the Management Committee of the Aberfan Disaster Fund*, pp. 34–35.
39 C. Geoffrey Morgan, *Second Report of the Management Committee of the Aberfan Disaster Fund*, 1970, p. 10.
40 Interview, MJ and fund trustee. B. Nightingale, *Charities* (London: Allen Lane, 1973), p. 184, claims that the Charity Commission felt that the donation would help rehabilitate Aberfan and was thus in accordance with the trust deed. We have been unable to get any confirmation of this claim.
41 Welsh Office, Background note for J Siberry [Assistant Secretary dealing with Aberfan], 25 July 1968. PRO BD 11/3804.
42 PRO COAL 73/2. Minutes of meeting on 6 March 1967.

43 *Western Mail*, 27 July 1968. When the extent of the government and NCB pressure on the Disaster Fund started to become publicly known, George Thomas (Lord Tonypandy) stated that he would have resigned had the Government not acceded to Aberfan's repeated requests. *Western Mail*, 1 August 1997. Thomas died less than two months later.

44 *Western Mail*, 27 July 1968.

45 *Western Mail*, 27, 29 July, 6 August 1968.

46 *ADF mins*, 8 August 1968. GRO D/D X 295/12/1/2.

47 PRO BD 11/3804, Background note for Siberry, 25 July 1968.

48 *ADF mins*, 8 August 1968. GRO D/D X 295/12/1/2.

49 *Western Mail*, 9 August 1968.

50 *Western Mail*, 14 August 1968.

51 *Merthyr Express*, 15 August 1968.

52 *ADF mins*, 8 August 1968. GRO D/D X 295/12/1/2.

53 H. Picarda, *The Law and Practice Relating to Charities* (London: Butterworths, 1977), p. 91.

54 *Aberfan Tribunal Report*, para. 161.

55 Aberfan Tribunal Report, Appendix D. Original copies of the Memorandum are in the Tribunal papers, PRO BD 52.

56 *Aberfan Tribunal Report*, para. 90.

57 *Aberfan Tribunal Report*, paras. 83–95

58 *Aberfan Tribunal Report*, paras. 279–80.

59 *Hansard*, Commons, 5th ser., vol. 751, cols. 1928–9, 2010–2011.

60 PRO BD 52/1/8, 'Proposed alternative methods of removing the whole of the tip complex', June 1967.

61 *Rylands v Fletcher* [1868] LR 3, HL 330; *Att Gen v Cory Bros & Co Ltd* [1921] 1 AC 521.

62 Such a duty was imposed in the Mines and Quarries (Tips) Act 1969, over the objections of the Coal Division of the Ministry of Power, who said that imposing a duty to protect the public 'would be a revolutionary innovation in the field of industrial safety legislation'. PRO POWE 52/68, Coal Division memo on Tribunal findings and recommendations.

63 Telephone interview, MJ and Aberfan Memorial Fund secretary, 29 January 1999.

64 *Western Mail*, 1 August 1997; *South Wales Echo*, 31 July, 1 August 1997.

65 *The Charity Commissioners: how they can help charity trustees* paras. 1, 3; cf also para. 10. In *Report of the Charity Commissioners for England and Wales for the Year 1967* (London: HMSO, 1968), pp. 33–37.

66 See, e.g., draft reply to letter from L R Beard to the Prime Minister, 13 March 1970. PRO BD 11/3791.

67 C. M. Parkes & D. Black, 'Disasters', in C. M. Parkes & A Markus (eds.), *Coping with Loss: Helping Patients and their Families* (London: BMJ Books, 1998).

68 Kathleen M. Wright, Robert J. Ursano, Paul T. Bartone, Larry H. Ingraham, 'The Shared Experience of Catastrophe: An Expanded Classification of the Disaster Community', *American Journal of Orthopsychiatry*, vol. 60, no. 1, January 1990, 35–42.

69 See, for example, Frank Prochaska, *The Voluntary Impulse: Philanthropy in Modern Britain* (London: Faber & Faber, 1988).

70 Quoted in Nightingale, *Charities*, p. 178.
71 Nightingale, *Charities*, p. 179.
72 Viz., a maximum of 27 who mentioned it in covering letters with their initial donations (ADA, Dowlais collection, H021), plus the 50 mentioned above, who gave their approval when approached by the Trustees.
73 John Humphrys, *Devil's Advocate* (London: Hutchinson, 1999), p. 63.
74 Helen Mason, 'All in a good cause?' *Sunday Times*, 27 September 1987, p. 59.
75 Tina Gaudoin, 'The Marchioness: The True Story', *The Times*, 22 July 1999.
76 *Hansard*, 5th ser., vol. 737, col. 618; vol. 743, col. 958.'
77 See Wells, *Negotiating Tragedy*, pp. 94–5.
78 See R. W. Suddards (ed), *Administration of Appeal Funds* (London: Sweet & Maxwell, 1991).
79 See P. Luxton, *Charity Fund-Raising and the Public Interest: An Anglo-American Legal Perspective* (Aldershot: Avebury, 1990), p. 124. The *Herald of Free Enterprise* fund was also split into two, with one being charitable and the other not.
80 S. Coleman, A. Jemphrey, P. Scraton & P. Skidmore, *Hillsborough and After: The Liverpool Experience, First Report* (Liverpool: Liverpool City Council, 1990), ch. 6. The problems over DSS benefits are a reminder of the class prejudices that dogged funds such as Senghennydd at the start of the century.
81 N. Deakin (chairman), *Meeting the Challenge of Change: Voluntary Action into the 21st Century*, The Report of the Commission on the Future of the Voluntary Sector, NCVO, 1996 (vol. 1), para. 3.2.6. Charity Commission, *RR1 – The Review of the Register of Charities.* . However, Peter Luxton notes that a redefinition would bring a flood of litigation attempting to clarify the meaning of charity. 'The Deakin Report: Its Legal Implications', *New Law Journal*, 146 (6771), Sup no 69, 6 December 1996, p. 15.
82 See, for example, Barbara Amiel, 'Behind disaster funds lie the best impulses of human nature, but the minute there is money, other instincts surface', *The Times*, 4 September 1987, p. 17.
83 *Review of Register of Charities*, paras. 1–2, 13–14, quoted at 2 and 13.

Chapter Seven

THE PRICE OF LIFE: BEREAVEMENT
DAMAGES

It's my opinion and that of many others in this deeply sad community that this effort by the NCB puts shame on us all and also those who made the law valid ... The life long grief and loneliness being shared by so many here is a condition we realize no amount of money can erase ... [but] my own child **** who was 9 ½ years when she was killed, was a healthy intelligent child who should have had a life expectancy of at least 60 years. Dividing £500 by 60 gives her last years a value of less than £8 per year. Some of the children were extremely capable and intelligent and, without doubt would have done credit to both community and country. All of them should be alive today. They are not. They died violently and most cruelly through no fault of their own and because of the neglect of others. ... This matter hurts us here deeply – adds to the feeling that our children – whatever they meant to us, and whatever values they may have been as citizens, are now dead, and being so, value little to this country, and also value little to those who caused them to die. They are now it seems and within the letter of the law, to be written off, as cheaply as possible, and the matter closed. ... Is there no room for social conscience in law and business?

Letter from a bereaved Aberfan mother to
Lord Robens of Woldingham PC,
Chairman of the National Coal Board,
23 May 1967.[1]

To anybody who is not a lawyer, this statement seems a matter of common sense, as well as strong emotional appeal. The low sums then awarded by the courts (and more recently by statute) also seem to be a long way out of line with the valuation of a human life in other areas of public policy.

Whenever a decision is made on safety spending, an implicit valuation of life has been made. There is now a broad consensus that society's willingness to pay for safety equates to its putting a valuation of around £1m–£2m on a life. For road schemes, the figure used is £700,000. For railway investment, the figure generally used is £2m.[2]

Legal justifications

After Aberfan, the NCB robustly defended its award of £500 to the family of each child who was killed. The NCB's insurance staff, who did not accept liability for the disaster on behalf of the NCB until April 1967, called the award 'a good offer' and urged Lord Robens, their chairman, to resist demands to pay more – 'It is only the hard core [of bereaved parents] who are trying to capitalize'.[3] The insurance staff pointed out that it was in line with the leading cases on loss of expectation of life, viz., *Benham v Gambling* ([1941] AC 157) and *Yorkshire Electricity Board v Naylor* ([1968] AC 529). By May 1967, the *Naylor* case had reached the House of Lords where the figure of £500, which the court of first instance had awarded, was confirmed.

In the words of the report of the Lords' decision in the first case:

> The respondent [Gambling] was the father and was constituted the administrator of the estate of his infant child of two and a half years who, while a passenger in a motor car, was so injured by that car being run into and overturned by a car driven by the appellant that he died the same day.
>
> Asquith J., sitting without a jury, had before him, with the assent of counsel on both sides, the tables of expectation of life prepared by the Registrar-General, and according to these, a newly born child has an expectation of life of about 58 years, but the judge said that this statistical material was "not real evidence in a matter of this kind." On a consideration of the evidence the judge fixed the damages at £1200, having arrived at the conclusion that this amount was "neither unreasonably excessive nor unreasonably deficient." On appeal Slesser L. J. and MacKinnon L. J. held that the award of £1200 should stand, while Goddard L. J. considered that the amount should be reduced to £350.

Up to that case, judges had not followed any set formula in making awards for loss of expectation of life. The size of the award had been left to the discretion of juries, which had the effect of producing widely divergent, and rapidly advancing, awards. Reference was sometimes made to life expectancy which thus tended to raise awards to deceased children.[4] For example, in *Turbeyfield v GWR Co* ([1937] 158 LT 135) £1,500 was awarded following the death of an eight-year-old girl. In *Bailey v Howard* ([1939] 1 KB 453) £1,000 was awarded after the death of a three-year-old girl. The initial award of

£1,200 in *Benham v Gambling* thus reflected this pattern. Benham however appealed to the House of Lords against the size of the award. They reduced the award to £200. Lord Simon, the Lord Chancellor, spoke for a unanimous court.

The case report shows that none of the judges, including the one who initially awarded £1200, thought that actuarial evidence of the child's expectation of life was directly relevant. However, Lord Simon appealed to actuarial reasoning in his comment that as the child had lived in a country village away from main roads, and as his father had a settled occupation, his life expectancy was above average immediately before the fatal accident. Average manual earnings in 1941 were £4.97 a week, or approximately £250 a year.[5]

An approach based on the earnings forgone (as might have applied had the child been injured rather than killed) would therefore have led to an award in the region of £5,000 on the basis of a yield of 5 per cent. No judge in the case contemplated an award of that order of magnitude. What was the reasoning of those (Goddard in the Court of Appeal, and Simon speaking for the House of Lords) who favoured reducing the initial £1200 to £350 or £200?

As quoted in the Lords judgement, Goddard's reasoning was as follows:

> Goddard L. J., on the contrary, considered that the damages were extremely high and indeed excessive. He pointed out the extreme difficulty of fixing a figure representing a solatium due to a person who is dead, and he construed the dictum in Lord Wright's judgement, to which I have referred, as meaning in the case of a dead infant "that you should take that" (i.e., the fact that the deceased is a very young child) "into account by way of minimising the damage." The Lord Justice continued: "With an infant you do not know that its parents will live or that it will have any education. It is far more exposed to certain dangers, and so forth, and it is altogether far more difficult with a baby of a few months, or even a few years, it seems to me, to come to a fair sum than in the case of another person. Certainly I should feel that in such a case any estimate based upon the probable length of life was entirely fallacious," and the Lord Justice reached the conclusion that there is no principle upon which such damages can be assessed "beyond saying that you are to give what is fair and moderate and to use your common sense." He gave it as his opinion that £350 would be a reasonable sum in all the circumstances.

Goddard thus rejects actuarial calculations. On any actuarial calculation, the damages payable for a child would be greater, the younger the child (because the number of years of life expectancy in actuarial tables declines as a person ages). He seems to have used two lines of argument: that the parents might not live, and that the infant was more exposed to danger than an older child. The first is false: the younger the child, the longer its parents' life expectancy. The second is true, but is more than outweighed by the longer life expectancy of those who do survive. Both factors are bundled into the tables of life expectancy at any given age, which Goddard's court already had before it as evidence. Having rejected the only extant relevant evidence, Lord Goddard had to fall back on 'common sense'.[6]

Lord Simon, speaking for the House of Lords, was subtler:

> In the first place, I am of opinion that the right conclusion is not to be reached by applying what may be called the statistical or actuarial test. Figures calculated to represent the expectation of human life at various ages are averages arrived at from a vast mass of vital statistics; the figure is not necessarily one which can be properly attributed to a given individual. And in any case the thing to be valued is not the prospect of length of days, but the prospect of a predominantly happy life. The age of the individual may, in some cases, be a relevant factor. For example, in extreme old age the brevity of what life may be left may be relevant, but, as it seems to me, arithmetical calculations are to be avoided, if only for the reason that it is of no assistance to know how many years may have been lost, unless one knows how to put a value on the years. It would be fallacious to assume, for this purpose, that all human life is continuously an enjoyable thing, so that the shortening of it calls for compensation, to be paid to the deceased's estate, on a quantitative basis. The ups and downs of life, its pains and sorrows as well as its joys and pleasures – all that makes up "life's fitful fever" – have to be allowed for in the estimate. In assessing damages for shortening of life, therefore, such damages should not be calculated solely, or even mainly, on the basis of the length of life that is lost. ...
>
> Asquith J. ... observed that the earlier decisions quoted to him assumed "that human life is, on the whole, good." I would rather say that, before damages are awarded in respect of the shortened life of a given individual under this head, it is necessary for the Court to be satisfied that the circumstances of the individual life were calculated to lead, on balance, to a positive measure of happiness, of which the victim has been deprived by the defendant's negligence. If the character or habits of the individual were calculated to lead him to a future of unhappiness or despondency, that would be a circumstance justifying a smaller award. ...
>
> Of course, no regard must be had to financial losses or gains during the period of which the victim has been deprived. The damages are in respect of loss of life, not of loss of future pecuniary prospects. The main reason, I think, why the appropriate figure of damages should be reduced in the case of a very young child is that there is necessarily so much uncertainty about the child's future that no confident estimate of prospective happiness can be made. When an individual has reached an age to have settled

prospects – having passed the risks and uncertainties of childhood and having in some degree attained to an established character and to firmer hopes – his or her future becomes more definite and the extent to which good fortune may probably attend him at any rate becomes less incalculable. I would add that, in the case of a child, as in the case of an adult, I see no reason why the proper sum to be awarded should be greater because the social position or prospects of worldly possessions are greater in one case than another. Lawyers and judges may here join hands with moralists and philosophers and declare that the degree of happiness to be attained by a human being does not depend on wealth or status. ...

It remains to observe, as Goddard L. J. pointed out, that, stripped of technicalities, the compensation is not being given to the person who was injured at all, for the person who was injured is dead. The truth, of course, is that in putting a money value on the prospective balance of happiness in years that the deceased might otherwise have lived, the jury or judge of fact is attempting to equate incommensurables. Damages which would be proper for a disabling injury may well be much greater than for deprivation of life. These considerations lead me to the conclusion that in assessing damages under this head, whether in the case of a child or an adult, very moderate figures should be chosen.

...[W]e are all agreed in thinking that the proper figure in this case would be £200, *and that even this amount would be excessive if it were not that the circumstances of the infant were most favourable.* (Our emphasis) In reaching this conclusion, we are in substance correcting the methods of estimating this head of loss, whether in the case of children or adults, which have grown up in a series of earlier cases, and which Asquith J. naturally followed, and are approving a standard of measurement which, had it been applied in those cases, would have led, at any rate in many of them, to reduced awards. I trust that the views of this House, expressed in dealing with the present appeal, may help to set a lower standard of measurement than has hitherto prevailed for what is in fact incapable of being measured in coin of the realm with any approach to real accuracy.

The central reasoning is that damages are awardable not for loss of earnings but for loss of a predominantly happy life. In the case of the two-and-a-half-year-old boy, there was no knowing whether his life would have been predominantly happy. (But the last paragraph of the judgement implies, undermining the rest of Lord Simon's reasoning, that in this case the odds had favoured the boy. This is actuarial reasoning, although Lord Simon apparently did not recognise it as such). The final paragraph of the judgement contains a clear instruction that it is to bind future English and Welsh decisions. Indeed, the reasoning was subsequently interpreted as having been primarily influenced by policy concerns rather than the concept of lost happiness: 'I cannot interpret that decision as anything other than a decision based on policy, but justified by assumptions more philosophical than legal'.[7] This was not untypical of Simon who did occasionally try to 'restate the law in the form of numbered propositions'. However, his arguments were not always seen as 'satisfactory', with difficulties glossed over in the interest of policy.[8]

So matters rested until the case of *Naylor v Yorkshire Electricity Board* ([1968] AC 531). The facts of the case are well summarised in the Jingle-like heading of the Lords decision:

> Damages – Personal injuries – Loss of expectation of life – Deceased happy, healthy young man – Engaged to be married – Settled prospects of employment – Basis of assessment – Fall in value of money – Whether to be taken into account – Whether £1,000 appropriate – ... Law Reform – Whether necessary – Damages – Loss of expectation of life – Awards of moderate sums – Shortened life of unconscious plaintiff – Awards of substantial sums – No real or logical difference between two cases.
>
> On April 23, 1964, a young man of 20 years of age was killed by an electric shock while employed by the appellants as a jointer's mate. He was a happy, healthy young man who would probably have become a jointer at the age of 21 had he lived. He had become engaged to be married one week before he was killed. In an action by his mother as administratrix of his estate under the Law Reform (Miscellaneous Provisions) Act, 1934, s.1 for damages on behalf of his estate, the appellants admitted liability, agreed the funeral expenses at £60 8 6, and offered £500 for loss of expectation of life. The respondent refused to accept that offer, contending that in view of the fall in the value of money it was too low. At the trial there was unchallenged expert economic evidence that since 1941 the purchasing power of the pound had declined by two-and-a-half times. Ashworth J. awarded £500 for loss of expectation of life and £60 8 6 funeral expenses, a total of £560 8 6 damages in all. On appeal, the Court of Appeal increased the damages under the head of loss of expectation of life to £1,000. The appellants appealed:- Held, allowing the appeal, that the trial judge had made a proper and correct estimate of the damages to be awarded, he having taken into account all relevant factors, including the decline in the value of money since 1941, in arriving at the sum of £500, and that, accordingly, there was no justification for interfering with his award.
>
> Per Lord Devlin. It would be a great improvement if this head of damage was abolished and replaced by a short Act of Parliament fixing a suitable sum which a wrongdoer whose act has caused death should pay into the estate of the deceased. While the law remains as it is, I think it is less likely to fall into disrespect if judges treat Benham v. Gambling (supra) as an injunction to stick to a fixed standard than if they start revaluing happiness, each according to his own ideas.

The first issue considered was the decline in the value of money between 1941 and 1964 (or 1968). The court of first instance heard evidence from a lecturer in economics and statistics that £200 in 1941 was the equivalent of £500 in 1967. (According to the officially published Retail Price Index, the amount should have been £554.64 in 1967).

By a 2 to 1 majority, the Court of Appeal raised the compensation payable to the Naylor estate from £500 to £1000. Lord Salmon, speaking for the majority, said:

> It seems to me to be manifest from what was stated in Benham v. Gambling that if the deceased in that case had been a young man in the position of the deceased here, the House of Lords would have assessed the damages at much more than £200 – probably at £400

However, the House of Lords unanimously rejected this argument, and restored the compensation payable to £500. It is rather a pity that they gave Lord Salmon's argument such short shrift. *If* one accepts Lord Simon's argument that the reason for holding down the award to the Gambling estate was the great uncertainty about the future happiness of a 2-year-old child, then it seems to follow that, as the future happiness of Mr Naylor was attested by his having good job prospects and having just become engaged, his happiness was more certain, and the award ought to have been higher.

Lord Morris of Borth-y-Gest conceded that

> If an infant aged 2 was subject to all the risks and uncertainties of childhood and if no view could be formed as to whether happiness could be anticipated an award might he very small. There might come a time when prospects were more settled.

However, he did not accept that that argument applied in this case, because that passage is in the middle of a quite different argument, viz., that

> He [Naylor] lost what is usually called his expectation of life. The loss was something personal to himself. No one knows what life would in fact have held for him had he lived. No one will ever know. No one could ever know. The chances, the changes and the vicissitudes of the future are in the future. He will not know them. No surmise can with any measure of confidence be made whether by his untimely death he was denied happiness or was spared unhappiness.

As in 1941, the judges agreed that there was no definite basis for the calculation of the damages due. Lord Devlin said,

The assessment being based on an estimate of prospective happiness, the ground given by Viscount Simon L.C. for the reduction was that there was so much uncertainty about a child's future that no confident estimate could be made. This is an exceptional principle to be applied in the law of damages, where difficulty in calculation is not ordinarily taken as a ground either for reducing or for increasing the award.

After observing that the tariff laid down in *Benham v Gambling* had been described as 'judicial legislation', Devlin went on,

> The law has endeavoured to avoid two results, both of which it considered would be undesirable. The one is that a wrongdoer should have to pay large sums for disabling and nothing for killing; the other is that the large sum appropriate to total disablement should come as a windfall to the beneficiaries of the victim's estate. To arrive at a figure which avoids these two undesirable results is a matter for compromise and not for judicial determination. I cannot think that a judge derives much assistance either from the artificialities – inevitable when convenience is cloaked with logic – in Viscount Simon's speech or from the customary exhortations to use common sense. It would, I think, be a great improvement if this head of damage was abolished and replaced by a short Act of Parliament fixing a suitable sum which a wrongdoer whose act has caused death should pay into the estate of the deceased.

In *Cain v Wilcox* ([1968] 3 All ER 817), which involved the death of a 2½-year-old child, Cairns, J. ruled that,

> in cases of the extremities of old age or childhood, it may be appropriate to award less that would be the case of the ordinary adult. ... [W]e are here in a realm where mathematical calculations do not come into it at all. On any view, that which is to be awarded for loss of expectation of life can only be an artificial figure, and really in the end the only guidance that one derives from the cases cited is that that artificial figure should be a moderate one. ... I think it would be disastrous if this appeal succeeded to the extent of persuading us to enter into minute calculations in a case of this character. If we were to take that course, I can only foresee that there would be a flood of litigation ... seeking to draw minute distinctions between the circumstances of deceased persons. That would be a wholly unwholesome development ...

This precedent allowed the conventional sum to be lowered in cases involving the very young or old but effectively reinforced the notion of a uniform small conventional sum. Again, at the heart of the above judgement were policy concerns over a flood of potential litigation should cases be assessed individually. The inheritors of the estates of 'one or two old people without dependants' killed at

Aberfan received £300 for loss of expectation of life.[9] Given that, according to *Benham v Gambling*, payments were not for the loss of length of life but the quality of life, then such smaller sums were unfair. Nonetheless, given that the heading remained 'the loss of expectation of life' smaller payments to the elderly probably seemed logical to NCB lawyers. Such were the contradictions of the law.[10]

The conventional sum itself was raised periodically to allow for inflation. Shortly before being superseded by a statutory amount, it had reached £1,750. (*Kralj v McGarth*, [1986] 1 All ER 54). However, the short Act that Devlin sought was not to be passed until 1982. It is convenient to break with chronology in order to trace what has happened since Devlin's remarks.

The Administration of Justice Act 1982 (section 1(1)(a)) allowed a fixed sum of £3,500. In doing so, it changed the heading under the payment was made. The heading of loss of expectation of life (payable to the estate of the deceased) was abolished and replaced by bereavement damages payable to a narrow class of relative. However in practice, where the estate was inherited by someone within this class, the two headings amounted to the same thing. The size of the award was increased to £7,500 by statutory instrument in 1990. 'Covered are spouses ... in respect of the other's death, and parents in respect of a minor child. The parents of young adult children, unless there was some dependency, are entitled to nothing'.[11] Thus the estates of Gambling, and of the child victims of Aberfan, would today receive the statutory amount. The estate of Naylor would not. Nor did those of the young adult victims of the *Marchioness*, and Hillsborough disasters.

The value of awards under this heading may be expressed in constant prices as in Table 7.1.

Table 7.1 shows that the amount in real terms has fluctuated wildly, because neither the courts nor the 1982 Act provided for automatic uprating to allow for inflation. The courts in the *Naylor*

Table 7.1 Damages for loss of expectation of life/bereavement, 1941

Year	Amount in current prices, £	Value (1941 = 100)
1941	200	100
1967	500	91.11
1968	500	86.24
1983	3500	120.13
1991	7500	165.03
1997	7500	134.29

Sources for Table 7.1: historical RPI tables constructed by Professor David Hendry (by kind permission), and *Annual Abstract of Statistics*, various issues.

cases need not have summoned a lecturer in economics. They need only have looked at the published Retail Price Index series, which has run since 1919. Despite the huge amount of time they devoted to the question of inflation since 1941, they got the answer wrong. £500 in 1967 pounds was worth only 91 per cent of the value of £200 in 1941 pounds. The further year that the *Naylor* case took to reach the House of Lords devalued the award by a further 5 percentage points – something which features nowhere in the very long judgement. The 1982 Act raised awards but because the amount was not indexed automatically, in contrast to (for instance) legislation setting social security benefits, it declined steeply in real terms until the 1990 Statutory Instrument imposed a steep increase, and has declined again since. This is not a very impressive performance for the best legal brains in England and Wales.

Commentaries on the law

Generally, the economic reasoning of the courts, in both of the key cases, was lamentably weak. Having discarded the only evidence available, namely actuarial evidence of life expectancy at various ages, the judges plucked numbers from the air. The best-informed remarks were those of Lords Morris of Borth-y-Gest and Devlin in 1968. In the Socratic sense that at least they knew that they did not know, they were the wisest judges. As Devlin said, the amount was fixed by judicial legislation and was quite arbitrary. It bore (and still bears) no relation either to the damages payable for injury or to the value of a human life used for cost-benefit analysis by government departments. Though it might be appropriate to set the amount below either of those ceilings (on the grounds that a huge settlement would be merely a windfall for the estate and would not bring the deceased back), the process has made no concessions to the bereaved Aberfan mother.

Devlin was not the only one uneasy about such payments. J. A. Jolowicz, a Professor of Comparative Law at Cambridge University, referred to loss of expectation of life as an 'absurd' heading for damages while another judge (Diplock, L. J.) called it 'the modern substitute of blood money'.[12] In 1973, the Law Commission reviewed the assessment of damages for personal injuries, including death.[13] It recommended the abolition of payments for loss of expectancy of life to victims' estates on the grounds that future happiness is impossible to calculate. In doing this, it considered whether there should be any place in the law for other forms of compensation for non-pecuniary loss suffered by others apart from the victim. The Law Commission concluded that such a payment should only be made for bereavement in the case of the loss of an infant child or a spouse. The reasoning for such a payment was that

> an award of damages, albeit small, can have some slight consoling effect where parents lose an infant child or where a spouse loses husband or wife. If money can, even minimally, compensate for such bereavement we think it should be recoverable.

As well as easing the grief, the award was also intended to encompass the loss of guidance and counsel that the Scottish Law Commission emphasised.[14] The English Commission recommended a fixed sum rather than a figure that varied according to circumstances and individuals. Their reasoning was:

> we are anxious that there should no judicial enquiry at all into the consequences of bereavement. Nor do we follow the South Australian example in distinguishing between the amounts recoverable in differing relationships; it is, we think, fruitless to try to distinguish between the loss suffered by a parent and that suffered by a spouse; we accept that the award is no more than an arbitrary figure, but, despite its arbitrariness, we think it is something that ought to be, in these two limited contexts, recoverable. We recognise that the effects of bereavement will be greater in some cases than others but to avoid any judicial enquiry into degrees of grief we are prepared to accept this disparity.

The figure recommended in the case of spouses and unmarried minor children was £1,000, recoverable from the negligent party under the Fatal Accident Acts. It further recommended a provision to vary that figure by statutory instrument.[15]

The 1978 Royal Commission, headed by Lord Pearson, on civil liability and compensation for personal injury also concluded, although not unanimously, that payments to immediate relatives for loss of life expectancy should be abolished and replaced with damages recoverable under the Fatal Accidental Acts. The damages were to be primarily for 'the loss of society' rather than sorrow or suffering. In other words, they were to compensate for the loss of non-pecuniary benefits from the deceased, such as help and guidance.[16] Jolowicz noted that it was presumably not intended 'that the court should investigate whether or not the plaintiff positively enjoyed the society of the deceased.'[17] Indeed, like the Law Commission, the Pearson Commission hoped that a small award that did not vary between cases would avoid the need to inquire into family relationships. The Pearson Commission however disagreed that the figure should be a sum permanently fixed at the same level. Instead, it made the sensible recommendation of a *variable* figure. It proposed a yardstick of half average industrial earnings. In 1977, that was approximately £2,000.[18] Although to set a one-off payment (a stock) in terms of an income (a flow) is confusing, it would at least have produced automatic uprating.

During its research, the Pearson Commission received evidence that many parents (including some bereaved at the Summerland and Moorgate disasters) who lost children felt that the sums they had been awarded were inadequate, or even derisory, acknowledgements of their losses.[19] (Lord Robens also gave evidence; parents from Aberfan did not.) The figure the Commission recommended was a rise on the earlier conventional £500 but still it did not take into account the likely length of life of the deceased or their likely earning potential. Neither the Law Commission or the Pearson Commission appear to have considered the possibility of making awards on this pecuniary basis and both rejected the practice in Scottish Law of bereavement payments being unlimited.[20] The previous convention, that calculating future earnings was impossible, was thus continued.

Under Scottish law, bereavement payments are not actually for the bereavement itself but 'loss of society'. In 1993, the scope of this heading was widened and defined as such:

(a) distress and anxiety endured by the relative in contemplation of the suffering of the deceased before his death;
(b) grief and sorrow of the relative caused by the deceased's death; and
(c) the loss of such non-patrimonial benefit as the relative might have been expected to derive from the deceased's society and guidance if the deceased had not died.

Although the 1973 Law Commission envisaged bereavement payments in England and Wales incorporating loss of society, the difference in headings means that Scottish payments are variable and thus potentially higher. However, this comes at a cost to the beneficiary. Applicants are required to provide the awarding board with sufficient family information to enable an evaluation of the loss of society and guidance of the deceased. It was such intrusive investigations that the Pearson Committee wanted to avoid.

The Pearson Commission was not even unanimous in proposing payments for loss of society. Three of its members wished to abolish all rights to claim in relation to bereavement where there was no dependency. Jolowicz claimed that retention of such payments

amounted to 'no more than an expectation that the abolition of
damages for loss of expectation of life ... without replacement would
be widely resented'.[21] P. S. Atiyah, Professor of English Law at the
University of Oxford, also felt that the Pearson Commission was
trying to meeting a 'strongly irrational and punitive element' in
public demands by retaining awards for the death of children or
spouses.[22] The commission did indeed acknowledge that such abolition would be widely resented but it pointed both to the Scottish
situation and to the 'slight consoling effect' of these payments.[23]

The recommendations of the Law Commission included draft
legislation which became the basis of the Administration of Justice
Act 1982 (s.3). The Act abolished damages for loss of expectation of
life and replaced them with bereavement damages set at the fixed
sum of £3,500. Only the married spouse or parents of an unmarried
minor child (but only the mother of an illegitimate child) qualify for
such a payment but it is not subject to proof of financial dependency
or an inquiry of the extent of grief. The Lord Chancellor was given
the power to raise the sum by statutory instrument.

The payment of awards under the 1982 Act continues to raise
objections in the legal profession. Peter Cane, a later editor of
Atiyah's standard book on compensation, notes that the motives of
relatives seeking such awards 'may be questionable'. He goes on to
maintain that it is arbitrary to pay 'what is still to many people a
substantial sum of money' when relatives of people seriously injured,
whose mental suffering may be prolonged and greater, receive
nothing. Cane also objects to the fixed rate of payments to claimants,
irrespective of the health or emotional bond between the spouse or
parent and the deceased. Finally, Cane feels that *solatium* payments
should be a low priority in a legal system that 'denies adequate
compensation for loss of income to so many of those injured in accidents or crippled by disabling illness'.[24] Cane also claims that there is
a punitive or penal element in non-pecuniary damages, particularly
in cases against corporations arising out of disasters. Given that such
awards are normally paid by the insurer, he concludes that punitive
damages as a penalty are 'wholly inappropriate'.[25]

But in a mature insurance market, as this one is, insurance companies give better rates to careful clients, and/or force them to adopt
appropriate safety rules. Gold has noted that in the maritime industry insurers are becoming more involved and interested in safety matters. Loss records are beginning to affect premiums more directly
than ever with the result that maritime management is becoming
more safety conscious.[26] The same applies to other industries where
pressure vessels (e.g. boilers) are used.

Celia Wells also rebuts Cane's arguments. She argues personal injury claims always involve a mixture of motives and it is unfair to single out this group without defining how such motivations should be judged.[27] Disaster victims themselves are often offended by the doubting of their motives. As Disaster Action repeatedly stress, their interest is in justice and a recognition of their loss rather than financial gain.[28] Wells also stresses that a comparison between death and injury is poor. The relatives of someone injured will benefit, directly or indirectly, through the awards made to the individual him or herself, while the different order of death to injury is recognised by legal systems in many ways. She argues that £7,500 to a very limited class of relatives could hardly be considered an unduly generous sum.[29] Richard Colbey, a barrister, adds that in the USA in 1997, the parents of a six-year-old boy who died after falling out of a badly designed van were awarded $262 million (£162 million).[30]

Justice or finance?

Public pressure for higher awards grew through the 1980s. The pressure of Citizen Action Compensation Campaign for higher awards for non-pecuniary damages to victims of disasters has been central in this.[31] The spate of disasters in the late 1980s drew wider attention to the plight of injured and bereaved parties and was a spur in the bringing of a 1989 private member's bill.[32] Weight has been added to the victims' cause by the large sums awarded by juries in defamation cases for loss of reputation. The high level of these awards contrasts strongly with the smaller sums given in the more serious cases of death and injury. Libel awards illustrate the problems of consistency that led to abandonment in 1966 of the use of juries in cases involving non-pecuniary awards for injuries and deaths.[33] More recently, the 1996 Defamation Act minimised the role of juries in libel cases.

The narrowness of the class of relatives entitled to claim bereavement damages has led to some resentment amongst bereaved relatives. The inability of children to claim for bereavement after the loss of a parent was one source of anger. The disasters of the 1980s exposed the ineligibility of parents whose young adult children are killed. Parents of *Marchioness* and *Herald* victims are said to have been particularly affected by this and it was a driving force behind one set of parents bringing an action for the pain and suffering suffered by their daughters who were killed at Hillsborough.[34]

Influenced by such concerns, in 1989 Lawrence Cunliffe MP (Labour, Leigh) introduced a private member's bill (Citizen

Compensation Bill) to raise the damages to £10,000 (subject to a maximum of £50,000 in respect of each death) with an extended class of persons entitled to claim (spouses, parents, children, and any other person whom the court thought had suffered through a special relationship with the deceased). The Government opposed the bill on the basis that the Law Commission had rejected a wider category of entitled relatives while the 1982 Act provided a mechanism for raising the level of damages. The bill failed to become to law but the Solicitor General did announce a review of the level of bereavement damages.[35]

That review presented three different options. Firstly, to raise the level, in accordance with the change in the value of money, to £5,000. Secondly, to raise the award by more than the rate of inflation to, 'say', £10,000. Thirdly, to retain the award at its existing level of £3,500.

In favour of the first award, the review noted that '[s]ince the sum is not intended to compensate for actual monetary loss, changes on the level are not called for every year' but argued that the value of money had changed sufficiently to justify a change. In favour of an award of £10,000, the review stated: 'it can be argued that damages for bereavement should be set at something more than a nominal sum to reflect the deep grief and suffering which the untimely death of a close relative can bring about.' Against this option the review pointed out that such a rise would change the nature of the award and it was arguable whether parliament had given the Lord Chancellor that power. The argument for the third option of maintaining the level of awards was that the change in the value of money was not yet sufficient to justify a rise. Despite hearing arguments for £10,000 from the Bar and the Law Society, the Lord Chancellor set the award at a figure of £7,500.[36]

Although a welcome development, that rise did nothing for those bereaved relatives not eligible. Since actions in tort can survive death, suing for losses (i.e. pain and suffering) sustained between the injury and death is one avenue open for relatives to gain financial compensation for their bereavement. However, identifying the medical difference between instantaneous death (for which compensation for pain and suffering in not recoverable) and non-instantaneous (for which compensation is recoverable) is difficult and distasteful. This was illustrated by a case brought by the parents of two teenage girls killed in the Hillsborough disaster (*Hicks v C.C. S. Yorkshire* [1992] 2 All ER 65). The House of Lords upheld the verdict of the High Court and Court of Appeal and ruled that from the evidence it was not possible to establish that there had been any physical injury and suffering before the two girls lost consciousness in the crush. The Lords also ruled that the fear of death felt by victims subsequently killed was not in itself grounds for recovery. As Wells points out, this is a fine line that illustrates a 'critical difference between the legal and cultural assessment of events'.[37] Mr and Mrs Hicks lost two daughters, aged 15 and 19, in the Hillsborough disaster. They received the statutory bereavement award for the loss of their youngest daughter but for the eldest, they received nothing. In contrast, sums of up to £200,000 were paid to certain (but not all) individual junior police officers who helped in the rescue operation to compensate them for the post-traumatic stress disorder.

The shortcomings of the law were further illustrated by a 1990 case where a seventeen-year-old sustained injuries in a road accident (*Doleman v Deakin* [1990] TLR 30 January 1990). He died from his injures after his eighteenth birthday. The court ruled that his parents were not entitled to bereavement damages because the deceased was not a minor at the time of the death.

Thus the sense of injustice felt by the bereaved Aberfan parent at the size of the award she received has resurfaced after other disasters and accidents. For those who lose a close loved one on whom they were not financially dependent, the financial compensation can seem derisory; for those who lose an adult child, such compensation is non-existent. The basis for those awards has changed from loss of expectation of life to bereavement. This change has arguably resulted in the law becoming less fair. The narrow class of dependants entitled to bereavement damages under the 1982 Administration of Justice Act is a regression from the previous position where the beneficiaries of the deceased's estate were entitled to a payment for loss of expectation of life.

At the heart of the injustices remains the uncomfortable task of trying to put a financial figure on the value of a life. Although that is not what the law intends as the purpose of the award, it is how many bereaved perceive it.[38] As the Aberfan parent pointed out, no figure can ever truly compensate for her loss. This has been used as argument not to pay such awards.[39] But as Lawrence Cunliffe argued during the second reading of his abortive bill 'It is true that damages can never adequately compensate for the loss of a member of one's family, but just because it is difficult to compensate does not mean that we should not try.' Money may not compensate for a life but it is the only tool available to the law and it would be an insult to the bereaved if nothing were available.[40] Such payments have often been interpreted as 'reflecting the significance that society attaches to a death caused by the negligence of another person.'[41] They are thus important to the bereaved. When compared to the sums received for injuries, their value seems not only ungenerous but derisory.[42] As another Aberfan parent asked thirty years later, 'is that all my child was worth, £500?'[43] The situation is not helped by the failure to index link bereavement damages.

One obvious way of putting a financial figure on the value of a life is to calculate what the deceased young person would otherwise have earned, and to base compensation on the net present value of this stream of income forgone. Economists have a more sophisticated objection to this than we have found in any court judgement or legal commentary:

> There are two economic arguments for parental compensation: i) emotional loss, trauma, etc. ii) financial loss to parents. The financial loss to parents is clearly not the same as the present value of the prospective future earnings stream of the child, since most of this income would be devoted to personal consumption during adulthood. In Britain it has long (for 200+ years) been the habit of young adults to leave the parental home in their early 20s and establish a new household on marriage. From the age of 18, most employed males and females would have been paying for their board and lodging, rather than handing over their earnings to their parents. In consequence, the parental income forgone by the premature death of a child can scarcely be more than the child's income from ages 14 to 17. This, of course, should be offset against the marginal household cost of that child if he/she lived to age 17. The overall financial loss calculated in this way is very small; it may even be a long-term financial gain to the household. It might be argued that children also provide transfers to their parents when the parents are elderly, and that these should also be factored into the calculation. In practice, however, family financial transfers have been shown in survey data to be very small (only 3.3% of elderly households in inter-war London reported receiving financial transfers from relatives). This type of calculation would, of course, produce very different, and very high, compensation values for the death of an adult who was supporting young dependants – then the compensation would need to cover their anticipated living costs until the age of 18.[44]

In response to this economic argument the following points can be made.

- The financial transfers from the middle-aged to their parents are probably a very small proportion of the value of care services that middle-aged people take on as their parents become elderly and dependent. The author of the letter at the head of this chapter, like the other surviving Aberfan parents, is now in her 70s, and of an age where her daughter, if she had lived, might be starting to give her considerable support.

• Again and again, the recipients of these sums for the loss of their children testify that they find them insulting to them and to the memory of their dead children. Until recently, they could contrast them with astronomical sums awarded to celebrities in libel damages. That anomaly has been partly corrected by reducing the amount of damages payable for defamation. But other stark anomalies remain, such as that between relatives of Hillsborough victims and some Hillsborough police officers.

• There is a perverse incentive for negligent parties. It is cheaper to kill than to injure, and it is cheaper to kill children than to kill adults. That is not an incentive structure that any society would wish to encourage.

• The case for higher payments is also related to promoting safety. As a representative of Disaster Action pointed out in 1993 'Paying out should at least teach corporations that there is a heavy price if they take safety responsibilities too lightly'.[45]

• Finally, bereavement damages are tied up with the issue of punishment. A 'significant number' of respondents to the Lord Chancellor's 1990 consultation paper argued for higher bereavement damages because of what they perceived as the inadequacy of criminal sanctions in fatal cases of negligence. This feeling is of course particularly strong regarding large companies which cause disasters.[46]

In 1997, the Law Commission rejected bereavement damages as a method of punishing the wrongdoer but it did propose increasing bereavement damages to £10,000 (the same figure as that payable by the Criminal Injuries Compensation Scheme following a death) and linking them to the RPI. As part of the proposals, damages would be paid to all eligible rather than the current single payment. The class eligible of relatives would be expanded to include parents of older children, children who lose parents and siblings and some unmarried partners (those with children or cohabiting for 2 years). Such changes, if enacted, would represent a welcome development but one too late for victims of disasters past. The Commission concluded that much of the unrest was concerned with false public perceptions about the purpose of the payments. It recommended that the legislation make clear that the awards were for:

(a) the grief and sorrow of the relative caused by the deceased's death
(b) the loss of such non-pecuniary benefit as the relative might have

been expected to derive from the deceased's care, guidance and society if the deceased had not died.[47]

Negligent parties are of course entitled to pay the families of the deceased more than the minimum sum statutorily required. Such gestures would represent a real acceptance of responsibility that has too often been lacking following disasters. Even where a financial responsibility is accepted to pay compensation, a court settlement or a no-fault out-of-court settlement is often interpreted as an attempt to evade moral responsibility that adds to the trauma of the bereaved. British Rail accepted complete responsibility for the Clapham rail disaster after just one day and offered an immediate hardship payment of £2,000 each to bereaved families. Within a month the British Railways Board had offered each bereaved family compensation of £10,000, £6,500 more than the sum stipulated by the 1982 Administration of Justice Act. Such sums were on top of any claimed for loss of dependency, injuries etc. Some other companies involved in disasters have similarly paid larger sums than required by law.

Table 7.2 Non-pecuniary compensation payments following certain disasters.

Company (disaster)	Bereavement payment	Pain & suffering payment
P&O (Zeebrugge)	£5,000	£5,000
London Underground (King's Cross)	£7,500	£3,500
British Rail (Clapham)	£10,000	£,4000

Source: Law Commission Consultation Paper no 148, *Claims for Wrongful Death* (London: HMSO, 1997), p. 92, note 273.

The pain and suffering was that endured by the deceased between the moment of the disaster and death; the same heading as the Hicks family's unsuccessful claim after Hillsborough. Cunliffe maintained in Parliament that the above settlements were due to the scale of the disasters and the 'sensational reporting'. This had meant that 'the defendants felt that it would be unconscionable to pay the statutory amount to the bereaved'.[48] The Law Commission argued that such payments should not guide legislation because of the 'highly charged and public circumstances' in which they took place.[49] For families who lose their children in road traffic accidents or other 'everyday' tragedies there is no accompanying publicity to shame a company, or a disaster fund to try and make up for legal inadequacies.

For those bereaved relatives whose subsequent grief and anger becomes a psychiatric disorder then there is the option of suing for compensation. Litigation after the sinking of the *Herald of Free Enterprise* established the validity of PTSD as grounds for compensation after a disaster. This included relatives who were suffering from 'pathological grief'. Yet such bereaved relatives can face considerable legal obstacles in succeeding their claims. After the Hillsborough disaster, a number of test cases were brought to court by bereaved relatives who had either witnessed the disaster on television or had actually been at the game itself but in another part of the stadium (*Alcock v Chief Constable of South Yorkshire Police* [1992] 1 AC 310). The cases went to the House of Lords where they eventually failed amid legal concerns over the proximity of the plaintiffs to the disaster and their relationship with the victims. None of the claimants had been in the ground *and* lost a spouse or child. In essence, the cases failed because of policy concerns that such a decision in favour of the plaintiffs would open the floodgates for future claims. According to one commentator, underpinning the Lords' concerns was a fear that the law would have to compensate people for the strains of life such as negligently caused bereavement.[50] In a world where images are broadcast across the world to millions, a further fear was that defendants would be subjected to 'indeterminate liability, to an indeterminate group of people, for an indeterminate length of time'.[51] Thus, as with bereavement damages, reluctance to overcompensate those who lose relatives because of the negligence of another has resulted in only narrow classes of people being able to claim for psychiatric damage caused by the horror of their experiences. In making their judgement, the House of Lords did not make a single explicit reference to the medical determinants of psychiatric injury.[52]

Aberfan was the first British disaster to receive intensive television coverage. As happened at Hillsborough, the NCB lawyers anticipated claims from parents for nervous shock on hearing of the disaster or seeing it on television. Although the lawyers said that this was a 'doubtful of issue of law' they decided to 'deal reasonably with genuine cases rather than to test the legal issue to the limit'.[53] Three decades later, the cases following Hillsborough did test that legal issue and the result did not favour the bereaved. One Hillsborough relative commented:

> ... we went through mental torture. But, according to the law because you're sitting at home, waiting for horrible news, you didn't suffer. I'm afraid there's something twisted and sick about the law.[54]

The issue at the heart of this chapter is not whether money can compensate families (or indeed help ease their psychological trauma) after the loss of a loved one on whom they were not financially dependent. Nor is it, as acknowledged by the judges and politicians discussed above, whether the law is compensating any financial loss by parents whose child is killed. (They may have been able to expect some form of support in their old age but such practice is far from the norm in Britain and to compensate for its loss is making predictions that no actuarial evidence can substantiate.) Instead, payments upon the death of a child represent a symbolic acceptance of guilt by the negligent party and a recognition of this by the State enforcing the payment. For that reason, bereavement damages should not be seen as 'blood money' but some recompense for the bereaved to illustrate that their loss has not gone unacknowledged. Compensation is as much about justice as finance.

Notes

1 PRO COAL 73/2. Names of author and her daughter withheld. Lord Robens did not reply.
2 British Railways Board, *Automatic Train Protection* (London: BRB 1994), p. 12.
3 PRO COAL 73/2: W. J. P. Webber to Lord Robens, 25 April 1967 (accepting liability); D. Haslam to same, 31 May 1967 ('good offer'); D. H. Kelly to same, 8 June 1967 ('hard core'); Secret Minute of the board 16 June 1967 (agreeing not to go above £500 per victim).
4 Law Commission Consultation Paper No 140, *Damages for Personal Injury: Non-Pecuniary Loss* (London: HMSO, 1995), para., 2.7.
5 Average industrial weekly earnings (manual workers, men over 21) in 1941 – 99s 5d. Source: *British Labour Statistics, Historical Abstract 1886–1968* (Dept of Employment & Productivity: HMSO, 1971), p. 99. The above is prior to the 1948 standard industrial classification, so that an exact comparison with figures for the 1960s is not possible. Nevertheless, the order of magnitude is correct.
6 'When Goddard went to Buckingham Palace to receive [his knighthood] from King George V, they discussed the recent increase in crimes of violence and the monarch remarked that he hoped the new judge would not hesitate to sentence violent criminals to flogging, advice which Goddard invariably took when he considered it appropriate. From the outset he proved himself a strong judge, dominating his court and giving short shrift to dilatory counsel and evasive witnesses, although he normally behaved with studied courtesy on the bench.' H. Montgomery Hyde, Rayner Goddard, Baron Goddard, *Dictionary of National Biography*, CD-Rom version (OUP, 1995).
7 Lord Reid in *West v Shephard* [1964] AC 326, 342.

8 *Dictionary of National Biography* (OUP, 1995). A. L. Goodhart, 'Viscount Simon, 1873–1954', (1954) 70 LQR 177, 179–180.
9 PRO COAL 73/2 Donald Haslam to Robens, 31 May 1967.
10 The NCB seemed to be aware of a potential problem and noted that the offer seemed to be 'acceptable' to the deceased's solicitors and 'as far as we know' the relatives. COAL 73/2 Donald Haslam to Robens, 31 May 1967.
11 Wells, *Negotiating Tragedy*, p. 126.
12 J. A. Jolowicz, 'Compensation for Personal Injury and Fault', in D. K. Allen, C. J. Bourn & J. H. Holyoak (eds.), *Accident Compensation after Pearson* (London: Sweet & Maxwell, 1979), p. 65.
13 The Law Commission (Report 56), *Report on Personal Injury Litigation – Assessment of Damages* (London: HMSO, 1973).
14 Scottish Law Commission Memorandum No. 17, 10 April 1972. Scots law already made provision for claims for solatium but the Scottish Law Commission recommended that this be replaced by a wider claim for loss of non-pecuniary benefits such as guidance and counsel.
15 Law Commission, *Report on Personal Injury Litigation*, paras. 172–177.
16 Lord Pearson, *Royal Commission on Civil Liability and Compensation for Personal Injury* (London: HMSO, 1978), para. 422.
17 Jolowicz, 'Compensation for Personal Injury and Fault', p. 60.
18 Pearson, *Royal Commission*, paras. 370, 418–427.
19 Pearson, *Royal Commission*, para. 370.
20 Damages (Scotland) Act 1976, amended by the Damages (Scotland) Act 1993.
21 Jolowicz, 'Compensation for Personal Injury and Fault', p. 65.
22 P. S. Atiyah, 'What now?' in Allen *et al. Accident Compensation after Pearson*, p. 244.
23 Pearson, *Royal Commission*, paras. 418–25.
24 Peter Cane, *Atiyah's Accidents, Compensation and the Law* (London: Butterworths, 5ᵗʰ edn., 1993), pp. 76–77.
25 Cane, *Atiyah's Accidents*, p. 146.
26 Edgar Gold, 'Learning from Disaster: Lessons in Regulatory Enforcement in the Maritime Sector', *Review of European Community and International Environmental Law*, vol. 8, no. 1, April 1999, 16–20.
27 Wells, *Negotiating Tragedy*, p. 127.
28 For example see *Disaster Action Newsletter*, Spring/Summer 1997 Issue 4.
29 Wells, *Negotiating Tragedy*, p. 127.
30 R. Colbey, 'New look at disaster pay-outs', *The Guardian*, 11 October 1997. The sum was divided into $12.5m for actual damages and $250m for punitive damages. Gary Slapper, 'Corporate Crime and Punishment, *The Criminal Lawyer*, March/April 1998, p. 7.
31 Cane, *Atiyah's Accidents*, p. 146.
32 See, for example, *Hansard*, 6ᵗʰ ser. vol. 148, col. 548.
33 Cane, *Atiyah's Accidents*, p. 141. Juries may still be used in exceptional cases.
34 Wells, *Negotiating Tragedy*, pp. 125–126. Also see, for example, *Hansard*, 6ᵗʰ ser. vol. 148, col. 544.
35 *Hansard*, 6ᵗʰ ser., vol 144, col. 456, vol. 148, cols. 511–569, vol. 156, cols. 637–649. Lord Chancellor's Department, *Damages for Bereavement: A Review of the Level* (London: Lord Chancellor's Department, 1990).

36 SI 1990/2575. See David Kemp (assisted by Peter Mantle), *Damages for Personal Injury and Death* (London: Sweet & Maxwell, 7th edn., 1999), pp. 74–75.

37 Wells, *Negotiating Tragedy*, p. 125.

38 Law Commission Consultation Paper no 148, *Claims for Wrongful Death* (London: HMSO, 1997), para. 3.136.

39 E.g., in the debates on the 1982 bill and its amendment in 1989, Lord Hailsham, Hansard (Lords), vol. 428, cols. 27–28, 45; & James Arbuthnot MP, a member of Lloyds, *Hansard*, vol. 148, col. 527.

40 Law Commission, *Claims for Wrongful Death*, para. 3.130.

41 Cunliffe in *Hansard*, 6th ser., vol. 148, col. 519. Alfred Morris (Manchester, Wythenshawe) *Hansard*, 6th ser., vol. 148, col. 544.

42 For example, in 1998 the recommended figure for very severe brain damage was £110–150,000, severe facial scarring in a young woman £22,500 to £42,500 and loss of a thumb £17,000 to £26,000. Like bereavement damages, such figures are of course arbitrary. Judicial Studies Board, *Guidelines for the Assessment of General Damages in Personal Injury Cases* (London: Blackstone, 4th edn., 1998).

43 MJ interview with bereaved Aberfan parent.

44 Summary of opinion of an academic economist presented to authors, Summer 1999.

45 Pamela Dix, 'Distress and Redress', *The Guardian*, 29 December 1993.

46 Law Commission, *Claims for Wrongful Death*, p. 81, note 213.

47 Law Commission, *Claims for Wrongful Death*, para. 3.138.

48 Cunliffe in *Hansard*, 6th ser. vol. 148, col. 520.

49 Law Commission, *Claims for Wrongful Death*, p. 92, note 273.

50 H. Teff, 'Liability for Psychiatric Illness after Hillsborough', *Oxford Journal for Legal Studies*, vol. 12 , Autumn 1992, p. 448.

51 Judge Cardozo, quoted in Shyamala Rajan-Vince, 'Nervous Shock!'. LAWTEL document no. 0981210. www.Lawtel.co.uk

52 See Teff, 'Liability for Psychiatric Illness'. However, the cases did establish that damages could be claimed by secondary victims where proximity to the disaster and a close relationship to the deceased were established.

53 PRO COAL 73/2 Aberfan Common Law Claims, Memo from Donald Haslam to Lord Robens, 31 May 1967.

54 Quoted in Davis & Scraton, *Beyond Disaster*, p. 45.

Chapter Eight

HOLDING CORPORATIONS TO ACCOUNT

A prosecution should only take place when the investigation into the disaster has uncovered evidence which indicates criminal culpability; and we are aware that not every disaster is necessarily the result of criminal conduct on the part of a company and their senior officers. However, the absence of any successful manslaughter prosecution, or indeed any other prosecution, for an offence which relates directly to causing a death after any of the disasters whose family groups we represent, has led us to seriously consider whether the reasons for this lie outside those relating to sufficiency of evidence.[1]

Disaster Action

Disasters involve varying degrees of failures and neglect. When does behaviour become so negligent that it should be classed as criminal? Criminal law uses concepts such as intent or recklessness to answer this question. Yet such matters are highly subjective, meaning that the law is essentially a social construct open to debate and conflict. The Aberfan tribunal saw its job as being the assignment of blame, not of liability in civil law, still less of criminal investigation.[2] But if companies were to be prevented from behaving as the NCB had behaved before (and, for that matter, after) Aberfan, there would have to be civil, regulatory, and/or criminal sanctions.

This chapter looks at two main routes towards holding companies responsible for safety: statutory regulation under the Health and Safety at Work Act 1974, and the threat of corporate manslaughter charges. It also considers other routes in passing, such as civil litigation and pressure from inquest juries. Changing cultural values and the evolving role of inquest juries have changed the social perception of negligent corporations. Consequently there have been calls for the law to be reformed to ensure that convictions for corporate killing are easier to achieve. However, such reform is problematic, as the Southall (1997) and Ladbroke Grove (1999) rail accidents have most recently shown.

Health and safety at work in 1966

In 1966, safety in the workplace was governed by a complex series of acts and inspectorates that had grown up as industry developed.[3] Primary enforcement of this legislation was criminal but a breach of statutory duty made it easier for injured plaintiffs to sue.[4] Independent regulators, rather than the police, had carried out the regulation and inspection of industry since the 1833 Factory Act. Breaches of such regulations were criminal offences but, through being enforced by an agency other than the police, they did not carry the same stigma. Even deaths in the work place were not normally considered as heinous criminal offences. Instead, like traffic crimes, workplace offences were seen as what has been labelled, 'quasi crime'.[5] Criminal law was traditionally based around notions of intent. In accidents at work or on the road, intent was not an issue, no matter how negligent the perpetrator. Thus the Aberfan disaster was commonly perceived, not as a criminal act, but as a tragic accident.

Breach of a regulatory statute could result in fines or imprisonment but such lines were rarely pursued, and when pursued often had meagre results. (And, as already explained, nobody at Aberfan committed a statutory offence under the Mines and Quarries Act 1954; the disaster was not a reportable accident as no miners were injured or killed). Inspectorates maintained that persuasion was more effective than prosecution. More effective compliance could be achieved by promoting safety procedures as good practice than as something to do because the law required it.[6] A sample of cases investigated by the Factory Inspectorate between 1961 and 1966 revealed that fewer than 4 per cent of contraventions of Acts and regulations resulted in prosecution or even the threat of it. Of the few firms that were found to be contravening for the third or later time, prosecution or the threat of it was still only used in ten per cent of cases. The Mines and Quarries Inspectorate took an even more co-operative approach. Perhaps because it was regulating a coal industry that, in theory, was answerable to a sponsoring government department, the Inspectorate had adopted a remarkably non-confrontational role. It believed that good relations with both the NCB and NUM would often ensure safety standards beyond the legal requirements.[7] From 1938 to 1946, the Inspectorate made 43 prosecutions (an annual average of 4.78) involving mines. From 1947 (the year of nationalisation of the coal industry) to 1969, the inspectorate brought 35 prosecutions involving mines (an average of 1.52 a year).[8] Its prosecution rate was very far below that of other inspectorates. Table 8.1 shows that the pattern continued into the 1970s.

Table 8.1 Number of Prosecutions instituted by or involving HSC enforcement
authorities, 1971–75

Premises subject to	1971	1972	1973	1974	1975
Factories Act	1330	1547	1782	1826	1433
Offices, Shops and Railway Premises Act	165	115	123	120	78
Mines and Quarries Act	2	–	3	3	2
Agriculture (Safety, Health and Welfare Provisions) Act	214	340	305	164	147

Source: Health and Safety Executive, *Health and Safety Statistics 1975*, HMSO, p. 7.

The Robens Committee

Barbara Castle became the first Secretary of State at the new Department of Employment and Productivity in April 1968. The title of the new department was meant to indicate that its responsibilities had expanded beyond those of the old Ministry of Labour. One responsibility it inherited was that of oversight of the various health and safety at work statutes. The first hint we have of a plan to rationalise and improve them is in Castle's diary entry for 11 October 1968:

> Faced with my determination to have new safety, health and welfare legislation in this Parliament, the office has come up with a new idea. Instead of struggling with a detailed bill we should have a simple measure setting up a new independent authority which would co-ordinate the safety provisions in all fields. It obviously has great possibilities, though a few probing questions by me reveal that the difficulties have not yet been thought through. I told them to prepare a more detailed submission to me.

The next reference, again from her diary, is this, on 9 April 1970:

> Alf Robens has jumped at my invitation to chair the inquiry into safety, health, and welfare. He came along for a drink and was all rearing [sic] to go. Ken Barnes [Deputy Under-Secretary at the Department of Employment and Productivity] and Sisson [C.H. Sisson, the poet, at the time the Assistant Under-Secretary responsible for the Safety, Health and Welfare Division of the DEP] were delighted: we haven't had anything go so smoothly for a long time.[9]

So smoothly did the setting up of the committee go that we have found no other surviving records of it. There is nothing in the surviving Private Office records from the Department. Nor did it go to an inter-departmental committee, at least not one that recorded any conclusions in the CAB 130 series of *ad hoc* ministerial committees.[10]

In some ways Robens was an appropriate choice for chairman. Fatalities and injuries per NCB manshift had come down sharply during his chairmanship. He devotes a chapter of his memoirs to the 'strong lead' he gave on accident reduction. During his chairmanship, fatal and serious accidents per 100,000 manshifts in the NCB declined from 1.34 in 1960 to 1.04 in 1970, a 22.4 per cent decline.[11] Robens was also a well-known figure in both trade union and business circles, which gave him an authority that crossed labour-capital divides.

In other ways, Robens was a very surprising choice. Firstly, it might be felt that the man who had presided over the Coal Board at the time of Aberfan was inappropriate for the job. As some of those writing about later disasters have pointed out, Robens had a personal vested interest in the committee's conclusions that apathy was the main cause of accidents, thus making criminal law generally inappropriate for dealing with workplace safety.[12] Second, ministers in general, and Castle in particular, thoroughly disliked and distrusted him. Earlier, while Secretary of State for Transport, she had had to appoint a chairman for British Rail. Finding her preferred nominee, Peter Parker, blocked by other ministers (and, in the end, by his unwillingness to do the job for the pay on offer), she recorded:

> Harold [Wilson] is now keen for me to see Alf Robens. What did Dick [Marsh] think of him? Utterly ruthless – and would think nothing of selling his Minister down the river. Not a very good administrator but with the sort of personality that inspires confidence. I am determined not to have Alf even if he would take it.[13]

She also described Aubrey Jones of the Prices and Incomes Board as 'rivalling Robens in megalomania ... Aubrey really is another Robens, though without the savagery'.[14] As a friend of Cecil King, Robens had been on the fringes of King's plans to topple Wilson as Prime Minister. Wilson noted

> [S]ubstantial sections of the press were again engaged on a 'Wilson-must-go' campaign.... It had the enthusiastic backing of Lord Shawcross. In no time at all, the other members of the trinity, Lord Robens and Mr Cecil King, were joining in with demands for a coalition of all the talents – Great Britain Limited ...[15]

Robens' involvement in the plot to topple the Wilson government and replace it by a military junta led by Earl Mountbatten and Sir Solly Zuckerman may not have been overt but it was known that he shared King's contempt for Government ministers and his view that the UK should be run by businessmen like themselves.

Why, if Robens was quite unacceptable to run the Railways Board in 1967, did he seem an ideal appointment for the health and safety job in 1970? By 1970 his ten year stint at the Coal Board was almost over. Ministers had worried about the risk of his attacking their energy policies once he had left the NCB. The health and safety job, unlike the chairmanship of British Rail, was removed from day-to-day politics. From Barbara Castle's point of view, it was an ideal siding into which to shunt such dangerous freight as Lord Robens.

The Robens Report

The Robens Report states that the general lack of prosecutions for health and safety offences was due to the difficulties in identifying those cases where it would be appropriate and to the problem of establishing a degree of direct personal responsibility that would justify a custodial sentence. Instead small fines were generally imposed that did not even meet the derisory maximum that legislation allowed. The result was that criminal proceedings in health and safety fell 'between two stools'. On the one hand criminal proceedings were felt inappropriate for the majority of situations, while doing little to help improve future standards, and on the other hand the penalties imposed were generally too light to have any real impact in cases where 'exemplary punishment' was needed.[16]

The solution of Robens and his committee was a system that, in the majority of incidents of unsafe practice, allowed for 'constructive remedial action' rather than criminal punishment. Voluntary standards and codes of practice should supplement, and where possible replace, statutory regulations. A system of self-regulation would encourage companies to act responsibly. Prosecution was only to be used in the minority of more serious 'flagrant, wilful or reckless' cases.[17] The Report justified this approach by arguing that

> ... the traditional concepts of the criminal law are not readily applicable to the majority of infringements which arise under this type of legislation. Relatively few offences are clear-cut, few arise from reckless indifference to the possibility of causing injury, few can be laid without qualification at the door of a particular individual. The typical infringement or combination of infringements arises rather through carelessness, oversight, lack of knowledge or means, inadequate supervision or sheer inefficiency. In such circumstances the process of prosecution and punishment by the criminal courts is largely an irrelevancy.[18]

As at Aberfan, deaths caused by carelessness or oversight were not deemed criminal.

The bulk of Robens' recommendations became law through the Health and Safety at Work etc. Act (HSWA) 1974. The Act has remained at the heart of British safety legislation ever since, although other later statutes cover specific areas such as environmental protection, road safety and the nuclear industry.[19] The Act also brought an extra eight million people not covered by previous health and safety legislation under its scope.[20] Jenny Bacon, the Director-General of the HSE at the time of writing, identifies four key areas where the Robens Report changed Health and Safety philosophy in the UK. The first was the Report's 'big idea' of self-regulation. Secondly, the report advanced the business and economic case for addressing health and safety issues. Thirdly, legislation should be goal rather than rule based in order to encourage emphasis on the causes of problems rather than symptoms. Finally, it advocated a consistent approach in standards, legislation and enforcement across the whole of industry.[21]

In terms of enforcement and punishing offenders, 'the Inspectorate and Commission have sharper, tougher and longer teeth' than Robens envisaged.[22] The Health and Safety Executive (HSE), as its name implies, has executive powers, broader than those of inspectorates under previous legislation. Robens had merely recommended an Authority, not an Executive. The 1974 Act provides both a general offence of failing to ensure the health, safety and welfare of employees and the continuation of specific regulations relating to particular industries. Breach of either is a criminal offence punishable, in some cases, by imprisonment.

The 1974 HSWA did not abolish all the existing legislation in the field. Instead, it instructed the Health & Safety Commission (HSC) and HSE to progressively replace statutes with a new system of regulations and approved codes. As well as this combination of specific statutes and regulations, the Act also created a basic requirement of a safe and healthy workplace within 'reasonable practicability'. This clause allowed companies to balance the risk against the financial and time costs of prevention.[23]

Underpinning both report and Act was the assumption that the interests of employer and employee were shared: a safe and healthy workplace was beneficial to both sides. It is symbolic of this that the 1974 Act was bipartisan. It was drafted under the 1970–4 Heath government, but fell at the dissolution of parliament. The Labour bill differed from the Conservative one only in giving a greater statutory role to trade unions, and in the 'grandfathering' of old law including the Mines & Quarries Act 1954, in s.1(2). Theo Nichols is one of several Marxist critics who argue that capital's first priority will always be profit and that workers are seen as simply components in the means of production.[24] However, even from a Marxist perspective, an uninjured worker is worth more to a capitalist than an injured one, unless you assume that there is a reserve army of the unemployed at the gate all the time. At least at times of high employment, the Marxist argument against self-regulation fails. But it does throw light on the controversy between codes and statutes. The Robens Committee, and the HSE, inherited statutes and wished to substitute codes. So do regulators world-wide. What is at stake, and are they right?

On codes and statutes

The Robens Committee found that 'there is too much law, [and] too much of the existing law is intrinsically unsatisfactory'.[25] Too much law because what was needed was not regulation by the state but self-ownership of safety. Too much of the existing law was intrinsically unsatisfactory because it had been drafted to minimise the particular risks that were obvious to those who drafted the law (sometimes in response to disaster). These risks might have changed or even disappeared since the statute was drafted.[26] Far better, thought the Robens committee, that those who worked in an industry should work together to define the main risks and how to minimise them. This has been the approach of the HSC/HSE ever since. In the transport industries, for instance, each operator works out its own Safety Case and submits it for approval to the relevant inspectorate.

Regulation of the coal industry by the Mines and Quarries Act 1954 was a prime example of the system the Robens Committee deplored. The 1954 Act updated the Coal Mines Act 1911, which itself consolidated various Victorian statutes.[27] The 1954 Act was too big, but (as we saw above) not only did it include nothing about tip safety but the Coal Division of the Ministry of Power thought it would be a 'revolutionary innovation' to incorporate a duty of safety to the public.

The mining industry was notorious for its bad industrial relations. That was so before, during, and after nationalisation. Nowhere, one might think, would the Marxist prediction that the interests of owners and workers were opposite be better borne out. But on this matter, owners and workers were on the same side, and equally myopic. And so were the inspectors who oversaw the 1954 Act. Apart from a few suggestions in the Tribunal Report that the former Powell Duffryn company had been more safety-conscious at Aberfan than its successor the NCB, Aberfan brought no comfort for any of the stakeholders in the coal industry. And yet, when the Health and Safety at Work etc Act was passing through the Commons, the mining group of Labour MPs was behind the addition of a clause that requires regulations under the Act to be 'designed to maintain or improve the standards of health, safety, and welfare'.[28] They wished to protect 'their beloved Mines & Quarries Act', according to one observer,[29] from precipitate repeal. No matter that its failings had contributed to the death of 144 people at Aberfan.

Therefore, whereas Marxist and other critics of regulation may complain that regulation by codes of practice is too cosy compared to regulation by statute, the mining industry does not offer persuasive evidence to help them. A better way to approach the question is by considering *Regulatory capture.*

Regulatory capture and the independence of inspectorates.

Regulation, in its most general definition, is 'the imposition of economic controls by government agencies on (usually) private businesses.'[30] Governments have regulated businesses for as long as both have existed. Among the things regulated are price, quantity of goods, quality of goods, entry and exit of firms, and (most relevant here) safety.

What is regulation for? To that, there are numerous internal and external answers. The internal answers come from legislators and regulators; the external, from academic analysts (mostly in Chicago). The internal case for safety regulation is that consumers lack information about product safety. Residents of Aberfan lacked expert knowledge of whether their tips were safe (although, as it turned out, they had a better idea than did the regulator). Therefore it is legitimate for the state to impose safety regulations on mining companies. The external analysis accepts that the case exists, but adds that all parties will act in their self-interest. Regulators will support regulation *per se* because it gives them a job. Industries will oppose it in so far as it raises their costs, but support it in so far as it protects existing firms from competitors. Politicians will maximise what Peltzman called their political support function. Peltzman defined it in terms of price and wage regulation, but the definition is general and may apply to any kind of regulation: 'the regulator adjusts ... until the marginal political support from ... change in any direction yields no further increase in political support'.[31] Regulation fails when it fails to achieve its stated aim. As we have shown, there was regulatory failure at Aberfan. The Mines and Quarries Inspectorate hardly ever prosecuted. HM Inspectors of Mines and Quarries were former colliery engineers, and therefore usually former NCB employees. They were as much moles being asked about the habits of birds as were the engineers they regulated.

The complaint that HM Inspectorate of Mines & Quarries was too close to the industry it regulated was not new in 1966. It emerged from the Gresford mining disaster in 1934, in which 261 miners, three rescuers and one surface worker were killed in an explosion in a North Wales colliery. The inquiry, chaired by Sir Henry Walker, the Chief Inspector of Mines and Quarries, faced a difficult task. The colliery's management had not kept many of the operational records required of it while part of the mine had to be sealed off because of the explosion and fire with the victims' bodies, and causal evidence, still inside. (In 1935, Gresford Colliery was reopened, and it continued to operate until 1973. The disaster seams were never unsealed.) This meant that verifying any of the evidence at the inquiry, much of which was contested, was often impossible.

The Walker report was not published until 1937; it had been delayed in the vain hope that the disaster seam could be reopened to recover the victims' bodies and search for evidence. The lack of evidence also impeded the subsequent prosecution of colliery managers under the Coal Mines Act 1911. They were fined a total of £140 plus £350 in costs, mostly for failure to keep prescribed records.[32] The report criticised the colliery management for a variety of technical failings but ultimately did not blame them directly for the disaster. However the two assessors to the inquiry both disagreed with aspects of Walker's report. John Brass, representing the owners, insisted that safety had not been comprised for financial reasons and that although there were technical infringements of mining legislation they did not contribute to the disaster. Joseph Jones, representing the workers, felt that visits by the Inspectorate had been 'insufficient and ineffective' and that this 'entire absence of effective supervision' had been a contributory factor in the disaster.[33]

Stafford Cripps, counsel for the miners, had made allegations against the Inspectorate at Gresford during the inquiry. Some of them seem to be borne out by evidence from Cripps' cross-examination of the local inspector. But Chief Inspector Walker reported that not only had inspectors acted honestly throughout the inquiry, but

that their duties had been misunderstood. They did not have the
resources or the remit to fully inspect every place of work, nor did the
inspectors' responsibilities remove the statutory safety responsibilities of the owners and officials of a colliery.[34] In his dissent, Jones
concluded that the

> Chief Inspector of Mines, or any of his assistants, should *not* in future be
> called upon to conduct formal investigations of this kind.
>   In stating this I do not impute incompetency or unfairness to the
> Commissioner at this Inquiry. I do assert, however, that it imposes upon
> any person directly associated with the Inspectorate a dual loyalty which
> must inevitably strain impartiality to the farthest limits.
>   The seriousness of such investigations demands that they be entrusted
> to members of the Judiciary, whose training and experience is required,
> but with whom there might sit persons of practical experience in mining
> to advise them only on matters concerning mining production and
> conditions.[35]

At Gresford such problems had contributed to a controversial
inquiry report that dogged industrial relations at the colliery for
years to come.[36] At Aberfan, Jones's recommendation was followed.
There is no evidence that Harold Wilson had read Jones's report. But
the public horror at the disaster led him to order an inquiry under the
Tribunals of Inquiry (Evidence) Act 1921, not one under the Mines
and Quarries Act 1954, the successor Act to that of 1911 under which
the Gresford inquiry was held. Edmund Davies refused to have a
miner as one of his assistants because that would mean having to
have an owners' representative too.[37] The Aberfan inquiry could
consider whether the Inspectorate was to blame. Its failure to do so
adequately is its most serious weakness.
   Gresford was not the last colliery disaster at which the ability of
the Inspectorate to inquire into its own alleged failings was queried.
At Bilsthorpe, Notts, in August 1993, three miners were killed by a
roof fall. HM Deputy Chief Inspector of Mines conducted the ensuing inquiry under the 1954 Act. It did not discuss the Inspectorate's
own role in approving practices that the accident showed to have
been dangerous and which the inquiry report recommended should
be discontinued. A campaign led by the local MEP led the HSE to
commission a second report from 'an independent person not connected with the mining industry'.[38] The Inspector of Mines who had
conducted the first inquiry was a witness at the second, at which he
was cross-examined. Although the second report did not explicitly
criticise either the first report or the Inspectorate, its first paragraph
of conclusions states:

The Public Hearing appears to have satisfied the demand for a Public Inquiry, and many of those present expressed their satisfaction. It allowed unions and individuals with experience of skin to skin driving of roadways ... to express their views and to question British Coal and the HMI. Though no particularly new evidence was forthcoming there was a considerable debate.... As was to be expected the presentations and discussion ranged much more widely than the HSE report on the accident.[39]

That statement echoes the experiences of victims and bereaved relatives such as the Aberfan man whose family was wiped out in the disaster, who said that the cross-examination of Lord Robens by Desmond Ackner was 'balm to his soul'. It speaks for independent inquiries and for inspectorates not drawn directly from the industry they inspect. The Mines and Quarries Inspectorate's lack of independence from the monopoly employer it regulated contrasts sharply with the contemporary situation of HM Inspectorate of Railways.

The authors of the first statutes regulating railways in the UK, in 1840, 1842, and 1844, saw the need for the inspectorate to be independent of the railway companies. This was no easy task, as most of the engineering expertise in the infant industry of railways was among the railways' own staff. However, there was one independent source of engineering expertise – the Army. The 1840 Act stipulated that railway inspectors must be officers of the Royal Engineers. The statutory requirement was actually repealed in Gladstone's railway regulation act of 1844, but the culture was already so deeply implanted that HM Inspectors of Railways were recruited almost exclusively from retired officers of the Royal Engineers until as recently as the 1980s. At the time of Aberfan, the Railway Inspectorate existed as a model for a reform of the Mines and Quarries Inspectorate that never took place. The Railway Inspectorate had the statutory duty to report on fatal (and some other) railway accidents, such as that at Hither Green in 1967.[40]

Other regulators meanwhile were, like the Mines and Quarries Inspectorate, far closer to the subjects of their attention. This was particularly true of the Department of Energy's regulation of the offshore oil industry. From the mid 1970s, North Sea oil made significant contributions to the British economy and was important in maintaining a surplus in her balance of payments. The Department of Energy rather than the HSE carried out inspections under an agency agreement. This 'political economy of speed' has been blamed for most of the 106 deaths that occurred in the industry up to December 1980.[41] Piper Alpha starkly highlighted this situation. The Cullen Report criticised the Department of Energy's inspections as 'superficial to the point of being little use as a test of safety on the platform'. Cullen questioned, 'in a fundamental sense, whether the type of inspection practised by the Department of Energy could be an effective means of assessment or monitoring the management of safety by operators.'[42] After the disaster, responsibility for safety in the off-shore oil industry was transferred to the HSC.

At the time of writing, a Department of Employment, Transport, & the Regions (DETR) working party is considering public responses to a consultation document on transport safety. The DETR asks consultees, among other things, whether the accident investigators for those modes of transport not under the HSE wing (sea, air, and perhaps road) should be brought under it. Consultees were asked to consider whether there were 'benefits in locating regulatory responsibilities in an *independent* body' [i.e., not reporting to a sponsoring department such as DETR] which might 'make it easier for staff to move between different areas of regulation, encouraging wider vision and guarding against too "cosy" a relationship with the regulated industry'.[43] This statement reflects current HSE practice. The HSE points out that independence of the regulated industry is a mixed blessing. Regulators who are too independent of the industry may not know enough about it to regulate, and investigate accidents, successfully. But it does rotate staff around its inspectorates in the way suggested by the DETR paper.[44]

There may be no right answer to the question, 'How independent should inspectors be'? This is a central issue in the aftermath of the Ladbroke Grove disaster of October 1999, which is ongoing as this book goes to press. In a flurry of activity in the first few days after the disaster, before even the tracks had been cleared and reopened:

- Lord Cullen was again appointed to head an inquiry into the disaster under Section 14(2)(b) of the 1974 Act. This means that it is an inquiry independent of the relevant Inspectorate, able to review and criticise the Railway Inspectorate itself. In this, it resembles Aberfan, Bilsthorpe II, King's Cross, Clapham and Cullen's own earlier inquiries into Piper Alpha and Dunblane, rather than Gresford or Bilsthorpe I.
- The Railway Inspectorate issued an interim report within two days of the disaster, stating that the immediate cause was a signal passed at red, but that 'Our belief is that it is a systems failure and that any action or omission on the part of the driver was only one factor'. It added, 'Early evidence suggests that the accident would have been prevented by the installation and correct operation of a Train Protection Warning System'.[45]

- The government announced that it would strip Railtrack plc of its safety responsibilities, in response to a pre-Ladbroke Grove HSE report which had raised the question of whether a profit-making corporation was the right home for a division responsible for safety standards on the network.[46]
- The HSE prohibited Railtrack and the operators from using the line leading to the signal which had been passed at red.
- The Rail Regulator announced that he would investigate whether any out of Railtrack and the two train operating companies involved had breached their licences, warning that if so, the licences might be revoked.[47] The shares of all three companies involved fell sharply within 48 hours of this announcement.
- The police remained on site for two weeks after the disaster, stating that they were treating it as a scene of crime.

This represents a massive change since 1966. The public bodies concerned immediately blocked off the option of laying all the blame on the driver who overran a red signal (who was killed in the accident), and focused attention on systems in the upper reaches of the companies concerned. On the other hand, both the Ladbroke Grove and the earlier Southall accidents showed that the corporate acceptance of blame has gone backwards in the privatised railway. Sir Robert Reid immediately accepted British Rail's responsibility after Clapham and his successor (also Sir Robert Reid!) appeared in court to represent British Rail when it was fined under the 1974 Act. After Southall and Ladbroke Grove, Railtrack and two train operators had incentives to blame one another.

Protecting the public from workplace negligence

Whether or not there is a common interest between workers and management, industry remains potentially dangerous to third parties. At Aberfan, the cosy relationship between the NCB and the Mines and Quarries Inspectorate was not in the public interest. Aberfan began a gradual shift towards companies considering the safety of the wider public as well as their employees. The Tribunal Report had recommended that the law should require the Mines Inspectorate 'to consider the safety, health and welfare of all persons going about their lawful business in the vicinity of a mine, including the safety of their property'.[48] The Coal Division of the Ministry of Power initially objected, calling this a 'revolutionary innovation in the field of industrial safety legislation'.[49] However, tips were dealt with separately by the Mines and Quarries (Tips) Act 1969, so that the general commitment to public safety that the Tribunal had envisaged was not implemented.[50]

In 1967, Lord Robens claimed that,

> We can never know what good may have come out of Aberfan – the number of lives that will be saved – simply because I know of other industries who have told their men to ensure that their safety regulations will protect not only their employees but the public as well.[51]

The Robens Committee was asked 'to consider whether any further steps are required to safeguard members of the public from hazards, other than general environmental pollution, arising in connection with activities in industrial and commercial premises and construction sites'.[52] In this, the legacy of Aberfan was obvious. Its report claimed that

> there is apparently a long-established and deep-seated reluctance on the part of the administering departments and inspectorates to accept any explicit responsibility in relation to the safety of the public. It is as if there were some invisible ring-fence around the occupational safety system, with the general public left outside.

In the light of senior NCB officers' attitudes to the public described in earlier chapters, this has its ironies. The Report recommended giving the health and safety authority power to make statutory regulations to safeguard the general public where there was cause to believe it could be affected by an industrial or commercial operation.[53] Section 3 of the 1974 Act did just that:

> It shall be the duty of every employer to conduct his undertaking in such a way as to ensure, so far as is reasonably practicable, that persons not in his employment who may be affected are not thereby exposed to risks to their health and safety.[54]

Putting the law into practice: the Health and Safety Executive

Although the Robens Report recommended the creation of a single inspectorate, separate inspectorates were maintained to look after factories, quarries and agriculture, railways, mines, nuclear and offshore safety. Following disasters there were moves to bring such inspectorates under the remit of the HSE. Responsibility for rail moved from the Department of Transport to the HSE in 1990 after the Clapham disaster and responsibility for offshore safety was transferred from the Department of Energy after Piper Alpha.

Nonetheless, the Health and Safety Commission was created to oversee and direct the whole area, while the Health and Safety Executive was created to enforce it. The Robens Report envisaged that government, trade unions and employers would work together at both local and national level to ensure an effective system of self-regulation. This tripartite approach was implemented and runs through the HSE, HSC and all connected advisory committees. Even aside from the problem of regulatory capture just discussed, the corporatist climate of that assumption is no longer prevalent. Today, employees are rarely involved in such levels of open consultation and protection.[55] In the individualistic climate of the 1980s and 1990s, with unions much weaker than in the 1960s, the institutional base for Robensite corporatism is much weaker.[56] Consequently, without union protection, some workers do not speak out about their safety concerns for fear of losing their job. Nichols argues that the decline in the power of trade unions during the 1980s has been responsible for a general rise in accident rates across industry.[57] The tripartite approach has also led to criticisms that the interests of small business and non-unionised or poorly organised workers are under-represented. Meanwhile, Baldwin criticises the tripartite approach for ensuring that consensus techniques are chosen rather than the kind of radical thinking that could reshape existing practices. The regulatory capture we have documented gives substance to Baldwin's fears.[58]

The 1989 HSC Annual Report states that, 'HSE inspectors do not approach their task with a view to seeking out legal violations and prosecuting error'.[59] The HSE's assumption is that that most employers who transgress are essentially ill-informed rather than ill-intentioned. However, different inspectorates retain different approaches to compliance and prosecution. A small factory may go two years without seeing an inspector but every nuclear plant is visited regularly. Hutter identified some of the variables that determine the approach favoured. The resources available are obviously important. The former Industrial Air Pollution Inspectorate had a high ratio of officers to premises. Detection of offences was thus hard to escape and therefore there was less need for prosecutions since compliance could be ensured through persuasion. The political context also shapes prosecution policies. Industries or areas where there is public concern, such as environmental health, are more likely to witness strict enforcement. However most health and safety offences are not matters of particular public concern, meaning there is little popular demand for prosecution until something goes terribly wrong. Finally, the relationship between the inspectorate and the regulated is important. Where an industry is in close geographical and social proximity to its inspectors then prosecution is less likely. Those inspectors with close relationships assume that the transgressors are essentially well-intentioned and are thus less likely to prosecute. However in more diverse industries there is a greater tendency for the regulators to be suspicious. This is illustrated by the Factory Inspectorate's tough stance towards the construction industry where employers tend to be more transient than the other businesses regulated by the inspectorate.[60]

In 1990, J. D. Rimington, HSE Director General, told the House of Commons Employment Committee that the HSE had wanted more cases to be tried in the Crown Court (which could levy higher fines than magistrates) but it was constrained by the extra staff time and cost involved.[61] In 1994–5, a two per cent cut was imposed on the HSE's budget, the following year there was a five per cent cut.[62] Even without such cuts, it would be impossible for the HSE to regularly inspect every employer. In 1995, there were just 638 Factory Inspectors to cover 400,000 workplaces, 171 agricultural Inspectors for 300,000 workplaces and 52 Railway Inspectors to cover all of Britain's railways.[63] The result was a heavy workload on inspectors. In 1999, it was claimed that the HSE only have the resources to investigate 5.5 per cent of all notified accidents.[64] Consequently, the HSE must rely on a strong degree of self-regulation if it is to be effective.

The UK's health and safety regime is generally a successful one by international standards. However when that system fails and people are killed or injured then the HSE's response and regulation has come under attack. Deaths in the workplace do not automatically lead to prosecution. In 1993–94, only 35 per cent of workplace deaths resulted in any prosecution by the HSE.[65] For the bereaved relatives, the result is a sense of anger and injustice. Gary Slapper estimates that 4,000 deaths in England and Wales since 1965 meet the criteria for consideration for corporate manslaughter.[66] Only two have resulted in manslaughter convictions.

Where prosecutions are brought, there have been complaints that the subsequent fines are too low. The majority of cases are prosecuted in a Magistrates' rather than Crown Court. Before 1991, Magistrates' Courts only had the power to impose fines of up to £2,000. Consequently, to the annoyance of the HSC, most workplace fatalities that led to prosecutions resulted only in small fines. In 1988–89, three per cent of prosecutions resulting from workplace fatalities were tried in the Crown Court where the average fine was £2,145. Of the remaining 97 per cent tried in Magistrates' Courts, the average fine was £505.[67] In 1992, the maximum fine in magistrates' courts was raised to £20,000. By 1997–98 the average fine in Magistrates' Court had risen to £6,223 for H&S offences.[68]

Since 1990, fines have been rising significantly where cases reach the Crown Court which has the power to impose unlimited fines. There have been a number of substantial and high profile fines. British Rail were fined £250,000 under the 1974 Act for failure to ensure the safety of employees and passengers following Clapham. In 1987 British Petroleum were fined £750,000 following three deaths at the Grangemouth refinery. The HSE believed it represented a landmark in the application of safety law. (Although as Slapper points out, the fine actually represented only 0.05 per cent of BP's profit after tax.[69]) In February 1997, the companies responsible for a walkway, that collapsed at Ramsgate port killing six people, were fined a total of £1.7 million. In 1998 the Court of Appeal decided that H&S fines should be large enough to make clear to management their health and safety responsibilities and that fines should be proportional to a company's ability to pay. The ruling also stressed that magistrates should consider carefully before accepting any H&S case where a large fine may be needed and that the size of fines should reflect ignored warnings and any deliberate breach with a view to profit.[70] This was welcomed by the HSC who agreed that because penalties for health and safety prosecutions had not in the past 'generally match[ed] the crime' they had been undermining attempts to ensure that the prevention of workplace deaths, injuries and ill-health was at the heart of company management practices.[71] In 1999, two companies were fined a total of £1.7m following the collapse of three tunnels during the construction of the Heathrow Express. No one was injured in the accident and the size of the fine was a clear reflection of the increasing conviction to ensure H&S offences are not treated lightly. A deterrent element is also important in this, although, as the HSE, conceded in 1990, sending senior individuals to prison would have a more significant effect.[72]

After the £1.7m fine for the Ramsgate port deaths, Disaster Action claimed that the actual charge of 'failing to ensure the safety of passengers' could be seen as an insult to the relatives of those who died.[73] Prosecutions under the 1974 Act do not distinguish between offences that resulted in injury or death and those that did not. It is the breach of health and safety regulations that is being tried, not its consequences. The growth in the size of fines represents a significant development but anger remains amongst relatives that the actual charges brought are for health and safety offences rather than manslaughter.

Before the 1990s there was some reluctance in the HSE to press for manslaughter charges after workplace deaths. In 1990, Rimington argued that those seeking to change to the system were overly concerned with punishment rather than justice. He said, 'I honestly do not think ... that a bloodthirsty attitude in these matters is the right one to adopt'.[74] Between 1974 and 1992, there were over 9,000 deaths at work but the HSE could not point to a single case referred to the CPS.[75] Even if the will to pursue manslaughter charges did exist, there were practical problems. The police did not have a clearly defined role in investigating workplace deaths while HSE inspectors concentrated on enforcement, not treating H&S offences as criminal acts in the ordinary sense.

The 1974 Act does allow imprisonment for certain offences (such as the contravention of licences and prohibition notices, the illegal use of explosives and the disclosure of confidential information) but such sentences are rare. The first imprisonment for a health and safety offence was not until 1994. Whatever the rights and wrongs of prosecution, such a situation compounds the perception of health and safety offences as quasi-crime.

The HSE's attitude to prosecutions has changed during the 1990s. Prosecution rates are rising and the HSE has lobbied for higher fines. A protocol drafted by the HSE, police and CPS lists their respective responsibilities after workplace deaths in England and Wales.[76] The HSE certainly does not feel that it is 'soft' on offenders. Jenny Bacon, its current director, stresses that Health and Safety offences are crimes.[77] As such they should not be taken lightly. Bacon also maintains that it is important for the law to be accepted by companies if it is to work and be enforceable. Stringent and confrontational enforcement could endanger the legitimacy of health and safety legislation.[78] Indeed in the aftermath of an accident, companies are more likely to concede to HSE demands for wider safety measures unrelated to the incident under investigation.[79] Thus by not taking a confrontational approach compliance can often be achieved.

The HSE also publicly supports calls for reforming the law on corporate manslaughter. The failure to bring more manslaughter prosecutions, and in particular, imprison individuals is a direct result of the current law on manslaughter. Convictions under the 1974 Health and Safety Act do not need to establish individual blame and are thus much easier to obtain than a manslaughter conviction where the guilt of an individual has to be established. Thus rather than risk losing a conviction altogether, the HSE often just prosecutes for the health and safety offences.

Disasters and prosecutions since Aberfan

The framework in which responses to workplace deaths are managed naturally also shapes the response to disasters too. None of the disasters of the 1970s witnessed any criminal proceedings. Despite evidence of poor architectural design contributing to the death toll at Summerland and a failure to heed the lessons of previous problems at Ibrox, both were essentially seen as tragic accidents. (The causes of the third major UK disaster of the 1970s, the Moorgate Tube crash, remain unclear.) Ignored warnings were also revealed at the inquiry into the 1985 Bradford fire. A court case established civil liability but again there were no criminal prosecutions. The instance of a football club being (at least partly) to blame for the death of its supporters made Bradford an unusual case. The strong emotional link between fans and their club made them reluctant to push for proceedings that could ultimately harm the team. The knowledge that the poor conditions at the Valley Parade ground were far from unique added to the acceptance of the fire as a 'dreadful blow' from fate and that attaching blame was pointless.[80] However, after Bradford a change began to emerge in the public perception and legal response to disasters in the UK. As with the increased pressure on the HSE to treat workplace deaths more seriously, disasters now began to become associated with corporate negligence. The first institutional evidence of this was in disaster inquests.

Legally, the role of an inquest is only to establish who the deceased was, and how, when and where the death occurred. However as the 1980s progressed, coroners have been unable (and occasionally unwilling) to keep them within these bounds in the way that the Aberfan coroner did. The Aberfan inquest was not held in front of a jury. The coroner thus had complete control over its verdict. Had there been a jury then the local anger at the conduct of the NCB might have resulted in an unlawful killing verdict. This was what happened, against the advice of the respective coroners, at the inquests into Zeebrugge, Glanrhyd and Clapham.[81] This was clear evidence that the perception of deaths inflicted by corporations was changing. The coroner who presided over both the Clapham and *Marchioness* inquests felt that juries were under pressure to return a

verdict of unlawful killing because of the strong emotions of the
inquests and an awareness of 'the near riot that would ensue if they
dismissed the suffering as 'an accident''.[82]

Despite their restricted legal standing, these three juries turned the
role of the inquest from merely deciding the circumstances of death
into determining liability. With an unlawful killing verdict open to
them, juries cannot but pass a verdict on criminal liability.[83] The
Clapham inquest postdated the decision not to prosecute for manslaughter. Wells sees it as a clear resistance to institutional pressure.[84]
The unlawful killing verdict at the Zeebrugge inquest led to the DPP
bringing charges against P&O. The large death toll, the damning
Sheen Report and high profile media coverage meant there was considerable public pressure for a prosecution. Yet this decision did not
mark the beginning of a new trend.

Table 8.2 shows the relationship between the inquests, the formal
inquiry, and any criminal proceedings after a number of disasters.
There is no standard pattern in the chronology of these three outcomes. For rail, sea, and air disasters, there is a statutory inquiry; for
some others including Aberfan there is not. Some coroners sit with
juries, some without. The damning inquiry reports into Zeebrugge
and Clapham must have influenced the unlawful killing verdicts of
the respective juries at the inquests.

Coroners (like chairmen of judicial inquiries) have considerable
leeway in drawing up their terms of reference. They have discretion as
to what evidence they take while, with no legal aid available, cross-
examinations can depend on the financial resources of the victims'
families. Again, the impact of this on the verdict, and thus the decision
to prosecute, can be significant. At Hillsborough, while the DPP was
completing his investigations into the possibility of criminal action,
inquests were held to establish the 'who' and 'where' of deaths but not
the 'how'. No cross-examinations were allowed and the process was
described as purely an 'information dissemination exercise'. The main
inquests were resumed after the DPP had decided not to prosecute.
The coroner decided not to accept any evidence from after 3.15 p.m.
on the day of the disaster despite the fact that it was not clear that all
the victims were actually dead by then. Therefore the role of the emergency response was not fully considered.[85] The coroner instructed the
jury to return a verdict of unlawful killing only if they found a degree
of recklessness in the management of the match. A verdict of accidental death was returned. Appeals to the Attorney General to quash the
verdicts were unsuccessful, as was an application to the High Court to
overturn the Coroner's imposition of a 3.15 cut-off time. After
considerable public campaigning, the whole case was re-examined by

Table 8.2 Disasters in England & Wales, 1966–99

Disaster	Date	Inquiry	Inquest	Death toll	Inquest	Criminal prosecution
Aberfan	21 Oct 66	Jul 67	Sep 67	144	A/D	DNP – Aug 67
Hither Green crash	05 Nov 67	Dec 67	Nov 67	49	A/D	(DNP)
Moorgate	28 Feb 75	Jun 76	Apr 75	42	A/D	(DNP)
Bradford City Fire	11 May 85	July 85 & Jan 86	Jan 86	56	A/D	(DNP)
Manchester Aircraft Fire	25 Aug 85	Mar 88 & Mar 89	Sep 86	55	A/D	(DNP)
Herald of Free Enterprise	06 Mar 87	Jul 87	Oct 87	193	Unlawful	DP – Jun 89
Glanrhyd	19 Oct 87	Apr 90	Jul 88	4	Unlawful	DNP – Sep 89
King's Cross fire	18 Nov 87	Nov 88	Oct 88	31	A/D	DNP May 89
Clapham train crash	12 Dec 88	Feb 89	Sep 90	35	Unlawful	DNP – May 90
Kegworth air crash	08 Jan 89	Feb 89 & Oct 90	May 90	47	A/D	(DNP)
Hillsborough	15 Apr 89	Aug 89 & Jan 90	Mar 91	96	A/D	DNP – Aug 90
Marchioness	20 Aug 89	Aug 91	Sep 89	57	*Adjourned	DNP – Sep 90
Ladbroke Grove	5 Oct 99	1)Oct 99 2)?2000 3)?2000	Oct 99	31	Not yet known	Not yet known

Key:
DNP = decision not to prosecute
(DNP) = prosecution apparently not considered
A/D = Accidental Death
DP = decision to prosecute for manslaughter
Where two or more dates are shown in the inquiry column the first refers to an interim report.
* After pressure from the bereaved, the Marchioness inquests were reopened in April 1995 and returned an unlawful killing verdict.
Source: adapted from Wells, 'Disasters: the role of institutional responses', p. 215; some extra cases added. The table excludes Scottish disasters because there is no inquest procedure there, and also Summerland (Isle of Man).

Lord Justice Stuart Smith on behalf of the Home Secretary soon after the change of government in 1997. However, he concluded that no new evidence justified reconsidering previous criminal, disciplinary, public inquiry or inquest decisions.[86] Yet the accidental death verdicts at Hillsborough contradicted the Taylor Report which blamed the police. Although the CPS decided not to prosecute, a private prosecution for manslaughter against the two senior police officers at Hillsborough is progressing through the courts as we write.

The Zeebrugge unlawful killing verdict led to the prosecution of P&O and seven individuals from the company for manslaughter. The judge dismissed the case while the prosecution was only part way through its examination of witnesses, and before any defence witnesses had appeared. The collapse was not on the principle that a company could not be prosecuted for manslaughter or the identification of officials with the appropriate seniority and responsibility, but on the judge's interpretation of 'involuntary' manslaughter. There are two categories of involuntary manslaughter – reckless and unlawful acts. The P&O prosecution alleged that the company and its directors had been reckless in their running of operations and regard for safety. The judge dismissed the charges on the basis that this could not be proved since sailing with the bow doors open was not an obvious and serious risk which the defendants failed to realise or ignored. Vessels of this class had worked largely without mishap for seven years during which time there had more than 60,000 sailings. There are doubts about the validity of the judge's decision. There had been previous sailings with open doors while after the tragedy warning lights were installed on P&O ferries to indicate that doors were not shut.[87]

The P&O prosecution nonetheless marked the legal recognition that corporations could be tried for manslaughter. Yet the prosecution's failure also clearly illustrated the problems in achieving a conviction. Significant in this was the ruling that the failures of directors could not be aggregated to determine a corporation's guilt. The judge ruled that for a corporation to be found guilty at least one of its senior officers must be individually guilty of manslaughter. It was not enough to aggregate individual failings that alone did amount to anything that could be deemed manslaughter. Smith and Hogan argue that such a doctrine may have no place in

> offences requiring knowledge, intention or recklessness; but, arguably, there is a place for it in offences of negligence ... [where a] series of minor failures by officers of the company might add up to a gross breach by the company of its duty of care.[88]

The Herald Families' Association said of the trial that

> simple truth and commonsense had given way under the weight of the legal arguments submitted by an exceptionally powerful battery of defence counsel whose costs (eventually recovered from public funds) had been underwritten by the corporate defendant.[89]

In 1994 four schoolchildren were killed in a canoeing accident in Lyme Bay, Dorset. The company, OLL Ltd, which ran a small activity centre under whose charge the children had been, was successfully prosecuted in 1994 for manslaughter. OLL Ltd was fined £60,000 while its managing director was sentenced to three years in prison. That was cut to two years on appeal, of which fourteen months were served.[90] The appeal judge noted the need to find a balance between relatives seeking long sentences and defendants who had no criminal intent and did not understand why they had been sent to prison.[91] Yet the case was the first successful prosecution of a company for manslaughter in English and Welsh legal history. The prosecution overcame many of the classic problems of corporate manslaughter because the managing director was clearly responsible for operations. The prosecution was also aided by an incidental change in the manslaughter law. 'Reckless' was now longer reliant on the obvious and serious risk applied in the P&O case. Instead, proving gross negligence was to be the basis of a successful conviction.[92]

The possibility of private prosecution

At Aberfan residents fought the reluctance of the state to address their grievances by forming pressure groups such as the Tip Removal Committee. This proved highly effective and the failure to bring public prosecutions has resulted in similar groups after more recent disasters. The Herald Families' Association began life as a victim support group before evolving into a litigation pressure group. Like similar groups formed after *Marchioness*, King's Cross and Hillsborough, it lobbied intensively for the bringing of criminal charges against the parties concerned. Where such moves fail then the victims' groups have become a vehicle for an alternative route to justice – a private prosecution.

Yet this is fraught with problems. It exposes the supporters to accusations of seeking revenge or financial gain.[93] More significantly, private prosecutions are expensive while the lawyers are disadvantaged compared to a state action by not having the police to gather evidence.[94] In January 1988, the Herald Families' Association had pledges of £50,000 to carry out a private prosecution if necessary. However it decided not to proceed after the failure of the public prosecution against P&O because of the potential cost in the event of another failure.[95] Survivor groups at King's Cross and Clapham also spoke of their wish to bring private prosecutions but none did.[96] The private prosecutions against two senior police officers at Hillsborough were only able to go ahead after considerable fund raising, helped by the support of famous rock bands and the wider community of football fans.

The problems of private prosecution were illustrated by the three *Marchioness* trials. In two successive trials juries failed to agree on charges brought against the captain of the dredger that had collided with the *Marchioness*, while in September 1990 the DPP decided not to bring charges against the dredger's owners. The widower of one of the deceased then launched a private prosecution. The DPP decided to intervene with a view to taking over and dropping the prosecution but then after public protest he recanted. However, the case was dismissed at the committal hearings. Although the MAIB report was published, it had taken evidence in private. There was no public inquiry into the deaths, and it was five-and-a-half years before the full inquests were held.[97]

Owning up

The desire for prosecutions might be less forceful if the companies responsible owned up voluntarily. The lack of public admissions of fault and remorse after disasters has been partly enabled by the existence of alternative and immediate culprits. The two identified boys who started the fire at Summerland and the anonymous individuals whose cigarettes started the fires at King's Cross and Bradford are prime examples, as is Captain Lord of the *Californian* (see chapter 9). They helped obscure the poor architecture at Summerland, the inadequate fire precautions at King's Cross, the known fire risk of combustible material under a wooden stand at Bradford and the regulatory failures of the Board of Trade that contributed to the loss of life aboard the *Titanic*. But for the efforts of Desmond Ackner, something similar might have happened after Aberfan.[98] Inquiries can identify such problems but, in such cases, they can not prevent the blame being deflected, if only partially, from the shoulders of the company responsible.

Scapegoating is particularly tempting where the culprit is an employee of the company responsible. After the Clapham disaster, although British Rail admitted full responsibility, the National Union of Railwaymen feared that blame would be placed on its members. Individuals, a spokesperson said, 'should not be pilloried while generals sit in bunkers.' Jimmy Knapp, the union's general secretary, said that 'One lesson must surely be that we can't let individuals work under the same stresses and strains that led to the accident.'[99] British Rail did not try to pass the buck on to one of its employees at Clapham but after Southall a different picture emerged. Great Western Trains pleaded guilty to failing to provide safe passage and claimed that its 'remorse and responsibility are unqualified'.[100] Yet it maintained that the disaster was primarily caused by the driver not doing what he was trained to do. The driver lost his job and charges of manslaughter against him had to be dropped because there were doubts whether he was mentally fit to give evidence and financially he would be unable to pay any fine levied. The company did not regard its allowing the train to proceed with the automatic stopping system not working as a 'significant cause'.[101] This was despite the fact that, when the fault in the train's protection system had been reported at Swansea, it would have been easy to turn the train on the triangle there so that the opposite end (with a working protection system) was at the front.

There is a strong parallel between Southall and Aberfan. Both the NCB and Great Western Trains had failed to provide the required assistance or direction to its staff to ensure safety should any mistakes be made. Although the NCB admitted that its failure to implement any kind of tipping policy had caused the Aberfan disaster, Lord Robens still felt that the essential cause of the disaster was the personal breakdown in communication between two employees. Lord Ackner felt that his role at the Tribunal was to push the blame upwards within the NCB as the board tried to push it downwards. Similarly after Zeebrugge, there was some feeling within P&O that the cause of the disaster was not its failure to ensure a system that informed the captain whether the bow doors were shut but the fact that the assistant bosun in charge of shutting them had fallen asleep. Such circumstances have enabled corporations to deflect blame from themselves.

A public acceptance of blame by corporations after disasters is important to the bereaved and survivors. After Zeebrugge one bereaved relative complained that even a letter saying sorry would have been of some comfort but none came. Similarly after the King's Cross fire, some survivors felt aggrieved because they had had no personal apology from London Transport.[102] British Rail seem to have a better record. At the investigation into the 1967 Hither Green disaster, British Rail began with a statement accepting complete liability for the disaster.[103] This may have been a direct lesson from the Aberfan Tribunal's criticism of the coal board.

Perhaps influenced by the criticisms of London Underground for delaying accepting responsibility for the King's Cross fire,[104] British Rail also immediately accepted blame after the Clapham disaster in 1988. The chairman, Sir Robert Reid, personally attended court to plead guilty when the Railways Board was fined £250,000. In his summing up the judge said

> At the very earliest possible opportunity an acceptance of responsibility on behalf of the Board was made plain ... [T]he clearest possible indications of ... "contrition" and what I might call "remorse" ... were plain to be seen, and indeed frankly put forward, by those on behalf of the British Railways Board, from the outset.
>
> The genuineness of those reactions, and the determination of the Board to remedy the faults that had appeared, can be very accurately gauged, in my judgement, by the fact that the Chairman of the Board has appeared before this Court in person to stand as the representative of his Board and to accept upon his own shoulders the criticisms that are being made.

Similar quick admissions of responsibility followed the Purley and Glasgow fatal crashes of 1989. However the break-up of British Rail broke the model. In 1999, the managing director of the post-privatisation Great Western Trains found himself rebuked by the judge trying the company after the Southall disaster for his failure to appear in court. Mr Justice Scott Baker said 'He is the man in charge of safety, yet he is not here. He has not taken the trouble to come to court. I would have thought he might have been here if your clients [Great Western Trains] were really concerned about this matter.'[105] Great Western were fined £1.5 million for health and safety offences and guilty of what the judge called a 'dereliction of duty'.

Reform? The Law Commission's proposals

The path to private prosecution may be problematic but it can still act as an agent for wider change. The CPS wishes to maintain control of serious cases and thus the threat of private prosecution influences it to bring public charges.[106] This was significant in the bringing of charges against P&O after Zeebrugge. The willingness of victims to resort to private prosecution was also influential in the decision to review the law on corporate manslaughter.

In 1991 a Royal Commission on Criminal Justice was set up to examine the effectiveness of the criminal justice system. It heard evidence from Disaster Action and the Hazards Campaign, which campaigns for justice for workplace deaths. Campaigning for a change to the law, which had proved 'farcically ineffective' in dealing with companies that had committed manslaughter, was central in the work of Disaster Action.[107] The group had commissioned its own research on the subject and utilised the media to help ensure corporate responsibility became a subject of public debate.[108]

The Commission published its finding in July 1993 but failed to make any references or recommendations regarding the issue of corporate or managerial culpability for work-related deaths.[109] However, in 1994, the Law Commission investigated the possibility of changing the law to ensure that blame was distributed appropriately. In a consultation paper, it recommended that a new offence of killing by gross carelessness be introduced to replace gross negligence manslaughter. The charge was to apply to corporations through the principle of identification.[110] When the final report was published in 1996, after wide consultation, the recommendations had altered significantly. The Commission recommended the introduction of a new offence of corporate killing. For a company to be convicted the following circumstances would have to apply:

> management failure by the corporation is the cause or one of the causes of a person's death; and
> that failure constitutes conduct falling far below what can be reasonably be expected of the corporation in the circumstances.

The risk would not have to be obvious nor would the defendants have to be capable of recognising it. The penalty upon conviction would be a fine and, if appropriate, a remedial order. As the Commission point out, P&O would have undoubtedly have been found guilty had they been charged under such a law. So too would the NCB after Aberfan. This reform would obviate the need to prove individual responsibility on the part of senior management or directors, as well as avoid problems in clarifying what constitutes an obvious risk.

The recommendations did not satisfy all campaigners in the area. A lawyer who acted for some of the Southall and *Marchioness* victims in their attempt to bring private prosecutions argued that fines have proved insufficient deterrents in matters of health and safety. She claimed that only a prison sentence would act as a sufficient deterrent and ensure that corporate entities were not used to mask the responsibility of individual directors.[111] The Law Commission did provide for the prosecution of individual directors who could be proved to have been personally responsible through the charges of reckless killing or killing through gross carelessness. However, the old problem of proving individual blame in the upper echelons of a company would remain in cases such as Zeebrugge. The

HSE is presently concerned that culpable directors hide behind their corporation and thus escape personal censure.[112] The Law Commission's recommendations offer little that will end this practice.

Lacey and Wells also criticise the Commission's recommendations for leaving unclear the relationship between the liability of corporations and individuals within it. The Commission fails to answer the question of whether both individual and company should be prosecuted. They argue that the realities of prosecution policy are such that it would be unlikely that, for the same offence, a company would be charged with corporate killing while its directors were charged with reckless killing or killing through carelessness. Even where there was evidence against directors, they feel that a prosecutor would be more likely to pursue the custom-made charge of corporate killing. The result would be that culpable directors would avoid criminal censure.[113]

Ridley and Dunford point out the probable complexities of the evidence in such cases. Trials may be long with highly talented defence lawyers. The resultant burden on the jury will be significant and they will have to make fine decisions about what constitutes reasonable practice. These problems will also put added pressure on the judge to ensure a satisfactory trial. Ridley and Dunford maintain that the biggest problem of the proposals is that they do not consider the role of the regulatory authorities in enforcement. The old problem of the HSE needing to pass on cases, which it may not be equipped professionally or politically to assess, to the CPS will remain.[114]

An incomplete cultural shift

It is clear that the Law Commission's proposals result from a significant shift in cultural attitudes towards holding companies responsible for their actions. Slapper claims that the State's reluctance to criminalise corporate conduct stems from an entrenched political and economic bias where companies are not treated as citizens capable of committing violent crimes for fear of harming their economic performance.[115] The law is thus a construct of the dominant political economy. Yet no longer does it appear that society is willing to tolerate the misdemeanours of corporations in the name of economic progress or well being. With lawyers' gradual acceptance of this, it appears that there has been a widespread cultural change, which Lacey and Wells ascribe to the cultural relativity of attitudes to risk. When accidents do happen we are no longer prone to accept them in the fatalistic way that magical and religious beliefs determined in the past. Allocating blame helps us make sense of our world and the things that go wrong in it. Thus new technologies have produced new responsibilities and provoked cultural reassessments; there are now new hazards against a new cultural background. Thus when disaster strikes, society's reaction will be different.[116]

Such arguments speak to the long term. They do not explain why the change in attitudes arrived so quickly between the 1970s and the Zeebrugge disaster. The disasters of the 1980s produced very different outcomes to those before, despite the common features of mismanagement. A 1991 sample of people involved in the Summerland fire showed that only 17 per cent felt that justice was not done.[117] This contrasts clearly with the anger so apparent after disasters in the 1980s. This change was not just grounded in the varying degrees of negligence or the reconciling power of time but instead in a developing perception of corporations and their responsibilities. Thus we must look for more specific cultural and political shifts that underpinned these different responses.

Accidents, and particularly disasters, have a powerful social and psychological impact. They bring home the realities of risk in a way that abstract possibilities can not. Disasters arouse emotions and command attention. This has social consequences and creates expectations and demands for action.[118] Before the 1980s, disasters produced specific legislation to ensure that they do not happen again. By the late 1980s, such specific measures were not considered sufficient with the number and frequency of disasters seemingly on the increase. Media coverage brought the horror of these disasters into the living room in full colour. The subsequent disaster inquiries repeatedly highlighted mismanagement, ignored warnings, and apathy towards safety. No longer were the specific safety measures – which, as was often pointed out, simply shut the stable door after the horse had bolted[119] – regarded as acceptable. The law's reluctance and inability to punish corporate wrongdoings seemed increasingly out of line with public opinion.

The growth of a litigation culture, influenced by trends in the United States, has meant that today harmed individuals are more likely to go to law.[120] At Aberfan most people's experience of the law was probably limited to divorce proceedings and other non-criminal proceedings. The 1980s saw a growth in, first, personal injury lawyers and then specialist disaster lawyers. Indeed, since Zeebrugge, the Law Society has brought together solicitors representing victims to pool resources and information.[121] The lifting of restrictions on solicitors' advertising enabled them to publicise their services. Underpinning this emerging litigation culture was the 1980s growth

in neo-liberalism which stressed the rights of the individual.
Although primarily directed towards the right to live and work free
from government constraints, neo-liberalism also espoused the individual's right to seek compensation and retribution if harmed by the
activities of others.

The catalogue of disasters seemed to have a wider cause in the
enterprise culture of the 1980s. If Aberfan was a disaster of
corporatism, then Zeebrugge was a disaster of under-regulated capi-
talism. Even the HSE conceded that the drive for profit was putting
lives at risk and this became starkly clear after Piper Alpha.[122] John
Prescott, as Shadow Transport Secretary, claimed that the government had 'reduced the whole consciousness and culture of safety'.[123]
In particular, Prescott argued that cuts in government subsidies for
public transport were causing safety problems. He criticised the
Fennell Inquiry into King's Cross fire because wider questions of
public subsidy were omitted.[124] Despite government denials of any
link, and accusations that Prescott was trying to make political
capital, the frequency of the disasters seemed to add credence to his
claims.[125]

Thus the willingness to turn to the law was also underpinned
by some loss of faith in corporations. Central to this has been a
growing awareness of corporate crime. Triumphalism about the
unregulated free market has declined sharply since the fall of
Margaret Thatcher in 1990. The first actual manifestations of
this were seen at the Zeebrugge case. The Sheen Report severely
criticised Townsend Thoresen, the owners of the *Herald of Free
Enterprise*: 'From top to bottom the body corporate was infected
with the disease of sloppiness.'[126] Being a private-sector company, Townsend Thoresen could not pass blame on to public
spending cuts. It seemed to typify the wider malaise in business
and commitment to profit above safety. The subsequent
unlawful killing inquest verdict and manslaughter charges represented a backlash against this. Society may not have the will to
economically rein in the power of corporations but it was
increasingly creating pressure that corporations should at least
be held accountable for their negligence. Once one case had
succeeded in reaching the courts, even if it had not resulted in a
conviction, then other disaster groups were bound to look to the
same course of action. As one lawyer involved in Hillsborough
said, 'the Herald case led us all to consider the possibility of
manslaughter'.[127]

Disentangling multiple inquiries

After Southall, Mr Justice Scott Baker ruled that the prosecution
had not identified a culpable individual within the company whose
actions could be deemed to be those of the company. Essentially, the
case failed on the same grounds as that against P&O. He went on
'There is little purpose in the law commission making recommendations if they are to be allowed to lie for years on a shelf gathering
dust'.[128]

The Ladbroke Grove disaster seems certain to blow off the dust.
The disaster happened only a few miles from Southall, on the same
track, involving several of the same parties. Both accidents resulted
from signals passed at danger. John Prescott was by this time the
minister in overall charge of transport. The firm and drastic
regulatory actions immediately after the Ladbroke Grove disaster –
including the threat to revoke the operating licences of the three companies involved – have no precedent after any other disaster in our
period. The cultural and political pressures for a more effective
attack on corporations responsible for deaths seem overwhelming.

And yet there is much to disentangle. Some of the immediate
anger at Ladbroke Grove arose because the Southall inquiry had
only just started, two years after that accident. Supporters of the
Ladbroke Grove victims pointed out that, had the Southall inquiry
proceeded, its recommendations might have been put into effect in
time to prevent the Ladbroke Grove disaster from occurring at all.
But the delay to the Southall inquiry had a very simple cause. The
manslaughter prosecutions had to take priority. And almost nobody
now doubts that it is appropriate to press for manslaughter charges
where there is *prima facie* evidence of gross negligence. This is part of
the cultural shift that began at Zeebrugge. The idea is no longer
rejected, in the words of J. D. Rimington, as 'bloodthirsty'. But it
comes at a cost.

In the end, the fact that violations of the 1974 Act are not seen as
'real' crimes turns out to have another side to it. Neither the courts
nor the HSE have felt that a prior inquiry prejudices a later health
and safety charge. That was the sequence at Clapham, and also at
Southall, where Mr Justice Scott Baker convicted Great Western
Trains of violations of the 1974 Act three weeks after throwing out
the manslaughter charges. Perhaps, when the dust of Ladbroke
Grove settles, it will turn out that this rather than manslaughter or
corporate killing is the best route for holding corporations to
account and preventing disasters.

Notes

1 Disaster Action, *Response to the Law Commission Involuntary Manslaughter Consultation Paper*, 1994, para. 2.1.
2 *Aberfan Report*, para. 77, p. 39.
3 There were 9 groups of statutes separately administered by 6 central government departments through 7 separate inspectorates. Robert Baldwin, *Rules and Government* (Oxford: OUP, 1995), p. 126; Robens, *Safety and Health at Work*, paras. 24-6.
4 Civil actions against employers for negligence of their employees in health or safety matters have always been possible, going back as least as far as *Priestley* v. *Fowler* (1837) 3 M&W, 1. But until recently they have been rare. For the case of asbestosis see N. Wikeley, 'Turner & Newall: Early Organizational Responses to Litigation Risk', *Journal of Law and Society* 24, 1997, pp. 252-75; and his 'The Asbestos Regulations 1931 - A Licence to Kill?', *Journal of Law and Society* 19 1992, pp. 365-78.
5 Nicola Lacey & Celia Wells *Reconstructing Criminal Law: Critical Perspectives on Crime and the Criminal Process* (London: Butterworths, 1998 2nd edn.), p. 495; W.G. Carson, 'The conventionalisation of early factory crime', *International Journal of the Sociology of Law*, 7, 1979, pp. 37-60.
6 See Gerald Rhodes, *Inspectorates in British Government: Law Enforcement and Standards of Efficiency* (London: George Allen, 1981), ch. 4.
7 See Rhodes, *Inspectorates in British Government*, pp 75, 78-80, 94.
8 Calculated from data in Robens Report, written evidence, p. 377.
9 Barbara Castle, *The Castle Diaries 1964-70* (London: Weidenfeld & Nicolson, 1984), entries for 11.10.68 and 9.4.70, pp. 528 and 785. Several people, both politicians and civil servants, would dispute the claim that it was all Barbara Castle's idea. Cf e.g., letter from Lord Walker of Doncaster to MJ, September 1999; discussion between IM and senior HSE staff, September 1999. HSE staff are inclined to give most credit to James Tye, at the time director of the British Safety Council.
10 A search of the online catalogue of the Public Record Office at drew a blank under all of the following class headings: CAB 128, CAB 129, CAB 130; LAB 14; LAB 16; LAB 43; LAB 77; LAB 96. There are copious papers, already open, relating to the progress of the Robens Committee from its appointment in 1970 to its report in 1972 in class LAB 96. Lady Castle has no specific memories of the setting up of the committee. Sir Kenneth Barnes and C. H. Sisson concur that it was not politically controversial. Letters to MJ, March to August 1999.
11 Robens, *Ten Year Stint* pp. 234-45 (quoted at p. 234) and table on p. 325.
12 David Bergman, *Disasters: Where the Law Fails: A New Agenda for Dealing with Corporate Crime* (Herald Families Association, 1993), pp. 20-24. Celia Wells, *Corporations and Criminal Responsibility* (Oxford: Clarendon, 1993), p. 42.
13 Castle, *Diaries*, 25 October 1967, p. 313.
14 Castle, *Diaries*, 7 and 8 February 1968, pp. 370-1.
15 Wilson, *Labour Government*, p. 493.
16 *Safety and Health at Work, Report of the Committee*, chairman Lord

Robens, Cmnd 5034/1972, para. 262

17 Robens, *Safety and Health at Work*, paras. 263-264 .

18 Robens, *Safety and Health at Work*, para. 261.

19 New regulations increasingly originate in European Union law. See Goddard, 'European Law: New Origins for Health and Safety Regulation', *Journal of Personal Injury Law*, 5, 1994.

20 Health and Safety Commission, *Health and Safety at Work etc Act: The Act Outlined*, HSC2, 1994, pp. 3-4.

21 Derived from A. J. P. Dalton, *Safety, Health and Environmental Hazards at the Workplace* (London: Cassell, 1998), p. 43. Dalton is a fierce critic, but on this point his perception is shared by HSE insiders.

22 J. R. Carby-Hall, 'Health, Safety and Welfare at Work', *Managerial Law*, vol. 31, no. 1/2, 1989, pp. 40, 36.

23 Baldwin, *Rules and Government*, p. 131.

24 Theo Nichols, *The Sociology of Industrial Injury* (London: Mansell, 1997). Cf also Frank Pearce and Steve Tombs, 'Policing Corporate "Skid Rows": A reply to Keith Hawkins', *British Journal of Criminology*, vol. 31 no. Autumn 1991, p. 415.

25 Robens, *Safety and Health at Work*, para. 29.

26 Railway safety regulation is a good example of evolution in response to successive disasters. See L.T.C. Rolt, *Red for Danger* (Newton Abbot: David & Charles, 1966).

27 Sir A. Bryan, *The evolution of health and safety in mines* London: Ashire Publishing Ltd, 1975, *passim*

28 Health & Safety at Work, etc., Act (1974 c.37), s. 1(2).

29 Interview, IM with a civil servant involved in health and safety regulation during the passage of the Act, September 1999.

30 T. E. Keeler and S. E. Foreman, 'Regulation and deregulation' in P. Newman (ed.), *The New Palgrave Dictionary of Economics and the Law* (London: Macmillan 3 vols 1998), vol. 3 pp 213—22, quoted at p. 213. For the Chicago theory of economic regulation see also G. Stigler, 'The theory of economic regulation', *Bell Journal of Economics and Management Science* 2 (1971) pp. 3—21; S. Peltzman, 'Toward a more general theory of regulation', *Journal of Law and Economics* 19 (1976), pp. 211—40; S. Breyer and P. W. MacAvoy, 'Regulation and deregulation' in J. Eatwell et al. (eds.), *The New Palgrave Dictionary of Economics* (London: Macmillan 4 vols. 1987), vol. 4 pp. 128—34.

31 Keeler and Foreman, 'Regulation and deregulation', p. 214.

32 Williamson, *Gresford*, p. 203.

33 Sir Henry Walker (chairman), *Report on the Causes of and Circumstances attending the Explosion which occurred at Gresford Colliery, Denbigh, on the 22nd September, 1934*, Cmd 5358 (London: HMSO, 1937); Joseph Jones at p. 146.

34 *Gresford Report*, pp. 89-90.

35 *Gresford Report*, Joseph Jones at p. 149.

36 For an examination of the legacy of the disaster see Roger Laidlaw, 'The Gresford Disaster in Popular Memory', *Llafur*, vol. 6, no. 4, 1995, 123-146; Stanley Williamson, *Gresford: The Anatomy of a Disaster* (Liverpool: Liverpool University Press, 1999). We were also much helped by a discussion between IM and Sir Geoffrey Wilson, who was one of Cripps' juniors at Gresford, September 1999.

37 PRO PREM 13/1280.

38 Crossland, (Sir) B, *Public Hearing following the extensive fall of roof at Bilsthorpe Colliery: a report to the Health and Safety Commission* [1994] no publication details shown. The original report is HSE, *Extensive fall of roof at Bilsthorpe Colliery: a report of HSE's investigation into the extensive fall of roof at Bilsthorpe Colliery, Notts on 18 August 1993* (London: HSE Books 1994).

39 Crossland, *Public Hearing*, para. 94, p.21.

40 After a visit from the Chief Inspector of Railways reporting progress in the inquiry into the Hixon level-crossing accident, Barbara Castle discussed with her diary whether she would have to resign as Secretary of State for Transport over the forthcoming report. Castle, *Diaries*, 8 February 1968, p. 371.

41 See Slapper, 'Corporate Manslaughter', pp. 437-483. Also see W. G. Carson, *The Other Price of Britain's Oil : Safety and Control in the North Sea* (Oxford: Martin Robertson 1981); Charles Woolfson, John Foster & Matthias Beck, *Paying for the Piper: Capital and Labour in Britain's Offshore Oil Industry* (London: Mansell, 1996), pp. 249-253;

42 *Public Inquiry into the Piper Alpha Disaster*, Cm. 1310 (HMSO, 1990), executive summary, ch.1, para. 1.15.

43 Department of Employment, Transport, & the Regions, *Consultation Document on Transport Safety* (London: DETR 1999); available at http://wwww.local-transport.detr.gov.uk/transsaf/index.htm, paras. 2.09-2.10

44 IM, interview with senior HSE staff, September 1999.

45 HSE, 'Train Accident at Ladbroke Grove Junction, 5 October 1999: First HSE interim report, 8 October 1999', at http://www.open.gov.uk/hse/railway/paddrail/interim.htm.

46 House of Lords statement by Lord Macdonald of Tradeston, 11 October 1999, at HSE, 'Review of Arrangements for Standard Setting and Application on the Main Railway Network: Interim Report', at http://www.open.gov.uk/hse/railway/standset.htm. This decision was not implemented.

47 Office of the Rail Regulator, Press Notice ORR 99/43, 11 October 1999, at http://www.rail-reg.gov.uk/pn99/pn43_99.htm

48 *Aberfan Report*, para. 295 (1).

49 POWE 52/68. Coal Division memo on Tribunal findings, 26 July 1967.

50 Robens committee, *Safety and Health at Work*, para. 286.

51 Lord Robens quoted in *Western Mail*, 11 September 1967.

52 Robens committee, *Safety and Health at Work*, para. 1.

53 Ibid. paras. 284, 287, 291.

54 Health and Safety at Work etc. Act 1974, s. 3 (1).

55 Bridget M. Hutter, 'Regulating Employers and Employees: Health and Safety in the Workplace', *Journal of Law and Society*, vol. 29, no. 4, Winter 1993.

56 IM interview with Jenny Bacon (Director General, HSE). For a first hand account of such problems see Ed Punchard, *Piper Alpha: A Survivor's Story* (London: W. H. Allen, 1989).

57 See Nichols, *Sociology of Industrial Injury*. Barbara Castle, pointing specifically to the Piper Alpha and Herald of Free Enterprise disasters, also maintained that the decline in unionism was undermining health

and safety provision in the workplace. Barbara Castle, *Fighting all the Way* (London: Macmillan, 1993), p. 588.
58 Baldwin, *Rules and Government*, p. 139.
59 HSC Annual Report, 1988/89, p. 4.
60 This paragraph is derived from Bridget M. Hutter, 'Variations in Regulatory Styles', *Law and Policy*, vol. 11, no. 2, April 1989, 153-174.
61 Employment Committee, *Work of the Health & Safety Commission & Executive*, para. 10.
62 Charles Woolfson & Matthias Beck, 'Deregulation: The Contemporary Politics of Health and Safety', in Aileen McColgan, (ed.), *The Future of Labour Law* (London: Cassell, 1996), p. 182.
63 Wells, *Negotiating Tragedy*, p. 55.
64 *File on Four*, 16 February 1999.
65 Ann Ridley & Louise Dunford, 'Corporate Killing – Legislating for Unlawful Death?', *Industrial Law Society*, vol. 26, no. 2, June 1997, p. 99.
66 *Guardian*, 9 December 1994.
67 Gary Slapper, 'Corporate Manslaughter: An Examination of the Determinants of Prosecutional Policy', *Social and Legal Studies*, vol. 2, no. 4, December 1993, p. 429.
68 Sections 2-6. Almost half the figures were less than £5,000. HSC News Release, C49:48, 16 November 1998.
69 Slapper, 'Corporate Manslaughter', pp. 429-430.
70 *R v F. Howe & Son (Engineers) Ltd*, Court of Appeal (Criminal Division), 6 November 1998.
71 HSC News Release, C49:48, 16 November 1998.
72 Employment Committee, *The Work of the Health and Safety Commission and Executive*, Minutes of Evidence, 14 March 1990. Publication number 293-I, paras. 118, 73.
73 *Disaster Action Newsletter*, Spring/Summer 1997, Issue 4.
74 House of Commons, Employment Committee, Session 1989-90, 'The work of the Health & Safety Commission and Executive', Oral Evidence, 14 March 1990, p. 14.
75 Gary Slapper, 'Crime without Conviction', *New Law Journal*, vol. 142, 14 February 1992, p. 192.
76 HSE, *Work-Related Deaths: A protocol for liaison*, 1998.
77 *File on Four*, Radio 4, 16 February 1999.
78 Bacon cited in Woolfson & Beck, 'Deregulation: Contemporary Politics of Health and Safety', p. 185.
79 See Bridget M. Hutter, & Sally Lloyd-Bostock, 'The Power of Accidents: The Social and Psychological Impact of Accidents and the Enforcement of Safety Regulations', *British Journal of Criminology*, vol. 30, no. 4, Autumn 1990, p. 417.
80 Letters from *The City Gent* (Bradford City FC fanzine) to MJ, 3, 26 August 1999.
81 Celia Wells, 'Disasters: the role of institutional responses', in Robert Lee & Derek Morgan (eds.), *Death Rites: Law and Ethics at the End of Life* (London: Routledge, 1994), pp. 198-201.
82 Paul A. Knapman, 'Hillsborough Lives On', *Justice of the Peace & Local Government Law*, 25 January 1997, 79-80. He argues that the law should not force juries into choosing between an accidental or unlawful

verdict. His solution would be to remove the need for a verdict and let juries 'decide on a form of words called "findings" '.

83 Wells, 'Disasters: the role of institutional responses', pp. 202-203
84 Ibid., p. 206.
85 Although the Taylor Report felt that 'no valid criticism' could be lev-elled against the responding emergency services, doubts remain on whether delays and confusion caused further loss of life. See Scraton, *Hillsborough*, pp. 124-125.
86 Home Office press release, 066/98. 18 February 1998.
87 Wells, 'Disasters: the role of institutional responses', p. 210.
88 Sir John Smith & Brian Hogan, *Criminal Law* (London: Butterworths, 8th edn., 1996), p. 189.
89 David Bergman, *Disasters: Where the Law Fails - A New Agenda for Dealing with Corporate Violence* (Herald Families Association, 1993), p. 1.
90 *R v. OLL Ltd* 144 *NLJ* 1735. *Guardian*, 9 February 1996.
91 Ridley & Dunford, *Corporate Killing*, pp. 102-103.
92 Wells, *Negotiating Tragedy*, pp. 172-173.
93 Disaster Action, *Response to the Law Commission Involuntary Manslaughter Consultation Paper* (LCCP No. 135), 1994, para. 2.3.
94 Bergman, *Disasters*, p. 6
95 Peter Spooner, *The HFA Story, 1987-1994* (London: Herald Families Association, 1994), pp. 18-19. Peter Spooner, 'Corporate Responsibility in an Age of Deregulation', in Dennis J Parker & John W Handmer, *Hazard Management and Emergency Planning: Perspectives on Britain* (London: James & James, 1992), p.101.
96 Celia Wells, 'Cry in the Dark: Corporate Manslaughter and Cultural Meaning', in Ian Loveland (ed.), *Frontiers of Criminality* (London: Sweet & Maxwell, 1995), p. 114.
97 Wells, *Negotiating Tragedy*, pp. 50-51.
98 See minute 7 of discussion between Richard Marsh, Minister of Power, and Lord Robens, 3 August 1967. 'Lord Robens said that … the Tribunal Report was a conspiracy of silence as a result of which only the Board had been accused. The real cause of the failure of the Board … was a breakdown of communication in that … Mr Roberts … and Mr Exley were not on speaking terms'. PRO POWE 52/94.
99 *Guardian*, 14 September 1990.
100 *Guardian*, 27 July 1999.
101 *Guardian*, 24 July 1999.
102 Cohen, *Aftershock*, pp. 77, 96
103 *The Times*, 24 November 1967.
104 London Underground had initially suggested that the fire was caused by arson and consequently were subject to public criticism.
105 Quoted in *The Guardian*, 24 July 1999, p. 4. GWT's legal representatives maintained that the Chief Executive had not appeared as a result of legal advice.
106 Carol Harlow & Richard Rawlings, *Pressure through Law* (London: Routledge, 1992), pp. 228-231.
107 Chairman of Disaster Action quoted in *Guardian*, 31 October 1991.
108 See Disaster Action Newsletter, 1995. The group's research was funded by a grant from the Joseph Rowntree Charitable Trust.

109 West Midlands, HASAC, *The Perfect Crime*, p.4.
110 Law Commission, *Criminal Law: Involuntary Manslaughter*, Consulta-
     tion Paper no. 135, HMSO, 1994, paras. 1.20, 4.1 – 4.2.
111 *Guardian*, 4 October 1997.
112 Lacey & Wells, *Reconstructing Criminal Law*, p. 522
113 Ibid., pp. 521-522.
114 Ridley & Dunford, 'Corporate Killing', pp. 111-112
115 Gary Slapper, 'Legal regulation of safety', *Health and safety at work*,
     April 1992.
116 Lacey & Wells, *Reconstructing Criminal Law*, p. 514. Wells, *Negotiating
     Tragedy*, pp. 177-182.
117 Michael J. Soloman & James Thompson, 'Anger and Blame in Three
     Technological Disasters', *Stress Medicine*, vol. 11, 1995, p. 202.
118 Bridget M. Hutter & Sally Lloyd-Bostock, ' The Power of Accidents:
     The Social and Psychological Impact of Accidents and the Enforcement
     of Safety Regulations', *British Journal of Criminology*, vol. 30, no. 4,
     Autumn 1990, p. 410.
119 For example, *The Times*, 15 August 1989.
120 For a critique of such a culture see Frank Furedi, *Courting Mistrust:
     The Hidden Growth of a Culture of Litigation in Britain* (London: Centre
     for Policy Studies, 1999).
121 Harlow & Rawlings, *Pressure through Law*, p. 123.
122 See Slapper, 'Corporate Manslaughter', pp. 437-438.
123 *Guardian*, 28 August 1989, p. 2.
124 *Hansard*, 6th Series, vol. 143, col. 143.
125 See, for example, *The Guardian*, 7 March 1989, 21 August 1989.
126 *M.V. Herald of Free Enterprise, Report of the Court, No 8074*, Depart-
     ment of Transport (London: HMSO, 1987), para. 14.1
127 See *The Times*, 20 October 1990.
128 Quoted in *The Guardian*, 3 July 1999, p. 4.

Chapter Nine

GOVERNMENT AND DISASTER

I wish to say that the Board of Trade has got many eyes and many ears,
but it does not seem to have any brains[1]

W.D. Harbinson, Counsel for the relatives of the
third class passengers lost on the Titanic.

Disasters often involve regulatory failure. Somebody was responsible for safety and failed to ensure it, through negligence or lack of imagination, or both. In Chapter 2 we argued that the failure to hold anyone accountable for the Aberfan disaster derives from the corporatist assumptions that pervaded British politics at the time. We begin this concluding chapter by revisiting the sinking of the *Titanic* in 1912. In 1912, as in 1966, the interests of government and industry overrode those of disaster victims. We then examine why the interests of the consumer are so often overlooked in the aftermath of disasters. Our case studies are two series of disasters and unlearnt lessons, in the post-war ferry and football industries. We conclude by examining the lessons and legacy of Aberfan.

The loss of the *Titanic*[2]

The loss of the *Titanic* was the UK's best-known and deadliest peacetime disaster since 1900. The liner sank on the night of 14/15 April 1912 with the loss of 1,490 lives; 711 people were saved. An inquiry into the disaster was set up under Lord Mersey, a retired Liverpudlian judge. The inquiry concluded that 'the loss of the said ship was due to collision with an iceberg, brought about by the excessive speed at which the ship was being navigated'. The deceased captain, not there to answer allegations, was spared criticism, as was the Board of Trade whose regulations had failed to specify that liners should carry sufficient lifeboats for all on board, or to regulate wireless telegraphy or visual disaster signals. In contrast, Stanley Lord, the Master of a ship in the vicinity, the *Californian*, was strongly condemned for not going to the *Titanic's* aid.

The inquiry was to report to the Board of Trade, but as one MP asked in the Commons how could it do so properly 'if they find that the Board of Trade has been culpable'? The Prime Minister, H. H. Asquith, said, 'There is no difficulty whatever.... They are perfectly entitled to find the Board of Trade culpable'.[3] The mechanics of the inquiry made this unlikely. The Board had set the inquiry's agenda by asking it to answer 26 specific questions. The Board's counsel was Sir Rufus Isaacs, the Attorney-General. Even more starkly than HM Inspectors of Mines at Gresford and Bilsthorpe (chapter 8), Isaacs had a vested interest in deflecting blame and apportioning praise. He ran the inquiry at many points, dragging a complaisant Lord Mersey along with him.

Isaacs had an agenda as a member of the Government and another one as a private citizen. Neither served the public interest. He had an interest in finding any convenient scapegoat other than an arm of the UK government. The Master of the *Californian* had already been scapegoated in the US inquiry into the disaster. Lord Mersey accepted the extraordinary procedural device of adding a question to the 26 that set the inquiry's agenda, after Captain Lord had already been heard, because the transcript shows that he, too, had convinced himself of Captain Lord's guilt. As a private citizen, Isaacs held a large block of shares in the American Marconi Company, whose shares would become more valuable, the more he was able to show that Marconi wireless had saved lives, and its extension would save more. The American inquiry questioned Guglielmo Marconi very sharply over his role in restricting information from the disaster in order to maximise the windfall profits of the wireless operators aboard the *Titanic* and the rescue ship, all of whom were his employees.[4] In contrast, Isaacs asked Marconi only a sequence of respectful questions.

The deepest failures identified in the Mersey Report are, as so often in disaster inquiries, failures of imagination. Ship designers, operators and regulators had never conceived of such a thing happening. The *Titanic* was believed to be able to act as her own lifeboat because her design of bulkheads and watertight doors was expected to survive any holing. In the event, Mersey concluded, 'The *Titanic* as constructed could not have remained afloat long with such damage as she received'. The watertight bulkheads did not go high enough into the passenger accommodation. First and second class passengers thus got unrestricted promenades from end to end of the ship; promenades which cost many of them their lives. But Mersey attaches no blame to her designers or builders, presumably because everybody thought the same, and everybody was wrong. Thus the Board of Trade's failure to update lifeboat regulation went uncriticised. The US inquiry[5] had not attacked the Board for this shortcoming but only because it expected the better placed Mersey to do so. In the subsequent parliamentary debate, the shipping industry blocked any serious discussion. There is a lively argument between the merits of self-regulation and those of regulation by Government agency. Self-regulation *by* a Government agency may be the worst of all worlds. The Board of Trade was all but judge in its own case.

This outcome was facilitated by the limited scope of the inquiry. It began as an essentially private conversation between the Government (Rufus Isaacs), and capital, in the shape of White Star. Both had strong motives for directing the inquiry away from their own culpability. A third actor was added when one (but only one) of the trade unions whose members had been aboard was let into the inquiry. This was classic tripartite corporatism involving government, suppliers of capital and suppliers of labour. The huge public interest in the disaster, and the non-corporatist American inquiry, forced the doors wider open, but Lord Mersey was very reluctant to let consumer interests be involved in the inquiry. Representatives of the bereaved relatives of passengers were allowed in on sufferance. Representatives of regular trans-Atlantic travellers were not admitted. Corporatism is often assumed to postdate 1945; it does not. After the loss of the *Titanic*, the lessons regarding the Board of Trade's inappropriate regulatory priorities before and after the disaster went largely unheeded: the captive regulator had failed the consumer.

Disaster victims: class, corporatism, high politics, and producer dominance

It is worth holding the *Titanic* and Aberfan tragedies in parallel for a moment. Remarkably similar allegations emerge from each. Some say the dead were victims of the class system, others that they died because they were unimportant peripheral people. The *Titanic* legend owes much to the belief that the third-class passengers who drowned were victims of the British class system, which had ensured that the first-class was evacuated in the limited number of lifeboats first. This is not exactly correct. Counsel for the third-class passengers at the inquiry accepted that there was no class discrimination in loading the boats. The effects of class were cross-cut by honour codes such as 'women and children first' and 'officers stay at their posts'. Not a single engineer officer survived; some stokers and firemen, released from their posts and permitted to fend for themselves, did. Class affected survival rates indirectly, by its influence on the design of the ship. The third-class passengers slept in the lower decks and thus learnt about the danger last and reached the boat deck last, mostly after all the boats had been launched. Many of them were Scandinavian or southern European emigrants. They did not speak English, may not have understood the crew's instructions, and had nobody to represent them at the inquiries or in the UK parliament.

Although working-class passengers and crew were not fully represented at the UK inquiry, in practice this made little difference to the outcome. Amongst the dead were some of the world's richest men, yet even their deaths were unable to place the interests of passengers at the forefront of the inquiry. The bias that did exist was an anti-consumer bias. Mersey treated a request by frequent trans-Atlantic passengers to be represented at the inquiry as 'one of the strangest' he had heard.[6] The shipping industry and its regulators ensured that their interests took priority.

Aberfan was a small working-class community isolated from the heart of UK politics. It is true that the Wilson government's decision to grant Legal Aid to pay for the legal representation of the Aberfan parents and residents at the Tribunal of Inquiry meant they were able to afford the best 'silk' of the day. The fearsome Desmond Ackner triumphed over the National Coal Board at the Tribunal. But in the aftermath of the disaster, a Labour government, whose support across South Wales was secure, ignored Aberfan's interests. The only electoral threat came from Plaid Cymru, and even that was essentially marginal (Chapter 2).

There has been much theoretical debate on whether or not the peripheries of the UK are neglected by London-based governments. Michael Hechter saw the 'Celtic' periphery as neglected and exploited by the English core. He argued that the values and interests of the periphery are gradually submerged and its resources are used to support the core.[7] Rather similarly, Jim Bulpitt spoke of territory and power in the UK. According to Bulpitt, the business – what he called 'statecraft' – of the centre was to keep those things which governing politicians cared about in the centre, the realm of high politics. The rest was the periphery, the realm of low politics.[8]

Is it true that Aberfan suffered because it was Welsh? (a fifty-year echo of the claims by Irish MPs that Irish emigrants suffered the worst loss of life in the *Titanic*). One scrap of evidence in Hechter's favour is a remarkable memorandum from the Prime Minister's Office to Harold Wilson in late October 1966. The *Western Mail* had been campaigning for a memorial service to the victims of Aberfan to be held in Westminster Abbey. Wilson's office advised him against asking the church authorities for a memorial service there, 'partly because the Welsh Church [is] disestablished and ha[s] no claim on Westminster Abbey'.[9]

But most of the evidence favours Bulpitt rather than Hechter. The London media, Royalty, and the Prime Minister all travelled to Aberfan to see the horror of the disaster for themselves. It was only a few hours drive away or an even shorter flight. Even Lord Robens got there, 36 hours later. Intensive media coverage, particularly television, ensured that the disaster was seen as a national one.[10] For all the rumblings of nationalism in 1960s Wales, she remained fundamentally part of the United Kingdom, politically, culturally and emotionally. Aberfan suffered because it was part of the periphery, not specifically because it was Welsh. Had it been in the Yorkshire coalfield, the dynamics of high and low politics would have been the same. As Chapter 3 demonstrated, the NCB dominated the valleys and ignored complaints or concerns about safety. The tips were tolerated as an inevitable by-product of mining, which had nowhere else to put them. The physical and environmental threat the tips presented was tolerated by the people of the coalfields, including South Wales, in a way that it would not be in, say, the south of England. Before Aberfan, no one spoke out against their existence per se. The only relevant difference between Aberfan and South Yorkshire was that, uniquely in the South Wales valleys, the tips were on the hillsides above the settlements.

Both Lord Robens and Lord Marsh have confirmed that they were fighting each other about government fuel policy in 1967.[11] Aberfan became a sideshow. In corporatist Britain the interests of a nationalised industry took precedence over those of the consumers or the public. The use of money from the disaster fund to pay for the removal of the tips is the most conclusive example of this.

Thus the failures to prioritise the interests of Aberfan were not because it was Welsh or working-class, but because the community was peripheral. Its cultural and social values were so remote from metropolitan ones that neither understood the other. George Thomas, originally a teacher from Tonypandy in the Rhondda, did initially protest at the decision to encourage the disaster fund to contribute to the payment of the removal of the tips. But his lone voice in the cabinet was not sufficient and in the end he acquiesced in the plan. The South Wales valleys consisted of safe Labour seats. Thus the valleys' interests were not the concern of high politics, whereas avoiding a coal strike was.

Aberfan and the spiral of hopelessness

Aberfan was the victim of high politics over and over again. There was psychological truth in Gwynfor Evans' complaint in the Aberfan debate that if the tips had been at Hampstead or Eton, the Government would have taken notice.[12] After the disaster, the factors we have identified in previous chapters interacted in the most baleful way. Aberfan's local government was weak because Merthyr Council was so small (chapter 3). The villagers of Aberfan were traumatised beyond the comprehension of outsiders who could see only their 'unpredictable emotions and reactions'[13] (chapter 5). The trustees of Bethania chapel, Aberfan, which was used as the mortuary after the disaster (chapter 1), pleaded with George Thomas to get the NCB to pay for it to be demolished and rebuilt, on the grounds that its members could not longer bear to worship there. Thomas passed the plea on to Lord Robens, who rejected it.[14] When Aberfan villagers demanded the removal of the tips, they were dismissed as irrational. Charity law seemed designed to protect only its own antique structure. Certainly it protected neither the donors to, nor the beneficiaries of, the Aberfan Disaster Fund (chapter 6). The £500-a-head compensation the villagers received for the deaths of their children seemed obscenely low to common sense, but 'a generous settlement' in the briefing note to Marsh for the Aberfan debate[15] (chapter 7). Even as insurers wrangled, the ruins of the school and empty houses remained for a year (see Laurie Lee's account, chapter 1).

Again and again, the newly released records on Aberfan show the mutual incomprehension of a Welsh village and the world of Westminster and Whitehall. But how unique was Aberfan? In the next section we follow two threads of related disasters – on ferries, and in football stadiums – to show how they, too, were insulated from high politics, with fatal results.

Ferry and football deaths

In one of the *Titanic* debates, an MP (Richard Holt, Lib., Hexham; partner in Alfred Holt & Co, shipowners) described ' "boats for all"

[as] one of the most ridiculous proposals ever put forward'. The grounds for objection were cost and the threat to the competitiveness of British shipping.

There have been concerns about the safety of roll-on, roll-off (ro-ro) ferries since their introduction in the early post-war years. The first ro-ro to be lost at sea was the *Princess Victoria* off Stranraer in 1953 at the cost of 133 lives. Cars on board shifted in rough seas and forced the car doors open, leading the vessel to sink very quickly. In 1982, the capsize of the *European Gateway* off Harwich (six people killed) led the Royal Institute of Naval Architects to call for a change in the design of ro-ro vessels before more lives were lost. Bulkheads were needed to divide the lower deck in order to delay a vessel capsizing should it bring in water. Safety changes were actively considered but not implemented. Then, in 1987, the *Herald of Free Enterprise* capsized with her bow doors open in just ninety seconds, at the cost of 192 lives.

More reports followed from marine engineers calling for the redesign of such ferries. At the impetus of the UK government, the International Maritime Organisation (IMO) passed regulations (known as SOLAS 90) to ensure that all vessels built after April 1990 had to able to remain upright for long enough to allow all passengers to evacuate. Although the UK had called for the regulations to apply to all ships, the member countries of the IMO felt the cost of converting existing ships was too high. However, after lobbying from the Herald Families Association, the UK Department of Transport persevered alone and introduced the full SOLAS 90 regulations for most ferries operating in its waters. Then in 1994 the ferry *Estonia* sank in the Baltic Sea. The vulnerability of the ro-ro design again increased the death toll as the ship rapidly sank. Over 900 people were killed.[16]

The *Estonia* disaster led to further calls for tighter safety regulations and IMO commissioned a complete review of the safety of roll-on roll-off ferries. It had taken a series of disasters to overcome the commercial concerns about the cost of the safety measures needed. The shipping industry itself was not unconcerned with safety but commercial interests dominated its agenda. Indeed the whole design of the ro-ro ferries was determined by the commercial need to sail quickly.[17] The Government too was concerned about safety but it had difficulties reconciling this with the commercial needs of the shipping industry. The specific political and financial links between individuals and companies within the industry and political parties complicated the matter further.[18] The creation of an over-riding commitment to safety faces many barriers.

In 1923 the inaugural Wembley FA Cup Final was in danger of descending into disaster. The official attendance was 126,047 but some estimates put the crowd at 250,000. The overcrowding caused thousands to spill on to the pitch and delayed the game. Miraculously no one was killed yet there were an estimated 1,000 injuries. The organisation of the match attracted severe public criticism. Consequently, the newly-elected first Labour government, perhaps conscious of its duty to protect the safety of working men in their recreation, set up an inquiry into 'abnormally large attendance on special occasions'.[19]

The FA refused a request from the inquiry for information. Although impressed by the fact that, free of any regulation, football had so far avoided any serious accident and was relatively free of trouble,[20] the committee did recommend a system where grounds were licensed. It envisaged that its recommendations would be implemented through pressure from sport's governing bodies who assured them that they were anxious that their sports take place 'under conditions which will promote the public safety'.[21] Given the FA's non-appearance at the inquiry, this was an optimistic stance. The committee's recommendations were not implemented or even debated in Parliament.

The lack of firm action following the Wembley debacle was assisted by the myths that grew up around the game. The appearance of the King was said to calm the crowds and a single policeman on a white horse was (said to have been) able to clear the pitch, allowing the match to go ahead. Thus instead of being remembered for the endangering of lives and breakdown in safety control, the game came to symbolise the supposed orderliness and good discipline of British crowds.[22] With such a discourse dominant, the match was hardly likely to spark a major review of crowd safety. Instead, the organisational legacy of the events was all-ticket FA Cup finals in order to avoid such chaos and embarrassment in the future.

In 1946, 33 people were killed and over 400 injured in overcrowding at an FA Cup match in Bolton. The official inquiry, chaired by Moelwyn Hughes, noted

> how simple and how easy it is for a dangerous situation to arise in a crowded enclosure. It happens again and again without fatal or even injurious consequences. But its danger is that it requires so little additional influences ... to translate the danger into terms of death and injuries. The pastime of football watching is on the increase and the chances of danger among the crowds are arising.[23]

Moelwyn Hughes recommended a licensing scheme run by local authorities with penalties for non-compliance.

Although initially supportive, the government (again Labour) proved to be uncertain about the measures while the football authorities viewed them with distrust. There was even a debate within government as to whether public safety should include spectators at a football match. The Home Office thought that the existing self-regulatory scheme based upon inspections by the police was failing because the relationship between clubs and police was already too close to be effective. Yet the football industry feared that any regulatory scheme run by local authorities might 'err on the side of excessive caution', resulting in clubs 'being put to considerable expense and being subject to a great deal of official interference'.[24] Specific post-war conditions further complicated the issue. The shortage of building materials meant that ground improvements were not easy and required special permission. From early 1946, the situation was also complicated by the fact that the government was trying to restrict mid-week sport, because of the economic crisis and fuel shortages, on a voluntary rather than legislative basis. There was strong criticism from both sides of the house of the irony of a Labour government restricting working-class sport. Building material shortages and the economic crisis were part of high politics. The safety of spectators at sports grounds was not.

The licensing plan met opposition in the cabinet where it was argued that the burden would be too great on local authorities, materials were in short supply and that no legislation could prevent accidents caused by illegal entry. It was thought that 'the risk of a serious incident was small enough to be taken'.[25] Thus instead of the system of regulation by local authority recommended by the Moelwyn Hughes inquiry, a system of self-regulation was adopted where clubs simply told the Football Association that their ground had been inspected by qualified persons.

It was ineffective. The safety of spectators had still not become firmly entrenched in the culture of football. Sir Norman Chester's 1968 inquiry into the state of the game and how it could be developed for the public good noted that there was a need for better facilities at many grounds from the viewpoint of crowd safety and behaviour.[26] Yet this brief mention was the only attention paid in the whole of the report to the question of safety.

An independent report in 1968 into the game noted that the recommendations of the Shortt and Moelwyn Hughes reports were often ignored, although they did carry some weight with football directors. The report felt that because of the absence of legislation some clubs did 'not feel obliged to put their grounds into a state considered by the police to be necessary for crowd control'.[27] A 1969 government report on crowd behaviour noted that although the self-regulation system worked 'satisfactorily' there was an advantage in replacing the 1948 certificates with up-to-date regular inspections.[28] Consequently, the football associations of England, Scotland and Wales asked those clubs whose grounds had a capacity of 10,000 or more for an annual certificate that their grounds had been inspected by (undefined) qualified personnel.

The failure of this system of self-regulation became clear in 1971 when 66 people were killed in a crush at Ibrox Park, Glasgow. The subsequent Wheatley Report also recommended a licensing system operated by local authorities.[29] However, the cost to small clubs of implementing large-scale safety measures in their stadia was potentially crippling. Wheatley felt that the risk was not large enough to jeopardise the existence of smaller clubs in the short term. Many fans would have agreed that the whole existence of these clubs was worth the safety risk in their grounds.

The 1975 Safety at Sports Grounds Act was based upon Wheatley's recommendations. It established a system of inspection by local authorities and established a series of technical safety requirements in football grounds. Because of the cost of the safety measures, the Act initially only applied to clubs in the English first division and Scottish Premier division (plus the three international rugby grounds in Britain). Clubs in the English second division were brought under the Act in 1979. This system created an anomaly where small grounds such as Shrewsbury (capacity 16,800) were designated under the Act but large stadiums such as Sheffield United's (capacity 44,000) were not.[30]

Nor were there any more vocal demands for more comprehensive legislation. By 1975, football hooliganism had begun to be seen as a significant problem. Football might still be the national sport but it had become a politically unfashionable pastime that had few vocal supporters in government. Thus the safety of its supporters was not a political issue. The matter was further complicated by the fact that for many supporters the culture and atmosphere of the terraces, complete with pushing, swaying and a sense of unpredictability, was actually part of the attraction of the game. Thus there was little consumer pressure for comprehensive safety legislation.

The Bradford fire, which would have been avoided had the ground been subject to the Act, shattered this complacency. Bradford saw the extension of the Act to all Football League clubs although some of the recommendations of the subsequent

Popplewell Report were not fully implemented. Popplewell's recommendation of adequate exits in perimeter fences could have
prevented the Hillsborough disaster. Hillsborough brought a radi-
cally different philosophy to safety within football through the
forced introduction of all-seater stadiums. It also awoke fans to the
importance of safe grounds. All-seater stadiums were forced upon
generally reluctant clubs[31] by a government who saw football as an
embarrassment and irritant. The Heysel tragedy of May 1985[32] and
the continuing problem of hooliganism meant that the government
was no longer content for football to govern its own affairs. Hooliganism, not safety, had brought football into the arena of high
politics. Such was its determination that money was made available
to the game for ground improvement by earmarking some of the
proceeds of the levy on football pools. Finally, a new body, the Football Licensing Authority, was set up to oversee the licensing and
regulation of grounds.

The history of football disasters in post-war Britain illustrates
how the safety of the consumer is submerged beneath wider
concerns. The failure to introduce a more comprehensive regulatory
scheme sprang from a tradition of excluding sport from legislation.
This tradition, which dated back into the nineteenth century days of
amateur idealism, was based upon a belief that sport's values were
divorced from those that the law regulated. Its competitive but
communal ethos, with an emphasis on fair play, had no need of intervention from the world of economics and politics.[33]

Finally, safety regulation in football had to compete against the
characterisation of fans as hooligans. The government and the industry's authorities were overly concerned with the misbehaviour of a
minority and thus measures to prevent violence overruled safety
concerns. The lethal fences at Hillsborough, designed to cage hooligans like animals, are the most tragic example of this. Even in the
wake of disaster, events were not divorced from the question of
hooliganism. After the Bradford disaster, Eldon Griffiths MP (Con.,
Bury St Edmunds) noted that 'a number of police officers plunged
into the fire to pull out fans who in other circumstances would have
been pelting them with rocks'. Much to the resentment of people in
Bradford, the inquiry into the fire was also asked to investigate the
hooliganism at the Heysel tragedy and a hooligan-related death at
Birmingham City FC.[34] The subsequent parliamentary debate on the
interim report was dominated by discussion of violence rather than
safety.[35] As after Aberfan and the loss of the *Titanic*, parliamentary
debates were shown to be inadequate in identifying the causes of disasters. In the aftermath of the Hillsborough disaster, the

investigations were influenced by media representations of fans as hooligans. The Taylor Report dismissed such allegations but the association between the disaster and hooliganism distorted the inquests. Even the final decision to take the hugely expensive step of all-seater stadia was as much influenced by its potential to reduce crowd trouble as it was to ensure crowd safety.[36]

The presence of safety regulations alone is not enough to create a climate of safety. The safety of consumers is just one interest competing in the aftermath of disaster. Whether it wins or not depends as much upon the power and influence of interests as it does on the validity of its own voice. After the Dunblane tragedy, there was a strong reluctance in the government to ban all handguns. This was despite very strong public and media pressure to do so. It took a change of government and some significant PR mistakes by the gun lobby before the campaigners achieved a total ban.[37] Public and media support for a safety cause is not enough to ensure its success.

Pro-consumer regulation?

Risk may be part of life but that hardly excuses failures on the part of regulatory bodies to minimise it. Regulation of industry in twentieth century Britain has too often been primarily concerned with the interests of the regulated rather than of the consumer. The litany of disasters from the *Titanic* to Aberfan through to the cluster of tragedies in the 1980s is evidence of the catastrophic consequences for the public. The last section showed that the potential victims of ferry sinkings and football ground disasters were ignored in the corporatist era. They were not part of high politics. Although, as the tables in chapter 4 show, these two categories of disaster have been among the most lethal, policy makers have not perceived them as the most disastrous. Ferry passengers are a temporary community. Football supporters are all too easily demonised.

But as Britain became less corporatist, the response to disasters changed. By the 1980s, an individualistic, consumer culture was emerging. Whatever social problems that may have created, it has been good news for disaster victims. They still face considerable legal obstacles but their interests are considered today by government to a far greater extent than in the 1960s. Government reviews of inquiry procedures, safety regulation and the like all clearly value the importance of the needs of the bereaved and survivors. The hints from the Blair Government in August 1999 that the law on corporate manslaughter and bereavement damages may be about to change are further evidence of an evolving commitment to the disaster victims. The immediate steps taken by government and regulators after the Ladbroke Grove disaster (Chapter 8) are the starkest possible contrast to Aberfan. Even devolution may be relevant. Kenneth O. Morgan has suggested that the Aberfan could not have been treated as badly as it was had there been a Welsh Assembly in 1967.[38] Analogously, after Ladbroke Grove, a government plan to hand partial control of the London Underground to Railtrack was immediately dead in the water. In a notable U-turn, Deputy Prime Minister John Prescott abandoned it in early December 1999. The reason? All the major candidates for the mayorship of London, beginning with the Labour maverick Ken Livingstone, had pledged themselves against it. The Blair government knew that if they persisted with the plan their favoured nominee for the Labour candidacy was doomed.

Economists expect regulators to operate in the interests of the regulated industry, rather than in the public interest when that can be identified (Chapter 8). Regulation by Parliament does not seem to work either. Parliamentary debates are typically captured by the producer interest in question. As well as after Aberfan (Chapter 2), this happened with the *Titanic*, and (for that matter) in the 1844 debates about Gladstone's proposals for railway regulation.[39] In 1993, Neil Hamilton MP (Parliamentary Under-Secretary of State, DTI) alleged that 'Our response to recent large scale disasters has been out of all proportion to the disasters themselves.' He was referring to the cost of the regulations implemented after tragedies such as the King's Cross fire and the sinking of the *Marchioness*. Hamilton saw disasters as exceptions that did not warrant regulatory responses that would unduly burden industry. In a statement reminiscent of the debate after the sinking of the *Titanic*, he asserted that 'we have to ask ourselves whether the costs of regulation are proportionate to the risk. After all risk is an essential part of life.'[40] Yet, despite Mr Hamilton, regulation is far more pro-consumer now than in the 1960s. We showed in Chapter 8 that this is the case in the HSE, although some of its inspectorates seem more independent of the industries they regulate than others. The Inspectorate of Mines and Quarries has made a long move away from Gresford and Aberfan, although the events at Bilsthorpe showed that the move was not yet been complete. The Charity Commission, too, has moved a long way. It now states its mission as being 'The Charity Commission's aim is to give the public confidence in the integrity of charity'. As to its current review of the register of charities it writes, ' The key premise of the Review is that it should be conducted openly and with as much input from the voluntary sector and the public as possible.'[41] That is a huge improvement, from a consumer perspective, on the situation described in Chapter 6.

Regulation cannot stop human negligence or folly but it can at least draw attention to possible fatal dangers. Yet even then rules are sometimes not enough. Perceptions of risk are socially constructed. There needs to be a commitment to compliance that does not allow safety regulations to be subsumed beneath the pressures of daily operation and profit seeking.[42] There needs to be a culture of safety in which regulation is internalised – those affected, whether managers or employees, must believe in the rules that they have to obey.

Disaster and responsibility

The public pressure in the aftermath of disasters is not just concerned with ensuring the tragedy is never repeated. There is also a strong public desire to establish why the disaster happened and, if appropriate, apportion blame. The desire to hold people responsible is sometimes seen as somewhat vulgar or revengeful. It is also criticised for sometimes obscuring the managerial, administrative and financial causes and lessons of disasters.[43] Indeed, the desire to name and blame culprits is also thought to encourage those possibly responsible to evade honest critiques of their actions and practices when things do go wrong.[44] The Aberfan tribunal may be one such example. Elliott and Smith have shown how football clubs' belief that the Hillsborough disaster was the fault of the police and/or fans' behaviour on the day may have discouraged them from 'taking responsibility for ensuring the safety of spectators' and created 'an illusion that safety management is beyond their control'.[45]

Yet naming and blaming can act as a deterrent and encourage a more safety-conscious culture. For the victims of a disaster it is not only a piece of the healing process but also an integral part of justice. Companies responsible for disasters too often seem unconcerned with this and more interested in protecting their own reputations.

Clear statements of responsibility and liability signify an acceptance of blame. The repeated absence of this means that an injustice is done not so much through failures to hold people legally accountable for disasters as through the lack of public recognition of wrong doing. Civil liability is not enough. Many cases are settled out of court and away from the public spotlight. Settling compensation is not the same as admitting clear fault. For example, South Yorkshire Police never gave a formal admission of liability for the Hillsborough disaster although they did not contest their financial liability.[46] The greater use of criminal charges in the aftermath of a disaster would help to overcome such problems. The Law Commission's recommendations for a charge of Corporate Killing may be criticised for failing to address the problem of how to handle individuals responsible. But the possibility that it provides for the symbolic and public punishment of a corporation is significant.

The Aberfan Tribunal in many ways provided that symbolic retribution. As one bereaved parent said of seeing Robens being attacked by Ackner on the witness stand 'it was a balm to my soul.'[47] A member of Lord Robens' private office later conceded that, although he felt the Tribunal was unfair to the NCB, Aberfan needed to see the board, in effect, put on trial.[48] Today, in a culture that views corporate crime more strictly, such a public pillorying is not regarded as sufficient. Some form of accompanying prosecution or even apology is required. The NCB accepted the findings of the Tribunal Report in public and attacked them in private (Chapter 2). It did not say sorry. However, on the 25th anniversary of the disaster British Coal gave a donation of £10,000, some of which was spent on the memorial garden. Its residuary successor supplies a wreath to the annual memorial service in Aberfan cemetery at 9.15 am every 21 October.

The legacy of Aberfan

The most obvious legacy of Aberfan was a change in attitudes towards the management of tips. The coal industry across the world began to assess the safety of its refuse disposal procedures and monitor the stability of its spoil heaps. Such caution continues to this day. The disaster also triggered a programme of land reclamation across Wales and was influential in ensuring the landscaping of many tips following Welsh colliery closures. In the UK, despite the privatisation of the National Coal Board, such redundant tips continue to be monitored. Yet this commitment was not immediately universal. Aberfan did not lead to any actual changes in US safety legislation before 1972. The collapse of a dam of liquid mining waste at Buffalo Creek in that year occurred despite the company responsible possessing copies of NCB literature produced to prevent another tip disaster. The president of the company had also corresponded with an NCB tip-expert because of the potential for such disasters in its operations. Yet despite this and a survey (triggered by Aberfan) identifying problems at Buffalo Creek, the disaster was not averted.

Subsequently, safety legislation was introduced covering mining waste disposal and both Aberfan and Buffalo Creek were cited in the ensuing Congress debate.[49] As with so many other disasters, Buffalo Creek was a testimony to the danger of ignoring warnings and experience.

The Aberfan disaster initiated little actual change in the management of disasters. Yet aspects of the rescue operation had been confused and uncoordinated. Lord Robens said of the operation: 'One only had to be remotely concerned with the Aberfan tragedy to know that the chaos of disaster was followed by the chaos of rescue. The heroes of the rescue operations were individual heroes. Men and women who despite the organization or lack of it stretched themselves to the limit in their desire to save life.'[50] Yet the Welsh Office were reluctant to disseminate the lessons of the rescue operation for fear of being seen as criticizing individuals and organisations. Aberfan did however establish a precedent for giving the police overall responsibility for disaster rescue operations. Yet the confusion after subsequent disasters (particularly Hillsborough) has confirmed the Welsh Office view that no two disasters are alike making learning specific lessons difficult.[51]

Merthyr Tydfil County Borough Council failed to cope with the disaster because of its limited resources and misunderstanding of the needs of disaster victims. Statutory requirements for disaster planning are still limited but guidelines are issued by the Home Office whose Emergency Planning Division feels that they are taken seriously and used as a code of practice.[52] Concerns over the Millennium Bug gave the subject a renewed public profile and the Home Office's Emergency Planning Division a new avenue of work. But this has done little to develop the handling of more 'conventional' disasters. Indeed, it is almost an accident that the EPD has this role at all. It evolved from the Home Office's civil defence responsibilities which, with the end of the Cold War, had lost their importance.

As Chapter 5 demonstrated, the lessons of Aberfan for the management of trauma were not learnt either. The absence of any research project and the contemporary lack of understanding of the long-term nature of post-disaster stress, meant that not until after Bradford was there any clear attempt to disseminate lessons on how to help the victims of disaster. The momentum that this process gained during the disasters of the 1980s has since subsided in the absence of more recent disasters. Reports on disaster management have been well received but then shelved.[53] A lack of clear evidence means that there is little agreement on the most effective methods of actually helping disaster victims cope with their short and long-term trauma.

The anger of disaster victims is now better understood as a normal, and often justified, response. We now know much more about how the inflexibility of the law and wider concerns can deepen the trauma that follows disasters. Yet the laws on corporate responsibility and compensation remain unjust and there are many who continue to feel that battles for justice simply prolong suffering. Government departments may act mechanistically and discourage the innovation required in the aftermath of a disaster. There is now a strong awareness that this can hurt the victims of disaster. A 1998 Emergency Planning Society report stresses the need for flexibility in legal processes and the approach of management. As the report points out such good practice may be self-evident but it is still often not implemented. Whether the report's desire to see the 'needs of all people affected by a disaster' at the heart of the official response will be realised remains to be seen.[54]

When people do see an event as a disaster, their sympathy can bring new problems. The size of the Aberfan Disaster Fund was clear evidence of this. The memory of the problems and the bitterness was long-lasting. It influenced the administration of later funds. The smooth running of the Bradford fund owed much to the lessons of Aberfan. The Bradford fund itself has become a model of how to run a disaster fund.

In Aberfan the legacy of the disaster continues. In October 1998 the village suffered severe flooding. An independent inquiry showed that the flooding was exacerbated by dumped spoil from the removed tips. One survivor of the disaster and victim of the flooding said 'I was buried alive in that tip in the disaster. Now it's the same tip again dumped outside my door. It's no wonder I am angry. This flooding was not an act of God – it was man made.'[55]

For the victims of disasters that shake the public's conscience, some form of financial compensation can be found through disaster funds. However adequate compensation from the negligent party is much harder to achieve if the bereaved were not dependants of the deceased. The growth of a litigation and victim culture and 'ambulance chasing' (where companies seek out and offer to represent injured parties charging no fee if unsuccessful) is the subject of disdain.[56] However the desire for greater bereavement damages is not part of this trend; the injustice suffered is not financial but symbolic. Payments are not the actual cost of the life lost but recognition of the wrongdoing by the negligent party. The small sums presently payable under the law to a narrow class of relatives do not adequately achieve that. Finally, it creates the perverse situation where it is cheaper to kill a child accidentally than to maim one. Such 'incentives' should not be the outcome of responsible law. A similar injustice is at the heart of the repeated failures to bring those responsible to trial. The need for this is not revenge or retribution but a social acknowledgement of the wrong doing allied to a strong deterrent that might help prevent future disasters. The importance of a deterrent is derived from the evidence that most disasters are not accidents or acts of gods but the result of mistakes, oversights or criminal negligence. If the Law Commission's recommendations for a charge of corporate killing are implemented then a much needed change will have been achieved.

The hardest thing is saying sorry. Again and again in this book, we have reported the same complaint from survivors and bereaved relatives: *If only they would admit they were to blame, we could get on with trying to rebuild our lives.* In our litany of disasters, Aberfan is the worst and Clapham the best. Of course there is no such thing as a good disaster. But, after Clapham, the successive chief executives of British Rail accepted corporate liability for themselves, did not try to push it down the line, and turned up in court to be reprimanded. Regrettably, disasters caused by human error will happen again in the UK. Let us hope the corporations responsible will read the record and try to live up to the Clapham standard. And that never again are disaster victims treated like the people of Aberfan.

Notes

1 Wreck Commissioner's Court, *Formal Investigation into the Loss of the S. S. "Titanic"*, Minutes of evidence, ten parts, (London: HMSO, 1912), day 29, part 8, p. 738.

2 This section is a précis of the much fuller evidence about the *Titanic* in our paper ' "Regulation run mad": the Board of Trade and the loss of the *Titanic*', forthcoming in *Public Administration*, vol. 78, 2000.

3 *Hansard* 5th series 37:2060 (PQ by Major Archer-Shee, reply by the Prime Minister).

4 In a telegram intercepted and read by the US authorities, Marconi had advised them not to tell their stories until he had secured them a handsome fee.

5 US Congress, Senate. 1912. *Report of the Senate Committee on Commerce pursuant to S. Res. 283, Directing the Committee to Investigate the Causes of the Sinking of the 'Titanic', with speeches by William Alden Smith and Isidor Rayner*, 62d Cong., 2d sess., 28 May 1912, S. Rept. 806 (6127). Washington, Government Printing Office. Some of this report is available in T. Kuntz, *The Titanic disaster hearings : the official transcripts of the 1912 Senate investigation*. (New York: Pocket Books, 1998).

6 *Formal Investigation into the Loss of the S.S. "Titanic"*, Minutes 1912, part 2, day 3, p. 46.

7 Michael Hechter, *Internal Colonialism: The Celtic Fringe in British National Development, 1536–1966* (London: Routledge, 1975).

8 J. Bulpitt, *Territory and Power in the United Kingdom: an interpretation* (Manchester: Manchester University Press 1983) and his 'The discipline of the new democracy: Mrs Thatcher's domestic statecraft', *Political Studies*, 34, 1986, 19–39.

9 'Note for the Record', n.d., c.27 October 1966. PRO: PREM 13/1280. Prime Minister's papers on the Aberfan Tribunal.

10 Harold Wilson noted that when he visited a Cornish school less than eight days after the disaster, he felt 'almost a sense of resentment at these happy innocent children, with all they had to look forward to, compared with the children of that Welsh valley, who had no future.' Wilson, *Labour Government*, p. 298. Cledwyn Hughes called the disaster 'the most appalling experience in the whole of my political period.' Letter to MJ, 6 July 1999.

11 Robens; *Ten Years Stint*, ch. 10. Lord Marsh interview.

12 *Hansard*, Commons, 5th ser., vol. 751, col. 1958.

13 J. Siberry [Welsh Office Assistant Secretary stationed in Aberfan] to P. Cousins, 10 February 1969. PRO BD 11/3807. 'Removal of Aberfan tips 1969/71'.

14 Thomas to Robens, 15.05.68; reply, 5 June 1968. PRO: COAL 73/4 Pt 1. The chapel was rebuilt, but at the expense of the disaster fund, not the NCB. The new chapel contains a memorial tablet to its members lost in the disaster.

15 Briefing note, sect 14. Aberfan Compensation, Claims and Payments by NCB, 9 September 1967. PRO POWE 52/68, 'Debate on the report of the Aberfan Inquiry'.

16 The above two paragraphs are derived from 'IMO and ro-ro safety' (January 1997), www.imo.org/focus/intro.htm; Gary Slapper & Steve Tombs, *Corporate Crime* (London: Longman, 1999), pp. 149–153 & Peter Spooner, *The HFA Story, 1987–1994* (London: Herald Families Association, 1994).

17 Crainer, *Zeebrugge*, ch. 3.

18 In 1987 P&O gave the Conservative Party £100,000. The company's chairman was later knighted by Mrs Thatcher, which led *The Daily Mirror* to dub him Lord Zeebrugge.

19 Rt Hon Edward Shortt KC (chairman), *Report of the Departmental Committee on Crowds*, cmd. 2088, London: HMSO, 1924. Hereafter Shortt Report.

20 In fact 25 people had been killed at Ibrox Park in 1902 when a wooden stand collapsed.

21 Shortt Report, paras. 46–47.

22 Jeff Hill & Francesco Varrasi, 'Creating Wembley: The Construction of a National Monument', *The Sports Historian*, 17 (2), November 1997, p. 38.

23 R. Moelwyn Hughes, Enquiry into the Disaster at Bolton Wanderers' Football Ground on the 9th March, 1946, Cmd. 6846 (London: HMSO, 1946), p. 12. Original syntax.

24 FA and Football League representatives quoted in Norman Baker, 'Have they forgotten Bolton?', *The Sports Historian*, 18 (1), May 1998, p. 143. The analysis presented here of the aftermath of the Bolton disaster is largely derived from this article.

25 Herbert Morrison (Lord President) quoted in Baker, 'Have they forgotten Bolton?' p. 144.

26 Norman Chester (chairman), *Report of the Committee on Football* (London: HMSO, 1968), para. 345.

27 *Soccer Hooliganism: A Preliminary Report*, Bristol: John Wright & Sons, 1968, p. 9.

28 John Lang (chairman), *Report of the Working Party on Crowd Behaviour at Football Matches* (London: HMSO, 1969), para. 12.

29 Rt. Hon. Lord Wheatley, *Report of the Inquiry into Crowd Safety at Sports Grounds*, Cmnd. 4952, (London: HMSO, 1972).

30 Inglis, *Football Grounds of Great Britain*, p. 35. The ground improvements required by the Act were partly funded through voluntary levies on 'spot the ball' competitions achieved in return for a government promise not to tax the competition. This was achieved through the work of the sympathetic sports minister Denis Howell. Denis Howell, *Made in Birmingham: The Memoirs of Denis Howell* (London: Queen Anne Press, 1990), pp. 260–261.

31 Dominic Elliott & Denis Smith, 'Waiting for the Next One: Management Attitudes to Safety in the UK Football Industry', unpublished paper. Also see Dominic Elliott, *Organisational Learning from Crisis: An Examination of the Football Industry, 1946–97*, Ph.D. thesis, University of Durham, 1998.

32 39 Juventus fans were killed when a wall collapsed following a charge by Liverpool fans at the European Cup final held in Heysel, Belguim.

33 Ken Foster, 'Developments in Sporting Law', in Lincoln Allison (ed), *The Changing Politics of Sport* (Manchester: Manchester University Press, 1993), p. 106.

34 *Hansard*, vol. 79, col. 36; vol. 80, col. 153 (speech by Mr Madden). Gerald Kaufman (Labour, Manchester, Gorton) called the joint inquiry 'insensitive and in the worst possible taste.' *Hansard*, vol. 79, col. 23, 3 June 1985.

35 *Hansard*, vol. 83, cols, 21–33.

36 Government concerns about hooliganism rather than safety were further indicated by the passing of the 1989 Football Spectators Act (which was to curb the civil liberties of fans in an effort to fight hooliganism) without waiting for Taylor to complete his inquiry into Hillsborough and crowd safety. In 1990 it was forced to abandon the national membership scheme, which the Act had legislated for, when Taylor expressed doubts about its implication for safety.

37 Stuart Thomson, Lara Stancich and Lisa Dickson, 'Gun Control and Snowdrop', in F. F. Ridley & Grant Jordan (eds.), *Protest Politics: Cause Groups and Campaigns* (Oxford: Oxford University Press, 1998).

38 K. O. Morgan, 'Welsh Devolution: The Past and Future' in Bridget Taylor and Katarina Thomson (eds) *Scotland and Wales: Nations Again?* (Cardiff: University of Wales Press, 1999), p. 213.

39 McLean and Johnes, 'Regulation run mad'; I. McLean, 'Railway regulation as a test-bed for rational choice' in K. Dowding and D. King, (ed.), *Preferences, Institutions, and Rational Choice* (Oxford: Clardendon Press, 1995), pp. 134–61.

40 Hamilton quoted in Woolfson and Beck, 'Deregulation: Contemporary Politics of Health and Safety' p. 195.

41 Charity Commission website, http//www.charity-commission.gov.uk, home page, and Review of the Register pages.

42 See, e.g., Timothy Hynes & Pushkala Prasad, 'Patterns of 'Mock Bureaucracy' in Mining Disasters: An Analysis of the Westray Coal Mine Explosion', *Journal of Management Studies*, 34 (4), July 1997, 601–623.

43 Tom Ellis, 'Aberfan: The Real Lesson?, *Planet*, 135 (July–August 1999). Geoffrey Howe, 'The Management of Public Inquiries', *Political Quarterly*, vol. 70, issue 3, July 1999, p. 296.

44 Nick Pidgeon, The Limits of Safety? Culture, Politics, Learning and Man-Made Disasters, *Journal of Contingencies and Crisis Management*, vol. 5, no. 1, March 1997, p. 9.

45 Elliott & Smith, 'Waiting for the Next One'; Elliott, *Organisational Learning from Crisis*.

46 In his review of the evidence relating to the disaster, Lord Justice Stuart Smith maintained there was 'no difference in principle between accepting liability and paying on a 100 per cent basis than there is making a formal admission of liability'. Quoted in Scraton, *Hillsborough*, p. 171.

47 *Timewatch*, BBC2.

48 Letter from John Taylor to MJ, 23 July 1999.

49 John Braithwaite, *To punish or persuade: enforcement of coal mine safety* (Albany: State University of NY Press, 1985), pp. 36–38. David J. Akers, *Overview of Coal Refuse Disposal in the United States*, Coal Research Bureau, West Virginia University, Report No. 172, January 1980, p. 3. Letter from Mine Safety and Health Administration (US Department of Labor) to MJ, August 1999.

50 Lord Robens, 'Mine Disasters', *Advancement of Science*, June 1969, p. 393.

51 A report on the rescue operation at Aberfan and the Welsh Office's concerns over how and if it should be circulated can be found in PRO BD 11/3803.

52 Letter from Home Office Emergency Planning Office to MJ, 2 August 1999.

53 Letter from Phil Scraton (co-author of *Beyond Disaster: Identifying and resolving Inter-agency Conflict in the Immediate Aftermath of Disasters*, A Research Report for the Home Office Emergency Planning Division, 1997) to authors, 13 July 1999.

54 Emergency Planning Society, *Responding to Disaster: The Human Aspects*, Guidance Document, 1998.

55 Quoted in *Western Mail*, 6 March 1999.

56 In particular see Frank Furedi, *Courting Mistrust: The Hidden Growth of a Culture of Litigation in Britain* (London: Centre for Policy Studies, 1999) & Humphrys, *Devil's Advocate*, ch. 1.

APPENDIX

The current definition of PTSD is as follows:

The essential feature of Posttraumatic Stress Disorder is the development of characteristic symptoms following exposure to an extreme traumatic stressor involving direct personal experience of an event that involves actual or threatened death or serious injury, or other threat to one's physical integrity; or witnessing an event that involves death, injury, or a threat to the physical integrity of another person; or learning about unexpected or violent death, serious harm, or threat of death or injury experienced by a family member or other close associate (Criterion A1). The person's response to the event must involve intense fear, helplessness, or horror (or in children, the response must involve disorganized or agitated behavior) (Criterion A2). The characteristic symptoms resulting from the exposure to the extreme trauma include persistent reexperiencing of the traumatic event (Criterion B), persistent avoidance of stimuli associated with the trauma and numbing of general responsiveness (Criterion C), and persistent symptoms of increased arousal (Criterion D). The full symptom picture must be present for more than 1 month (Criterion E), and the disturbance must cause clinically significant distress or impairment in social, occupational or other important areas of functioning (Criterion F).[1]

Other symptoms such as anger and guilt are also sometimes present in PTSD sufferers but are not defined as part of the disorder itself.

Note

1 American Psychiatric Association, *Diagnosis and Statistical Manual of Mental Disorders: DSM-IV* (Washington: American Psychiatric Association, 4th edition, 1994), p. 424.

BIBLIOGRAPHY

I. Archival Sources

Aberfan Disaster Archive
Merthyr Collection (Merthyr Tydfil Central Library)
Dowlais Collection (Dowlais Library)
For catalogue of these archives, see our Web site at
               http://www.nuff.ox.uc.uk/aberfan/home.html

Merthyr Tydfil Central Library
Merthyr Tydfil County Borough Council, minutes and accounts

Glamorgan Record Office
British Coal Records, South Wales Area Files, D/D NCB 67/4.
Llewellyn and Hann papers, Powell Duffryn solicitors at the Tribunal of
    Inquiry, D/D LH
Police records on Aberfan disaster, GRO D/D Con 289/4
Aberfan Disaster Fund, Management committee and sub-committee
    papers, 1967–73
Glamorgan County Council Civil Defence papers on the Aberfan disaster,
    GCC/CD

Public Record Office
Board of Trade Establishment Division papers, BT 13/50
Board of Trade Marine Department papers, MT 9/920/E24382

Board of Trade Consultation Marine papers, MT 15
Cabinet office papers, CAB 128, CAB 164
Charity Commission papers, CHAR 9, CHAR 10
Foreign Office papers, FO 115/1710, FO 369/522
Ministry of Labour papers LAB ????????
Ministry of Power papers, POWE 52
NCB papers, COAL 29, COAL 73
Prime Minister's Private Office papers, PREM 13
Treasury Solicitor papers, TS 58
Tribunal of Inquiry papers, BD 52
Welsh Board of Health papers MH 96/2179
Welsh Office papers, BD 11, BD 28, BD 50, BD 61

South Wales Coalfield Collection; University of Wales, Swansea
Coal Industry National Consultation Council minutes
S. O. Davies papers
National Union of Mineworkers, Annual conference reports
National Union of Mineworkers, South Wales Area minutes
Tŷ Toronto archive

National Library of Wales
Lord Edmund Davies Papers
Alun Talfan Davies Papers
Diocese of Llandaff papers
Cyril Moseley papers
Eilfryn Peris Owen Papers
Lord Morris of Borth y Guest Papers
Rev. Evan Wyn Williams Papers
Harri Webb Papers

II. Interviews and Correspondence

Interviews and/or correspondence with the authors
Ackner, Desmond (Counsel, APRA)
Bacon, Jenny (Director General, HSE)
Barnes, Kenneth (former Deputy Secretary, Department of Employment and Productivity)
Berkley, J. B. (Disaster Action)
Billnitzer, Dave
Blackshaw, Alan (former private secretary to Richard Marsh [q.v.], Ministry of Power)
Castle, Barbara (former Secretary of State for Employment and Productivity)
Cooksey, A. (HM Deputy Chief Inspector of Railways)
Cuthill, J. M. (Psychiatrist)
Davies, Ron, (former Secretary of State for Wales)

Davis, Gerald (former Secretary, Aberfan Disaster Fund)
Dearing, Ron, (former Assistant Secretary, Coal Division, Ministry of Power)
Evans, Andrew (Centre for Transport Studies, UCL)
Gates, Terry (HSE Policy Unit)
Hillsborough Families Support Group
Hodgkinson, Peter (Centre for Crisis Psychology)
Howe, Geoffrey (Counsel at Aberfan Tribunal)
Hughes, Cledwyn (former Secretary of State for Wales)
Lang, J. S. (Chief Inspector of Marine Accidents)
Langdon, B. (HM Chief Inspector of Mines)
Leiper, Elizabeth (Psychotherapist)
McKinlay, R. C. (AAIB)
McQuaid, Jim (Director of Science and Technology, HSE)
Marsh, Richard (former Minister of Power)
Morgan, Geoffrey (former Secretary Aberfan Disaster Fund)
Moseley, Cyril (solicitor, APRA)
O' Connell, Morgan (Consultant Psychiatrist)
Parkes, Colin Murray, (bereavement consultant at Aberfan)
Sisson, C.H. (former Director of Occupational Safety and Health,
    Department of Employment and Productivity)
Spooner, Peter (Herald Charitable Trust)
Talfan Davies, Alun, (former trustee Aberfan Disaster Fund)
Taylor, John, (Lord Robens' private office)
Thatcher, Margaret (Former Shadow Spokesperson on Fuel and Power)
Tudor, W. & Tudor, J. (Aberfan)
Walker, Harold (former Parliamentary Under-Secretary of State,
    Department of Employment and Productivity)
Watkin, Hugh, (teacher, Aberfan)
Watkins, Tasker, (former trustee Aberfan Disaster Fund)
Wilson, Geoffrey (Assistant counsel for the Miners' Federation of Great
    Britain, Gresford disaster inquiry)

*Aberfan Study [series of interviews]: An unknown spring (1986),
South Wales Coalfield Collection, University of Wales, Swansea*
Richards, Emlyn and Elaine. AUD/519
Lewis, Sheila (Mrs). AUD 520
Beale, John. AUD/521
Williams, Howell. AUD/522
Williams, Hetty. AUD/523
Davey, Audrey. AUD/524
Jones, Raymond Gwynfryn. AUD/525
Jones, Mair. AUD/526
Vaughan, Joan and Cyril. AUD 527
Hayes, Kenneth (Rev), Carpenter, Bryn and Pearson, Doug. AUD/528.
Jones, Elwyn- (Lord). AUD/530

The authors have also informally spoken to many people involved in differing capacities at Aberfan and other disasters.

III. Newspapers and periodicals

Birmingham Post
British Medical Journal
Colliery Guardian
Daily Express
Daily Mail
Daily Mirror
Daily Telegraph
Financial Times
Independent
Locomotive Journal
Merthyr Express
Private Eye
The Guardian
The Observer
The Sun
The Times
Times Higher Education Supplement
Transport Review
South Wales Argus
South Wales Echo
Sunday People
Sunday Times
Wales on Sunday
Washington Post
West Virginian Gazette
Western Mail

IV. Official publications

British Labour Statistics, Historical Abstract 1886–1968 (Dept of Employment & Productivity: HMSO, 1971).
Charity Commission, *Annual Reports.*
Chester, Norman (chairman), *Report of the Committee on Football* (London: HMSO, 1968).
Crossland, Bernard, *Public Hearing following the Extensive Fall of Roof at Bilsthorpe Colliery: A Report to the Health and Safety Commission* (no date).
Cullen, Douglas (Lord) (Chairman), *Inquiry into the circumstances leading up to and surrounding the events at Dunblane Primary School on*

Wednesday 13 March 1996 (Edinburgh: HMSO for the Scottish Office, 1996).

Cullen, Douglas (Lord) (chairman), *The Public Inquiry into the Piper Alpha Disaster*, Cm. 1310 (London: HMSO, 1990).

Davies, Edmund (chairman), *Report of the Tribunal appointed to inquire into the Disaster at Aberfan on October 21st 1966*, HL 316, HC 553 (London: HMSO, 1967).

Department of Employment, *The Flixborough Disaster: Report of the Court of Inquiry* (London: HMSO, 1975).

Department of the Environment, Transport and the Regions, *Consultation Document on Transport Safety* (London: DETR, 1998).

Disasters Working Party, *Disasters: Planning for a Caring Response, Part One: The Main Report* (London: HMSO, 1991).

Dunne, Laurence R. (chairman), *Report on an Inquiry into the Accident at Bethnal Green Tube Station Shelter on the 3rd March 1943*, Cmd 6583 (London: HMSO, 1945).

Emergency Planning Society, *Responding to Disaster: The Human Aspects*, Guidance Document, 1998.

Employment Committee, *The Work of the Health and Safety Commission and Executive*, Minutes of Evidence, 14 March 1990.

Fennell, Desmond (chairman) *Investigation into the Kings' Cross Underground Fire*, Cm 499 (London: HMSO, 1988).

Hansard

Hayes, John W., *Report of the Enquiry into River Safety*, Cm 1991 (London: HMSO, 1991).

Health and Safety Commission, *Health and Safety at Work etc Act: The Act Outlined*, HSC2, 1994.

– *Annual Reports*

– *Enforcement Policy Statement*, 1995.

Health and Safety Executive, *Reducing Risks, Protecting People*, Discussion Document (London: HSE, 1999).

– *Extensive Fall of Roof at Bilsthorpe Colliery: A Report of the HSE's investigation into the Extensive Fall of Roof at Bilsthorpe Colliery, Nottinghamshire on 18 August 1993* (London: HSE, 1994).

– *Work-Related Deaths: A protocol for liaison* (London: HSE, 1998).

– *Review of Arrangements for Standard Setting and Application on the Main Railway Network: Interim Report* (London: HSE, 1999).

– *Train Accident at Ladbroke Grove Junction, 5 October 1999: First HSE interim report, 8 October 1999* (London: HSE, 1999).

Hidden, Anthony (chairman), *Investigation into the Clapham Junction Railway Accident*, Cm. 820 (London: HMSO, 1989).

Home Office, *Report of the Disasters and Inquests Working Group* (London: Home Office, 1997).

– *Dealing with Disaster* (London: HMSO, 1992 & 1997 edns.).

– *Press release, 066/98. 18 February 1998*.

Hughes, R. Moelwyn, *Enquiry into the Disaster at Bolton Wanderers' Football Ground on the 9th March, 1946*, Cmd. 6846 (London: HMSO, 1946).

Lang, John (chairman), *Report of the Working Party on Crowd Behaviour at Football Matches* (London: HMSO, 1969).

Law Commission, *The Actions of Loss of Services, Loss of Consortium, Seduction and Enticement*, Published Working Paper no. 19 (London: HMSO, 1968).

– *Report on Personal Injury Litigation – Assessment of Damages*, Report No. 56 (London: HMSO, 1973).

– Criminal Law: Involuntary Manslaughter, Consultation Paper No. 135 (London: HMSO, 1994).

– Damages for Personal Injury: Non-Pecuniary Loss, Consultation Paper No 140, (London: HMSO, 1995).

– *Legislating the Criminal Code: Involuntary Manslaughter*, Report No.237 (London: HMSO, 1996).

– *Claims for Wrongful Death*, Consultation Paper 148 (London: HMSO, 1997).

Local Government in Wales, Cmnd. 3340 (Cardiff: HMSO, 1967).

Lord Chancellor's Department, *Damages for Bereavement: A Review of the Level* (London: Lord Chancellor's Department, 1990).

Leigh, C., *Reports of HM Inspectors of Mines and Quarries (under the Mines and Quarries Act 1954) for 1966, South Western Division* (London: HMSO, 1967).

Marriott, P. B., *Report of the Chief Inspector of Marine Accidents into the collision between the passenger launch Marchioness and MV Bowbelle with loss of life on the River Thames on 20 August 1989* (London: HMSO, 1991).

Mersey, Lord (chairman), *Report of a Formal Investigation into the circumstances attending the foundering on 15th April, 1912, of the British steamship "Titanic," of Liverpool, after striking ice in or near Latitude 41° 46' N., Longitude 50° 14' W, North Atlantic Ocean, whereby loss of life ensued.* Cd 6352 (London: HMSO, 1912).

Office of the Rail Regulator, Press Notice ORR 99/43, 11.10.99.

Pearson, Lord, *Royal Commission on Civil Liability and Compensation for Personal Injury*, Cmnd 7054 (London: HMSO, 1978).

Pennington Group, *Report of the Circumstances Leading to the 1996 Outbreak of Infection with E. Coli O157 in Central Scotland, The Implications for Food Safety and the Lessons to be Learnt* (HMSO, 1998).

Popplewell, Oliver (Chairman), *Committee of Inquiry into Crowd Safety and Control at Sports Grounds, Interim Report* (London: HMSO, 1985), Cmnd. 9585.

– *Committee of Inquiry into Crowd Safety and Control at Sports Grounds, Final Report*, Cmnd. 9710 (London: HMSO, 1986).

Stephenson, H. S., *Report of HM Chief Inspector for Mines and Quarries (under the Mines and Quarries Act 1954) for 1966* (London: HMSO, 1967).

Reports of the Charity Commissioners for England and Wales.

Registrar General's Statistical Review of England and Wales for the Year 1966 (London: HMSO 1967),

Robens, Lord (chairman) *Safety and Health at Work, Report of the Committee*, Cmnd 5034 (London: HMSO, 1972).

Sheen, Barry, *MV Herald of Free Enterprise: report of Court no. 8074, formal investigation* (London: H.M.S.O for Department of Transport, 1987)

Taylor , Peter, *The Hillsborough Stadium disaster, 15 April 1989: Inquiry by the Rt. Hon Lord Justice Taylor: Interim Report*, Cm 765 (London: HMSO, 1989).

Taylor, Peter, *The Hillsborough Stadium disaster, 15 April 1989: Inquiry by the Rt. Hon Lord Justice Taylor: Final Report*, Cm 962 (London: HMSO, 1990).

US Congress, Senate. *Report of the Senate Committee on Commerce pursuant to S. Res. 283, Directing the Committee to Investigate the Causes of the Sinking of the 'Titanic', with speeches by William Alden Smith and Isidor Rayner, 62d Cong.*, 2d sess., 28 May 1912, S. Rept. 806 (6127). Washington, Government Printing Office, 1912.

Walker, Sir Henry (chairman), *Report on the Causes of and Circumstances attending the Explosion which occurred at Gresford Colliery, Denbigh, on the 22nd September, 1934*, Cmd 5358 (London: HMSO, 1937).

Wheatley, Lord (chairman), *Report of the Inquiry into Crowd Safety at Sports Grounds*, Cmnd. 4952, (London: HMSO, 1972).

V. Law cases cited

Alcock v Chief Constable of South Yorkshire Police [1992] 1 AC 310

Attorney-General v Cory Brothers & Co Ltd [1921] 1 AC 521

Bailey v Howard [1939] 1 KB 453

Benham v Gambling [1941] AC 157

Cain v Wilcox [1968] 3 All ER 817

Crocker v British Coal Corporation, *The Times*, 5 July 1995; [1996] JPIL Issue 1/96

Doleman v Deakin [1990] TLR 30 January 1990

DPP v P&O European Ferries (Dover) Ltd [1991] 93 Cr. App. R. 73

DPP v Kent & Sussex Contractors Ltd [1944] KB 146

Frost and others v Chief Constable of South Yorkshire Police and others, TLR, 4 December 1998

Hicks v C.C. S. Yorkshire [1992] 2 All ER 65

Kerria Developments Ltd and another v Reporter Ltd, The Times, 31 July 1984, HC Lexis

Kralj and another v McGrath and another [1986] 1 All ER 54

Moore v Bresler [1944] 2 All ER 515

Priestley v Fowler [1837] 3 M&W 1

Re Gillingham Bus Disaster Fund [1957] 3 WLR 1069

R v Cory Brothers and Company, Limited. Feb. 2, Glamorgan Assizes [1927] 1 KB 810

R v ICR Haulage Ltd [1944] 30 Cr App R 31

R v F. Howe & Son (Engineers) Ltd, Court of Appeal, 6 November 1998

R v Northern Strip Mining Construction Ltd, *The Times*, 2, 4 & 5 February 1965
R v OLL Ltd [1994] 144 NLJ 1735
Rylands v Fletcher [1868] LR 3 HL 330
Turbeyfield v GWR Co [1937] 158 LT 135
Yorkshire Electricity Board v Naylor [1968] AC 529

VI. Other published material

Adam Smith Research Trust, *But Who Will Regulate the Regulators?* (London: Adam Smith, 1993).
Allen, D. K., Bourn, C. J. & Holyoak, J. H., (eds.), *Accident Compensation after Pearson* (London: Sweet & Maxwell, 1979).
Allen, Simon, 'Rescuers and Employees – Primary Victims of Nervous Shock', *New Law Journal*, 7 February 1997, 158–160.
Allison, William, *Rangers: The New Era, 1873–1966* (Glasgow: Glasgow Rangers FC, 1966).
Alvey, Norman, *From Chantry to Oxfam: A Short History of Charity and Charity Legislation* (Chichester: British Association for Local History, 1995).
American Psychiatric Association, *Diagnosis and Statistical Manual of Mental Disorders: DSMI-IV* (Washington: American Psychiatric Association, 4th edition, 1994).
Anon., 'Disasters', *Which?*, September 1988, 426–429.
– 'Disasters Update', *Which?*, November 1989, 558–560.
– (Editorial) 'Disaster Planning – Fact or Fiction?', *British Medical Journal*, 24 May 1975, 406–407.
– (Editorial), 'Prepared for a Disaster?', *British Medical Journal*, 27 September 1975, 723.
– 'Disasters as a catalyst for civil and/or criminal proceedings', *P&I international*, December 1996, 238–239.
– 'Time to reform railway safety', *Modern Railways*, 760, December 1997.
Arnheim, Michael, 'Zeebrugge: is it a good offer?', *Solicitors Journal*, vol. 131, no. 19, 8 May 1987, 606–608.
Arnott, Hilary, 'Justice: Hillsborough's Final Victim?', *Legal Action*, April 1992, 7–8.
Ashworth, William, *The History of the British Coal Industry, Vol. 5, 1946–1982: The Nationalized Industry* (Oxford: Clarendon Press, 1986).
Austin, Tony, *Aberfan: The Story of a Disaster* (London: Hutchinson, 1967).
Bailey, Eric, 'Post-Traumatic Stress Disorder: A Contrasting View', *Disaster Prevention & Management*, vol. 2, no. 3, 1993, 22–25.
Baker, Norman, 'Have they forgotten Bolton?' *The Sports Historian*, no. 18(1), May 1998, 120–151.

Baldwin, Robert, *Rules and Government* (Oxford: Clarendon, 1995).

Ballard, Paul H. & Jones, Erastus (eds.), *The Valleys Call: A Self-Examination by People of the South Wales Valleys during the 'Year of the Valleys, 1974* (Ferndale: Ron Jones Publications, 1974).

Barton, Allen H., *Communities in Disaster: A Sociological Analysis of Collective Stress Situations* (Ward Lock Educational, 1969).

Bayliss, R. W., *Symptoms in the Operational Failure of Public Administration: Aberfan, Hither Green, Hixon Crossing*, Occasional Papers no. 10 (Birmingham: University of Birmingham, 1969).

Bedfordshire County Council, *Picking up the Pieces: Report of a Multi-agency workshop to develop post-major incident psycho-social support plans* (Bedford, 1996).

Benson, John, 'Charity's Pitfalls: The Senghenydd Disaster', *History Today*, vol. 43, November 1993, 5–7.

Benthall, John, *Disasters, Relief and the Media* (London: I. B. Tauriss, 1993).

Bergman, David, *Deaths at Work: Accidents or Corporate Crime* (London: WEA, London Hazards Centre & Inquest, 1991).

– 'A Killing in the Boardroom', *New Statesman & Society*, 15 June 1990, 15–16.

– *Disasters: Where the Law Fails: A New Agenda for Dealing with Corporate Violence* (London: Herald Charitable Trust, 1993).

Biel, Steven, *Down with the Old Canoe: A Cultural History of the Titanic Disaster* (New York: W.W. Norton, 1996).

Bignell, Victor, Peters, Geoff, Pym, Christopher, & Hunter-Brown, Caryl, *Catastrophic Failures* (Milton Keynes : Open University Press, 1977).

Birch, Anthony H., *The Concepts and Theories of Modern Democracy* (London: Routledge, 1993).

Bovens, Mark, *The Quest for Responsibility: Accountability and Citizenship in Complex Organisations* (Cambridge: Cambridge University Press, 1998).

Bradford Metropolitan Council, *Out of the Valley: Bradford MDC's Response to the Bradford City Fire Disaster, 1985–86* (Bradford: City of Bradford Metropolitan Council, 1986).

Braithwaite, John, *To Punish or Persuade? Enforcement of Coal Mine Safety* (Albany: State University of New York Press, 1985).

Braithwaite, John, 'Shame and Modernity', *British Journal of Criminology*, vol. 33, no. 1, Winter 1993, 1–18.

Breyer S. and MacAvoy, P. W., 'Regulation and deregulation', in J. Eatwell *et al.* (eds), *The New Palgrave Dictionary of Economics* (London: Macmillan 4 vols 1987), vol. 4, 128–34.

British Psychological Society, *Psychological Aspects of Disaster* (Leicester: British Psychological Society, 1990).

British Railways Board, *Automatic Train Protection* (London: BRB 1994).

Brittain, Victoria, 'New Grass in the Valley but Scars on the Mind Remain', *The Times*, 12 October 1971.

Brook, Richard, *An Introduction to Disaster Theory for Social Workers* (Norwich: Social Work Monographs, 1990).

Brotchie, Jane, 'When Nightmares Come True', *New Statesman & Society*, 12 May 1989, 19–20.

Brown, John H., *The Valley of the Shadow: An Account of Britain's Worst Mining Disaster: The Senghenydd Explosion* (Port Talbot: Alun Books, 1981).

Bryan, Sir Andrew, *The Evolution of Health and Safety in Mines* (London: Ashire Publishing, 1975).

Bulpitt, Jim, *Territory and Power in the United Kingdom: An Interpretation* (Manchester: Manchester University Press, 1983).

Butt Philip, Alan, *The Welsh Question: Nationalism in Welsh Politics 1945–1970* (Cardiff: University of Wales Press, 1975).

Cairns, Elizabeth, *Charities: Law and Practice* (London: Sweet & Maxwell, 3rd edn, 1997).

Cane, Peter, *Atiyah's Accidents, Compensation and the Law* (London: Butterworths, 5th edn, 1993).

Cannon, Tom, *Corporate Responsibility: A Textbook on Business Ethics, Governance, Environment: Roles and Responsibilities* (London: Pitman, 1994).

Carby-Hall, J. R., 'Health, Safety and Welfare at Work', *Managerial Law*, vol. 31, no. 1/2, 1989, 1–57.

Carson, W. G., *The Other Price of Britain's Oil: Safety and Control in the North Sea* (Oxford: Martin Robertson, 1982).

Castle, Barbara, *The Castle Diaries 1964–70* (London: Weidenfeld & Nicolson, 1984).

–– *Fighting all the Way* (London: Macmillan, 1993).

Chesterman, Michael, *Charities, Trusts and Social Welfare* (London: Weidenfeld & Nicholson, 1979).

Claricoat, John & Phillips, Hillary, *Charity Law, A-Z: Key Questions Answered* (Bristol: Jordans, 1995).

Clarke, Peter, *Hope and Glory: Britain, 1900–1990* (London: Allen Lane, 1996).

Clarkson, C. M. V., 'Corporate Culpability', *Web Journal of Current Legal Issues*, http://webjcli.ncl.ac.uk/1998/issue2/clarkson2.html

Clegg, Francis, 'Disasters: Can Psychologists help the Survivors?', *Psychologist*, April 1988, 34–35.

Cohen, David, *Aftershock: The Psychological and Political Consequences of Disaster* (London: Paladin, 1991).

Colbey, Richard, 'New Look at Disaster Pay-outs', *The Guardian*, 11 October 1997.

Cole, David (ed.), *The New Wales* (Cardiff: University of Wales Press, 1990).

Coleman, Sheila, Jemphrey, Ann, Scraton, Phil & Skidmore, Paula, *Hillsborough and After: The Liverpool Experience, First Report* (Liverpool: Liverpool City Council, 1990).

Coles, Eva, 'What Price Emergency Planning? Local Authority Civil Protection in the UK, *Public Money and Management*, October-December, 1998, 27–32.

Collins, Henry E., *Mining Memories and Musings: Autobiography of a Mining Engineer* (Letchworth: Ashire Publishing, 1985).

Collins, Valerie, *Recreation and the Law* (London: Spon, 2nd edn, 1993).

Cook, Judith, *An Accident Waiting to Happen* (London: Unwin, 1989).

Couto, Richard A., 'Catastrophe and Community Empowerment: The Group Formulations of Aberfan's Survivors', *Journal of Community Psychology*, vol. 17, July 1989. 236–248.

– 'Economics, Experts, and Risk: Lessons from the Catastrophe at Aberfan', *Political Psychology*, vol. 10, no. 2, 1989, 309–324.

Coward, Ros, 'Death Watch', *New Statesman & Society*, 28 April 1989, 12–13.

Crainer, Stuart, *Zeebrugge: Learning from Disaster, Lessons in Corporate Responsibility* (London: Herald Charitable Trust, 1993).

Crenson, Matthew A., *The Unpolitics of Air Pollution: A Study of Non-Decisionmaking in the Cities* (Baltimore: John Hopkins University Press, 1971).

Crossman, R. H. S., *The Diaries of a Cabinet Minister. Vol. 2: Lord President of the Council and Leader of the House of Commons 1966–68* (London, 1976).

Dalton, A. J. P., *Safety, Health and Environmental Hazards at the Workplace* (London: Cassell, 1998).

Davie, Michael, *The Titanic: The Full Story of a Tragedy* (London: Bodley Head, 1986).

Davis, Howard & Scraton, Phil, *Beyond Disaster: Identifying and Resolving Inter-Agency Conflict in the Immediate Aftermath of Disasters*, A Research Report for the Home Office Emergency Planning Division, 1997.

– Failing the Bereaved: Inter-Agency Relationships in the Immediate Aftermath of Disaster' in *Picking Up the Pieces: Report of a Multi-Agency Workshop to develop Post-Major Incident Psycho-Social Support Plans* (Bedford: Bedfordshire County Council, 1996).

Davison, Gerald C., & Neale, John M., *Abnormal Psychology* (New York: John Wiley, 7th edn, 1997).

Dawson, Sandra, Willman, Paul, Clinton, Alan & Bamford, Martin, *Safety at Work: The Limits of Self-Regulation* (Cambridge: CUP, 1988).

De Courcy, Anne, 'A Generation was wiped out that day', *Daily Mail Weekend*, 5 October 1996, 10–13.

Deakin, N. (chairman), *Meeting the Challenge of Change: Voluntary Action into the 21st Century*, The Report of the Commission on the Future of the Voluntary Sector (London: NCVO, 1996).

Dimbleby, Jonathan, 'Aberfan: Four Years After', *New Statesman*, 25 December 1970, 862.

Dix, Pamela, 'Corporate Responsibility for Public Safety', *Consumer Policy Review*, vol. 5, no. 6, Nov/Dec 1995, 200–202.

– 'Distress and Redress', *The Guardian*, 29 December 1993.

– 'A Hard Crusade', *The Guardian*, 25 July 1998.

Doel, Melanie & Dunkerton, Martin, *Is it Still Raining in Aberfan? A Pit and its People* (Little Logaston: Logaston Press, 1991).

Donaldson, David, *The Medico-Legal Investigation of Mass Disasters*, www.donaldson.freeserve.co.uk/disaster.html

Douglas, Mary, *Risk and Blame: Essays in Cultural Theory* (London: Routledge, 1992).

Drabek, Thomas E., *Social Dimensions of Disaster: Instructor Guide* (Emmitsburg: Federal Emergency Management Agency, 1996).

– 'Following Some Dreams: Recognizing Opportunities, Posing Interesting Questions, and Implementing Alternative Methods', *International Journal of Mass Emergencies and Disasters*, March 1997, vol. 15, no. 1, 21–46.

Duckham, Helen, *Great Pit Disasters: Great Britain, 1700 to the Present Day* (Newton Abbot: David & Charles, 1973).

Elliott, Dominic & Smith, Denis, 'Football Stadia Disasters in the United Kingdom: Learning from Tragedy?', *Industrial and Environmental Crisis Quarterly*, vol. 7, no. 3, 1993, 205–229.

– 'Waiting for the Next One: Management Attitudes to Safety in the UK Football Industry', unpublished paper.

Ellis, Tom, *Mines and Men: The Career of a Mining Engineer* (Reading: Educational Explorers, 1971).

– 'Aberfan: The Real Lesson?, *Planet*, July-August 1999.

Elwyn-Jones, Lord, *In My Time: An Autobiography* (London: Futura, 1988).

England, Edward, *The Mountain that Moved* (London: Hodder & Stroughton, 1967).

Erikson, Kai T., *In the Wake of the Flood* (London: Allen and Unwin, 1979).

Evans, Andrew W., 'Fatal Accidents on Britain's Main Line Railways', *Journal of the Royal Statistical Society Series: Statistics in Society*, forthcoming.

Evans, Neil, 'Community, Memory and History', *Planet*, 115, February/March 1996, 47–55.

Evans, R. S., 'The Development of Local Government', in *Merthyr Tydfil: A Valley Community* (Merthyr: Merthyr Teachers Centre Group, 1981).

Eyre, Anne, 'Faith, Charity and the Free Market', in Gee, Peter & Fulton, John (eds.), *Religion and Power, Decline and Growth: Sociological Analyses of religion in Britain, Poland and the Americas* (British Sociological Association, Sociology of Religion Study Group, 1991).

– 'More than PTSD: Proactive Responses Among Disaster Victims', *The Australasian Journal of Disaster and Trauma Studies*, 1998–2.

– 'Bridging the Gap: Research-based Emergency Management', *Emergency Management*, Spring 1999, 9.

Fishlock, Trevor, *Wales and the Welsh* (London: Cassell, 1972).

Follis, Richard, 'Case Review: Davis v Central Health Authority', *AVMA Medical and Legal Journal*, April 1991, 11.

Ford, Roger, 'Southall: emotion versus cold fact', *Modern Railways*, November 1997, 697.

Foster, Dennis, *Claiming Compensation for Criminal Injuries* (Croydon: Tolley, 2nd edn., 1997).

Foster, Ken, 'Developments in Sporting Law', in Allison, Lincoln (ed.), *The Changing Politics of Sport* (Manchester: Manchester University Press, 1993).

Francis, Hywel & Smith, David, *The Fed: A History of the South Wales Miners in the Twentieth Century* (Cardiff, 2nd edn, 1998).

Frederick Place Chambers, *Health and Safety at Work: Legislation and Cases* (Birmingham: CLT Professional Publishing, 1995).

Fritz, Charles E., 'Disaster', in Robert K. Merton & Robert A. Nisbet (eds.), *Contemporary Social Problems* (New York: Harcourt, 1961), 651–694.

– 'Disasters' in *International Encyclopaedia of the Social Sciences*, vol. 4 (New York: Macmillan & Free Press, 1968).

Furedi, Frank, *Culture of Fear: Risk-Taking and the Morality of Low Expectation* (London: Cassell, 1998).

– *Courting Mistrust: The Hidden Growth of a Culture of Litigation in Britain* (London: Centre for Policy Studies, 1999).

Gardiner, Robin, & Van Der Vat, Dan, *The Riddle of the Titanic* (London: Weidenfeld and Nicolson, 1995).

Gaudoin, Tina, 'The Marchioness: The True Story', *The Times*, 22 July 1999, 37, 42.

Gist, Richard & Lubin, Bernard (eds.) *Psychosocial Aspects of Disaster* (New York: Wiley, 1989).

Gleser, Goldine C., Green, Bonnie L. & Winget, Carolyn N., *Prolonged Psychosocial Effects of Disaster: A Study of Buffalo Creak*, (New York: Academic Press, 1981).

Gold, Edgar, 'Learning from Disaster: Lessons in Regulatory Enforcement in the Maritime Sector', *Review of European Community and International Environmental Law*, vol. 8, no. 1, April 1999, 16–20.

Goodhart, A. L., 'Viscount Simon, 1873–1954', *Law Quarterly Review*, 70, 1954, 177–180.

Gourvish, Terry & O'Day, Alan, *Britain since 1945* (London: Macmillan, 1991).

Green, Bonnie L., Grace, Mary C., Lindy, Jacob D., Gleser, Goldine C., Leonard, Anthony C. & Kramer, Teresa L., 'Buffalo Creek Survivors in the Second Decade: Comparison with Unexposed and Nonlitigant Groups', *Journal of Applied Social Psychology*, 20 (13), August 1990, 1033–1050.

Green, Bonnie L., Lindy, Jacob D., Grace, Mary C., Gleser, Goldine C., Leonard, Anthony C., Korol, Mindy, Winget, Carolyn, 'Buffalo Creek Survivors in the Second Decade: Stability of Stress Symptoms, *American Journal of Orthopsychiatry*, 60 (1), January 1990, 43–54.

Greenfield, Steve & Osborn, Guy, 'The Legal Regulation of Football and Cricket: "England's Dreaming" ' in: Roche, Maurice (ed.), *Sport, Popular Culture and Identity* (Brighton: Chelsea School Research Centre edn, 1998), 193–209.

Gregory, Robert, 'Political Responsibility for Bureaucratic Incompetence: Tragedy at Cave Creek', *Public Administration*, vol. 76, Autumn, 1998, 519–538.

Griffiths, Robert, *S. O. Davies: A Socialist Faith* (Llandysul: Gomer Press, 1983).

Habermas, Jürgen, 'Learning from Disaster: A Diagnostic Look Back at the Short 20th Century', *Constellations*, 5 (3), 1998, 307–320.

Haines, Fiona, *Corporate Regulation: Beyond 'Punish or Persuade'* (Oxford: Clarendon, 1997).

Hamer, Mick, 'Lessons from a disastrous past: Victorian disasters in public places have much in common with more recent tragedies, except that many more lives were lost', *New Scientist*, 22 December 1990, vol. 128, no. 1748.

Hamilton, Paula, 'Memory Remains: Ferry Disaster, Sydney 1938', *History Workshop Journal*, 47, Spring 1999, 192–210.

Handmer John, & Parker, Dennis, 'British Disaster Planning and Management: An Initial Assessment, *Disasters*, vol. 15, no. 4, 1991, 303–317.

Hannon, Patrick (ed.), *Wales on the Wireless: A Broadcasting Anthology* (Llandysul: Gomer, 1988).

Harlow, Carol & Rawlings, Richard, *Pressure through Law* (London: Routledge,1992).

Harrison, Paul, 'Aberfan: A Hope of Community', *New Society*, 15 March 1973, 587–589.

Harrison, Shirley (ed.), *Disasters and the Media* (Basingstoke: Macmillan, 1998).

Hart, R .J., Lee, J. O., Boyles, D. J. & Batey, N. R., 'The Summerland Disaster', *British Medical Journal*, 1 February 1975, 256–259.

Hattenstone, Simon & O'Sullivan, Tom, 'Those who were left behind', *The Guardian Weekend*, 8 May 1999, 23–30.

Hawkins, Keith, 'Compliance Strategy, Prosecution Policy and Aunt Sally', *British Journal of Criminology*, vol. 30, no. 4, Autumn 1990, 444–466.

– 'Enforcing Regulation: More the Same from Pearce and Tombs', *British Journal of Criminology*, vol. 31, no. 4, Autumn 1991, 327–430.

Hechter, Michael, *Internal Colonialism: The Celtic Fringe in British National Development, 1536–1966* (London: Routledge, 1975).

Henderson, Ian, 'The British Approach to Disaster Management: A Fresh Look at the Tay Bridge Disaster, 1879', *Northern Scotland*, vol. 18 (1998), 57–74.

Henderson, Ian, 'Local Government's Role in Emergency Planning', *Local Government Studies*, vol. 12, no. 4, July/August 1986, 10–16.

Henderson, Sondra Milne, 'Great Britain: Disaster Zone', *The Guardian*, 15 June 1988.

– 'Working towards Relief', *The Guardian*, 16 June 1988.

Herman, Judith Lewis, *Trauma and Recovery: From Domestic Abuse to Political Terror* (London: Pandora, 1994).

Heyer, Paul, *Titanic Legacy: Disaster as Media Event and Myth* (Westport: Praeger, 1995).

Hill, Jeff & Varrasi, Francesco, 'Creating Wembley: The Construction of a National Monument', *The Sports Historian*, vol. 17 (2), November 1997.

Hillman, Judy & Clarke, Peter, *Geoffrey Howe: A Quiet Revolutionary* (London: Weidenfeld & Nicolson, 1988).

Hills, Alice, 'Seduced by recovery: the consequences of misunderstanding disasters', *Journal of Contingencies and Crisis Management*, vol. 6, no. 3, September 1998, 162–170.

Hinton, Peter (ed), *Disasters: Image and Context* (Sydney: Sydney Association for Studies in Society and Culture, 1992).

Hodgkinson, Peter E., 'Technological Disaster: Survival and Bereavement',
Social Science and Medicine, vol. 29, no. 3, 352–356.

Hodgkinson, Peter E. & Stewart, Michael, *Coping with Catastrophe: A
Handbook of Disaster Management* (London: Routledge, 1991).

Holloway, Sally, *Moorgate: Anatomy of Railway Disaster* (Newton Abbot:
David & Charles, 1988).

Horlick-Jones, Tom, 'Modern Disasters as Outrage and Betrayal',
International Journal of Mass Emergencies and Disasters, vol. 13, no. 3,
305–315.

Howard, Michael, 'Health and Safety at Work', *The Magistrate*,
July/August 1990, 128–129.

Howe, Geoffrey, 'The Aberfan Disaster', *Medico-Legal Journal*, 38, 1968,
107–21.

– *Conflict of Loyalty* (London: Macmillan, 1994).

– 'Procedure at the Scott Inquiry', *Public Law*, Autumn 1996, 445–460.

– 'The Management of Public Inquiries', *Political Quarterly*, vol. 70, issue 3,
July 1999, 294–304.

Howell, Denis, *Made in Birmingham: The Memoirs of Denis Howell*
(London: Queen Anne Press, 1990).

Hughes, Maureen (ed.), *Aberfan – Our Hiraeth* (Aberfan: Aberfan &
Merthyr Vale Community Co-operative, 1999).

Humphrys, John, *Devil's Advocate* (London: Hutchinson, 1999).

Hutter, Bridget M. & Lloyd-Bostock, Sally, 'The Power of Accidents: The
Social and Psychological Impact of Accidents and the Enforcement of
Safety Regulations', *British Journal of Criminology*, vol. 30, no. 4,
Autumn 1990, 409–422.

Hutter, Bridget M., 'Regulating Employers and Employees: Health and
Safety in the Workplace', *Journal of Law and Society*, vol. 20, no. 4,
Winter 1993, 452–470.

– 'Variations in Regulatory Styles', *Law and Policy*, vol. 11, no. 2, April
1989, 153–174.

Hynes, Timothy & Prasad, Pushkala, 'Patterns of 'Mock Bureaucracy' in
Mining Disasters: An Analysis of the Westray Coal Mine Explosion',
Journal of Management Studies, 34 (4), July 1997, 601–623.

Hyslop, Donald, Forsyth, Alastair & Jemima, Sheila, *Titanic Voices*
(Southampton: Southampton City Council, 1994).

Inglis, Simon, *The Football Grounds of Great Britain* (London:
CollinsWillow, 1987).

James, Arnold J. & Thomas, John E., *Wales at Westminster: A History of the
Parliamentary Representation of Wales, 1800–1979* (Llandysul: Gomer,
1981).

James, Brian, 'The New Tragedy of Dunblane', *Night&Day*, 19 July 1998.

Jardine, Casandra, 'Aberfan's 'lucky' one', *Daily Telegraph*, 18 October 1996.

Jasanoff, Sheila, *Learning from Disaster: Risk Management after Bhopal*
(Philadelphia: University of Pennsylvania, 1994)

– 'The political science of risk perception', *Reliability Engineering and System Safety*, vol. 59, 1998, 91–99.

Jefferson, Michael, *Criminal Law*, (London: Pitman, 3rd edn, 1997).

Johnes, Martin, 'Disasters and Responsibility: Lessons from Aberfan', *Planet*, 135, June–July 1999, 13–18.

Jones, Erastus, 'Working in Aberfan and the Valleys', *Social & Economic Administration*, 9 (1), 1975, 30–40.

– 'Aberfan – 'The village that refused to be destroyed' ', *Merthyr Express*, 16 October 1986.

Jones, T. Mervyn, *Going Public* (Cowbridge: D. Brown, 1987).

Jones, Michael A., *Textbooks on Tort* (London: Blackstone, 6th edn, 1998).

Jones, Michael Wynn, *Deadline Disaster: A Newspaper History* (Newton Abbot: David & Charles, 1976).

Joseph S., Dalgleish T., Williams R., Yule W., Thrasher S., Hodgkinson P. (1997), 'Attitudes towards emotional expression and post-traumatic stress in survivors of the *Herald of Free Enterprise* disaster', *British Journal of Clinical Psychology*, Feberuary, vol. 36, part 1, 133–138.

Judicial Studies Board, *Guidelines for the Assessment of General Damages in Personal Injury Cases* (London: Blackstone, 4th edn, 1998).

Keller, A. Z., Wilson, H. C., & Al-Madhari, A., 'Proposed Disaster Scale and Associated Model for Calculating Return Periods for Disasters of Given Magnitude', *Disaster Prevention and Management*, vol. 1, no. 1, 1992, 26–33.

Kelly, Charles, 'A Review of Contributions to Disasters: 1977–1996, *Disasters*, 22 (2), 1998, 144–156.

Kemp, David (assisted by Peter Mantle), *Damages for Personal Injury and Death* (London: Sweet & Maxwell, 7th edn, 1999).

Kendell, R. E. & Zealley, A. K. (eds.), *Companion to Psychiatric Studies* (Edinburgh: Churchill Livingstone, 5th edn, 1993).

King, Cecil, *The Cecil King Diary, 1965–1970* (London: Cape, 1972).

Kletz, Trevor, 'Are Disasters Really getting Worse?', *Disaster Prevention & Management*, vol. 3, no. 1, 1994, 33–36.

– *Learning from Accidents in Industry* (London: Butterworth, 1988).

Knapman, Paul A., 'Hillsborough Lives On', *Justice of the Peace & Local Government Law*, 25 January 1997, 79–80.

Kuntz, Tom (ed.), *The Titanic Disaster Hearings: The Official Transcripts of the 1912 Senate Investigation* (New York: Pocket Books, 1998).

Lacey, Gaynor N., 'Observations on Aberfan', *Journal of Psychosomatic Research*, vol. 16, 1972, 257–260.

Lacey, Nicola & Wells, Celia, *Reconstructing Criminal Law: Critical Perspectives on Crime and the Criminal Process* (London: Butterworths, 2nd edn, 1998).

Laidlaw, Roger, 'The Gresford Disaster in Popular Memory', *Llafur*, vol. 6, no. 4, 1995, 123–146.

Laurence, Jeremy, 'Disastrous Disaster Funds', *New Society*, 20 March 1987, 10–11.

Lee, Laurie, *I Can't Stay Long* (Harmondsworth: Penguin edn, 1977).

Lee, Robert & Morgan, Derek (eds.), *Death Rites: Law and Ethics at the End of Life* (London: Routledge, 1994).

Lewis, Jerry M. & Veneman, J. Michael, 'Crisis Resolution: The Bradford Fire and English Society', *Sociological Focus*, vol. 20, no. 2, April 1987, 155–168.

Lieven, Michael, *Senghennydd, the Universal Pit Village, 1890–1930* (Llandysul: Gomer, 1994).

Littlewood, Jane, *Aspects of Grief: Bereavement in Adult Life* (London: Routledge, 1992).

Llewelyn, Chris, *Learning Lessons from Disasters* (Cardiff: Welsh Consumer Council, 1998).

Llewellyn, Richard, *How Green was my Valley* (London : Michael Joseph, 1939).

Luxton, Peter, *Charity Fund-Raising and the Public Interest: An Anglo-American Legal Perspective* (Aldershot: Avebury, 1990).

– 'The Deakin Report: Its Legal Implications', *New Law Journal*, 146 (6771), Sup no. 69, 6 December 1996, 15–16, 18–20.

McBryde, William & Barker, Christine, 'Solicitors' Groups in Mass Disaster Claims', *New Law Journal*, 12 April 1991, 484–487.

McGregor, Ian, 'The Public Inquiry Maze', *Civil Protection*, issue 47, Spring 1997, 6–7.

McLean, Iain, 'The Political Economy of Regulation: Interests, Ideology, Voters and the UK Regulation of Railways Act 1844', *Public Administration*, vol. 70, Autumn 1992, 313–331.

– 'On moles and the habits of birds: the unpolitics of Aberfan', *Twentieth Century British History* vol. 8, no. 3, 1997, 285–309.

– 'It's not too late to say sorry', *Times Higher Education Supplement*, 17 January 1997.

McLeod, John, *An Introduction to Counselling* (Buckingham: Open University Press, 2nd edn, 1998).

MacDonald, Alistair, 'The Bradford Football Fire', *New Law Journal*, 22 May 1987, 481–484.

Madgwick, Gaynor, *Aberfan, Struggling out of the Darkness: A Survivor's Story* (Blaengarw: Valley and the Vale, 1996).

Manning, Maria, 'Like it or Lump it', *New Statesman and Society*, 10 August 1990, 10–11.

Mansfield, C. P., 'Keeping Drama out of a Crisis', *Police Review*, 24 June 1988, 1320–1321.

March, Paul, 'The End of the Libel Story', *Entertainment Law Review*, vol. 9, no. 6, August 1998, 222–226.

Marks M, Yule W, de Silva P, 'Post-traumatic stress disorder in airplane cabin crew attendants', *Aviat Space Environ Med Mar*; 66(3), 1995, 264–268.

Marsh, Richard, *Off the Rails* (London: Weidenfeld & Nicolson, 1978).

Marwick, Arthur, *British Society Since 1945* (Harmondsworth: Penguin edn, 1990).

Mason, Helen, 'All in a good cause?' *Sunday Times*, 27 September 1987, 59.

Mead, Christine (ed.), *Journeys of Discovery: Creative Learning from Disasters* (London: National Institute for Social Work, 1996).

Members of the Medical Staff of Three London Hospitals, 'Moorgate Train Disaster', *British Medical Journal*, 27 September 1975, 727–731.

Millar, Stuart, 'Blood and Black Gold', *The Guardian*, 6 July 1998.

Millburn, Geoffrey & Miller, Stuart T. (eds.) *Sunderland: River, Town and People: A History from the 1780s* (Sunderland: Borough of Sunderland, 1988).

Miller, Joan, *Aberfan: A Disaster and its Aftermath* (London: Constable, 1974).

– 'Community Development in a Disaster Community', *Community Development Journal*, 8 (3), October 1973, 161–168.

Monahan, Jerome, 'Jupiter's Children', *The Guardian*, 20 October 1920.

Monbiot, George,' Unsafe to Criticise', *The Guardian*, 21 May 1998.

Moore, Roger, *The Price of Safety: The Market, Workers' Rights and the Law* (London: Institute of Employment Rights, 1991).

Morgan, Alun, 'The 1970 Parliamentary Election at Merthyr Tydfil', *Morgannwg*, XXII, 1978, 61–81.

Morgan, K. O., *Rebirth of a Nation: Wales, 1880–1980* (Cardiff/Oxford: Oxford University Press & University of Wales Press, 1981).

– *The People's Peace: British History, 1945–1990* (Oxford: Oxford University Press, 1990).

– 'Welsh Devolution: The Past and the Future' in Taylor, Bridget & Thomson, Katarina (eds.), *Scotland and Wales: Nations Again?* (Cardiff: University of Wales Press, 1999).

Morton, Andrew, 'Diana Wars: Memorial Fund in Turmoil', *The Times Weekend*, 22 August 1998.

Munroe, Neil, 'Still Shaking from the Nightmare', *Times Education Supplement*, 13 January 1989.

Murray, Bill, *The Old Firm: Sectarianism, Sport and Society in Scotland* (Edinburgh: John Donald, 1984).

Napier, Michael, 'Medical and Legal Trauma of Disasters, *Medico-Legal Journal*, vol. 59 (3), 1991, 157–184.

– 'Zeebrugge: the way forward', *Law Society's Gazette*, no. 40, 7 November 1990, 2.

– 'Group Litigation: Past, Present and Future', *Nottingham Law Journal*, vol. 2, 1993, 1–27.

Newburn, Tim, *Making a Difference? Social Work after Hillsborough* (London: National Institute for Social Work, 1993).

Newburn, Tim (ed.), *Working with Disaster: Social Welfare Interventions During and After Tragedy* (London: Longman, 1993).

Newman, P. (ed.), *The New Palgrave Dictionary of Economics and the Law* (London: Macmillan 3 vols 1998).

Nichols, Theo, *The Sociology of Industrial Injury* (London: Mansell, 1997).

Nilson, Douglas, 'Disaster Beliefs and Ideological Orientation', *Journal of Contingencies and Crisis Management*, vol. 3, no. 1, March 1995, 12–17.

Nightingale, Benedict, *Charities* (London: Allen Lane, 1973).

Norrie, Alan, *Crime, Reason and History: A Critical Introduction to Criminal Law* (London: Weidenfeld & Nicolson, 1993).

Nossiter, Bernard D., 'Aberfan: Tragedy Molds New Spirit', *Washington Post*, 27 May 1973.

Nunn, Charles, 'The Disaster of Aberfan', *Police Review*, 16 October 1987, 2069–2071.

Parker, Dennis J., & Handmer, John, *Hazard Management and Emergency Planning: Perspectives on Britain* (London: James & James, 1992).

Parkes, Colin Murray, 'Planning for the Aftermath', *Journal of the Royal Society of Medicine*, vol. 84, January 1991, 22–25.

– *Bereavement: Studies of Grief in Adult Life* (London: Routledge, 3rd edn, 1996).

Parkes, Colin Murray & Black, Dora, 'Disasters', in Colin Murray Parkes & Andrew Markus (eds), *Coping with Loss: Helping Patients and their Families* (London: BMJ Books, 1998), 114–125.

Payne, Christopher F., 'Handling the Press', *Disaster Prevention & Management*, vol. 3, no. 1, 1994, 24–32.

Paynter, Will, *My Generation* (London: Allen & Unwin, 1972).

Pearce, Frank and Tombs, Steve, 'Ideology, Hegemony, and Empiricism', *British Journal of Criminology*, vol. 30, no. 4, Autumn 1990, 423–443.

– 'Policing Corporate 'Skid Rows': A reply to Keith Hawkins', *British Journal of Criminology*, vol. 31 no. 4, Autumn 1991, 415–426.

– 'Hazards, Law and Class: Contextualizing the Regulation of Corporate Crime', *Social and Legal Studies*, vol. 6 (1), 1997, 79–107.

Peltzman, S. 'Toward a more general theory of regulation', *Journal of Law and Economics*, 19, 1976, 211–240.

Pendreigh, Brian, 'Cold Light of Day', *The Scotsman*, 15 March 1996.

Phillips, Jim & French, Michael, 'Adulteration and Food Law, 1899–1939', *Twentieth Century British History*, vol. 9, no. 3, 1998, 350–269.

Picarda, Hubert, *The Law and Practice Relating to Charities* (London: Butterworths, 1977).

Pidgeon, Nick, 'The Limits of Safety? Culture, Politics, Learning and Man-Made Disasters', *Journal of Contingencies and Crisis Management*, vol. 5, no. 1, March 1997, 1–14.

Pimlott, Ben, *Harold Wilson* (London: HarperCollins, 1992).

Power, Helen & Dowrick, Brian, 'Issues in Corporate Crime?: An Introduction', *Web Journal of Current Legal Issues*, http://webjcli.ncl.ac.uk/1998/issue2/power2.html

Prochaska, Frank, *The Voluntary Impulse: Philanthropy in Modern Britain* (London: Faber & Faber, 1988).

Punchard, Ed. (with Syd Higgins), *Piper Alpha: A Survivor's Story* (London: Star, 1989).

Quarantelli, E. L., 'The Environmental Disasters of the Future will be More and Worse but the Prospect is not Hopeless', *Disaster Prevention and Management*, vol. 2, no. 1, 1993, 11–25.

– 'Disaster Studies: The Consequences of the Historical Use of a Sociological Approach in the Development of Research', *International*

Journal of Mass Emergencies and Disasters, March 1994, vol.12, no. 1, 25–49.

Quarantelli, E. L. (ed.), *What is a Disaster? A Dozen Perspectives on the Question* (London: Routledge, 1998).

Raftery, John, 'Doing Better than the Media: Ethical issues in Trauma Research', *The Australasian Journal of Disaster and Trauma Studies*, 1997–2.

Raphael, Beverley, *When Disaster Strikes: A Handbook for the Caring Professions* (London: Unwin Hymen edn, 1990).

Rhodes, Gerald, *Inspectorates in British Government: Law Enforcement and Standards of Efficiency* (London: George Allen, 1981).

Richardson, Bill, 'Socio-Technical Disasters: Profile and Prevalence', *Disaster Prevention and Management*, vol. 3, no. 4, 1994, 41–69.

Riddell, Peter, *The Thatcher Era and its Legacy* (Oxford: Blackwell, 2nd edn., 1991).

Ridley, Ann & Dunford, Louise, 'Corporate Killing – Legislating for Unlawful Death?', *Industrial Law Journal*, vol. 26, no. 2, June 1997, 99–113.

Ridley, F. F. & Jordan, Grant, *Protest Politics: Cause Groups and Campaigns* (Oxford: Oxford University Press, 1998).

Robens, Lord, 'Mine Disasters', *Advancement of Science*, June 1969, 391–394.

– *Ten Year Stint* (London: Cassell, 1972).

Roberts, Ken, *The Reconstruction of 'Community': A Case Study of Post-Disaster Aberfan* (Coventry: Warwick Working Papers in Sociology, 1985).

Robertson, E. H., *George: A Biography of Viscount Tonypandy* (London: Marshall Pickering, 1992).

Robins, L. N.,' Steps towards evaluating Post-traumatic Stress Reaction as a Psychiatric Disorder', *Journal of Applied Social Psychology*, 20, 1990, 1674–1677.

Rock, Paul, *After Homicide: Practical and Political Responses to Bereavement* (Oxford, Clarendon Press, 1998).

Rocket, J. P., 'A Constructive Critique of United Kingdom Emergency Planning', *Disaster Prevention & Management*, vol. 3, no. 1, 1994, 47–60.

Rosenhan, David L. & Seligman, Martin E. P., *Abnormal Psychology* (New York: W. W. Norton, 3rd edn, 1995).

Rowan-Robinson, Jeremy, Watchman, Paul, & Barker, Christine, *Crime and Regulation: A Study of the Enforcement of Regulatory Codes* (Edinburgh: T & T Clark, 1990).

Russell, Dave, *Football and the English: A Social History of Association Football in England, 1863–1995* (Preston: Carnegie, 1997).

Scanlon, T Joseph, Luukko, Rudy & Morton, Gerald, 'Media Coverage of Crises: Better than Reported, Worse than Necessary,' *Journalism Quarterly*, Spring 1978, 68–72.

Scraton, Phil, *Hillsborough: The Truth* (Edinburgh: Mainstream, 1999).

– 'The Lost Afternoon', *The Observer*, 11 April 1999.

Scraton, Phil, Jemphrey, Ann & Coleman, Sheila, *No Last Rights: The Denial of Justice and the Promotion of Myth in the Aftermath of the Hillsborough Disaster* (Liverpool: Liverpool City Council, 1995).

Scraton, Phil, Berrington, Eileen & Jemphrey, Ann, 'Intimate Intrusions? Press Freedom, Private Lives and Public Interest', *Communications Law*, vol. 3, no. 5, 1998, 174–182.

Selwyn, Norman, *The Law of Health and Safety at Work* (London: Butterworths, 6th edn 1997).

Shader, Richard I. & Schwartz, Alice J., 'Management of Reactions to Disaster', *Social Work*, vol. 11, no. 2, April, 1966, 98–104.

Shearer, Ann, *Survivors and the Media* (London: Broadcasting Standards Council, 1991).

Shiels, Robert S., 'The Ibrox Disaster of 1902', *Juridical Review*, 4, 1997, 230–240.

– 'The Fatalities at the Ibrox Disaster of 1902', *The Sports Historian*, vol. 18 (2) November 1998.

Siddle, H. J., Wright, M. D., Hutchinson, J. N., 'Rapid failures of colliery spoil heaps in the South Wales Coalfield', *Quarterly Journal of Engineering Geology*, 29, 103–132.

Slapper, Gary, 'Crime without Conviction', *New Law Journal*, vol. 142, 14 February 1992, 192–193.

– 'Corporate Manslaughter: An Examination of the Determinants of Prosecutional Policy', *Social and Legal Studies*, vol. 2, 1993, 423–443.

– 'Crime without punishment', *The Guardian*, 1 February 1994.

– 'Corporate Crime and Punishment, *The Criminal Lawyer*, March/April 1998, 6–7.

– 'Cost of Corporate Crime', *The Times*, 22 June 1999.

– 'Corporate homicide and legal chaos', *New Law Journal*, 9 July 1999, 1031.

Slapper, Gary & Tombs, Steve, *Corporate Crime* (London: Longman, 1999).

Smith, Dai, 'The Valleys: Landscape and Mindscape', in Prys Morgan (ed.), *Glamorgan County History vol. VI: Glamorgan Society 1780–1980* (Cardiff: Glamorgan County History Trust, 1988), 129–149.

Smith, Denis & Toft, Brian, ' Editorial: Issues in Public Sector Risk Management', *Public Money and Management*, October-December 1998, 7–10.

Smith, Sir John & Hogan, Brian, *Criminal Law* (London: Butterworths, 8th edn, 1996).

Smith, Tom, *Robens Revisited: An examination of Health and Safety law 25 years after the Robens Report with particular emphasis on the Explosives Industry*, hompages.enterprise.net/saxtonsmith/robens.htm

Soloman, Michael J. & Thompson, James, 'Anger and Blame in Three Technological Disasters', *Stress Medicine*, vol. 11, 1995, 199–206.

Soloman, Susan D. & Green, Bonnie L., 'Mental Health Effects of Natural and Human-Made Disasters', *PTSD Research Quarterly*, vol. 3, no. 1, 1992, 1–3.

Spooner, Peter, 'Developing the Corporate Mindsets which will Help to Reduce Man-made Disasters', *Disaster Prevention & Management*, vol. 1, no. 2, 1992, 28–36.

– *The HFA Story, 1987–1994* (London: Herald Families Association, 1994).

Stigler, G., 'The theory of economic regulation', *Bell Journal of Economics and Management Science*, 2, 1971, 3–21.

Stuart, Mark, *Douglas Hurd: The Public Servant* (Edinburgh: Mainstream, 1998).

Stuart, Paul, 'Southall Rail Disaster due to Privatisation and Cost Cutting', *International Worker*, no. 240, 11 October 1997.

Suddards, Roger W., *Administration of Appeal Funds* (London: Sweet & Maxwell, 1991).

Suedfeld, Peter, 'Reactions to Societal Trauma: Distress and/or Eustress', *Political Psychology*, vol. 18, no. 4, 1997, 849–861.

Taylor, Ian, 'English Football in the 1990s: taking Hillsborough seriously?', in: Williams, John & Wagg, Stephen (eds.), *British Football and Social Change: Getting into Europe* (Leicester: Leicester University Press, 1991).

Taylor, John, 'Death's Grim Bazaar', *New Statesman & Society*, 15 December 1989, 30–32.

Taylor, Shelley E., *Health Psychology* (New York: McGraw-Hill, 3rd edn 1995).

Teff, H., 'Liability for Psychiatric Illness after Hillsborough', *Oxford Journal for Legal Studies*, vol. 12, Autumn 1992, 440–452.

Thatcher, Margaret, *The Downing Street Years* (London: HarperCollins, 1993).

– *The Path to Power* (London: HarperCollins, 1995).

Thomas, George, *Mr Speaker: The Memoirs of the Viscount Tonypandy* (London: Century Publishing, 1985).

Tidmarsh, Sheila, *Disaster* (Harmondsworth: Penguin, 1969).

Toft, Brian, 'The Failure of Hindsight', *Disaster Prevention & Management*, vol. 1, no. 3, 1992, 48–60.

Toft, Brian & Reynolds, Simon, *Learning from Disasters: A Management Approach* (Oxford: Butterworth-Heinemann, 1994).

Tombs, Steve, 'Law, Resistance and Reform: 'Regulating' Safety Crimes in the UK', *Social and Legal Studies*, vol. 4 (1995), 343–365.

Tumelty, David, *Social Work in the Wake of Disaster* (London: Jessica Kingsley, 1990).

Turner, Barry A., with Pidgeon, Nick F., *Man-Made Disasters* (Oxford, Butterworth-Heinemann, 2nd edn, 1997).

Wade, Wyn Craig, *Titanic: End of a Dream* (London: Weidenfeld & Nicolson, 1979).

Walker, John, *Disasters* (London: Studio Vista, 1973).

Walsh, Mike, *Disasters: Current Planning and Recent Experience* (London: Edward Arnold, 1989).

Walter, Tony, 'The Mourning after Hillsborough', *Sociological Review*, vol. 39, no. 3, 1991, 599–625.

Walters David & James, Philip, *Robens Revisited: The Case for a Review of Occupational Health and Safety Legislation* (London: Institute of Employment Rights, 1998).

Ware, Alan, 'Introduction: The Changing Relations between Charities and the State' in Alan Ware (ed.), *Charities and Government* (Manchester: Manchester University Press, 1989).

Watkins, Hugh, ' "From Chaos to Calm" The Diary of the Gordon-Lennox Education Centre, Nixonville, Aberfan from Thursday November 3rd, 1966 to Thursday, December 1st, 1966', *Merthyr Historian*, vol. 7, 1994, 58–69.

Weaver, Colin, 'Counselling in a Disaster' in Palmer, Stephen, Dainow, Sheila & Milner, Pat, (eds.), *Counselling: The BAC Counselling Reader* (London: Sage, 1996), 266–271.

Wells, Celia 'Inquests, inquiries and indictments: the official reception of death by disaster', *Legal Studies*, vol 11, 1991, 71–84.

– *Corporations and Criminal Responsibility* (Oxford: Clarendon, 1993).

– *Negotiating Tragedy: Law and Disasters* (London: Sweet & Maxwell, 1995).

– 'Cry in the Dark: Corporate Manslaughter and Cultural Meaning', in Ian Loveland (ed.), *Frontiers of Criminality* (London: Sweet & Maxwell, 1995).

– 'Corporate Manslaughter: A Cultural and Legal Form', *Criminal Law Forum*, vol. 6, no. 1, 1995, 45–72.

Welsby, Catherine, 'Warning her as to her future behaviour': The Lives of the Widows of the Senghenydd Mining Disaster of 1913', *Llafur*, vol. 6, no. 4, 1995, 93–109.

West Midlands Health and Safety Advice Centre, *The Perfect Crime? How Companies Escape Manslaughter Prosecutions* (Birmingham: West Midlands Health and Safety Advice Centre, 1994).

Whitham, David & Tim Newburn, *Coping with Tragedy: Managing the Responses to Two Disasters* (Nottingham: Nottinghamshire County Council, 1992).

Wikeley, Nick, 'The Asbestos Regulations 1931 – A Licence to Kill?', *Journal of Law and Society* 19 1992, pp. 365–78.

– 'Turner & Newall: Early Organizational Responses to Litigation Risk', *Journal of Law and Society*, vol. 24, no. 2, June 1997, 252–275.

Williams, R. M., & Murray Parkes, C., 'Psychosocial Effects of Disaster: Birth Rate in Aberfan', *British Medical Journal*, 10 May 1975, 303–304.

Williamson, Stanley, *Gresford: The Anatomy of a Disaster* (Liverpool: Liverpool University Press, 1999).

Wilson, Harold, *The Labour Government 1964–70: A Personal Record* (Harmondsworth: Penguin, 1974).

Winetrobe, Barry K., 'Inquiries after Scott: the return of the tribunal of inquiry', *Public Law*, Spring 1997, 18–31.

Witcomb, Henry, 'Disaster Claims – long overdue or reform?', *New Law Journal*, 17 August 1990.

Wood, Bruce, *The Process of Local Government Reform, 1966–74* (London: George Allen, 1976).

Woolf, Anthony D., 'Robens Report – The Wrong Approach', *Industrial Law Journal*, 2, 1973, 88–95.

Wolfenstein, Martha, *Disaster: A Psychological Essay* (Glencoe: The Free Press, 1957).

Woolfson, Charles, Foster, John & Beck, Matthias, *Paying for the Piper: Capital and Labour in Britain's Offshore Oil Industry* (London: Mansell, 1996).

Woolfson, Charles & Beck, Matthias, 'Deregulation: The Contemporary Politics of Health and Safety', in McColgan, Aileen (ed.), *The Future of Labour Law* (London: Cassell, 1996).

Wright, Kathleen M., Ursano, Robert J., Bartone, Paul T., Ingraham, Larry H., 'The Shared Experience of Catastrophe: An Expanded Classification of the Disaster Community', *American Journal of Orthopsychiatry*, vol. 60, no. 1 January 1990, 35–42.

Yehuda, Rachel & McFarlane, Alexander, 'Conflict between Current Knowledge about Posttraumatic Stress Disorder and its Original Conceptual Basis', *American Journal of Psychiatry*, 152 (12), 1995, 1705–1713.

Young, Peter, *Disasters: Focussing on Management Responsibility* (London: HFA, 1993).

Yule, William, 'The Effect of Disasters on Children', *Bereavement Care*, vol. 9, no. 2, Spring 1990.

– 'Work with Children following Disasters', in Martin Herbert (ed.) *Clinical Child Psychology: Social Learning, Development and Behaviour* (Chichester: John Wiley, 1991).

VII. Other unpublished material

Aberfan Tribunal of Inquiry, transcripts of oral evidence.

Akers, David J., *Overview of Coal Refuse Disposal in the United States*, Coal Research Bureau, West Virginia University, Report No. 172, January 1980.

Cathcart, Brian, 'We're all tabloids now', Paper given to the Institute of Historical Research, June 1997.

Clapham Junction Disaster Fund, *The report of the Trustees of the Fund*, May 1990.

Cuthill, James M., *The Aberfan Disaster – A Study of the Survivors*, Unpublished, no date.

Davis, Gerald, *The First Report of the Management Committee of the Aberfan Disaster Fund*, 1968.

Disaster Action, *Newsletters*

– *Response to the Law Commission Involuntary Manslaughter Consultation Paper (LCCP No. 135)*, 1994.

Elliott, Dominic Paul, *Organisational Learning from Crisis: An Examination of the Football Industry, 1946–97*, Ph.D. thesis, University of Durham, 1998.

Eyre, Anne, 'Calling for a Disasters Study Group: A Proposal', Paper given at British Sociological Association Conference, 1999.

Morgan, C. Geoffrey, *The Second Report of the Aberfan Disaster Fund*, 1970.

Owen, Douglas, *Some Organisational Aspects of a Public Inquiry*, Working Paper for Seminar 26th January 1977, Lancaster University.

Park, W. R. *et al.*, *Interim Report of Retaining Dam Failure, No. 5 Preparation Plant, Buffalo Mining Company, Saunders, Logan Country, West Virginia*, no date.

Slapper, Gary, *Law and Political Economy: Legal Responses to Deaths at Work*, LSE, Ph.D. thesis, 1995.

VIII. Select Broadcasts

Aftermath: Zeebrugge, ITV, 4 March 1988.

Disaster [series], BBC2, March 1999.

Lockerbie: A Night Remembered, Channel 4, 29 November 1998.

File on Four, BBC Radio 4, 16 February 1999.

Hillsborough: The Legacy, BBC1, 11 April 1999.

Survivors – Evil Acts, Partners in Motion (Canadian television broadcast).

Timewatch: Remember Aberfan, BBC2, 15 October 1996.

Wales this Week, HTV Wales, 25 October 1990.

INDEX

NB. Job titles in [square brackets] are those held on 21 October 1966, or other material time.